Police Supervision and Management

In an Era of Community Policing

Second Edition

KENNETH J. PEAK
University of Nevada, Reno

LARRY K. GAINES
California State University, San Bernardino

RONALD W. GLENSOR
Reno, Nevada, Police Department

PEARSON
Prentice
Hall

Upper Saddle River, New Jersey 07458

Library of Congress Cataloging-in-Publication Data

Peak, Kenneth J., 1947-
    Police supervision and management : in an era of community policing / Kenneth J. Peak,
Larry K. Gaines, Ronald W. Glensor.--2nd ed.
    p. cm.
    Rev. ed. of: Police supervision / Ronald W. Glensor, Kenneth J. Peak, Larry K. Gaines. c1999.
    Includes bibliographical references and index.
    ISBN 0-13-039472-6
    1. Police—Supervision of.   I. Gaines, Larry K.   II. Glensor, Ronald W.   III. Glensor,
Ronald W. Police supervision.   IV. Title.

HV7936.S8P39 2004
363.2'068'3—dc21   2003045615

Editor-in-Chief: Stephen Helba
Director of Production and
    Manufacturing: Bruce Johnson
Executive Editor: Frank Mortimer, Jr.
Assistant Editor: Sarah Holle
Editorial Assistant: Barbara Rosenberg
Marketing Manager: Tim Peyton
Managing Editor—Production: Mary Carnis
Manufacturing Buyer: Cathleen Petersen
Production Liaison: Denise Brown

Full Service Production: Naomi Sysak
Composition Management and Page
    Makeup: The GTS Companies
Design Director: Cheryl Asherman
Design Coordinator: Miguel Ortiz
Cover Design: Carey Davies
Cover Printer: Phoenix Color
Cover Images: Donovan Reese/Getty Images-Stone
    and Don Farrall/Getty Images-PhotoDisc
Printer/Binder: RR Donnelley & Sons

Pearson Education LTD.
Pearson Education Singapore, Pte. Ltd
Pearson Education Canada, Ltd
Pearson Education—Japan
Pearson Education Australia PTY, Limited
Pearson Education North Asia Ltd
Pearson Educaçion de Mexico, S.A. de C.V.
Pearson Education Malaysia, Pte. Ltd

10 9 8 7 6 5 4 3 2 1
ISBN 0-13-039472-6

—❖—

To Emma Olivia Peak, my beautiful and eventually very intelligent new granddaughter (written without any bias whatsoever)

—K. J. P.

To my loving family, Jean, Ashley, Courtney, and Cody, who tolerated me through this endeavor and the many other projects over the years.

—L. K. G.

To my wife Kristy for her supervision and leadership of our very busy lives. And to my daughter Breanne—a college graduate entering the world of science—and son Ronnie, who pursues his baseball dream in college.

—R. W. G.

Contents

---❖---

Preface

❖

A comparatively large number of textbooks on police management and administration have been written over the past several decades, addressing the roles and responsibilities of chiefs of police or sheriffs. This text, however, focuses on first-line supervisors and middle managers and is grounded on the assumption that the reader is an undergraduate, possibly even a graduate, student or a neophyte practitioner, possessing but a fundamental knowledge of police organizations and operations. It is intended to help those persons learn more about the field of policing, as well as help those practitioners who are preparing for promotion, and new and experienced supervisors who are seeking to improve their skills. It will help to lay the foundation for the reader's future study and experience.

This text also assumes that a *practical* police supervision perspective is often lost in many administrative texts; therefore, while necessarily delving into some theory, this text is intended to focus on the practical aspects of a supervisor's or manager's job.

Those of us who have held a job or position, unless self-employed, have had a supervisor to whom we reported. That individual probably had a hand in showing us how to do our work and certainly was responsible for making sure that we did it properly. Even persons who have not yet entered the working world have experienced supervision in school, in sports, in the Boy Scouts or Girl Scouts, or in other nonwork settings. Supervision is a crucial element of any organized activity and is present in all organizations.

Our supervisors often reported to *their* supervisors, or managers. The managers coordinated and supervised the efforts of the lower-level supervisors as well as ensuring that the unit functioned as higher-level administrators envisioned. Supervisors and managers are the keys to quality work in any organization.

This book specifically concerns *police* supervision and management. In order to address these topics thoroughly and to provide as much useful information as possible, we must maintain a dual approach by looking at supervision and management broadly, while also focusing narrowly on these areas in police organizations. All supervisors and managers, whether in police departments, construction, or business firms, share similar concerns and duties. They manage people and activities.

It is also true that each and every organization is unique. Police departments in particular are different from most other organizations, for the simple reason that police work is different from most other vocations and occupations. Police officers have the unique authority to arrest people and investigate their activities. Also, police departments are not all made from the same mold. The New York City Police Department and the Chicago Police Department, the two largest departments in the United States, are different from the Las Vegas Police Department or the Nashville Police Department. Although all of these departments have the same or similar responsibilities, substantial variation within the police profession itself makes the job of police supervisors or managers unique and challenging. In addition, the police supervisors' and managers' jobs have recently been made even more specialized as a result of the implementation of community policing. Community policing has placed many new responsibilities on the police sergeant and manager.

During the course of a workday, police supervisors and managers directly oversee several employees in the performance of their activities and may even supervise a life-threatening situation or a critical incident or disaster. While a supervisor may not have ultimate command and control over critical incidents or disasters, he or she is often the first responder at the scene; his or her actions and directions to subordinates will be vital in determining the eventual success of the police in dealing with the problem. Managers are called to the scenes of major critical incidents to supervise groups of officers and to coordinate actions with other police units or agencies, such as the fire department or emergency medical services. Supervisors and managers essentially ensure that police operations unfold as planned.

KEY TERMS

Although the terms *administration, management,* and *supervision* are often used synonymously, it should be noted that each is a unique concept that occasionally overlaps with the others. **Administration** encompasses both management and supervision. Administration is a process whereby a group of people are organized and directed toward achievement of the group's objective. The exact nature of the organization will vary among the different types and sizes of agencies, but the general principles used and the form of administration are often similar. Administration focuses on the overall organization and its mission and its relationship with other organizations and groups external to it. Administrators are often concerned with the department's direction and its policies and with ensuring that the department has the resources to fulfill its community's expectations. Police administrators generally include the chief, assistant chiefs, and high-ranking staff who support the chief in administering the department.

Management, which is also a part of administration, is most closely associated with the day-to-day operations of the various elements within the organization. For example, most police departments have a variety of operational units such as patrol, criminal investigation, traffic, gang enforcement, domestic violence, or community relations. The Los Angeles Police Department, the third largest police department in the country, has more than 200 specialized units. Each of these units is run by someone who is most aptly described as a manager. In most cases, these managers are captains or lieutenants. These managers ensure that their units fulfill their departmental mission and work closely with other units to ensure that conflict or problems do not develop. They also attend to planning, budgeting, and human resource or personnel needs to ensure that the unit is adequately prepared to carry out its responsibilities.

Supervision involves the direction of officers and civilians in their day-to-day activities, often on a one-to-one basis. Supervisors ensure that subordinate officers adhere to departmental policies, complete tasks correctly and on a timely basis, and interact with the public in a professional manner. Supervisors often observe their subordinates completing assignments and sometimes take charge of situations, especially when a deployment of a large number of officers is needed. They also work closely with managers to ensure that officers' activities are consistent with the unit's mission and objectives.

In the police organization, the first-line supervisor is usually a sergeant. We say *first-line* because sergeants are responsible for supervising those officers who are engaged in providing basic police services. Captains and lieutenants (called middle managers) also supervise, but they supervise persons who are also supervisors, and are more concerned with a unit's activities rather than with an individual officer's activities. In actuality, all ranking personnel from the chief to the sergeant supervise, but this text is concerned with supervision by sergeants and mid-level managers.

Finally, the terms *police officer, law enforcement officer,* and *peace officer* are also generally interchangeable. The primary difference is that peace officer refers to anyone who has arrest authority and usually includes correctional officers, probation officers, parole officers, and persons with special police powers. Correctional officers have specific police powers in their correctional facility workplace, and investigators of welfare or Medicaid fraud have limited peace officer powers. In this text, we are primarily concerned with police officers, who include municipal or rural officers; deputy sheriffs; highway patrol; troopers; state police; and others holding local, state, or federal law enforcement officer status. For the purpose of this text, the term *police officer* will generally be used to refer to all the positions noted.

ORGANIZATION OF THE BOOK

The 14 chapters of this book are organized to provide the reader with an understanding of the key elements of police supervision and management from both the theoretical and applied perspectives. To understand the challenges of police supervision and management, we must first place it within the "big picture" of a police organization. Thus, Part One, "The Supervisor in a Police Organization," introduces the concepts of supervision and management, the roles and responsibilities of supervisors and middle managers, leadership and motivation, and effective communication and negotiation in an organization.

Part Two examines the supervision of human resources. This section addresses training, evaluation, stress and wellness, ethics and liability, and subordinates' rights and discipline. It essentially provides information on the "people" in the police organization. Somewhere between 75 and 90 percent of a police department's budget is for personnel. It is therefore important for the supervisor and manager to learn how to manage this important resource. These chapters elaborate how the police department via the supervisor and manager work with people, motivate them, and ensure that the department's mission is achieved.

Part Three, "Supervising the Work of Police," contains information that is more applied in nature and reviews supervisors and managers at work, both on and off the street. It addresses what they need to know concerning officer deployment and scheduling, patrol and special operations, tactical operations and critical incidents, and community oriented policing and problem solving (COPPS). COPPS is now policing's primary paradigm and, as seen in Chapter 13, has had a profound impact on how police departments operate; this impact has filtered down to the supervisor and middle manager. Although it could have been placed in Part One or Two, this chapter on COPPS is purposely located at the end of the book, in Part Three's discussion of police work, because the challenge for police agencies is to *make COPPS a part of daily practice.* The authors want to emphasize to readers that it is more than merely a philosophical concept. It is *one that must be put into practice.*

Part Four provides a look at future trends and challenges. It examines what technology will offer law enforcement in the future.

Also note that at the end of each chapter are *case studies*—27 in all throughout the book—that allow the reader to contemplate the kinds of problems that are routinely confronted by police supervisors and managers and to apply the chapter materials. Discussion questions are also provided at the end of each chapter, to assist the reader in understanding the information contained in the chapter. With a fundamental knowledge of the criminal justice system and a reading of the chapters, the reader should be in a position to engage in some critical analysis—and even, it is hoped, some spirited discussions—of the issues involved and arrive at several feasible solutions to the problems presented.

ACKNOWLEDGMENTS

This book, and our collaborative effort in bringing it to fruition, was made possible with the input, counsel, guidance, and moral support of several people. The authors wish to acknowledge Frank Mortimer, Executive Editor; Sarah Holle, Assistant Editor; and Denise Brown, Production Liaison at Prentice Hall. In addition, we would like to acknowledge Naomi Sysak, Project Manager; and Linda Benson, copyeditor.

We are also grateful to the book's reviewers, who provided their insights and guidance and contributed a great deal toward making this a better effort (of course, we bear sole responsibility for any shortcomings in the final product): Terry Hoffman, Nassau Community College, Garden City, NY; James Albrecht, John Jay College, New York, NY; Alex del Carmen, University of Texas–Arlington, Arlington, TX; and Jeffrey Magers, SUNY College–Brockport, Brockport, NY.

Kenneth J. Peak
Larry K. Gaines
Ronald W. Glensor

About the Authors

---------------------------------- ❖ ----------------------------------

Ken Peak is professor and former chairman of the Department of Criminal Justice, University of Nevada, Reno, where he was named "Teacher of the Year" by the university's Honor Society. He entered municipal policing in Kansas in 1970 and subsequently held positions as a nine-county criminal justice planner in Kansas; director of a four-state Technical Assistance Institute for the Law Enforcement Assistance Administration; director of university police at Pittsburg State University (Kansas); acting director of public safety, University of Nevada, Reno; and assistant professor of criminal justice at Wichita State University. He has published 12 textbooks (on community policing, criminal justice administration, and police supervision and management), two historical books (on temperance and bootlegging), and more than 50 additional journal articles and book chapters. He served as chairman of the Police Section of the Academy of Criminal Justice Sciences and president of the Western and Pacific Association of Criminal Justice Educators. He received two gubernatorial appointments to statewide criminal justice committees while residing in Kansas and holds a doctorate from the University of Kansas.

Larry K. Gaines currently is a professor and chair of the Criminal Justice Department at California State University at San Bernardino. He received his doctorate in criminal justice from Sam Houston State University. He has police experience with the Kentucky State Police and the Lexington, Kentucky, Police Department.

Additionally, he served as the executive director of the Kentucky Association of Chiefs of Police for 14 years. Dr. Gaines is also a past president of the Academy of Criminal Justice Sciences. His research centers on policing and drugs. In addition to numerous articles, he has co-authored a number of books in the field: *Police Operations; Police Administration; Managing the Police Organization; Community Policing: A Contemporary Perspective; Policing Perspectives: An Anthology; Policing in America; Drugs, Crime, and Justice; Criminal Justice in Action;* and *Readings in White Collar Crime.* His current research agenda involves on the evaluation of police tactics in terms of their effectiveness in reducing problems and fitting within the community policing paradigm. He is also researching the issue of racial profiling in a number of California cities.

Ronald W. Glensor is a deputy chief of the Reno, Nevada, Police Department (RPD). He has more than 26 years of police experience and has commanded the department's patrol, administration, and detective divisions. He has been active in the development of, and training for, the RPD's community oriented policing and problem solving (COPPS) initiative since 1987 and has also provided COPPS training for more than 250 police agencies throughout the United States and in Canada, Australia, and the United Kingdom. He was the 1997 recipient of the prestigious Gary P. Hayes Award conferred by the Police Executive Research Forum for contributions in the policing field, served a six-month fellowship as problem-oriented policing coordinator with the Police Executive Research Forum in Washington, DC, and received an Atlantic Fellowship in public policy, studying repeat victimization at the Home Office in London. He is co-author of five textbooks and has also published in several journals and trade magazines. He is an adjunct professor at the University of Nevada, Reno, and instructs at area police academies and criminal justice programs. He holds a doctorate in political science from the University of Nevada, Reno.

PART ONE

The Supervisor in a Police Organization

PART ONE

The Supervisor and Police Organization

1
The Dynamics of Police Organizations

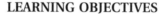

LEARNING OBJECTIVES

After reading this chapter, the student will:

- understand the concept of organizations
- be able to explain how organizational theory evolved
- describe several major elements of administrative theory
- understand rationales and purposes of police organizational design
- know how informal organizations, inertia, and unionization affect police organizations
- understand the basic philosophy underlying community policing and problem solving, and how organizations must be modified in order to accommodate this strategy

We are born in organizations, educated by organizations, and most of us spend much of our lives working for organizations. We spend much of our leisure time paying, playing, and praying in organizations. Most of us will die in an organization, and when the time comes for burial, the largest organization of all—the state—must grant official permission.

—Amitai Etzioni

No organization, regardless of its character, can rise higher than the quality and competency of its supervisory officials.

—August Vollmer

INTRODUCTION

Supervision and management are extremely important factors in determining whether or not an organization achieves its mission and goals.

This chapter looks closely at organizations, first in general terms, and then examines the evolution of organizational theory, including scientific management and bureaucratic management. Next, we examine administrative theory, which includes universal methods of administration and a number of important concepts that have been used to help in the smooth operation of organizations. Rationales and purposes of police organizational design are then reviewed, followed by some influencial factors to consider: informal organizations, inertia, and employee unions. The chapter concludes with a view of how organizational change must accompany community policing and problem solving.

THE CONCEPT OF ORGANIZATIONS

Organizations are entities consisting of two or more people who cooperate to accomplish an objective(s). In that sense, certainly the *concept* of organization is not new. Undoubtedly, the first organizations were primitive hunting parties. Organization and a high degree of coordination were required to bring down huge animals, as revealed in fossils from as early as 40,000 B.C. Organizations today are much more complex, often involving thousands of people. The New York City Police Department has more than 39,000 officers who must be supervised and managed. Most organizations are much smaller. The majority of police departments in the United States have 10 or fewer officers. Regardless of size, all organizations are organized and managed.

An *organization* may be formally defined as "a consciously coordinated social entity, with a relative identifiable boundary, that functions on a relatively continuous basis to achieve a common goal or set of goals" (Robbins, 1990:4). The term *consciously coordinated* implies supervision. *Social entity* refers to the fact that organizations are composed of people who interact with one another and with people in other organizations. *Relatively identifiable boundary* alludes to the organization's goals and the public served (Gaines, Southerland, and Angell, 1991:43). Following is an analogy to assist in understanding organizations:

> Organization corresponds to the bones which structure or give form to the body. Imagine that the fingers were a single mass of bone rather than four separate fingers and a thumb made up of bones joined by cartilage so that they are flexible. The mass of bones could not, because of its structure, play musical instruments, hold a pencil, or grip a baseball bat. A police department's organization is analogous. It must be structured properly if it is to be effective in fulfilling its many diverse goals. (Gaines et al., 1991:9)

An organization, especially a police department, can be just as complex as the human body. All sorts of managerial processes occur in the police department: decision making, planning, leadership, motivation, and control of subordinates' behavior. Moreover, the many parts or units in a police department may include patrol, criminal investigation, traffic, juvenile services, gang unit, drug interdiction, or domestic violence. These processes and parts must operate in harmony if the department is to achieve its goals and objectives.

It is the supervisors and managers who are most often responsible for ensuring harmonious coordination in the police department. Supervisors are concerned with *tasks* and *human resources*. With the former, they are responsible for ensuring that subordinate officers attend to their duties in a manner that is consistent with departmental expectations. They see that officers do their jobs the best way possible. Human resources refers to the fact that supervisors are responsible for people. People, especially in the workplace, often have problems and difficulties. Supervisors attempt to solve these problems and difficulties through training, supervision, and the provision of direction. Managers essentially have the same responsibilities, only at a higher level. In addition to being concerned with tasks and human resources, managers must ensure that the efforts of supervisors and officers collectively fulfill the unit's departmental responsibilities.

THE EVOLUTION OF ORGANIZATIONAL THEORY

The following section examines the development of organizational theory, which explains how an organization operates and provides the background for understanding productivity and leadership.

Scientific Management

Frederick Winslow Taylor, whom many consider to be the "father of scientific management," sought to refine management techniques by studying how workers might become more complete extensions of machines. Taylor (1911) was primarily interested in discovering the best means for getting the most out of employees—mostly the blue-collar workers at Bethlehem Steel in Pennsylvania where Taylor worked as chief engineer in 1898. Taylor maintained that management knew little about the limits of worker production and was the first to introduce time and motion studies to test his argument.

Taylor believed that by observing workers in action, wasted motions could be eliminated and production increased. He began by measuring the amount of time it took workers to shovel and carry pig iron. Taylor then standardized the work into specific tasks, improved worker selection and training, established workplace rules, and advocated close supervision of workers by a foreman.

The results were incredible; worker productivity soared. The total number of shovelers needed dropped from about 600 to 140, and worker earnings increased from $1.15 to $1.88 per day. The average cost of handling a long ton (2,240 pounds) dropped from $0.072 to $0.033.

Although criticized by unions for his management-oriented views, Taylor nonetheless proved that administrators must know their employees. His views caught on and soon emphasis was placed entirely on the formal administrative structure; later, such terms as *authority, chain of command, span of control,* and *division of labor* (discussed later) became part of the workplace vocabulary.

Taylor's work also spawned the idea of functional supervision, which is applicable to policing. In Taylor's time, supervisors were assigned to jobs but did not always have the technical expertise to adequately supervise their subordinates. *Functional supervision* entailed having several different supervisors on a job so that each one oversaw a particular aspect or part of the job—a part he or she had expertise in and could provide adequate supervision. Functional supervision is important in policing. For example, a sergeant supervising criminal investigations must have expertise in investigations, while a sergeant in traffic must have expertise in accident investigation and selective enforcement techniques.

Bureaucratic Management

Police agencies certainly fit the description of an organization. First, they are managed by being organized into a number of specialized units. Administrators, managers, and supervisors exist to ensure that these units work together toward a common goal; each unit working independently would lead to fragmentation, conflict, and competition and would subvert the entire organization's goals and purposes. Second, police agencies consist of people who interact within the organization and with external organizations, and they exist to serve the public.

The development of an organization requires careful consideration, or the agency may be unable to respond efficiently to community needs. For example, the creation of too many specialized units in a police department (e.g., street crimes, bicycle patrol, media relations, or domestic violence) may obligate too many officers to these functions and result in too few patrol officers. As a rule of

A patrol supervisor's day begins by giving officers vital information in briefing.
Courtesy Riverside, California, Police Department.

thumb, at least 55 percent of all sworn personnel should be assigned to patrol (Guyot, 1979:253–284). Indeed, a recent survey by the U.S. Department of Justice, Bureau of Justice Statistics (1999) found that an average of 63 percent of sworn officers in local police agencies were uniformed, with regular duties that included responding to calls for service.

Police administrators, through a mission statement, policies and procedures, a proper management style, and direction, attempt to ensure that the organization maintains its overall goals of crime suppression, order maintenance, and investigation, and that it works amicably with other organizations and people. As the organization becomes larger, the need becomes greater for people to cooperate to achieve organizational goals. (Formal organizational structures, which assist in this endeavor by spelling out areas of responsibility, lines of communication, and the chain of command, are discussed later.)

Police organizations in the United States are also *bureaucracies,* as are virtually all large organizations in modern society, such as the military, universities, and corporations (Gaines and Swanson, 1999). In popular terms, a bureaucracy has often come to be viewed in a negative light, as slow, ponderous, routine, complicated, and composed of "red tape," which frustrates its members and clients (Crozier, 1964). This image is far from the ideal or pure bureaucracy developed by Max Weber, the German sociologist, who claimed in 1947 that a bureaucratic organization

> from a purely technical point of view, [is] capable of attaining the highest degree of efficiency and is the most rational known means of carrying out imperative control over human beings. It is superior to any other form in precision, in stability, in the stringency of its discipline, and in its reliability, and is formally capable of application to all kinds of administrative tasks. (Weber, 1947:337)

The administration of most police organizations is based on the traditional, pyramidal, quasi-military organizational structure containing the elements of a bureaucracy: specialized functions, adherence to fixed rules, and a hierarchy of authority. This pyramidal organizational environment is undergoing increasing challenges, especially as a result of departments implementing community policing.

A simple structure indicating the hierarchy of authority or chain of command is shown in Figure 1–1.

To a large extent, police agencies are similar in their structure and management process. The major differences between agencies exist between the large and the very small agencies; the former will be more complex, with much more specialization, a hierarchical structure, and a greater degree of authoritarian style of command.

In the 1970s, experts on police organization, such as Egon Bittner (1970:51), were contending that the military-bureaucratic organization of the police was a serious handicap that created obstacles to the development of a truly professional police system. The reasons for this disillusionment include the quasi-military rank and disciplinary structures within police organizations; the lack of opportunity of management to match talent and positions; the organizational restrictions on personal freedom of expression, association, and dress; communication blockage in the tall structure; the organizational clinging to outmoded methods of operation; the lack of management flexibility; and the narrowness of job descriptions in the lower ranks of police organizations (Johnson, Misner, and Brown, 1981:53). This criticism continues today as proponents of community policing advocate that bureaucratic police departments should be decentralized so that decisions are made at lower levels of the department, allowing operational units to better meet citizen demands (Gray, Bodnar, and Lovrich, 1997; Sparrow, Moore, and Kennedy, 1990).

Notwithstanding this growing disenchantment with the traditional bureaucratic structure of police organizations, this structure continues to prevail; for many administrators, it is still the best structure when rapid leadership and division of labor are required in times of crises (Gaines and Swanson, 1999). The traditional school of thought that each police supervisor can effectively supervise only seven employees is part of the reason for this "tall" organizational structure. A number of agencies have experimented with other approaches, and the results have been mixed. Most departments have elected to retain the classical police structure (Maguire, 1997).

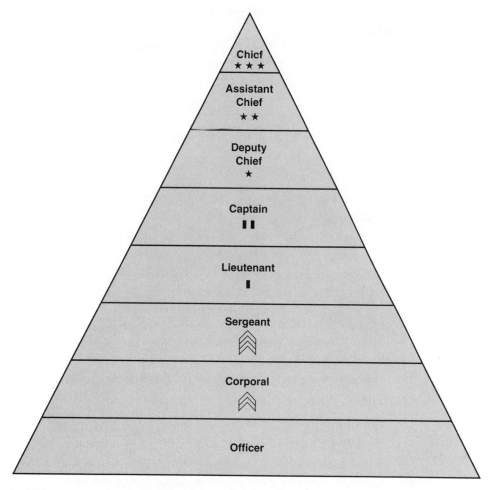

FIGURE 1–1 Traditional Pyramidal Chain of Command

Indeed, when police agencies have attempted to flatten the organizational structure, they have most often returned to the traditional organizational configuration. Perhaps an alternative is to keep a few features of the military model (such as police officers taking orders from superiors during critical incidents) and a few features of the bureaucratic model and then go beyond these to create a reasonably professional organization.

ADMINISTRATIVE THEORY

Administrative or management theory seeks to identify generic or universal methods of administration. Further, administrative theory is more compatible with the bureaucratic model than with scientific management, because it concentrates on broader principles. Key contributors to this school are Henri Fayol, Luther Gulick, and Lyndall Urwick.

The greatest contributions of Fayol, a French engineer, came from his experiences as a manager. His fame rests largely on his *General and Industrial Management* (1949), which includes the following principles:

1. Division of work: specialization
2. Authority: the right to give orders and to extract obedience
3. Discipline: the obedience, energy, behavior, and outward signs of respect as agreed upon by the organization and its employees
4. Unity of command: an employee receiving orders from only one supervisor
5. Unity of direction: with one leader and one plan for a group of activities having the same objective
6. Subordination of individual interest to the general interest
7. Remuneration of personnel
8. Centralization: a natural order of things
9. Scalar chain: the chain of superiors ranging from the ultimate authority to the lowest ranks, or chain of command
10. Order: a place for everyone and everyone in his or her place
11. Equity: the combination of kindness and justice
12. Stability of tenure of personnel: allowing employees to become familiar with their jobs and to be productive
13. Initiative at all levels of the organization
14. Esprit de corps and harmony: providing great strength

POSDCORB

Gulick and Urwick (1937) examined the role of administration in organizations and identified several key management functions. They articulated these functions using the acronym POSDCORB (for *p*lanning, *o*rganizing, *s*taffing, *d*irecting, *co*ordinating, *r*eporting, and *b*udgeting) as noted in Figure 1–2. Gulick and Urwick were most interested in how organizations might be structured and the role of managers within them. POSDCORB identified the key administrative activities that occupy the majority of a manager's time.

Gulick and Urwick also emphasized the need for coordinating the work by dividing labor within organizations. In police departments, this is known as specialization. *Specialization* means that similar tasks are grouped together so that they can be performed more efficiently. For example, many police departments have traffic units

---

Planning—working out in brad outline the things that need to be done and the methods for doing them to accomplish the purpose set for the enterprise.

Organizing—establishment of the formal structure of authority through which work subdivisions are arranged, defined, and coordinated for the defined objective.

Staffing—the whole personnel function of bringing in and training the staff and maintaining favorable conditions at work.

Directing—the continuous task of making decisions, embodying them in specific and general orders and instructions, and serving as a leader of the enterprise.

Coordinating—the all-important duty of interrelating the various parts of the work.

Reporting—keeping those to whom the execution is responsible informed about what is going on, which includes keeping himself and his subordinates informed through records, research, and inspection.

Budgeting—all that goes with budgeting in the form of fiscal planning, accounting, and control.

FIGURE 1–2 POSDCORB

Source: Luther H. Gulick and Lyndell Urwick, eds., *Papers on the Science of Administration* (New York: Institute of Public Administration, 1937), p. 13.

that handle all police activities related to the enforcement of traffic laws. The division of labor in police agencies is evident when examining an organizational chart. (See Figure 1–4, an organizational chart for the Portland, Oregon, Police Bureau, p. 20.)

Gulick and Urwick also saw the need in organizations for a hierarchy, whereby supervisors used a chain of command to coordinate orders and information from the top to the bottom of the organization. Sparrow, Moore, and Kennedy (1990) found that large American police departments averaged from nine to thirteen levels of rank or hierarchy.

Gulick and Urwick also believed that work should be coordinated in groups with one supervisor in charge. This concept, referred to as *span of control,* identified the number of persons reporting to a supervisor. Six to ten officers reporting to one supervisor is a commonly accepted span of control in policing, especially considering that patrol officers are assigned to a wide geographical area and that detectives often are investigating complicated criminal cases.

Taylor's scientific management theory and Gulick and Urwick's principles of administration, with their emphasis on the technical and engineering side of management, became known as *classical organizational theory.* Classical theory was quickly adopted by police in the first training schools in New York City and Berkeley, California, and influenced some of the early writers on police administration, including O. W. Wilson, V. A. Leonard, and August Vollmer. These theories remain the foundation for police management and supervision today.

Unity of Command

A related, important principle of hierarchy of authority is *unity of command,* an organizational principle that dictates that every officer should report to one and only one superior (following the chain of command). The unity of command

Interpersonal skills are essential for a supervisor's success.
Courtesy San Bernardino County, California.

principle applies to administrators and managers as well. That is, they do not skip over a sergeant or supervisor and give commands directly to an officer.

Ambiguity over authority occurs frequently in police organizations. Detectives and patrol officers often dispute who has authority over a criminal case; officers in two different patrol beats may disagree over who has responsibility for a call for service that is located on a beat boundary line. Numerous situations result in conflict because the lines of authority are unclear; as departments become larger and more complex, the amount of conflict naturally increases. The nature of conflict in the police setting is addressed in Chapter 4.

The unity of command principle also ensures that multiple and/or conflicting orders are not issued to the same police officers by several supervisors. For example, a patrol sergeant might arrive at a hostage situation and deploy personnel and give all the appropriate orders, only to have a shift lieutenant or captain come to the scene and countermand the sergeant's orders. This type of situation would obviously be counterproductive for all persons concerned. It is also important that all officers know and follow the chain of command at such incidents. In this example, the shift lieutenant or captain normally should consult with the sergeant before taking charge of the situation or giving any orders.

Span of Control

Span of control refers to the number of persons a superior officer can effectively supervise. The limit is small, normally three to five at the top level of the organization, and often larger at the lower levels, depending on factors such as the capacity of the supervisor and those persons supervised, the type of work performed, the complexity of the work, the area covered by it, distances between elements, the time needed to perform the tasks, and the type of persons served. Normally, a patrol sergeant will supervise six to ten officers, while a patrol lieutenant may have four or five sergeants reporting to him or her. This distribution of supervisors and managers applies to most of the units in a police department.

The tendency in modern police operations is to have the supervisors spread too thinly. Police supervisors and managers must be accessible to police officers. A patrol officer or detective may periodically encounter a situation that he or she does not know how to handle. It may not have been covered in the department's policies and procedures or it may be a unique situation. The officer must have the ability to discuss the issue with a superior. Also, sergeants are sometimes expected to back up officers on calls. This not only affords the responding officer support, but it also allows the supervisor to evaluate a subordinate's performance. If there are problems with an officer's performance, the supervisor can take action before the problem becomes a major issue. The supervisor can counsel the subordinate or assign him or her to the appropriate training. The supervisor must be in a position to monitor officers' activities and deal with problems before they become more serious.

Policies, Procedures, and Rules and Regulations

In policing, policies, procedures, and rules and regulations are important for defining role expectations for officers. In essence, they specify how officers should do their jobs. The department relies on these directives to guide or control officers' behavior and performance. Because police agencies are intended to be service oriented in nature, they must work within well-defined, specific guidelines designed to ensure that all officers conform to behavior that will enhance public protection (Alpert and Smith, 1999). Police supervisors must control officer behavior, but, it is hoped, officers have the initiative and dedication to perform up to departmental standards.

Police agencies normally distribute their policies, procedures, and rules and regulations in the form of General Orders. Larger agencies may have as many as a hundred General Orders, covering topics such as code of conduct, use of force, and pursuit driving. The General Order normally begins with a policy statement about the subject and then follows with detailed procedures concerning how the order will work in practice. Figure 1–3 is an example of a police agency's General Order. Notice how the General Order provides fairly specific guidelines. Such orders provide officers specific guidance about various tasks and responsibilities.

ANYWHERE USA POLICE DEPARTMENT GENERAL ORDER

Legal Advisor:	Approving Deputy Chief:	Chief of Police:

General Order No: 3/254.000

DOMESTIC VIOLENCE

Date Issued: November 4, 2002	**Last Review:** MAR/03

I. POLICY

The Anywhere USA Police Department recognizes that domestic violence has serious consequences to the family involved and necessitates prompt and thorough investigation. The Anywhere USA Police Department will investigate all calls for service involving domestic violence, recognizing that an aggressive policy of arresting domestic violence assailants leads to the reduction of domestic violence crimes and domestic homicides.

II. PROCEDURES

Officers will adhere to the arrest requirements as set forth under State Law PC 170.137:

170.137 Domestic violence: When arrest required; report required; compilation of statistics.

　1. Except as otherwise provided in subsection 2, whether or not a warrant has been issued, a peace officer shall, unless mitigating circumstances exist, arrest a person when he has probable cause to believe that the person to be arrested has, within the preceding 24 hours, committed a battery upon his spouse, former spouse, any other person to whom he is related by blood or marriage, a person with whom he is or was actually residing, a person with whom he has had or is having a dating relationship, a person with whom he has a child in common, the minor child of any of those persons or his minor child.
　2. If the peace officer has probable cause to believe that a battery described in subsection 1 was a mutual battery, he shall attempt to determine which person was the primary physical aggressor. If the peace officer determines that one of the persons who allegedly committed a battery was the primary physical aggressor involved in the incident, the peace officer is not required to arrest any other person believed to have committed a battery during the incident. In determining whether a person is a primary physical aggressor for the purposes of this subsection, the peace officer shall consider:
　　(a) Prior domestic violence involving either person;
　　(b) The relative severity of the injuries inflicted upon the persons involved;
　　(c) The potential for future injury;
　　(d) Whether one of the alleged batteries was committed in self-defense;

FIGURE 1–3   Example of a Police Agency's General Order

　　　Police officers have a great deal of discretion when answering calls for service or performing investigations (Walker, 1993). The task for the supervisor is to find the middle ground between wide discretionary authority possessed by the police and total standardization. The police role is much too ambiguous to become totally standardized, but it is also much too serious and important to be left completely to the total discretion of the officer. Officers will often seek a supervisor's opinion and guidance in discretionary matters. This requires that a supervisor is well informed about all policies, procedures, and rules and regulations. In some cases, the supervisor must seek clarification from his or her manager, especially in abnormal situations.

Policies are quite general and serve as guides to thinking, rather than action. Policies reflect the purpose and philosophy of the organization and help interpret those elements to the officers. An example of a policy might be that when answering calls at locations with a history of multiple calls, officers should attempt to identify the cause of the problems and take remedial action. A number of departments today are expanding on the idea of policies or guides and developing mission statements and value statements for officers. These mission and value statements are overarching guides that attempt to provide direction to officers as they perform their various job duties.

Procedures are more detailed than policies and provide the preferred methods for handling matters pertaining to investigation, patrol, booking, radio procedures, filing reports, roll call, use of force, arrest, sick leave, evidence handling, promotion, and many more job elements. Procedures describe how officers are to complete a specific task.

Rules and regulations are specific guidelines that leave little or no latitude for individual discretion. Some examples are requirements that police officers not smoke in public, check the operation of their vehicle and equipment before going on patrol, not consume alcoholic beverages within a specified number of hours of going on duty, arrive in court or at roll call early, or specify the type of weapons that officers carry on or off duty. Rules and regulations are not always popular, especially if perceived as unfair or unrelated to the job. Nonetheless, it is the supervisor's responsibility to ensure that officers perform these tasks with the same degree of professional demeanor as other job duties. As Thomas Reddin, former Los Angeles police chief, stated:

> Certainly we must have rules, regulations and procedures, and they should be followed. But they are no substitutes for initiative and intelligence. The more a [person] is given an opportunity to make decisions and, in the process, to learn, the more rules and regulations will be followed. (1966:17)

The Emergence of Humanism

Dissatisfaction with classical organizational theory began to develop in the 1930s. The emergence of labor unions had begun to put pressure on management to develop more humane and effective ways of managing and supervising workers. The human relations school of management evolved as a result of this dissatisfaction as well as from the Hawthorne experiments in the early 1930s.

The Hawthorne experiments provided the first glimpse of human relations theory. The Western Electric Company conducted a number of scientific management studies at its Hawthorne facilities in Chicago from 1927 through 1932. The experiments were an attempt to determine the level of illumination (light) and pattern of employee breaks that produced the highest levels of worker productivity. The researchers segregated a group of workers in an area and made numerous and varied changes in the levels of illumination and the length and number of work breaks. It was believed that if the optimal level of illumination and number and duration of work breaks could be discovered, employees would be more productive. Productivity increased as these two variables were manipulated. Ultimately, however, no consistent pattern in the changes in production relative to the changes in lighting and work breaks emerged. Productivity increased when work breaks were increased, and it increased when work breaks were reduced. The same pattern occurred when illumination was increased and reduced. Given the inconsistencies, the researchers could not discern why productivity was changing. Finally, the increases in productivity were attributed to worker job satisfaction from increased involvement and concern on the part of management. In essence, management's displayed concern for the workers, as evidenced in the experiment itself, resulted in higher morale and productivity.

Prior to the Hawthorne experiments, employers were not concerned with employees or their feelings. It was assumed that employees followed management's dictates. The Hawthorne experiments spurred a significant change in the relationship between management and employees. Management realized that individual workers and the work group itself could have just as much impact on productivity as management. The experiments signaled a need for management to harness worker energy and ideas so that management and workers could mutually benefit.

During the 1940s and 1950s, this research led to both private and public organizations recognizing the strong effect of the working environment and informal structures on the organization. In policing, attention was being paid to job enlargement and enrichment techniques to generate interest in the profession as a career. *Employee-centered* management approaches such as participatory management began to appear in policing. By the 1970s, there was also a move away from the traditional pyramid-shaped organizational structure to a more flattened structure with fewer mid-levels of management (Tenzel, Storms, and Sweetwood, 1976). This has resulted in an increase in responsibilities for managers and first-line supervisors as more responsibilities were delegated downward in the department.

McGregor's Theory X/Theory Y

Douglas McGregor (1966) was a proponent of a more humanistic and democratic approach to management. His work was based on two basic assumptions about people: Theory X, which views employees negatively and sees the need for structured organizations with strict hierarchal lines and close supervision; and Theory Y, which takes a more humanistic view toward employees, believing that they are capable of being motivated and productive. A further explanation of the assumptions about human nature and behavior that emerge from these divergent theories follows:

Theory X

- The average employee dislikes work and will avoid it whenever possible.
- People are lazy, avoid responsibility, and must be controlled, directed, and coerced to perform their work.
- People are inherently self-centered and do not care about organizational needs.
- People will naturally resist change.

Theory Y

- The average employee does not inherently dislike work.
- People will exercise self-control and are self-directed when motivated to achieve organizational goals.
- People are capable of learning and will not only accept, but will seek responsibility.
- People's capacity for imagination, ingenuity, and creativity are only partially utilized.

Theory X portrays a dismal view of employees and their motivation to work and supports the traditional model of direction and control. In contrast, Theory Y is more optimistic and leads one to believe that motivated employees will perform productively. Also, Theory Y assumes some responsibility on the part of managers to create a climate that is conducive to learning and achieving organizational goals.

Although it may appear that Theory X managers are bad and Theory Y managers are good, McGregor did not support one style over the other. Administrators may need the flexibility of employing one or both theories, depending on the personnel involved and the situation. For example, a supervisor dealing with an officer resisting attempts to remediate unacceptable behavior may need to rely on a Theory X approach until the officer is corrected. On the other hand, a self-motivated and skilled officer given the task of developing a briefing training lesson plan may require limited supervision and therefore can be guided through the task by employing Theory Y.

The human relations approach, however, is not without its critics. There is concern that shifting the emphasis away from administration and structure to social rewards for employees would distract from the accomplishment of organizational goals. Critics also argue that it can lead employees to expect more rewards for less effort (Lynch, 1986). Gaines (1978) noted that classical theory was organization without people, while human relations theory was people without organization.

As a general rule, the police field found bureaucratic management to be more acceptable. In the first half of the last century, police managers were strongly influenced by the reform movement that swept the nation. Corruption was rampant and the key words for resolving the problems were "efficiency" and "control." The goals of progressive chiefs were to gain control of their departments and to reduce political influence. Human relations was viewed as vague, and the military model with its rank and structure was viewed as almost a perfect panacea for resolving the problems of police managers (More and Wegener, 1992). Moreover, police departments and police chiefs were accountable to the public. One method for the chief to ensure that people and units were operating as envisioned was to enact controls, which were best facilitated by the principles of classical management.

The Systems Approach

By the mid-1950s, it was apparent that classical organizational theory and the human relations approach were inadequate to ensure a productive organization. Consequently, a new theory, *systems theory,* began to evolve. Systems theory has its roots in biology. An organization is similar to a living organism. It absorbs energy, processes the energy into some kind of output such as services, and attempts to maintain an equilibrium with its environment.

The systems approach emphasizes the interdependence and interrelationship of each and every part to the whole. According to Luthans (1985:94), "A system is composed of elements or subsystems that are related and dependent upon one another. When these sub-systems are in interaction with one another, they form a unitary whole."

The main premise of the theory is that to fully understand the operation of an entity, the entity must be viewed as a system or as a whole. The system can be modified only through changes in its parts. A thorough knowledge of how each part functions and the interrelationships among the parts must be present before modifications can be made (Certo, 1989).

This view opposes the way law enforcement agencies traditionally have been organized and have functioned. For example, detective units often work separate and apart from the remainder of the police department. It is not uncommon for other specialty units such as gangs, traffic, and street crimes to work in isolation as well. Functionally, what often occurs is that there are isolated subsystems with a limited interrelationship. The systems approach to management attempts to deal with this problem, trying to unify the various parts of the organization into a functioning whole.

A systems-oriented supervisor and other leaders must look at the big picture and continually analyze and evaluate how the entire organization is performing with respect to its missions, goals, and objectives. For example, in the case of a new policy regarding police pursuits, a systems-oriented supervisor would be conscious of how the new policy would affect all the organizational divisions, including patrol, investigations, administration, and training. A systems approach also takes into account the potential impact of decisions on external factors, such as the general public, political environment, and other criminal justice agencies. The goal is that all agencies and their units work together to resolve problems.

This section provided a brief introduction to organizational theory. Over time, three different schools of organizational thought have evolved: classical, human relations, and systems. Although various parts of human relations and systems theory can be applied to police organizations, most departments today still use classical theory as the basis for organizing (Maguire, 1997). Wycoff (1994) found that 61 percent of police administrators in her study reported that there was no need to change the organizational structure of their departments to implement community policing. Thus, it appears that many police administrators are content with current arrangements.

RATIONALES AND PURPOSES OF POLICE ORGANIZATIONAL DESIGN

All organizations have an organizational structure, be it written or unwritten, basic or highly complex. Administrators, managers, and supervisors use this organizational chart as a blueprint for action. The size of the organization depends on the demand placed on it and the resources available to it. Growth precipitates the need for more people, greater division of labor, specialization, written rules, and other such elements. Police administrators modify or design the structure of their organization to fulfill its mission.

An organizational chart reflects the formal structure of task and authority relationships determined to be most suited to accomplishing the police mission. The major concerns in organizing are

1. Identifying what jobs need to be done, such as conducting the initial investigation, performing the latent or follow-up investigation, and providing for the custody of evidence seized at crime scenes
2. Determining how to group the jobs, such as those responsible for patrol, investigation, and the operation of the property room
3. Forming grades of authority, such as officer, detective, corporal, sergeant, lieutenant, and captain
4. Equalizing responsibility—if a sergeant has the responsibility to supervise seven detectives, that sergeant must have sufficient authority to discharge that responsibility properly or he or she cannot be held accountable for any results (Robbins, 1976)

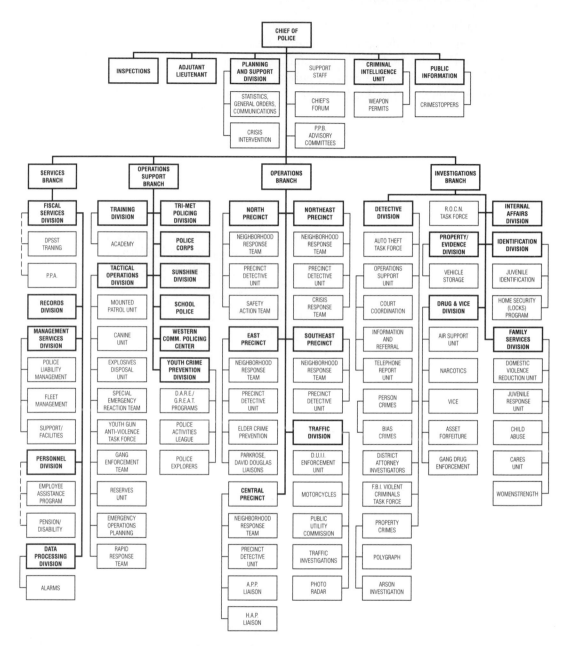

FIGURE 1–4   Portland Police Department Organizational Chart

Perhaps the best way to understand police supervision and management is to examine a police organization. Figure 1–4 shows the organizational chart for the Portland Police Bureau, including the division of labor and responsibilities common to a fairly large department. Notice that each of the four major branches in the department has a number of units. For example, the Investigations Branch has six major divisions. Detective, Property/Evidence, Drug and Vice, Internal Affairs, Identification, and Family Services. Each of these divisions are further divided into smaller subunits. The Family Services Division has five different subunits such as Domestic Violence Reduction, Juvenile Response, and Child Abuse. Drug and Vice Division includes Air Support, Narcotics, Vice, Asset Forfeiture, and Gang Drug Enforcement. Each unit would be composed of several detectives managed by a supervisor. Each of those units also has a set of distinctive goals and objectives and is commanded by a manager, a captain in large units and possibly a lieutenant or sergeant in the smaller ones. The lieutenants and sergeants who command units have the same responsibilities as the captains who command larger units.

What distinguishes the higher-ranking officers from supervisors is that they also perform planning, organizing, staffing, and other managerial functions. Higher-ranking managers have executive as well as supervisory responsibilities. They are responsible for both organization-wide functions and the supervision of their immediate subordinates.

Since all managers, regardless of their level in the organization, must supervise their subordinates, they are all responsible for directing and controlling. Higher-level managers, because of their other responsibilities, generally are unable to devote as much attention as first-line supervisors to these two important tasks. Thus, the brunt of direction and control in most organizations, including police departments, usually falls on the shoulders of supervisors. Managers cannot neglect supervision, however, because they ultimately are responsible for the operation of larger units in the organization.

FACTORS THAT INFLUENCE ORGANIZATION

The Informal Organization

Existing side by side with the formal organizational structure of a police organization is the informal organization. The structure and functions of a police organization will be shaped in large measure by several powerful forces—forces that often have a much stronger influence over how a department conducts its business than do managers of the department, the courts, legislatures, politicians, and members of the community.

Police agencies have a life and culture of their own. Within any organization, some people emerge as leaders, regardless of whether or not they are in a leadership position. In addition, within organizations, people will form their own groups, which may operate without official recognition and may influence agency performance (Bennett and Hess, 2001). This informal organization may help or harm the goals of the formal organization and can carry gossip, misinformation, and malicious rumors (communication within organizations is discussed in

Chapter 4). Therefore, supervisors and managers must recognize the informal organization that exists within their agency.

Police Culture and Inertia

The willingness to change is a fundamental requirement of today's police leaders, especially under community oriented policing and problem solving. Police agencies must modify their culture from top to bottom. Change is never easy, however, because there is so much uncertainty accompanying it. It is much easier to proceed with the status quo, because "we've always done it this way."

Indeed, probably the most common characteristic of change is people's resistance to it. Adapting to a new environment or methods often results in feelings of stress or other forms of psychological discomfort. Resistance to change is likely when employees do not clearly understand the purpose, mechanics, or consequences of a planned change because of inadequate or misperceived communication.

Those who resist change are sometimes coerced into accepting it. Change in police agencies, particularly a major change, is frequently characterized by the use of centralized decision making and coercive tactics. Through the use of task forces, ad hoc committees, group seminars, and other participatory techniques, employees can become more directly involved in planning for change. By thoroughly discussing and debating the issues, a more accurate understanding and unbiased analysis of the situation is likely to result.

Any police executive contemplating change should do so in a manner that offers the greatest possibility of success. As Swanson, Territo, and Taylor (2001:642) noted:

> Conventional wisdom about change states that the way to change an organization is to bring in a new top executive, give the individual his or her head (and maybe a hatchet), and let the individual make the changes that he or she deems necessary. What the conventional wisdom overlooks are the long-term consequences of unilateral, top-down change.

The problem, then, with radical and unilateral change is the possibility of a severe backlash in the organization; a complementary problem for changes that are made gradually is that after many months or a few years of meetings, discussion, and planning sessions, nothing much has actually happened in the organization. Finding an appropriate pace for change to occur—neither too quickly and radically nor too slowly and gradually—is one of the most critical problems of planned organizational change.

Therefore, police managers and supervisors must be *viable change agents*. In any hierarchy, a person who oversees others is responsible for setting both the policy and the tone of the organization. Many police organizations boast talented and creative chief executives who, when participating in the change process, will assist in effecting change that is beneficial and lasting. As James Q. Wilson (1997:3) put it,

> The police profession today is the intellectual leadership of the criminal justice profession in the United States. The police are in the lead. They're showing the world how things might better be done.

Employee Organizations and Unions

Another factor that will affect police organization and practices is unionization. Although police unionization as a viable force has existed in this country less than 40 years, its impact has been considerable. Unions do in fact result in fewer administrative and management prerogatives; at the bargaining table, they have shaped the way policy decisions have been made in many ways. They have thwarted the creation of civilian review boards, advocated the election of "law and order" candidates, resisted the replacement of two-officer patrol cars with one-officer cars, litigated against personnel layoffs, lobbied for increased budgets, and caused the removal of chiefs and other high-ranking administrators. When the objectives of the union and the police leaders are the same, the union can be a powerful ally, however. Nonetheless, unions often compete with the administration for control of the department; many chiefs have left their posts in order to move to an agency that has a less powerful union. This raises the issue of accountability: To what extent can chief executives and managers be held responsible for the operation of the department (Swanson et al., 2001)? (Unions are discussed further in Chapter 10.)

CONTEMPORARY APPROACHES: COMMUNITY POLICING AND PROBLEM SOLVING

New Philosophy and Practices

Policing has now entered the era of community oriented policing and problem solving; this policing strategy has expanded across the United States and indeed around the world. There are, however, some important organizational considerations that arise if COPPS is to be accommodated within the police agency.

As we discussed earlier in this chapter, the traditional, bureaucratic form of policing, with its tight control and clear-cut rules, enforced by rigorous disciplinary systems, has some positive contributions for today's policing organization; however, many of these same features are counterproductive under COPPS. The professional era of policing of the early and mid-1900s inculcated a militaristic style of management and established rigid hierarchical lines of control. As a result, chief executives often placed great emphasis on their officers "going by the book" (the operations manual) and trying to avoid any chance of something going awry that would make their department look bad. Discipline was the watchword, managers were not to "rock the boat," and sergeants were expected to maintain strict control over patrol officers.

Under COPPS, police leaders must also be pioneers. This means

1. shifting from telling and controlling employees to helping them develop their skills and abilities;

2. listening to the customers in new and more open ways;

3. solving problems, not just reacting to incidents;

4. trying new things and experimenting, realizing that risk taking and honest mistakes must be tolerated to encourage creativity and achieve innovation; and

5. avoiding, whenever possible, the use of coercive power to effect change (California Department of Justice, 1992).

COPPS forces a cultural transformation of the entire department, including a decentralized, more flattened organizational structure (to encourage officer initiative) and changes in recruiting, training, awards systems, evaluation, promotions, and so forth.

A related subject is that of values in police organizations. Police departments are powerfully influenced by their values—the beliefs that guide their practices. COPPS reflects a set of values, including a customer-driven, service orientation, with which citizens are to be treated with respect at all times, and supervisors and managers must listen for the "talk of the department" to see if values expressed by officers reflect those of the department.

A Case Study in Change: Hayward, California

A good example of a police organization that modified its structure to adapt to COPPS is Hayward, California (Kocher, 1998). First, after determining that the city had a diverse ethnic composition, changes were made in the department's recruiting, hiring, training, and evaluation processes. The city's personnel and police departments began exploring the following questions:

1. Overall, what type of candidate, possessing what type of skills, is being recruited?

2. What specific knowledge, skills, and abilities reflect the COPPS philosophy—particularly problem-solving abilities and sensitivity to the needs of the community?

3. How can these attributes best be identified through the initial screening process?

Next, all personnel, both sworn and civilian, received training in the history, philosophy, and transition to COPPS. The department's initial training was directed

Collaborating with residents to resolve neighborhood problems is the foundation of community policing.
Courtesy Charlotte, North Carolina, Police Department.

to management and supervisory personnel to ensure they understood the agency's values, modifying the existing police culture, moving the organization from traditional policing to the new philosophy, and focusing on customer relations.

Performance and reward practices for personnel were also modified. Emphasizing quality over quantity (e.g., arrest statistics, number of calls for service, response times), new criteria included an assessment of how well a call for service was handled and what type of problem-solving approach was used to reach a solution for the problem. The department's promotional process was retooled, and a new phase was added to the department's promotional test (the "promotability" phase) to evaluate the candidate's decision-making abilities, analytical skills, communication skills, interpersonal skills, and professional contributions.

Obviously, the importance of having enlightened police executives, managers, and supervisors cannot be overemphasized under a COPPS philosophy.

SUMMARY

This chapter has set the stage for the study of police supervision and management, defining organizations generally, then placing police agencies within the context of organizational and bureaucratic structures.

The reader will now have a better frame of reference for understanding the always challenging, and at times very difficult, positions of police supervisors and managers. The important part people in these positions play in human resource management is undisputed; they communicate, negotiate, train, evaluate, discipline, and deploy and must be sensitive to subordinates' needs and administrative goals and objectives. It will be seen in later chapters that, as first responders, supervisors must have a fundamental knowledge of a variety of major incidents and operations.

ITEMS FOR REVIEW

1. Explain what is meant by an organization.
2. Describe scientific management and bureaucratic management.
3. List the key management functions under POSDCORB.
4. Explain the differences among policies, procedures, and rules and regulations.
5. Explain McGregor's Theory X/Theory Y.
6. Review how the informal organization, resistance to change, and unionization can impact police organizations.
7. Discuss how organizational structures and functions might be modified in order to accommodate community policing and problem solving.

REFERENCES

Alpert, G. P., and Smith, W. C. (1999). Developing police policy: An evaluation of the control principle. In L. Gaines and G. Cordner, eds., *Policing perspectives: An anthology.* Los Angeles: Roxbury Press, pp. 353–362.

Bennett, W. W., and Hess, K. (2001). *Management and supervision in law enforcement,* 3d ed. Belmont, CA: Wadsworth.

Bittner, E. (1970). *The functions of the police in a modern society.* Public Health Service Publication 2059. Washington, DC: U.S. Government Printing Office.

California Department of Justice, Attorney General's Office, Crime Prevention Center (1992). *COPPS: Community oriented policing and problem solving.* Sacramento, CA: Author, pp. 67–68.

Certo, S. C. (1989). *Principles of modern management: Functions and systems,* 4th ed. Boston: Allyn & Bacon.

Crozier, M. (1964). *The bureaucratic phenomenon.* Chicago: University of Chicago Press.

Fayol, H. (1949). *General and industrial management,* trans. Constance Storrs. London: Sir Isaac Pitman.

Gaines, L. K. (1978). Overview of organizational theory and its relation to police administration. In L. Gaines and T. Ricks, eds., *Managing the police organization.* St. Paul: West, pp. 151–178.

Gaines, L. K., Southerland, M. D., and Angell, J. E. (1991). *Police administration.* New York: McGraw-Hill.

Gaines, L. K., and Swanson, C. R. (1999). Empowering police officers: A tarnished silver bullet? In L. Gaines and G. Cordner, eds., *Policing perspectives: An anthology*. Los Angeles: Roxbury Press, pp. 363–371.

Gerth, H. H., and Mills, C. W. (1946). *From Max Weber: Essays in sociology*. New York: Oxford University Press.

Gray, K., Bodner, J., and Lovrich, N. P. (1997). Community policing and organizational change dynamics. In Q. Thurman and E. F. McGarrell, eds., *Community policing in a rural setting*. Cincinnati: Anderson Publishing, pp. 41–48.

Gulick, L., and Urwick, L. (1937). *Papers on the science of administration*. New York: Institute of Public Administration.

Guyot, D. (1979). Bending granite: Attempts to change the rank structure of American police departments. *Journal of Police Science and Administration* 7:253–284.

Johnson, T. A., Misner, G. E., and Brown, L. P. (1981). *The police and society: An environment for collaboration and confrontation*. Englewood Cliffs, NJ: Prentice Hall.

Kocher, C. J. (1998). A blueprint for developing responsible change. *Community Policing Exchange* (November/December): 1–6.

Luthans, F. (1985). *Organizational behavior*. New York: McGraw-Hill.

Lynch, R. G. (1986). *The police manager: Professional leadership skills*. Englewood Cliffs, NJ: Prentice Hall.

Maguire, E. R. (1997). Structural change in large municipal police organizations during the community policing era. *Justice Quarterly* 14(3):547–576.

McGregor, D. (1966). The human side of enterprise. In W. Bennis and E. Schein, eds., *Leadership and motivation*. Cambridge: MIT Press, pp. 5–16.

More, H. W., and Wegener, W. F. (1992). *Behavioral police management*. New York: Macmillan.

Reddin, T. (1966). Are you oriented to hold them? A searching look at police management. *The Police Chief* 3:17.

Robbins, S. P. (1976). *The administration process*. Englewood Cliffs, NJ: Prentice Hall.

Robbins, S. P. (1990). *Organizational theory: Structure, design and applications*. Englewood Cliffs, NJ: Prentice Hall.

Sparrow, M. K., Moore, M. H., and Kennedy, D. M. (1990). *Beyond 911: A new era for policing*. New York: Basic Books.

Swanson, C. R., Territo, L., and Taylor, R. W. (2001). *Police administration: Structures, processes, and behavior,* 5th ed. Upper Saddle River, NJ: Prentice Hall.

Taylor, F. W. (1911). *The principles of scientific management*. New York: Harper & Bros.

Tenzel, J., Storms, L., and Sweetwood, H. (1976). Symbols and behavior: An experiment in altering the police role. *Journal of Police Science and Administration* 4(1):21–27.

U.S. Department of Justice, Bureau of Justice Statistics (1999). *Law enforcement management and administrative statistics, 1997*. Washington, DC: Author.

Walker, S. (1993). *Taming the system*. New York: Oxford Press.

Weber, M. (1947). *The theory of social and economic organization*, trans. A. M. Henderson and Talcott Parsons. New York: Free Press.

Wilson, J. Q. (1997, September/October). Six things police leaders can do about juvenile crime. In *Subject to Debate* (newsletter of the Police Executive Research Forum).

Wycoff, M. (1994). *Community policing strategies*. Unpublished report, Police Foundation.

2

Role and Responsibilities

---❖---

LEARNING OBJECTIVES

After reading this chapter, the student will:

- understand the nature of supervisors' and managers' roles, and how both operate within the organizational structure
- be able to explain how one prepares for and obtains promotion
- describe how the police culture and agency size affect supervision and management
- understand how supervision and management operate with patrol and investigative functions

Surround yourself with the best people you can find, delegate authority, and don't interfere.

—Ronald Reagan

A man is known by the company he organizes.

—Ambrose Bicrce

Responsibility is the price of greatness.

—Winston Churchill

INTRODUCTION

Now that we have obtained a fundamental understanding of supervision, management, and organizations from Chapter 1, we realize that the supervisor, who is directly and regularly in touch with those employees who actually do the work of the organization and interact with its customers and clients, is one of the most important members of an organization (Brown, 1992). If the supervisor fails to ensure that employees perform correctly, the unit will not be successful, causing difficulties for the manager—the lieutenant or captain. A police department is really nothing more than the sum total of all the units, and one problem unit can adversely affect other units and detract from the department's total effectiveness. This is particularly true for police organizations, because substantial interdependence exists among the various units in a police department. For example, if patrol officers do a poor job of writing reports when they respond to crimes, then the workload of detectives who later complete the case's follow-up investigation will increase.

This chapter continues that general theme by identifying some important characteristics of policing and police organizations that make police supervision and management complex and distinctive. First, we discuss the supervisor's and manager's roles in terms of actual tasks performed. Next, we describe in broad terms how one goes about assuming the supervisory and managerial roles; this chapter section examines the various systems used by police departments to promote officers, the influence of agency size, some considerations for supervising and managing various units in the police organization, and the influence of the police culture. Then, we examine managers' and supervisors' operations with regard to patrol and criminal investigations. The chapter concludes with two case studies.

THE SUPERVISORY ROLE

A Complex Position

From an organizational standpoint, the supervisor is often on the front line and caught in the middle. The supervisor deals with working employees on the one hand, and middle and upper management on the other. The concerns, expectations, and interests of labor and management are inevitably different and to some extent in conflict (Reuss-Ianni, 1983). Labor and management are, respectively, at the bottom and the top of the organization. It is management's responsibility to ensure that officers follow the dictates of policies and procedures and complete their assignments within the scope and mission of the department. Management has definite ideas about what officers should be doing and how they should do it. To some extent, management has developed a blueprint of the organization, and that blueprint outlines everyone's place and responsibilities. When officers do not follow the dictates outlined in the blueprint, the department is not effective.

Subordinate officers, on the other hand, have their own ideas about what is important and how they should perform their jobs. Officers often emphasize law enforcement tasks and deemphasize service tasks. Officers sometimes view the public negatively and act accordingly. This perception of the job often comes into conflict with management's, especially when management is implementing community policing. To help clarify this situation, Table 2–1 provides a listing of managers' and officers' expectations for supervisors.

Perhaps the best example of this today is the controversy over racial profiling. Officers sometimes are overly aggressive and stop minority drivers to investigate them. Management expects officers in these situations to be courteous and to follow the letter and spirit of the law. Management in many departments has voluntarily begun programs in which officers collect racial profiling data and information. Management expects supervisors to investigate or counsel officers whose statistics indicate biases or other problems. Their subordinates expect them to be understanding, to protect them from management's unreasonable expectations and arbitrary decisions, and to represent their interests. Management, though, expects supervisors to keep employees in line and to represent management and the overall department's interests.

There are several ways to place the supervisor's role in perspective. First, Likert (1961) visualized a *linking pin system* whereby each supervisor in the chain of command was a coordinator and conduit of information between the higher level of management and the lower level of workers. In this fashion, the supervisor is able to maintain a balance between upper-level expectations and subordinate expectations. When a directive flows downward in the department, the supervisor can explain it, put it in perspective relative to officers' needs and expectations, and sell the directive to subordinates. Such a process helps ensure that the directive is followed.

TABLE 2–1 Management's and Officers' Expectations of Supervisors

---

Management's Expectations

- Interpret departmental policies, procedures, and rules and regulations and ensure that officers follow them.
- Initiate disciplinary action when officers fail to follow policies.
- Ensure that officers' paperwork and reports are accurate and filed on a timely basis.
- Train officers when they are deficient or unskilled.
- Complete performance evaluations.
- Ensure that officers treat citizens with respect, act professionally, and show equality.
- Ensure that officers' equipment and appearance are in order.
- Back up officers and review their performance when they answer calls for service.
- Take charge of high-risk or potential critical-incident situations.
- Make assignments to ensure that the objectives of the unit are met.

Officers' Expectations

- Interpret departmental policies, procedures, and rules and regulations to meet the needs of the officers.
- Handle disciplinary actions informally rather than taking direct action, especially regarding minor infractions.
- Advocate for officers when they request vacation or time off.
- Support officers when there is a conflict with citizens.
- Provide officers support and back-up at high-risk calls.
- Assist officers in getting better assignments and shifts.
- Emphasize law enforcement activities over providing services, community policing activities, or mundane assignments such as traffic control.
- Understand that officers need to take breaks and sometimes attend to personal needs while on duty.

Others might view the position as a cushion where higher-level directives are mediated once they are issued. This softening of administrative intent sometimes results in less than desirable results. For example, a departmental policy may require officers to remain at the scene of an alarm until the owner arrives. Supervisors may allow officers to leave once the premise has been checked. A balance between departmental direction and subordinate needs must be maintained. Even when maintaining this balance, the manager or supervisor must ensure that the integrity of the directive is maintained. This is critical to the police organization.

Adding to the complexity of the supervisor's role is that the supervisor is the lowest managerial position in the department. A new supervisor, and especially one who is younger than some members of the department, has to go through a transitional phase to learn how to exercise command and get cooperation from subordinates. The new supervisor is no longer responsible solely for her or his own personal behavior, but instead is responsible for the behavior of several other employees. The step from officer to supervisor is a big one that calls for a new set of skills and knowledge largely separate from that learned at lower levels in the organization.

Since supervisors are promoted from within the ranks, they are often placed in charge of their friends and peers. Long-standing relationships are put under stress when a new sergeant suddenly has official authority over former equals. Leniency or preferential treatment oftentimes is expected of new sergeants by their former peers. When new supervisors attempt to correct deficient behavior, their own previous performance may be recalled as a means of challenging the reasonableness or legitimacy of their supervisory action. Supervisors with any skeletons in their closets can expect to hear those skeletons rattling as they begin to use their new-found authority. This places a great deal of pressure on the supervisor.

The supervisor's role, put simply, is to get his or her subordinates to do their very best. This task involves a host of actions, including communicating, motivating, leading, team building, training, developing, appraising, counseling, and disciplining. Getting subordinates to do their best includes figuring out each one's strengths and weaknesses, defining good and bad performance, measuring

Promotion can put relationships under stress, as it brings official authority over former equals.
Courtesy San Bernardino County Sheriff's Office.

performance, providing feedback, and making sure that subordinates' efforts coincide with the organization's mission, values, goals, and objectives.

Supervising a group of subordinates is made more difficult because of the so-called "human element." People are complex and sometimes unpredictable. Rules and principles for communicating, leading, and similar supervisory tasks are rarely hard and fast because people react differently. What works for a supervisor in one situation may not work for that supervisor in another situation, much less for some other supervisor. Thus, supervisors have to learn to "read" subordinates and diagnose situations before choosing how to respond. Supervisors have to become students of human behavior and of behavioral science disciplines such as psychology and sociology.

Effective supervision is also difficult because the job is dynamic, not static. Even without any turnover of personnel, subordinates change over time as they age, grow, mature, and experience satisfaction and dissatisfaction in their personal and work lives. In addition, turnover is common as a result of retirements, promotions, and transfers to other units within the department. When new subordinates come under the supervisor's wing, the supervisor must learn the best way to handle these new subordinates and also be attuned to the new officers' effects on other subordinates and on the work group as a whole.

It is not only one's subordinates who change; the organization and its environment change over time. The organization's rules and expectations may change. The public may make new demands. Societal values evolve and change. Effective supervision over the long haul requires continuous monitoring and adaptation. The department expects the supervisor to keep up with such changes in order to better supervise subordinates. Subordinates, on the other hand, expect the supervisor to help them interpret and adapt successfully to this changing environment. The nature of the supervisor's role is reflected in Figure 2–1.

Police Supervisory Tasks

Police supervision shares with general supervision an emphasis on the direction and control functions. One illustration of this are the results of a job analysis of the sergeant position in the 500-officer Lexington, Kentucky, Police Department. A job analysis is used by human resource experts to document what incumbents in a position do. In Lexington, the following 10 tasks were rated most important according to incumbent sergeants. They are listed with the most important first:

1. Supervises subordinate officers in the performance of their duties
2. Disseminates information to subordinates
3. Ensures that general and special orders are followed
4. Observes subordinates in handling calls and other duties

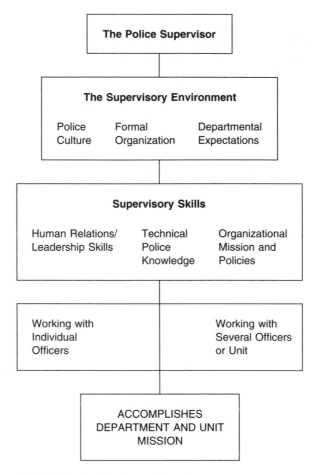

FIGURE 2–1   The Supervisory Process

5. Reviews and approves various departmental reports
6. Listens to problems voiced by officers
7. Answers backup calls
8. Keeps superiors apprised of ongoing situations
9. Provides direct supervision on potential high-risk calls or situations
10. Interprets policies and informs subordinates

Tasks 1 and 9 on this list are global supervisory tasks that incorporate both direction and control. Tasks 2 and 10 are aspects of the directing function, while tasks 3, 4, and 5 are elements of control. Thus, 7 of these top 10 sergeant's tasks involve directing and controlling. The remaining three tasks provide interesting glimpses into some of the other duties and responsibilities performed by police supervisors: listening to subordinates' problems, notifying superiors of problems, and directly assisting subordinates in performing their work. Police supervisors provide an important communications link in the hierarchy between workers and management, as well as acting as a sounding board for problems and grievances. They also get involved in performing street police work from time to time.

Supervisory tasks can range from the mundane (such as typing and filing reports, operating dictation equipment) to the challenging (assigning priorities to investigations, training personnel in forced-entry procedures and handling barricaded persons). Tasks may be administrative (preparing monthly activity reports, scheduling vacation leave), operational (securing major crime scenes, assisting stranded motorists), general (maintaining inventory of equipment, training subordinates), or specialized (conducting stakeouts, training animals for use in specialized units).

Types of Supervisors

Engel (2001) studied police supervisors and found four distinct types: traditional, innovative, supportive, and active. Each of these types of supervisors can be found in any police department. A particular supervisor's type is largely dependent on his or her experiences on the job and training and the department's organizational climate.

The *traditional* supervisor is law enforcement oriented. Traditional supervisors expect their subordinates to produce high levels of measurable activities such as traffic citations and arrests. They expect officers to efficiently respond to calls for service. They place a great deal of emphasis on reports and other paperwork. They provide officers with a substantial amount of instruction and oversight. To a great extent, traditional supervisors are task oriented. They tend to place greater emphasis on punishment than rewards and often believe that they do not have a great deal of power in the department. These supervisors see their primary role as controlling subordinates. Traditional supervisors often have morale and motivation problems with their subordinates.

The second type is the *innovative* supervisor, who is most closely associated with community policing. To some extent, innovative supervisors are the opposite of traditional supervisors. Innovative supervisors generally do not place a great deal of emphasis on citations or arrests. They also depend more on developing relationships with subordinates as opposed to using power to control or motivate. Innovative supervisors usually are good mentors, and they tend to coach rather than order. They are open to new ideas and innovations. Their ultimate goal is to develop officers so that they can solve problems and have good relations with citizens. Innovative supervisors sometimes have problems with officers who are task oriented or who emphasize enforcement and neglect community relations.

The *supportive* supervisor, like the innovative supervisor, is concerned with developing good relations with subordinates. The primary difference is that the supportive supervisor is concerned with protecting officers from what are viewed as unfair management practices. They see themselves as a buffer between management and officers. They attempt to develop strong work teams and motivate officers by inspiring them. Their shortcoming is that they tend to see themselves as "one of the boys," and they sometimes neglect to emphasize departmental goals and responsibilities.

The final category of supervisors according to Engel is the *active* supervisor, who tends to involve herself or himself in the field. Active supervisors sometimes are police officers with stripes or rank. They often take charge of field situations rather than supervising them. They are able to develop good relations with subordinates, because they are perceived as being hard working and competent. Their shortcoming is that by being overly involved in some field situations, they do not give their subordinates the opportunity to develop.

In another study, Engel (2002) examined police supervision in Indianapolis, Indiana, and St. Petersburg, Florida. She found that the four types of supervision were fairly evenly distributed in the departments. The most effective form of supervision, however, was the active supervisor. Active supervisors are those who patrol, write tickets, and back calls. Subordinates working for active supervisors performed better in a number of areas, including problem solving and community policing. This led Engel to conclude that active or working supervisors were able to develop a more productive work unit because of their ability to lead by example. It seems that working supervisors inspire subordinates to be productive.

Engel did identify one issue with active police supervisors; they reported a higher incidence of use of force relative to other supervisors. The Christopher Commission (1991) examined use-of-force problems in the Los Angeles Police Department and cautioned police administrators that aggressive use of force is transmitted to subordinates through sergeants. Since active supervisors participate in the provision of police services, efforts should be made to ensure that they follow policies as well as that subordinates adhere to policies and procedures. Supervisors must not only be well trained and selected carefully, but they also must receive a measure of supervision from their superior.

THE MANAGER'S ROLE

Thus far, we have given substantial consideration to the supervisor. This section examines the role of the manager, especially the middle manager, in the police organization. Although every ranking officer in the police department exercises some managerial skills and duties, here we are concerned with the managers to whom first-line supervisors report, for they generally are unit commanders. In a mid-sized or large police agency, a patrol shift or watch may be commanded by a captain, who will have several lieutenants reporting to him or her. The lieutenants may assist the captain in running the shift, but when there is a shortage of sergeants as the result of vacations or retirements, the lieutenant may assume the duties of a first-line supervisor. The lieutenant's position in some departments may be a training ground for future mid-level managers or unit commanders.

Perhaps the best way to understand what these shift commanders do is to examine the tasks they perform, using as an example the medium-sized police department in Lexington, Kentucky. The 15 most important responsibilities for lieutenants include the following (this list is based on the frequency they are performed and their level of importance):

1. Assisting in supervising or directing the activities of the unit
2. Performing the duties of a police officer
3. Ensuring that departmental and governmental policies are followed
4. Preparing duty roster
5. Reviewing the work of individuals or groups in the section
6. Responding to field calls requiring an on-scene commander
7. Holding roll call
8. Preparing various reports
9. Reviewing various reports
10. Coordinating the activities of subordinates on major investigations
11. Meeting with superiors concerning unit operations
12. Maintaining time sheets
13. Notifying captain/bureau commander of significant calls
14. Answering inquiries from other sections/units, divisions, and outside agencies
15. Serving as captain/bureau commander in absence of same

Notice that some of the tasks (i.e., 4, 7, 8, and 12) performed by the lieutenants are purely administrative in nature. These administrative activities occur in every operational unit in the police department. The lieutenants in Lexington also perform supervisory functions in tasks 1, 3, 5, 6, 9, and 10. These functions include lieutenants overseeing officers and sergeants to ensure that different tasks are completed. This direct supervision generally focuses on the most critical tasks or those tasks that when performed incorrectly can result in dire consequences. Tasks 11, 13, 14, and 15 are managerial in nature. These are responsibilities that are generally vested with a unit commander, but many lieutenants perform them, especially in the absence of the captain. Finally, lieutenants perform the duties of a police officer (task 2). With their supervisory and managerial responsibilities, they engage in a limited amount of police work. It is seen from this list that lieutenants are involved in a wide scope of supervisory, managerial, and police duties.

Next, we examine the tasks generally performed by the captain, again using the Lexington Police Department as an example. The 15 most critical or important tasks performed by captains are as follows:

1. Issuing assignments to individuals and units within the section
2. Receiving assignments for section/unit
3. Reviewing incoming written complaints and reports
4. Preparing routine reports
5. Reviewing final disposition of assignments
6. Ensuring that subordinates comply with general and special orders
7. Monitoring crime and other activity statistics
8. Evaluating the work of individuals and units within the section
9. Maintaining sector facilities
10. Discussing concerns and problems with people
11. Attending various staff meetings
12. Maintaining working contacts and responding to inquiries from other sections of the division
13. Reviewing and approving overtime in section/unit
14. Monitoring section/unit operations to evaluate performance
15. Fielding and responding to complaints against subordinates

A review of these tasks shows that captains have more administrative responsibilities than lieutenants or sergeants. Tasks 2, 4, 7, 9, 10, 11, 12, 13, and 14 are administrative in nature. These tasks indicate that captains spend a substantial amount of time coordinating their units' activities with the activities of other units and overseeing the operation of their units. As an officer progresses up the chain of command, his or her responsibilities become more administrative. At the same time, captains also have supervisory responsibilities. Tasks 1, 3, 5, 6, 8, and 15 are basically supervisory in nature. Whereas a sergeant or lieutenant may be supervising individual officers, a captain is more concerned with tasks, unit activities, and the overall performance of the officers under his or her command.

Every commander and administrator in the department, including the police chief, possesses administrative and supervisory responsibilities to some extent. As can be seen from the previous lists, the unit commander functions like a police chief. The unit commander has many of the same responsibilities as the chief, but on a smaller scale. The chief performs these functions for the total department, while the unit commander is concerned only with one unit.

GETTING THAT FIRST PROMOTION: ASSUMING THE SUPERVISORY ROLE

This section first describes the means by which officers are promoted to supervisory positions. Then, we examine some of the more important aspects of policing and police organizations that distinguish police supervision from supervision in general. These include the wide variety of tasks found in and among police organizations, characteristics of police officers, the strength of the police culture, and the nature of police work itself.

Seeking Promotion

For most officers, the opportunity to attain the rank of supervisor or sergeant is an attractive one. Generally, lateral entry from one department to another in a supervisory or managerial rank does not occur. Lateral transfers happen, for the most part, at the officer level, and many police departments will select chiefs from outside the department, which perhaps is a form of lateral transfer. Officers' promotional opportunities, to a great extent, are limited to their present agency, and the waiting period for sergeant's vacancies to arise through retirement or promotion—especially in smaller agencies—can seem an interminable one.

Another administrative consideration that can filter into the promotional process is the knowledge that good officers do not automatically become good supervisors. Many good officers who are promoted to the rank of sergeant cannot divorce themselves from being "one of the troops" and are unable to flex their supervisory muscles when necessary. In short, a good sergeant must wear two hats, one of being a people-oriented, democratic leader with concern for subordinates, and another of a task-oriented leader who has the ability to command officers in field situations. Von der Embse (1987) notes that a good supervisor should spend at least 50 percent of his or her time managing. If less than 50 percent of a supervisor's time is spent on managing the unit, then the supervisor is not doing his or her job. The supervisor is spending too much time being a line officer.

At the same time, a good sergeant does not always make a good lieutenant or captain. A supervisor's job essentially entails the supervision of tasks and people. Positions above sergeant require more conceptual skills, such as planning, organizing, staffing, and budgeting. The police manager deals with groups of people and problems that encompass large geographical areas, while the supervisor generally interacts with individual officers and performs specific tasks. Substantial differences exist between the supervisor and the manager.

Obtaining Promotion

It is probably not uncommon for 60 to 65 percent or more of eligible officers to take the supervisor's test. Competition for promotion in most police agencies is normally quite keen. This is especially true because there are more people at the rank of officer than at any other rank in any given police department.

It should also be noted that, for several reasons, many excellent street cops do not wish to be promoted. Perhaps they want to remain one of the troops and do not believe that they could maintain the personal distance, perspective, or disciplinary authority needed at a higher rank. In addition, they might lose a lot of overtime pay if promoted or might be transferred to what they deem to be an undesirable shift. Others work in a particular unit, such as domestic violence, enjoy the work, and do not want to take the chance of being promoted away from their work. Some police officers find themselves a niche in the department and strive to stay there.

Others test for the wrong reasons. Many officers test simply for the experience, because of pressure from peers, through curiosity, or just to get off the streets for a short while (Van Maanen, 1989). Some have a need for power, but these individuals generally do not make good supervisors. Some officers see promotion as a means to obtaining a raise in salary, better working conditions, or

A newly promoted sergeant. The rank of sergeant is one of the most difficult and challenging positions in a police organization.
Courtesy Washoe County, Nevada, Sheriff's Office.

an easier life. These officers, if promoted, do not make good superior officers. Promotions should be only for those who have a genuine interest in serving and improving the department.

Promotions in most agencies are governed by departmental and civil service procedures, intended to guarantee legitimacy and impartiality for the process. In some jurisdictions, this is a fairly complicated process in which each step is strictly governed by law or regulation. Larger departments generally use a multifaceted procedure in which officers must compete in a series of tests or exercises. In smaller departments, the promotion examination may be nothing more than an interview with the chief of police, city manager, mayor, or city council. Supervisors are generally chosen from a final, rank-ordered list of names, often based on scores from written and oral tests. Some agencies include factors such as seniority, performance evaluations, and experience in the process. The most common promotion process in policing consists of a written test involving departmental policies, state statutes, and a reading list consisting of supervision, management, and criminal investigation books; an oral interview board; and the most recent performance evaluation.

One of the most effective methods for promoting the best personnel is the assessment center, which is a multifaceted process whereby candidates are subjected to a variety of tests and testing formats. Some of the exercises in the assessment center include

- Interviews in which candidates explain their experiences and motivations for promotion
- Psychological tests to determine if candidates have the right temperament to be a superior officer
- In-basket exercises in which the applicant receives an abundance of paperwork and problems to be prioritized and dealt with in a prescribed amount of time
- Management tasks that ask the candidate to project a unit budget or plan a program to solve a problem
- Group discussions that evaluate candidates on their ability to interact with others
- Simulations of interviews with subordinates, the public, and news media to see how well applicants can deal with other important actors or groups.
- Fact-finding or planning exercises that give the officer a problem and ask him or her to evaluate it given the department's current resources and to develop a solution
- Oral presentation exercises that ask candidates to provide training to officers, a presentation to a community group, or an oral report at a staff meeting
- Written communications exercises that measure candidates' writing ability

The assessment center is superior to other methods because it allows the promoters to assess candidates in a number of varied situations. The simulations in assessment centers provide better information about how candidates will perform when confronted with real-life situations and allow the department to test on issues that are "current." For example, if the department has implemented community policing, a number of the exercises can reflect that orientation and organization. Although assessment centers are obviously more costly than conventional testing procedures, they are worth the extra investment and can help to avoid promoting the wrong person and possibly save untold dollars in lawsuits and problems for many years to come. A police department should spare no expense when promoting officers—such decisions are too important.

After being promoted, several dynamics work to make the transition difficult. The new supervisor or manager confronts a solitary process. Many departments provide newly promoted officers with training prior to or after promotion and require that they complete a structured field-training program similar to the one new officers receive before being assigned to their new responsibilities. In some states, training for various supervisory and managerial ranks is mandated by statute. For example, in California, all lieutenants must complete the Commission on Police Standards and Training (POST) management training program. This multi-week course is designed to prepare lieutenants for their new jobs and includes topics such as leadership, motivation, scheduling, and complaint investigations. In many agencies, however, training is simply not available, and the newly promoted officer must rely on advice and counsel from peers and superiors.

Differences by Agency Size

A great deal of variety exists among the 18,760 or so police departments in the United States (Reaves and Goldberg, 2000). Included in this group are general purpose police agencies, state police, sheriff's offices, highway patrols, state investigative agencies, and campus police departments. The agencies service small and large municipalities, merged metropolitan areas, counties, and entire states. Included also are federal law enforcement agencies and the police and security branches of the military.

Perhaps the greatest source of police organizational variation is size. A large number of American police agencies have fewer than 10 full-time sworn personnel. In many of these departments, especially those with five or fewer officers, the chief of police may be the only supervisor. In this situation, the chief must fulfill all the supervisory and managerial functions for the organization, a tall order that is made even more difficult by the 24-hour-a-day, 7-day-a-week nature of the police business. If the chief is the only supervisor, and if he or she works a normal 40-hour week, then for 128 hours each week, no supervisor is on duty. In other words, these chiefs are responsible for supervising their

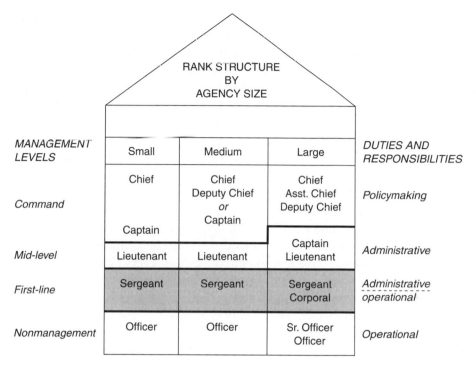

MANAGEMENT LEVELS	RANK STRUCTURE BY AGENCY SIZE			DUTIES AND RESPONSIBILITIES
	Small	Medium	Large	
Command	Chief	Chief Deputy Chief or Captain	Chief Asst. Chief Deputy Chief	Policymaking
	Captain		Captain	
Mid-level	Lieutenant	Lieutenant	Lieutenant	Administrative
First-line	Sergeant	Sergeant	Sergeant Corporal	Administrative operational
Nonmanagement	Officer	Officer	Sr. Officer Officer	Operational

FIGURE 2–2   Rank Structure by Agency Size

officers even though they are not usually on-duty with the officers. Often, these chiefs also perform police activities while they are on duty and serve as follow-up criminal investigators.

In slightly larger police organizations, particularly those with six to ten officers, the one or two sergeants in the agencies are, for all intents and purposes, assistant chiefs. They typically share both supervisory and managerial duties with the chief of police and are in operational command of the department much of the time. Out of necessity, they usually perform patrol, investigative, and other direct service activities as well. Figure 2–2 shows the varying ranks and managerial and supervisory duties that may exist in departments of varying size.

The larger the police agency, the more likely that the duties of supervisors (usually sergeants, but sometimes corporals as well) will be focused on overseeing their subordinates rather than on either doing police work or helping the chief manage the agency. In larger agencies, supervisors will ordinarily have a sufficient number of subordinates so that the supervisor is not expected to do much of the actual police work (handling calls, investigating crimes, and so forth), and overseeing the subordinates is, in and of itself, a full-time job. The same goes for managers. In larger departments, they spend the majority of their time overseeing the operations of specific units.

Another important difference between small and large police agencies is the degree of specialization that affects supervisors. In small agencies with one or two supervisors, the subordinates under their direction and control do everything—engage in patrol, respond to calls for service, investigate crimes, organize crime prevention groups, present school-based programs, and so forth. Supervisors in small departments, like their officers, have to be experts in all facets of police work. In a larger agency, by contrast, a supervisor may be responsible only for a squad of detectives, or a squad of burglary detectives, or even a squad of residential burglary detectives. The range of activity under the supervisor's authority is generally narrower in larger agencies. On the other hand, the volume of work under the supervisor's control may be greater, as may be the number, expertise, and sophistication of subordinates.

Differences also exist between *large* and *medium-sized* departments at the middle-management levels. In a medium-sized department (with less specialization), the entire detective division might be commanded by a captain or lieutenant, with sergeants assigned to supervise detectives in units such as robbery/homicide, burglary, fraud, vice/narcotics, and juvenile crimes. A larger agency, however, might have a deputy chief of police in charge of the detectives, with one lieutenant managing crimes against property (such as burglary, fraud, cyber crimes, and auto theft units) and another responsible for crimes against persons (robbery/homicide, sexual assaults, juvenile crimes); furthermore, each of these specialized units would have a sergeant supervising its detectives. Finally, larger agencies might also have lieutenants and/or sergeants supervising regional task forces that address gang, narcotics, cyber, and juvenile crimes.

One implication of these size differences is that in a small police agency all supervisors perform the same job, whereas in a large agency any two sergeants or managers may have quite different jobs. Both probably are engaged primarily in directing and controlling their subordinates. But the kind of work performed by their subordinates may vary widely: general patrol, emergency operations, specialized investigations, crime analysis, or community relations. Also, the functions that the supervisors and managers are called on to perform over and above directing and controlling will likely differ. Not all sergeants or managers will be expected to maintain records on grant projects, but some will. Some will review accident statistics while others will not. Some, but not all, will have civilian subordinates. These and many other variables in larger police organizations create diversity among supervisory positions.

One final important source of variation in police supervision has to do with time and place. Police supervision is complicated by the 24-hour-a-day nature of the business and by the fact that the police still make house calls. Those supervisors and managers who work at the same time and in the same place as their subordinates, such as a patrol team assigned to swing shift or a burglary unit in detectives, have a tremendous advantage over their colleagues who are separated from their subordinates by time, space, or both. For example, a lieutenant in a medium sized department may be responsible for patrol officers assigned to all three shifts, but he or she may seldom see many of the officers. Directing and controlling are much easier when one can continuously observe subordinates. Of course, the reality of most police supervision, especially in patrol and investigations, is that officers do their work alone and out of sight of supervisors. For that reason, police supervisors and managers must find other methods for overseeing officers' performance.

Supervision of Patrol Officers

One of the most influential leadership theories holds that the nature of subordinates is the key determinant of which style of management will be most successful (Hersey and Blanchard, 1988). Every indication is that this situational or contingency theory is quite applicable to police supervision (Southerland and Reuss-Ianni, 1992), and we will examine it in detail in Chapter 3. Here, we consider if any general characteristics of police officers have a pervasive impact on police supervision and management.

Some early studies suggested that policing attracts certain kinds of people with distinct personalities and philosophies. It was believed that conservative, authoritarian individuals with a preference for uniforms, weapons, and discipline were drawn to police work. Later studies, however, found that new police recruits scored surprisingly "normal" on psychological and intelligence tests. The most compelling characteristics that these recruits have in common are a desire to help others, an interest in job security, and perhaps some inclination toward risk taking and adventure. Otherwise, a police recruit class generally provides a good cross section of the population at large (Burbeck and Furnham, 1985).

Veteran police officers, however, clearly are different from the general population. As recruits, they may have started out much like their friends and neighbors, but police officers frequently become more rigid, more conservative, more cynical, and more suspicious as a result of adopting the police role and doing police work (Gaines and Kappeler, 2003). This is understandable, because they experience more anger, fear, and frustration than workers in most other fields. They see some of the worst things that people do to each other in the form of neglect, abuse, crime, and violence. And they have a good deal of lying, deception, suspicion, hatred, and violence directed at them. Given the rather dramatic and intense nature of policing and the police role, it would be odd if police officers' personalities and viewpoints were not affected. One manifestation of these effects on police officers is stress, a topic that is addressed fully in Chapter 7.

Also, and of equal importance, police superiors must attend to the emotional and psychological development of their subordinates and, in so doing, counter the occupational tendencies toward cynicism and stress-related mental and physical

Assisting and guiding officers in the field is one of the primary functions of supervisors.
Courtesy Riverside, California, Police Department.

ill health just described. Perhaps the greatest responsibility given to police supervisors is that of guiding the moral and intellectual development of their subordinates (Muir, 1977). We discuss ethics, values, and liability issues in Chapter 8.

The superior's challenge is to restore balance in officers' lives, which are
often thrown out of balance by the experience of policing. Today's superior cannot function like a military commander; he or she needs more than just unquestioned strength and toughness. Successful management and supervision utilize
personal attributes such as empathy, caring, and nurturing, as well as street-wise
attributes such as decisiveness, boldness, and toughness.

The Police Culture

As we discussed in Chapter 1, the role of the supervisor and manager is affected
by the strength of the police culture, which is a determining factor in work behavior. For example, the number of traffic citations issued or number of arrests by
officers is frequently determined by norms established by the work group—a condition we termed the informal organization in Chapter 1. And, on rare occasions,

police cultures support flagrant forms of deviance: drinking on duty, brutalizing prisoners, selling drugs, corruption (see Kappeler, Sluder, and Alpert, 1994; Kleinig, 1996). These behaviors do occur and are a major concern to managers and supervisors. Major scandals such as those occurring in Los Angeles (planting evidence), New York (officers involved in drug corruption), and New Orleans (officers committing robbery-homicides) in recent years cause substantial damage to the police department.

Most police officers do not engage in flagrant deviance, of course, and not all police organizational cultures encourage or even allow such behavior. The police supervisory or managerial responsibility is to be especially familiar with the norms and values of the organization's culture. If these norms and values are consistent with official expectations, the superior officer can use the culture in directing and controlling subordinates' behavior. When the organizational culture supports unhealthy attitudes and deviant behavior, the job of managing or supervising is made much more difficult. Either subordinates must be convinced to reject the culture's deviant norms and values, or the culture itself must be changed. In some departments, speeding in marked patrol cars is routinely accepted by officers and the police culture. Yet, when officers speed while on duty but not while responding to an emergency call, it is not only dangerous, but it also undermines citizen satisfaction with the police. Citizens expect their police to abide by the same laws under which they are held accountable. In this case, supervisors must make an extraordinary effort to bring police behavior into compliance with laws and larger societal expectations.

Other characteristics of the police business provide supervisors with opportunities to resist a deviant organizational culture. For example, if a group of officers is separated geographically from the rest of the organization, or works at a different time from other officers, the impact of the organizational culture may be reduced, and the supervisor's opportunity to develop an alternative culture is heightened. Indeed, it is quite common in police departments to find distinct behavioral styles among different squads, shifts, and units; these styles are frequently the result of supervisors' own varying philosophies, styles, and values. This not only applies to deviant behavior, but also to day-to-day activities. Supervisors can have an impact on individuals' priorities. If a sergeant thinks the issuance of traffic citations is most important, then subordinates will likely make an effort to write more tickets. The police manager can reinforce this as well as provide some direct supervision of the sergeants.

The Ideal Versus the Real

Since supervision is such an important ingredient in police administration, it is necessary to examine how effective supervision is. Recall that supervision is not only conducted by first-line supervisors, but it also is an integral part of management. Police chiefs, their subordinate commanders, and unit commanders are engaged in the supervision of subordinates and police activities. Officers located at each higher level in the chain of command are responsible for supervising their immediate subordinates and ensuring that they, in turn, supervise officers under their command.

Research indicates that supervision is extremely weak in most police departments. For example, Engel (2000) examined supervision in Indianapolis, Indiana, and St. Petersburg, Florida. She found that supervisors who were active influenced officers' decisions in making arrests and in using force but did not exert a substantial amount of influence in other areas. Moreover, active supervisors constituted only about one-quarter of the supervisors in the department. Other supervisors had even less influence on officers.

There are several explanations for this occurrence. First, Van Maanen (1989) and Jermier and Berkes (1979) suggested that only when subordinates encounter a task that is unpredictable or has a high level of uncertainty associated with it do they rely on their supervisors to make decisions for them. Otherwise, subordinates tend to rely on their discretion and complete the task without conferring with a superior officer. Thus, it is unusual for officers to seek supervisory advice or intervention. Historically, police supervisors have been comfortable with this arrangement.

Along these same lines, many supervisors use the rule of *management by exception,* which states that a superior does not have the time to supervise all the activities under his or her control and, therefore, should devote energy and time only to those exceptional tasks or activities. When adhering to this rule, many supervisors and managers may neglect the daily activities that are part and parcel of the unit's overall responsibilities. This allows some critical activities to occur without supervision, and officers may deviate from departmental expectations.

Some may suggest that this lack of supervision is partially a consequence of the strong emphasis within police administration over the past decade or two on the human relations approach to management, which has accompanied the implementation of community policing. This is not the case, however. First, Gaines and Swanson (1999) suggest that in the past, police organizations have not been authoritarian but have been more lackadaisical. They have had the appearance of authoritarianism as a result of the uniforms and military rank, but for the most part police officers of the past had as much, if not more, discretion than today's officers. Police departments now likely have less discretion, as they have instituted more comprehensive policies and procedures and provided officers with better training.

Second, research indicates that community policing has not had much effect on the police organization. Zhao, Lovrich, and Robinson (2001) found that community policing has not changed the core mission of the police. Law enforcement remains committed to crime fighting as opposed to a greater orientation toward the maintenance of order. The implementation of community policing should result in a mission shift to order maintenance. In his survey of police departments, Maguire

(1997) also found that police organizational structure has not changed appreciably as a result of community policing. Thus, community policing does not result in lax supervision. It also appears that some departments have not fully adopted community policing.

MANAGING AND SUPERVISING POLICE OPERATIONS

As the previous discussion indicates, many supervisory and managerial activities are similar across police organizations. At the same time, a number of subtle differences result from the activities and responsibilities associated with various assignments. The following section details some of these similarities and differences.

Patrol

The most common work assignments in police departments are patrol and investigation. Patrol officers, the most numerous of all police personnel, are generalists who perform a wide variety of duties. In small departments, patrol officers sometimes do everything. In larger departments, many police duties are assigned to specialized units. The following are among the major activities vested with patrol units:

1. *Call Handling*: Patrol officers handle the entire range of calls for service, from crimes in progress to domestic disputes to parking complaints. Officers often make reports or refer an incident to a specialized unit in the department.

2. *Routine Patrol*: Most patrol officers spend 30 to 50 percent of their available time on routine patrol. It is during this time that they should be attentive to the needs of businesses, neighborhoods, and citizens on their beat. Officers should maximize their attempt to get to know citizens and business owners, learn their needs and problems, and provide information and coordinate other services in order to address their problems. Community policing and problem solving activities in which officers can engage as part of their patrol time are discussed thoroughly in Chapter 13.

3. *Targeted Assignments*: Police departments today, especially under a community policing orientation, target recurring problems and assign patrol officers to those problems during their free patrol time. These assignments are usually based on information produced by crime analysis or dispatched calls for service data. This data helps officers identify "hot spots" (locations), individuals (offenders and victims), or types of crimes that are occurring with some frequency.

4. *Emergency Situations:* Patrol officers respond to criminal and noncriminal emergency situations. Criminal situations include armed robberies, hostage situations, and barricaded persons. Noncriminal emergencies include accidents involving chemical spills or the aftermath of a natural disaster such as an earthquake or tornado.

5. *Special Assignments*: Patrol officers are sometimes given special assignments such as controlling traffic at a ball game, providing security to visiting dignitaries, or escorting business persons making large bank deposits.

Table 2–2 provides a list of supervisory and managerial duties that are associated with the patrol function.

Criminal Investigations

Criminal investigation entails the examination of crimes that are reported to the department. Generally, patrol officers take the initial or preliminary report, which

---

TABLE 2–2   Managerial and Supervisory Responsibilities in Patrol

---

Managerial
- Request additional resources (officers, patrol vehicles, etc.) so that the unit can function properly.
- Meet with other managers to coordinate patrol activities with the activities of other units.
- Analyze crime data to identify problems.
- Provide direct supervision of patrol sergeants to ensure that they and the patrol unit are performing at an acceptable level.
- Review patrol schedules to ensure that beats are covered.
- Review performance evaluations.
- Examine the productivity of the unit to ensure that officers are working efficiently.

Supervisory
- Hold roll call to ensure that officers have their beat assignment and are familiar with crimes and wanted persons.
- Back up officers on dangerous or high-liability calls.
- Complete performance evaluations.
- Notify superiors of any problems or issues.
- Supervise officers to ensure that they follow departmental procedures and other legal mandates such as court decisions and procedural laws that guide how officers enforce the law.
- Make assignments to individual officers.
- Talk with citizens about problems and complaints.
- Recommend disciplinary action for officers.
- Recommend training programs for officers.
- Inspect officers and their equipment.
- Review officers' reports to ensure completeness and accuracy.

---

then is forwarded to detectives for a follow-up investigation. The detective assigned the case gathers physical evidence, interviews victims and witnesses, works with informants, interrogates suspects, writes reports, prepares applications for arrest and search warrants, meets with prosecutors, and testifies in court. Detectives may also work undercover, sometimes for extended periods of time, particularly to investigate vice and drug-related crimes. Thus, detectives have a fairly complex job.

Three categories of investigative work that have somewhat differing implications for supervision are crimes against property, crimes against persons, and vice and narcotics crime. Detectives involved in property crime investigations, such as burglary, theft, fraud, and cyber crimes, tend to have heavy caseloads, making this a high-volume activity. A primary role for the supervisor of property crime investigators is caseload management—setting priorities, screening out low-priority cases, monitoring caseload sizes, and so forth. Also, these kinds of investigations frequently involve informants, so monitoring their detectives' relations with informants is an important concern for supervisors.

Detectives view a suspect photo lineup. Supervising a specialized unit in detectives, training, or administration requires additional skills, knowledge, and abilities.
Courtesy NYPD Photo Unit.

Crimes against persons, which include robbery and homicide, rape, child abuse, and child sex offenses, normally involve smaller caseloads but each investigation is more intensive, in-depth, and longer. Because these crimes are generally more serious than property crimes, more is at stake in their investigation. Detectives may have to withstand pressure from victims, family, friends, the media, politicians, and even police superiors. The chances of detectives becoming personally involved in individual cases is great, as is the possibility of burnout caused by repeated exposure to violence and human suffering. Thus, supervisors must give careful attention both to the details of particular investigations and to the emotional health and well-being of their detective subordinates.

Supervisors of vice, narcotics, and undercover investigators should have an even greater concern than supervisors of personal-crime detectives for the well-being of their subordinates. Detectives who focus on vice and drugs and those who work undercover operate on the fringes of society and are exposed to a variety of temptations, including drugs, sex, and money. Undercover investigators sometimes become so immersed in lies and deception that they become confused about their occupational role and lose track of legal and professional ethics and responsibilities (Kleinig, 1996).

A different problem sometimes arises, particularly in narcotics investigation. Detectives feel so strongly about the evils of drugs and become so frustrated by the difficulty of making good cases that they may take the law into their own hands by fabricating evidence, planting drugs, using excessive force, and routinely lying in court (Barker and Carter, 1990; Kappeler et al., 1994). Although such behaviors are rare, supervisors of undercover and vice detectives must be alert to these possibilities; besides overseeing the investigation of particular cases, they must be especially attuned to the moral and psychological health of their subordinates.

As can be seen, criminal investigation is a comprehensive set of activities. In order to provide more clarity to the roles of supervisors and managers, their functions are listed in Table 2–3. Note that some activities occur only in specific units within the overall detective bureau. Not all detective units are addressed in the table, but several of the more critical ones are.

Table 2–3 shows a number of management functions that are consistent across the units in the detective bureau. It should be noted, however, that one of the most important managerial functions is the review of unit activities, which necessitates substantial expertise on the part of the manager. Supervisors in the detective units have a number of similar responsibilities, but at the same time, several responsibilities are unique to the type of investigative unit being supervised.

Other Responsibilities

Supervisors must direct and control their subordinates' use of discretionary authority. Supervisors must also make sure that when officers do stop, search, detain, and charge citizens that they do so using proper techniques and that they

---

TABLE 2–3   Managerial and Supervisory Responsibilities in Criminal Investigation

---

Managerial

- Request additional resources (detectives, clerical staff, forensic equipment, and photography equipment) so that the unit can function properly.
- Meet with other managers to coordinate patrol activities with the activities of other units.
- Analyze crime data to identify problems.
- Provide direct supervision of detective sergeants to ensure that investigations are performed correctly.
- Review detectives' schedules to ensure that enough detectives are assigned to each type of investigation.
- Review performance evaluations.
- Examine the productivity of the unit to ensure that officers are working efficiently.
- Review expenditures for informants and drug buys.

Supervisory

- Notify superiors of major crimes and breaks in investigations.
- Supervise officers to ensure that they follow departmental procedures, criminal procedures, and other legal mandates such as court decisions.
- Assign cases to individual detectives.
- Talk with citizens about problems and complaints.
- Recommend disciplinary action for officers.
- Recommend training programs for officers.
- Complete performance evaluations.
- Review officers' reports to ensure completeness and accuracy.
- Maintain register of confidential informants.
- Keep records on monies spent for confidential informants and drug buys.
- Discuss cases with detectives to determine if investigations are complete.
- Discuss cases with prosecutors.
- Establish case priorities.
- Have deals with suspects approved by superiors and the court.
- Look for patterns of abuse or corruption.
- Ensure that detectives enter information into departmental gang registry program.

---

act within the law. This includes proactively observing and reviewing subordinates' actions as well as responding to citizens' complaints about officers' behavior. Supervisors must ensure that their officers are not prone to use force unnecessarily or excessively. Most agencies have "early warning systems" in place that trace officer conduct and provide information about trends among groups and individual officers in order to address problems before they become serious or endemic. Still, supervisors must carefully review each instance of a subordinate's use of force to make sure that it was proper, legal, and within departmental guidelines. Early warning systems are discussed thoroughly in Chapter 9.

Police supervisors must enhance officer safety and help officers deal with the psychological effects of danger. Supervisors must also be wary of another reaction:

Some officers see so much danger in every situation that their approach to citizens becomes uniformly heavy handed and oppressive. Ultimately, police supervisors need to develop their officers into consistent and reliable decision makers.

Supervisors also need to ensure that their officers recognize and respect the varied functions of policing and overcome the view that work relating to order maintenance and social services is "not real police work." Supervisors should use performance appraisals, assignments, commendations, and other rewards and punishments under their control to drive home the message that all the varied functions of policing are legitimate aspects of police work.

In these situations, managers have the responsibility of reviewing the work of their supervisors. If a patrol sergeant becomes lax and does not ensure that officers follow the dictates of departmental policies, it is up to the manager to catch and correct such omissions. This is usually accomplished by reviewing complaints against officers and use-of-force and other routine reports and by frequently meeting with supervisors and discussing priorities and problems. Managers must hold their supervisors accountable and remain abreast of what is occurring in their units.

⎯⎯ Case Studies ⎯⎯⎯⎯⎯⎯⎯⎯⎯⎯

Following are two case studies that enable the reader to consider some of the substantive issues described in the chapter and to consider some options as solutions to problems.

Adapting to the Role: The Laissez-Faire Supervisor

Sgt. Tom Gresham is newly promoted and assigned to patrol on the graveyard shift; he knows each officer on his shift, and several are close friends. Sgt. Gresham was an excellent patrol officer and prided himself on his reputation and ability to get along with his peers. He also believed this trait would benefit him as a supervisor. From the beginning, Sgt. Gresham believed that he could get more productivity from his officers by relating to them at their level. He made an effort to socialize after work and took pride in giving his team the liberty of referring to him by his first name. Sgt. Gresham also believed that it was a supervisor's job to not get in the way of "good" police work. In his view, his team responded tremendously, generating the highest number of arrest and citation statistics in the entire department. Unfortunately, his shift was also generating the highest number of citizen complaints—yet, few complaints were sustained by internal affairs. It was Gresham's opinion that complaints are the product of good, aggressive police work. He had quickly developed the reputation among subordinates as being "a cop's cop." One Monday morning, Sgt. Gresham is surprised when he is called in to his patrol captain's office; the internal affairs lieutenant is also present. They show Gresham a number of use-of-force complaints against his team over the past week while Sgt. Gresham was on vacation. Despite his captain's efforts to describe the gravity of the situation, Gresham failed to grasp the seriousness of the complaints, and how his supervisory style may have contributed to them.

1. What do you think are some of Sgt. Gresham's problems as a new supervisor?
2. As his captain, what kind of advice would you give to Gresham?
3. What corrective action must Sgt. Gresham take immediately with his team of officers?

Seeing the Big Picture

Sgt. Henry Garcia, a college-educated 18-year veteran, scored near the top in his promotional exam. His career has essentially involved time spent in the planning/research and the training divisions. He also teaches report writing at the area academy. Garcia believes very strongly that officers are only as good as the reports they write. He believes his officers should write exceptional reports, and he devotes most of his time to reviewing officers' reports, counseling them on report content, and recommending changes and revisions. His demands require officers to spend inordinate amounts of time with their report-related duties (accruing much overtime in the process). Garcia often uses his team's reports at the recruit academy as examples of "good" police work. Arrests in his division are the lowest in the agency, but the division has the highest number of reported offenses. Sgt. Garcia often asks his officers why the arrest and crime statistics are so poor, but they fail to respond to him. Frustrated, he schedules an appointment to see his superior, a lieutenant, to discuss the problems.

1. As the lieutenant, what would you tell Sgt. Garcia are the reasons for the crime problem in his district and his relations with his team?
2. What might you suggest to rectify this situation?

SUMMARY

This chapter focused on the complex demands and considerations of police management and supervision. A number of important characteristics of policing and police organizations were identified that indicate that police management and supervision are complex and problematic. To a great extent, supervision at all levels of a police department is the fuel that makes the department operate. When there are supervisory problems at any level in the police department, it will negatively affect officers and units.

We learned how managers and supervisors assigned to different units, particularly patrol and investigations, are affected by their unit's mission and activities. We described how one goes about assuming a supervisory or managerial position, using a variety of promotional processes, as well as the supervisor's and manager's roles in terms of actual tasks performed. The influence of agency size and the police culture were also shown to be important considerations. The chapter's two case studies provided some substantive issues for the reader to use for applying chapter information.

ITEMS FOR REVIEW

1. Explain how the supervisor's and manager's roles are uniquely difficult and complex.

2. Delineate the means by which one is promoted to a supervisory level, some of the factors that influence whether or not one is promoted, and some of the problems that one faces on assuming the role.

3. What are the supervisor's and manager's tasks?

4. What are some of the major aspects of patrol work that supervisors and managers must oversee?

5. What kinds of supervisors exist in the police organization and how effective are they?

REFERENCES

Barker, T., and Carter, D. (1990). Fluffing up the evidence and covering your ass: Some conceptual notes on police lying. *Deviant Behavior* 11:61–73.

Brown, M. F. (1992). The sergeant's role in a modern law enforcement agency. *The Police Chief* (May):18–22.

Burbeck, E., and Furnham, A. (1985). Police officer selection: A critical review of the literature. *Journal of Police Science and Administration* 13:58–69.

Christopher Commission (1991). *Report of the independent commission on the Los Angeles Police Department.* Los Angeles: City of Los Angeles.

Engel, R. S. (2002). Patrol officer supervision in the community policing era. *Journal of Criminal Justice* 30:51–64.

Engel, R. S. (2001). Supervisory styles of patrol sergeants and lieutenants. *Journal of Criminal Justice* 29:341–355.

Engel, R. S. (2000). The effects of supervisory styles on patrol officer behavior. *Police Quarterly* 3(3):262–293.

Gaines, L., and Kappeler, V. (2003). *Policing in America.* Cincinnati: Anderson.

Gaines, L. K., and Swanson, C. (1999). Empowering police officers: A tarnished silver bullet? In L. Gaines and G. Cordner, eds. *Policing perspectives: An anthology.* Los Angeles: Roxbury Press, pp. 363–371.

Hersey, P., and Blanchard, K. H. (1988). *Management of organizational behavior: Utilizing human resources,* 5th ed. Englewood Cliffs, NJ: Prentice Hall.

Jermier, J. M., and Berkes, L. J. (1979). Leader behavior in a police command bureaucracy: A closer look at the quasi-military model. *Administrative Science Quarterly* 24:1–23.

Kappeler, V., Sluder, R., and Alpert, G. (1994). *Forces of deviance: Understanding the dark side of policing.* Prospect Heights, IL: Waveland.

Kleinig, J. (1996). *The ethics of policing.* Cambridge, England: Cambridge University Press.

Likert, R. (1961). *New patterns of management.* New York: McGraw-Hill.

Maguire, E. R. (1997). Structural change in large municipal police organizations during the community policing era. *Justice Quarterly* 14(3):547–576.

Muir, W. K., Jr. (1977). *Police: Streetcorner politicians.* Chicago: University of Chicago Press.

Reaves, B. A., and Goldberg, A. (2000). *Local police departments, 1997.* Washington, DC: Bureau of Justice Statistics.

Reuss-Ianni, E. (1983). *Two cultures of policing: Street cops and management cops.* New Brunswick, NJ: Transaction Books.

Southerland, M. D., and Reuss-Ianni, E. (1992). Leadership and management. In G. W. Cordner and D. C. Hale, eds., *What works in policing? Operations and administration examined.* Cincinnati, OH: Anderson, pp. 157–177.

Van Maanen, J. (1989). Making rank: Becoming an American police sergeant. In R. G. Dunham and G. P. Alpert, eds., *Critical issues in policing: Contemporary readings.* Prospect Heights, IL: Waveland, pp. 146–151.

Von der Embse, T. (1987). *Supervision: Managerial skills for a new era.* New York: Macmillan.

Zhao, J., Lovrich, N., and Robinson, T. H. (2001). Community policing: Is it changing the basic functions of policing? Findings from a longitudinal study of 200+ municipal police agencies. *Journal of Criminal Justice* 29:365–377.

3

Leadership and Motivation within the Police Organization

❖

LEARNING OBJECTIVES

After reading this chapter, the student will:

- know the basic leadership theories, and how leadership skills are developed
- have a working knowledge of motivating personnel in the workplace, and how motivational strategies may be applied in the police agency
- understand the difference between leading and managing
- be able to discuss how leadership can fail in a police department
- be able to develop work teams that engage in problem solving and enhance productivity
- know which leadership styles are best for the police agency

Of the best leader, when he is gone, they will say: We did it ourselves.

—Chinese proverb

It is time for a new generation of leadership, to cope with new problems and new opportunities. For there is a new world to be won.

—John F. Kennedy

Individual commitment to a group effort—that is what makes a team work, a company work, a society work, a civilization work.

—Vince Lombardi

INTRODUCTION

Previous chapters identified the first-line supervisor and the middle manager as two of the most important and influential members of a police organization, whose primary functions involved directing and controlling the work of subordinates. That discussion was limited to the functional duties and tasks, or the mechanics of these positions. Here we delve deeper, exploring the motivational side of supervision and management, or the "art of leadership." We explore why some supervisors and managers are capable of capturing the hearts and minds of their subordinates and arouse their passion to perform extraordinary tasks, while others struggle to gain officers' compliance to simple directions.

After opening the chapter with a consideration of relevant definitions and the kinds of traits that make good leaders, we look at the difference between *power* and *authority.* Next, we examine early theories of motivation (both content and process theories) that have stood the test of time, and then we look at several prominent theories concerning leadership, as well as leadership styles that do and do not work in the policing setting. We then discuss leaders who adopt a customer focus, team building, and why leaders fail. The chapter concludes with two case studies that provide the reader with an opportunity to view relevant issues and to integrate the information and possible solutions presented in the chapter.

It is important to remember that behind every good practice lies a good theory. Theory and practice are inextricably intertwined. Thus, we look at the primary theories behind employee satisfaction, motivation, and leadership. We might also point out that many books examine leadership theories in length; thus, in this chapter we limit our coverage to comparatively brief overviews of related theories for policing.

SUPERVISORS AND MANAGERS AS LEADERS

A Problem of Definition

Leadership is the heart and soul of any organization. The idea of leadership has been with us for quite a long time, yet widespread debate and disagreement as to its characteristics and meaning continue. As Bennis and Nanus (1985:5) observe, there has been long-standing difficulty in defining leadership: "Like love, leadership . . . is something everyone knew existed but nobody could define." It is clear that leadership is elusive, and everyone in a supervisory or managerial position must make every attempt to possess it.

Early ideas about leadership assumed that it was a matter of birth: the so-called "Great Man" theory of leadership. Leaders were born into leadership positions (e.g., monarchs). History has shown, however, that many of these born leaders were actually ineffective ones. When this view failed to explain leadership, it was replaced by the notion that great events made leaders of people who excelled in extraordinary situations. Moses, Julius Caesar, Martin Luther, Winston Churchill, Harry Truman, Gandhi, Martin Luther King Jr., and many others sought to assert their influence when time and social events intersected to make them great leaders. This definition is also inadequate, because there have been many instances requiring a leader, but one has failed to materialize. For example, one might conjecture that Los Angeles police executives failed to exert proper leadership in the Rodney King incident and during the riots in its aftermath.

Many other leadership theories have gained interest. Some looked at the leader; others looked at the situation. None, Bennis and Nanus (1985) argue, has stood the test of time. Now, they believe, we have an opportunity to appraise our leaders and ponder the essence of power. They maintain that today's leadership environment must be examined in three major contexts: commitment (maintaining a strong work ethic, with employees working at full potential); complexity (keeping abreast of legal, financial, and technological changes that have profound effects on organizations); and credibility (being recognized by other members of the department as a leader).

The word *leadership* is widely used and has resulted in as many definitions as there have been studies of the subject. Some commonly used definitions include the following:

- "Leadership is the process of directing the behavior of others toward the accomplishment of some objective." (Certo, 1989:351)
- "The process of influencing the activities of an individual or a group in efforts toward goal achievement in a given situation." (Hersey and Blanchard, 1988:86)

- "The process of directing and influencing the task-related activities of group members." (Stoner and Freeman, 1992:472)

Another leadership perspective that must be considered is subordinate acceptance of leadership. Bernard (1938) notes that followers must respect and accept a leader's orders and directives if they are to be followed. This entails that the leader develop relationships with followers, and directives must be within the boundaries of organizational norms and established policies. It means that leaders must sometimes sell their instructions to subordinates to gain compliance. Too often there is a *zone of indifference* in which subordinates do not respect their leader or question his or her directives. When this occurs, compliance is, at best, minimal. This means, as Bernard notes, that a leader's authority is delegated upward, not downward.

It is clear that supervisors use various methods for motivating officers. There is no one best way to manage and lead people in every situation. Leader style is largely dependent on the situation and the capabilities of those being led. In fact, supervisors may need to rely on a combination of strategies to be effective leaders. A number of leadership and motivation theories are addressed in this chapter, and an effective leader will need to rely on several of them, depending on the situation at hand.

Developing Leadership Skills

Katz (1975) identified three essential skills that leaders should possess: technical, human, and conceptual. Figure 3–1 illustrates these skills and how they apply to managers and supervisors. Notice that technical skills are most important at the lower supervisory ranks while conceptual skills preoccupy the higher ranks in an organization. Katz defined a *skill* as the capacity to translate knowledge into action in such a way that a task is accomplished successfully. Each of these skills, when performed effectively, results in the achievement of objectives and goals, which is the primary thrust of management and supervision.

Technical skills are those a manager needs to ensure that specific tasks are performed correctly. They are based on proven knowledge, procedures, or techniques. A supervisor's technical skills may involve knowledge in areas such as high-risk tactics, law, and criminal procedures. The police sergeant usually depends on training and departmental policies for technical knowledge. The areas in which managers need technical skills include computer applications, budgeting, strategic planning, labor relations, public relations, and human resources management. The manager must also have a knowledge of the technical skills required for the successful completion of tasks that are within his or her command.

Human skills involve working with people and include being thoroughly familiar with what motivates employees and how to utilize group processes. Katz

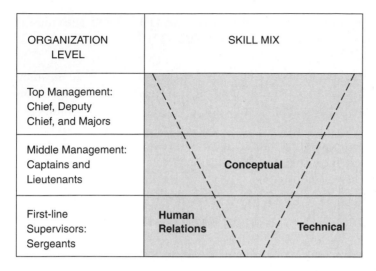

FIGURE 3–1   Leadership Skills Matrix
Source: Charles R. Swanson, Leonard Territo, and Robert W. Taylor, *Police Administration: Structures, Processes, and Behavior,* 3d ed. (New York: Macmillan, 1993), p. 169.

visualized human skills as including "the executive's ability to work effectively as a group member and to build cooperative effort within the team he leads" (p. 63). Katz added that the human relations skill involves tolerance of ambiguity and empathy. Tolerance of ambiguity means that the manager is able to handle problems when insufficient information precludes making a totally informed decision. Empathy is the ability to put oneself in another's place or to understand another's plight. The practice of human skills allows a manager to provide the necessary leadership and direction, ensuring that tasks are accomplished in a timely fashion and with the least expenditure of resources.

Conceptual skills, according to Katz, involve "coordinating and integrating all the activities and interests of the organization toward a common objective" (p. 65). Katz considered such skills to include "an ability to translate knowledge into action" and emphasized that these skills can be taught to actual and prospective managers and supervisors. Thus, good managers and supervisors are not simply born but can be trained to assume their responsibilities.

All three of these skills are present in varying degrees for each management level. As one moves up the hierarchy, conceptual skills become more important and technical skills less important. The common denominator for all levels of management is *human* skills. In today's unionized and litigious environment, it is inconceivable that a manager or supervisor could neglect the human skills.

Power, Authority, and Leadership

While considering the nature of leadership, it is important to remember that organizations exist to accomplish missions and goals that citizens cannot or will not achieve alone. Within organizations, and certainly within those of the police,

The higher one's rank in a police hierarchy, the more important it becomes to be able to conceptualize and develop necessary policies and procedures.
Courtesy Lexington, Kentucky, Police Department.

employees are granted the authority and power to morally and legally accomplish their tasks. Authority and power are related but separate concepts, however. *Authority* is a grant made by the formal organization to a position, which the person occupying that position wields in carrying out his or her duties. This fact does not mean that the person receiving that authority is automatically able to influence others to perform at all, let alone willingly (Swanson, Territo, and Taylor, 2001).

Power is the foundation of leadership. It is a necessary ingredient in influencing others to act or perform. While the leader whose subordinates refuse to follow is not totally without power (subordinates may be reprimanded, suspended, terminated, fined, and so on), such power must be used judiciously; both invoking it without just cause or failing to invoke it when necessary may contribute to a breakdown in discipline and performance, morale problems, and other negative side effects.

Power also arises in the informal side of an organization; members of a work group give one or more of their members power by virtue of their willingness to follow them on the basis of that person's charisma, experience, or heroism (such as the fictional "Dirty Harry," who was respected by peers while criticized by his superiors for constantly engaging in firefights and going "against the book").

The distinction between *power* and *authority* may be seen in the following example:

> A 10-year veteran, female, uniformed officer (Jones) is dispatched to a domestic violence scene and finds that a woman has clearly been assaulting her husband. The officer's sergeant, Blair, who has only recently been promoted from an office position, hears the call on the radio and shows up at the scene just as the female officer is preparing to leave without effecting an arrest. Sgt. Blair wants to know why Jones is not taking the woman to jail; it is clear that she is the assailant and the municipal ordinance requires an arrest. Jones tells her sergeant that she has personal knowledge from previous calls to the residence that the husband has until now been beating the wife with frequency, and therefore she will not take the woman into custody. The sergeant then directs Jones to make the arrest anyway, and she refuses, gets in her patrol car, and leaves. Later, Sgt. Blair files charges for refusal to obey the direct order of a superior, and Jones is suspended without pay for four days. Although wearing the "stripes" and possessing the *authority* they carry, Sgt. Blair's lack of experience contributed to his inability to influence Officer Jones to handle the situation according to the city ordinance. This led to Blair's relying on and invoking his *power* to discipline Jones. Jones, in this example, refused to recognize Blair's authority as a sergeant. Blair then resorted to power to force Jones to recognize or understand his authority and to solve the problem.

MOTIVATION THEORY

Toward Attaining Goals

Motivation generally refers to "the set of processes that arouse, direct, and maintain human behavior toward attaining some goal" (Greenberg and Barron, 1995:126). This definition implies that motivation consists of several areas. First, "arousal" refers to getting subordinates interested in performing some action. Some people are self-motivated and do not require a stimulus from a supervisor. Others, however, require direction or prodding. Second, this definition implies that people make choices about their behavior, such as about the amount and quality of their work. Management, through policies, direction, and consultation, can assist employees in making the correct choices. Finally, motivation is about maintaining productive behavior. Leaders must strive to have their subordinates working constantly to achieve goals. At its most fundamental level, motivation involves a *needs-goal model,* in which an individual seeks to fulfill a need (Figure 3–2). The need is then transformed into some behavior that is directed toward satisfying that need. For example, when someone becomes hungry, behavior becomes directed toward buying, preparing, and eating food. If a person is unable to satisfy a need, he or she becomes frustrated. This frustration may

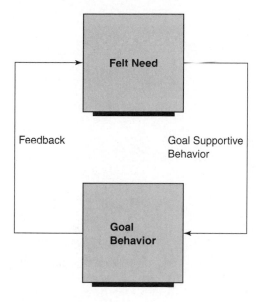

FIGURE 3–2 Needs–Goal Model of Motivation
Source: Samuel Certo, *Principles of Modern Management: Functions and Systems,* 4th ed. (Needham Heights, MA: Simon and Schuster, 1989), p. 377.

lead to greater effort by the employee or withdrawal and mediocre productivity. When a subordinate cannot achieve his or her goals, problems may arise.

Motivating employees on the job is not so simplistic. Therefore, motivation theory helps us understand the "why" of people's behavior. It is often misunderstood as something that supervisors do to employees. In reality, it is more internal and relates to an individual's needs, wants, and desires. But what exactly sparks an employee's desire to achieve a higher level of performance is not easily identified. What is clear, however, is that what motivates one employee to perform may not at all motivate another employee.

Motivation theories may be divided into two general categories: content theories and process theories. Content theories focus on the individuals' needs, wants, and desires and attempt to explain internal needs that motivate people's behavior. Process theories attempt to explain how people are motivated and focus on the interplay of the individual with forces in the workplace.

Content Theories

Maslow's Hierarchy of Needs

Abraham Maslow founded the humanistic school of psychology during the 1940s. Maslow's (1954) work focused on human needs and wants. He viewed people as perpetually "wanting" in nature and described their needs as insatiable. According to Maslow, people's needs are not random but progress in a "hierarchy of needs" from survival to security, social, ego-esteem, and self-actualization needs, as shown in Figure 3–3.

Self-actualization Needs — **Job-related Satisfiers**

Self-actualization Needs	Job-related Satisfiers
Reaching Your Potential	Involvement in Planning Your Work
Independence	Freedom to Make Decisions Affecting Work
Creativity	
Self-expression	Creative Work to Perform
	Opportunities for Growth and Development

Esteem Needs	Job-related Satisfiers
Responsibility	Status Symbols
Self-respect	Merit Awards
Recognition	Challenging Work
Sense of Accomplishment	Sharing in Decisions
Sense of Competence	Opportunity for Advancement

Social Needs	Job-related Satisfiers
Companionship	Opportunities for Interaction with Others
Acceptance	
Love and Affection	Team Spirit
Group Membership	Friendly Coworkers

Safety Needs	Job-related Satisfiers
Security for Self and Possessions	Safe Working Conditions
Avoidance of Risks	Seniority
Avoidance of Harm	Fringe Benefits
Avoidance of Pain	Proper Supervision
	Sound Company Policies, Programs, and Practices

Physical Needs	Job-related Satisfiers
Food	Pleasant Working Conditions
Clothing	Adequate Wage or Salary
Shelter	Rest Periods
Comfort	Labor-saving Devices
Self-preservation	Efficient Work Methods

FIGURE 3–3   Maslow's Hierarchy of Needs
Source: A.H. Maslow, *Motivation and Personality,* 2d ed. (New York: Harper & Row, 1970).

Maslow asserted that people are motivated by their lowest level of unsatisfied need. Once a lower need is satisfied, higher needs are sought. An important implication to motivation theory is understanding that a satisfied need is no longer a motivator of behavior. Simply stated, people who have their security needs met can be motivated only by higher needs.

What are the implications of this theory for the police organization? According to Maslow's hierarchy, a supervisor will better understand officers' performance and what motivates them by identifying their unfulfilled needs. There must also be a recognition that different officers may be at various levels in the hierarchy of needs and, therefore, are not necessarily motivated by the same wants. For example, a rookie officer may be most concerned with successfully completing the probationary period; therefore, security is that officer's primary concern and motivator. For the more veteran officer interested in promotion, motivation may derive from the esteem and status level. The supervisor may be successful in motivating this officer by delegating team leader duties and assisting the officer in preparing for the sergeant's exam.

Many of the tasks performed by field officers are self-directed.
Courtesy NYPD Photo Unit.

Argyris's Maturity-Immaturity Theory

Argyris's (1957) maturity-immaturity continuum also furnishes insight on human needs. According to Argyris, people naturally progress from immaturity to maturity. They develop needs for more activity and relative independence and often behave in many different ways. They also have deeper interests, consider a relatively long-term perspective, and show more awareness of themselves and more control of their own destiny. Argyris viewed an effective organization as one requiring employees to be self-responsible, self-directed, and self-motivated. He argued that motivation can be maximized when each employee pursues goals and experiences psychological growth and independence. He noted that the organization has a responsibility to structure the work environment so that employees can grow and mature.

Herzberg's Motivation-Hygiene Theory

In 1968, Frederick Herzberg developed a motivation theory based on a study of 200 engineers who were queried about when they were satisfied and dissatisfied with their jobs. The findings led Herzberg to identify two vital factors that are found in all jobs: (1) items that influence the degree of job dissatisfaction, called maintenance or *hygiene* factors, which relate mostly to the work environment, and (2) factors that influence the degree of job satisfaction, called *motivators,* which relate to the work itself. The items that comprise Herzberg's hygiene and motivator factors are shown in Figure 3–4.

Herzberg distinguished between job satisfaction and motivation. Indeed, using his scheme, an officer can be dissatisfied and motivated at the same time. If negative hygiene factors are present in a job, workers will become dissatisfied. Addressing these factors, such as by increasing salary, generally will not motivate people to do a better job, but it will keep them from becoming dissatisfied. In contrast, if motivating factors are high in a particular job, workers generally are motivated to do a better job. People tend to be more motivated and productive as more motivators are built into their job situation (Certo, 1989).

Dissatisfaction: Hygiene or Maintenance Factors	Satisfaction: Motivating Factors
1. Company policy and administration	1. Opportunity for achievement
2. Supervision	2. Opportunity for recognition
3. Relationship with supervisor	3. Work itself
4. Relationship with peers	4. Responsibility
5. Working conditions	5. Advancement
6. Salary	6. Personal growth
7. Relationship with subordinates	

FIGURE 3–4   Herzberg's Hygiene–Motivating Factors

The process of incorporating motivators into a job situation is called *job enrichment.* Subordinates are given more responsibilities, allowed to be involved in more complex cases, and have the opportunity to provide input into those decisions that directly affect them. The most productive employees are involved in work situations with desirable hygiene factors and motivating factors. This relates to Maslow's hierarchy of needs as well; for example, hygiene factors (such as a pay raise) can help to satisfy physical, security, and social needs, while motivating factors (for example, an award for outstanding performance) can satisfy employees' esteem and self-actualization needs.

According to Herzberg, hygiene factors may attract people to join an organization, but they do not provide the intrinsic satisfaction in the work itself that motivates people to perform at higher levels. Intrinsic motivation can only come from what the individual does through job responsibilities and subsequent satisfaction gained from job accomplishment. It appears that people are influenced more by intrinsic motivators than by hygiene factors. Put more simply, job satisfaction appears to be more important to most people than pay and benefits. A supervisor who conducts frequent team meetings to keep officers informed about departmental matters and to dispel rumors, who delegates additional duties to those officers ready to accept new challenges and compliments their work, and who solicits officers' participation in decision making whenever possible is appealing to their intrinsic motivators.

McClelland's Achievement, Power, and Affiliation Motives

McClelland (1964), another humanistic theorist, believed that individual needs were acquired over time and as a result of experience. From his studies, he identified three motives or needs that are important to an individual within an organizational environment:

1. *Need for achievement*—the need to succeed or excel. Some individuals must have standards or benchmarks to separate success from failure, and they have an internal force (motivation) that drives them toward accomplishment.

2. *Need for power*—the need to exert control over one's environment. Some individuals have an internal desire to make decisions and ensure that others abide by those decisions.

3. *Need for affiliation*—the need to establish and maintain friendly and close interpersonal relationships (social need).

Individuals who have a compelling drive to succeed are more interested in personal achievement than the rewards for their success. Such people have a desire to do things better; they seek situations in which they can attain greater personal responsibility; and they quickly volunteer for complex, challenging assignments. As they work through an assignment, they must have immediate and continuing feedback on their performance. If not carefully monitored and controlled, such individuals may develop a workaholic personality.

McClelland notes that power and affiliation needs are closely related to success. Successful managers and supervisors have a greater need for power and a lower need for affiliation. This type of individual is willing to take charge of a situation and act without undue regard for the social implications of decisions. If the need for power overshadows the affiliation need, however, managers and supervisors may become Machiavellian types who concentrate on their own success rather than on that of the organization or its personnel.

McClelland's theory has broad implications. The administrator should identify the high achievers and place them in positions where their attributes would best meet the department's needs. Some positions call for affiliation-oriented people, while others require achievers. When there is a crisis situation, a problem area within the department, or a new program is being developed and implemented, planning and operations are best handled by a high achiever. This internally motivated individual will take charge and exert all his or her energy toward ensuring that the assignment is completed successfully.

Some might argue that McClelland's theory overemphasizes authoritarian practices by concentrating on the need for task-oriented supervisors and managers, as opposed to those who are concerned with how their subordinates feel about them. To the contrary, a task orientation is not necessarily authoritarian. Authoritarian leaders often are more concerned with form than substance. That is, they frequently are caught up in making decisions and imposing their rules in an exercise of power while they give little regard to the task at hand. Said somewhat differently, they tightly control activity to the neglect of results. These managers and supervisors often are no more successful in attaining organizational goals than commanders who are overly concerned with how well they are accepted by their subordinates.

McClelland's successful manager or supervisor is an achiever who is goal directed and will do what is necessary to accomplish a given task. In most instances, the achievement of goals is impossible without high motivation within the work group. Therefore, the high achiever must maximize the resources of subordinates in order to be effective; this necessitates not only keeping an eye toward unit achievement, but also looking after the higher-order needs of others within the work group.

In sum, the content theorists attempt to explain behavior in terms of internal drives. In doing so, they raise a number of questions: How many needs are there? How many must be satisfied? Is there a hierarchy of needs? Which needs are most important? Are needs consistent across occupations? How can managers satisfy needs? It is no simple matter to apply content need theories. The managers and supervisors must, according to these theorists, provide avenues whereby subordinates can achieve their internal needs. Such a move requires better selection procedures for unit assignments, the opportunity for officers to have input into decision making, and a work climate in which officers' pay and benefits are at least satisfactory.

Process Theories

Expectancy Theory

In reality, the motivation process is much more complex than is depicted by the needs-goal model shown in Figure 3–2 and advocated by the content theorists. Content theories focus solely on the individual and, to a great extent, neglect the effects of the work environment on the individual. Vroom's (1964) expectancy theory was developed in the 1960s and addresses some of the complexities. This theory holds that people are motivated primarily by a felt need that affects behavior; however, Vroom's theory adds the issue of motivation *strength*—an individual's degree of desire to perform a behavior.

Vroom's expectancy model is shown in equation form in Figure 3–5. According to this model, motivation strength is determined by the perceived value of performing a task or job and the perceived probability that the work performed will result in an appropriate reward. That is, an individual is motivated if he or she perceives that the effort will be rewarded and if the value of the reward is equal to or greater than the amount of effort or work. Generally, individuals tend to perform the behaviors that maximize rewards over the long term.

Expectancy theory suggests that officers who experience success will feel more competent and therefore will be more willing to take risks in improving performance levels. When officers know that certain behaviors will produce anticipated departmental rewards, they are motivated. For example, an officer may be motivated to participate in a community policing project knowing that it could result in a higher performance rating, departmental letter of commendation, and improved promotional prospects. If such rewards are not forthcoming, the officer will be less enthusiastic when participating in similar projects in the future.

Equity Theory

Equity, from a motivational perspective, refers to the perceived fairness of rewards and the reward system itself. Adams (1963) formulated one of the best-known equity theories. He contended that when people believe that inequity exists in the way they are being treated, they will attempt to eliminate the discomfort, in order to restore a sense of equilibrium to the situation. Inequities exist

Individual's level of productivity and rewards	=	Other's level of productivity and rewards	=	Motivation strength

FIGURE 3–5 Adam's Equity Theory

because people believe the rewards or incentives they receive for their work are unequal to the rewards other workers appear to be receiving. Everyone wants to be treated equitably (not equally) and will engage in some type of social comparison to determine whether or not equity exists.

For example, police officers often compare their work and treatment to those of others in the department. Patrol officers might compare their workload and rewards with those of officers assigned to criminal investigation or traffic. If they perceive that other officers are working less but receiving better rewards, their levels of motivation likely will diminish. Comparisons of this type can negatively affect officer morale, especially among veteran officers who sometimes see less experienced officers assigned to specialty units such as traffic or training, and detectives receiving the benefits of additional pay, preferred hours of work, and more recognition and prestige.

It does not matter what managers and supervisors believe is fair and equitable, because fairness and equity are in the minds of those affected: "Perception is reality." Even if officers are rewarded in exactly the same way, inequities might still be perceived and can be caused by factors such as pay differentials, access to resources, preferential assignment, and promotion. Inequities and perceived inequities must be ferreted out by managers and supervisors, and when they are identified, they must be dealt with.

Departments embarking on community policing must also be careful that they do not allow officers engaged in community policing activities to be held in higher esteem or receive benefits not available to other patrol officers. This can have a significant negative impact on officer morale. It is for this reason that some have argued that specialized community policing units should not be established. It is more effective to have everyone or no one involved in the strategy.

The motivation theories discussed earlier help us to understand the many factors that influence workers' job satisfaction and willingness to perform their duties. It seems clear that employees want meaningful and challenging work. To deny this may result in frustration and poor performance. This is especially true of employees entering the workplace today. They are a new breed of worker: better educated, less resistant to change, motivated by varied job experiences and upward mobility, and less tolerant of militaristic structure and controls. This change presents a tremendous challenge for the supervisor to maintain the officers' interest in their work.

These theories may also tell us that the conventional bureaucratic structures and administrative practices that most police agencies were built on may be outdated for today's officer. Attention must be paid to job enrichment, participation, and human resources. By doing so, it becomes easier for the supervisor to ensure that employees' personal goals coincide with those of the organization.

LEADING VERSUS MANAGING

Leading is related to managing. In this chapter, however, we maintain that effective leadership goes well beyond the basic management functions described at the beginning of the chapter. Bennis and Nanus (1985:21) help us understand the broader role of supervision in their discussion of management and leadership: "To be a manager is to bring about, to accomplish, to have charge of, responsibility for, to conduct. Leading, on the other hand, is influencing, guiding in direction, course, action, opinion." They go on to say that managers are people who "do things right," and leaders are people who "do the right things." Managers are more efficiency driven and focus on mastering routine activities, while leaders are driven by vision and judgment. Managers tend to be bean counters, while leaders focus on achieving desired results.

In this regard, the following statement was developed by United Technological Corporation and provides much food for thought:

> People don't want to be managed. They want to be led. Whoever heard of a world manager? World leader[s], yes. They don't manage. The carrot always wins over the stick. Ask your horse. You can *lead* your horse to water, but you can't *manage* him to drink. If you want to manage somebody, manage yourself. Do that well and you'll be ready to stop managing. And start leading. (Quoted in Bennis and Nanus, 1985:22)

Another clear distinction between the leader and the manager is organizational consensus on overall goals—having a vision. According to Bennis and Nanus (1985:92), by focusing attention on a vision, the leader operates on the *emotional* and *spiritual resources* of the organization, on its values, commitment, and aspirations. The manager, by contrast, operates on the *physical resources* of the organization, its capital, human skills, raw materials, and technology. As they put it,

> Any competent manager can make it possible for people to earn a living [and] see to it that work is done productively and efficiently, on schedule, and with a high level of quality. It remains for the effective leader, however, to help people in the organization know pride and satisfaction in their work. (Bennis and Nanus, 1985:92)

They added: "The essential thing in organization leadership is that the leader's style *pulls* rather than *pushes* people on. Leading is a responsibility, and the effectiveness of this responsibility is reflected in the attitudes of the led" (Bennis and Nanus, 1985:80–81).

We concur that a successful police supervisor must be a good manager as well as a good leader. As Whisenand and Ferguson explained (1996:13), "If you're a competent manager, you are getting the most out of your resources. If you're a competent leader, you are pointing their energy in the right direction." It is therefore important that the supervisor manage departmental resources in as efficient a manner as possible, while also motivating and inspiring employees to perform to the best of their ability. Therein lies the influential art of leadership that instills the sense of esprit de corps or common purpose that imbues successful cohesive teams.

LEADERSHIP THEORIES

We now discuss trait, behavioral, situational, and contingency theories that attempt to explain leadership behavior. Whereas trait theories are based on the intrinsic qualities a leader possesses, behavioral theories explain leadership by examining what the leader does. Situational theories maintain that effective leadership is a product of the fit between the leader's traits or skills and the situation in which he or she is to exercise leadership. Contingency theories, to a degree, merge and extend trait and behavioral theories by examining how the environment or workplace affects leadership and the leader. Finally, transformational leadership theory examines how a leader can change or transform an organization. This is particularly important as police executives continue to adopt community policing.

Trait Theory

Early leadership studies of the 1930s and 1940s focused on the individual and assumed that some people were born leaders, and that good leaders could be studied to determine the special traits that leaders possess. From an organizational standpoint, this *trait theory* had great appeal. For example, in the police field it was assumed that all that was needed was for leaders with these special traits to be identified and promoted to managerial positions within the department.

Researchers have attempted to identify those special traits that separate successful leaders from poor leaders for more than 50 years. For example, Davis (1^40) found 56 different characteristics or traits that he considered important. While admitting it was unlikely that any manager would possess all 56 traits, he said the following 10 traits were required for executive success: intelligence, experience, originality, receptiveness, teaching ability, knowledge of human behavior, courage, tenacity, and a sense of justice and fair play.

The age-old assumption that leaders are born and develop their technical, human, and conceptual skills was completely discredited, because researchers have been unable to agree or present empirical evidence to support its claims (Tannenbaum and Weschler, 1961). There are too many traits that a good leader must possess, and some good leaders possess some of the traits, while other good leaders do not. Additionally, there are traits that good leaders possess that bad leaders also possess. Consequently, it is now believed that certain traits and skills increase the *likelihood* that a given person will be an effective manager. There are no guarantees, however.

Behavioral Theories

The *behavioral* approach focuses on a leader's behavior in relation to the environment. Studies at the University of Michigan and Ohio State University and Blake and Mouton's "managerial grid" led the early research of behavioral theories leadership. These studies were important because they studied leadership in real-life situations.

University of Michigan and Ohio State University Studies

The University of Michigan conducted a series of studies of leadership behavior in relation to job satisfaction and productivity in business and industrial work groups. The researchers determined that leaders must have a sense of the task to be accomplished as well as the environment in which the followers worked. They found the following to be the beliefs of a successful leader:

1. The leader assumes the leadership role is more effective relative to managers who fail to exhibit leadership.

2. The closeness of supervision will have a direct bearing on the production of employees. High-producing units had less direct supervision; highly supervised units had lower production. Conclusion: Employees need some area of freedom to make choices. Given this, they produce at a higher rate.

3. Employee-orientation is a concept that includes the manager's taking an active interest in subordinates. It is the leader's responsibility to facilitate employees' accomplishment of goals. (Bennett and Hess, 2001)

Ohio State University began its study of leadership in 1945 and identified leadership behavior in two dimensions: initiating structure and consideration. *Initiating structure* referred to supervisory behavior that focused on the achievement of organizational goals and included characteristics such as assigning subordinates to particular tasks, holding subordinates accountable for following rules and procedures, and informing subordinates of what is expected of them. *Consideration* was directed toward a supervisor's openness concerning subordinates' ideas and respect for their feelings as persons and included characteristics such as listening to subordinates, being willing to make changes, and being friendly and approachable. It was assumed that high consideration and moderate initiating structure yielded higher job satisfaction and productivity than did high initiating structure and low consideration (Sales, 1969).

The Managerial Grid

The managerial grid, developed by Robert Blake and Jane Mouton (1962), has received a lot of attention since its appearance and is based on and expands the research conducted at Ohio State and Michigan Universities.

The managerial grid (Figure 3–6) has two dimensions: concern for production and concern for people. Each axis or dimension is numbered from 1, meaning low concern, to 9, indicating a high concern. The horizontal axis represents the concern for production and performance goals, and the vertical axis represents the concern for human relations or empathy. The way in which a person combines these two dimensions establishes a leadership style in terms of one of the five principal styles identified on the grid.

The points of orientation are related to styles of management. The lower–left-hand corner of the grid shows the 1,1 style (representing a minimal concern for task or service and a minimal concern for people). The lower–right-hand corner of the grid identifies the 9,1 style. This type of leader would have a primary concern for the task or output and a minimal concern for people. People are seen as tools of production. The upper–left-hand corner represents the 1,9 style, often referred to as "country club management," with minimum effort given to output or task. The upper right, 9,9, indicates high concern for both people and production—a team management approach of mutual respect and trust. In the center, a 5,5, "middle-of-the-road" style, the leader has a "give a little, be fair but firm" philosophy, providing a balance between output and people concerns (Favreau and Gillespie, 1978).

These five leadership styles can be summarized as follows:

1. Authority-compliance management (9,1)
2. Country club management (1,9)
3. Middle-of-the-road management (5,5)
4. Impoverished management (1,1)
5. Team management (9,9)

Swanson and Territo (1982) attempted to investigate the extent to which Blake and Mouton's various styles are utilized by police managers. They surveyed managers from 166 different departments and found that almost 40 percent of the participants reported that they primarily used the team style of leadership. Twenty-nine percent reported the task or middle-of-the-road style as their primary form of leadership, 15 percent reported using the impoverished style, 11 percent reported using the authority-compliance form, and only 9 percent said they were country club managers. Swanson and Territo's research indicates a variety of styles being used by police leaders. The predominate style they found was the team style. The leaders who were not team leaders need to move in that direction.

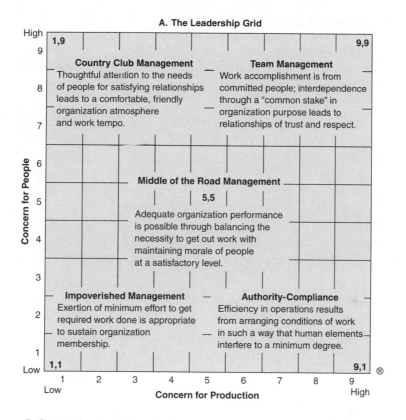

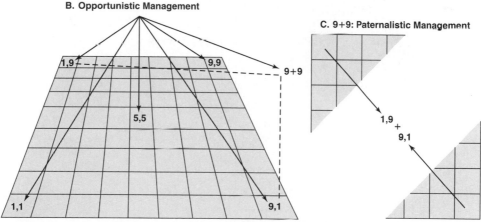

FIGURE 3–6 The Leadership Grid

Source: The Leadership Grid® figure, Paternalism Figure and Opportunism from *Leadership Dilemmas—Grid Solutions,* by Robert R. Blake and Anne Adams McCanse (Formely the Managerial Grid by Robert R. Blake and Jane S. Mouton). Houston: Gulf Publishing Company, (Grid Figure p. 29, Paternalism Figure: p. 30, Opportunism Figure: p. 31). Copyright 1991 by Scientific Methods, Inc. Reproduced by permission of the owners.

Situational Leadership

Situational leadership theories recognize that the workplace is a complex setting subject to rapid changes. Therefore, it is unlikely that one best way of managing these varying situations would be adequate. Simply, the best way to lead depends on the situation.

Hersey and Blanchard (1988) presented a model of situational leadership that has been used in training by many major corporations and the military services. Their model emphasizes the leader's behavior in relationship to followers' behavior (Figure 3–7). This approach requires the leader to evaluate follower responsibility in two ways: willingness (motivation) and ability (competence).

Situational leadership takes into account worker maturity; *maturity* is defined as the capacity to set high but attainable goals, the willingness to take responsibility, and the education and/or experience of the individual or the group. Figure 3–7 defines the various levels of worker maturity as follows:

M1:   The followers are neither willing nor able to take responsibility for task accomplishment.

M2:   The followers are willing but are not able to take responsibility for task accomplishment.

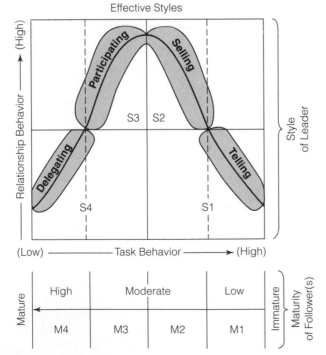

FIGURE 3–7   Situational Leadership Model
Copyrighted material. Reprinted with permission of Center for Leadership Studies, Escondido, CA 92025. All rights reserved.

M3: The followers are not willing but are able to take responsibility for task accomplishment.

M4: The followers are willing and able to take responsibility for task accomplishment. (Hersey and Blanchard, 1988)

Task behavior, shown in Figure 3–7, is essentially the extent to which a leader engages in one-way communication with subordinates; relationship behavior is the extent to which the leader engages in two-way communication (by providing positive reinforcement, emotional support, and so on). Four basic styles of leadership are associated with task accomplishment. They operate similarly to those on the managerial grid. They are characterized as follows:

S1: *Telling.* High task–low relationship style characterized by one-way communication in which the leader defines the roles of followers and tells them what, how, when, and where to do various tasks.

S2: *Selling.* High task–high relationship behavior is provided by two-way communication and socioemotional support to get followers to voluntarily buy into decisions that have been made.

S3: *Participating.* High relationship–low task behavior indicates both leader and follower have the ability and knowledge to complete the task.

S4: *Delegating.* Low relationship–low task behavior gives followers the opportunity to "run their own show" with little supervision. (Swanson, Territo, and Taylor, 2001)

The bell-shaped curve in the style-of-leader portion of Figure 3–7 means that as the maturity level of followers develops from immaturity to maturity, the appropriate style of leadership moves in a corresponding way (Hersey and Blanchard, 1988). For example, a police supervisor who has a subordinate whose maturity is in the M3 range would be most effective employing an S3 style of leadership.

Hersey and Blanchard asserted that leaders could reduce their close supervision and direction of individuals and increase delegation as followers' readiness to complete tasks increased. The difficulty of this style of leadership is its dependence on leaders to diagnose follower ability and then adjust their leadership style to the given situation. This is often easier said than done.

Contingency Theory

Several researchers (Burns and Stalker, 1961; Woodward, 1965) attempted during the late 1950s and early 1960s to show that no one leadership style was appropriate for all job situations. Some jobs require one type of leadership, while another may require a different one. For example, a leader's style in a barricaded-person situation would be different from that of the same leader working with officers confronting a burglary problem. Therefore, situational theories of leadership are based on the concept of leader flexibility: Successful leaders must change their leadership style as they confront different situations. But can leaders be so flexible as to employ all major styles? Obviously, not all leaders are capable of such flexibility. It may be that leaders are locked into a particular style as a result of their personalities and job experiences.

Fred Fiedler (1965) developed one strategy for overcoming these obstacles, which is to change the organizational situation to fit the leader's style, and not vice versa. According to Fiedler, leader–member relations (the degree to which the leader feels accepted by the followers), task structure (the degree to which the work to be done is outlined clearly), and power of the leader (discussed later) should be considered when assigning leaders. Police departments commonly move sergeants with investigative experience into detective units to capitalize on their knowledge. According to Fiedler, it may be just as important to evaluate the sergeant's leadership style and ability to ensure that it matches the leadership situation.

The basic components of *contingency theory* then are that (1) among people's needs is a central need to achieve a sense of competence, (2) the ways that people fulfill this need vary from person to person, (3) competent motivation is most likely to occur when there is a fit between task and organization, and (4) a sense of competence continues to motivate people even after competence is achieved (Plunkett, 1983). It seems that not only are subordinates unhappy when they have a leader whose style does not match the job, but the leader may be just as unhappy and unmotivated. Contingency theory argues that authoritarian leaders are more effective in performing structured and organized tasks. Human relation–type leaders are best suited for performing unstructured and uncertain tasks. Understanding this distinction requires that managers and supervisors tailor jobs to fit people or give people the skills, knowledge, and attitudes they will need to become competent (Burns and Stalker, 1961; Plunkett, 1983).

Transformational Leadership

A recent development in leadership theory is called *transformational leadership.* It is an employee-centered approach to leadership that seeks to elevate employees' level of performance by teaching and articulating organizational values. Transformational leadership occurs when leaders and followers interact in such a way that they are elevated and committed to some great cause external to the relationship. An example is the transformational role played by many police chiefs who moved their departments into community policing. Transformational leadership is most appropriate when the leader desires to initiate substantial change in the department or unit.

Transformational leadership is dynamic in that leaders enter into a purposeful and mutually supportive relationship with followers who are activated, motivated, and sustained by it. In the police field, the challenge for the manager or supervisor is to help police officers redefine their role and accept responsibility for following in a constantly changing, transformational environment. The key ingredients in developing an effective leadership–followership strategy are genuine participation, communication, shared decision making, equity, self-control, and interdependence.

Kotter (1995) has identified eight steps in the transformation process:

1. Establishing a sense of urgency or importance
2. Forming a guiding coalition to work as a team
3. Creating a vision that encompasses the desired change
4. Communicating this vision to all members of the department
5. Empowering other members of the organization to act on the vision
6. Ensuring that there are short-term wins or accomplishments
7. Building on improvements and continuing to pursue change
8. Ensuring that new approaches are adopted throughout the organization

The transformational approach emphasizes the importance of people, commitment, leadership, and empowerment. Here, leadership is not the exercise of power, but the empowerment of others to help set and achieve mutually acceptable goals or objectives. Good police managers and supervisors cultivate effective followership by creating and nurturing collective ownership of the enterprise based on common culture, shared values, mutual respect, trust, problem solving, and collaborative risk taking (Rippy, 1990).

Power and Leadership

Perhaps the two most often confused terms in management and supervision are *power* and *authority*. Authority is the right to command or give orders and is based on one's rank or position in the department. The extent to which an individual is able to influence others so they respond to orders is power. The greater this ability, the more power an individual is said to have. Further, a person can have rank but little or no power, and conversely, a person can have power but no rank within the department.

The total power a manager possesses is made up of position power and personal power. *Position power* is power derived from the organizational position a manager holds. In general, moves from lower-level management to upper-level management accrue more position power for a manager. *Personal power* is power derived from a manager's relationships with others (Certo, 1989).

Managers and supervisors can increase their total power by increasing their position power or their personal power. Position power can generally be increased by a move to a higher organizational position, but managers and supervisors usually have little personal control over moving upward in the department. They do, however, have substantial control over the amount of personal power they hold over other organizational members. To increase personal power, a manager can attempt to develop

1. *A sense of obligation in other organizational members that is directed toward the manager.* If a manager is successful in developing this sense of obligation, other workers think they should rightly allow the manager to influence them, within certain limits. Doing personal favors for others is a basic strategy.

2. *A belief in other organizational members that the manager possesses a high level of expertise within the organization.* To increase the perceived level of expertise, the manager must quietly make significant achievement visible to others and rely heavily on a successful track record and respected professional reputation.

3. *A sense of identification that other organizational members have with the manager.* The manager can strive to develop this identification by behaving in ways that other organizational members respect and by espousing goals, values, and ideals commonly held by them.

4. *The perception in other organizational members that they are dependent on the manager.* The main strategy the manager should adopt is a clear demonstration of the amount of authority that he or she possesses over organizational resources. This is aptly reflected in the managerial version of the Golden Rule: "He who has the gold makes the rules." (Kotter, 1977)

LEADERSHIP STYLES

We now examine the styles of leadership that are sometimes displayed in police organizations. When researchers could not agree on universally accepted leadership traits, they began to study leadership styles. An early focus of the style theory of leadership resulted in the adoption of a single style based on a manager's rank or position in the department. Here, we examine two different typologies of leadership styles, one by Likert and another proposed by Downs. We also present research by Van Maanen (1984), who examines police leadership in terms of station house sergeants and street sergeants.

Likert's Leadership Systems

Likert's (1961) management systems are a good way to conceptualize the differences across organizational theories. Likert examined a number of industrial plants in an attempt to discover the style of leadership used by various managers. He was primarily interested in determining those leaders who were successful and why. Likert identified four distinct leadership types: exploitive-authoritarian, benevolent-authoritarian, consultative, and participative. Figure 3–8 shows these types in a continuum from low employee involvement to high involvement and interaction.

- *Exploitive-Authoritarian Leadership:* The exploitive-authoritarian leader has no confidence or trust in subordinates, and subordinates are not allowed to provide input into decisions. Policies and decisions are formulated by top management and filter down the chain of command. There is little superior-subordinate interaction, and when there is, it is usually negative or directive in nature. Superiors generally attempt to motivate subordinates through fear, threats, and punishment. Employees become frustrated and join together in informal groups to protect themselves from top management and to oppose unpopular policies. The exploitive-authoritarian style of leadership thwarts motivation and causes officers to concentrate only on attaining minimum productivity levels. This style of leadership is obviously inappropriate in policing, because police officers' activities cannot be highly or easily controlled as a result of the types of activities performed and the high degree of discretion officers must have when dealing with crime and calls for service. Moreover, first-line supervisors seldom provide close supervision of officers, which is a key component of the exploitive-authoritarian style. If this style of leadership exists in law enforcement, it exists only in a few isolated cases.

- *Benevolent-Authoritarian Leadership:* The benevolent-authoritarian style is somewhat more positive than the exploitive-authoritarian style. With this style, most policies and decisions are made by top management and are distributed through the chain of command, but sometimes managers and supervisors listen to subordinates' problems. More interaction takes place between first-line supervisors and line employees than in the exploitive-authoritarian style. Superiors frequently are willing to listen, but they continue to make all the decisions. Subordinates still view superiors with caution and distrust, but not to the point that they oppose organizational goals. They feel somewhat frustrated because they have little input into daily activities, especially those that directly affect them. This style of leadership permeates many traditionally organized police

Likert's System Organizational Characteristics

Operating Characteristic	Exploitive-Authoritarian System	Benevolent-Authoritarian System	Consultative	Participative
Motivation	Economic security marked with fear and threats	Economic and occasionally status rewards coupled with some punishment	Economic, ego, and desire for new experiences. Occasional punishment	Economic, ego, and full involvement in the organization and shared power
Communication Processes	Very little and downward	Little and mostly downward	Quite a bit, up and down the organization	Substantial throughout the organization
Character of Interaction-Influence	Little interaction, usually distrustful	Some interaction with caution on the part of subordinates	Moderate interaction and a moderate level of trust and confidence	Extensive collegial interaction with a high degree of trust and confidence
Decision Making	Centralized with top administrators	Policy dictated by top administrators with some decisions resting with mid-level managers	Broad policies made at top with lower level echelons having input into programs	Decisions made throughout the organization with lower level subordinates having input in all decisions
Goal Setting	Goals set by top administrators and orders issued by administrators. Directives resisted by subordinates	Goals set by top administrators and orders issued by administrators with some discussion by subordinates	Goals and orders issued after discussion with subordinates. Goals and orders have some level of acceptance by subordinates	Goals established through group participation with high levels of acceptance by work group
Control Processes	Formalized controls established by top management, which are resisted by subordinates	Control rests primarily at the top with resistance from subordinates	Moderate delegation of authority and responsibility with subordinates having some input in performance expectations	Concern for performance throughout the organization coupled with collegiality
Productivity	Mediocre productivity	Fair to good productivity	Good productivity	Excellent productivity

FIGURE 3–8   Likert's Leadership Systems
Adapted from Likert, R. (1967). *The Human Organization: Its Management and Value.* New York: McGraw-Hill Book Co., pp. 14–24.

departments and is responsible for many of the motivational problems in these departments. (A possible reason for the existence of authoritarian leaders in police work is that the enforcement aspect of policing is, to a great extent, authoritarian, thereby attracting this type of individual.) Many officers working under this leadership style concentrate on accomplishing their assigned tasks, but they seldom go beyond them because of the lack of encouragement and the possibility of getting into trouble with their superiors. Hence, there is no real motivation to succeed, which is a necessary part of a successful organization. No statistics are available on the extent to which particular leadership styles exist in police organizations, but many police leaders likely are benevolent-authoritarian or consultative.

- *Consultative Leadership:* The consultative style of leadership is a process whereby management establishes goals and objectives for the department with subordinates making some of the decisions on methods of goal achievement (i.e., strategic and tactical decisions). A more positive relationship exists between superiors and line personnel as problems and possible solutions are discussed openly and freely. Employees are encouraged to become involved by providing input into some decisions and unit goals. Positive rewards are emphasized and punishment is used to motivate only in extreme cases. Whole or parts of police departments formally or informally adhere to this leadership style. This is especially true in larger police departments in which operational units have a great deal of autonomy (Toch, 1997). For example, the leadership style in drug units often is consultative. Officers in these units likely have substantial discretion in how they attack an area's drug problem. This style of leadership tends to emphasize involvement and esteem rewards and leads to a more positive motivational climate.

- *Participative Leadership:* The participative leadership style involves subordinates having input not only into tactical decisions, but also into policy formulation. It is a team approach whereby everyone has input in the organization's goals and objectives and operational strategies and tactics. The participative style implies that police officers provide direct input into what the department should be doing. Witte, Travis, and Langworthy (1990) found that officers at all levels within police departments favored the use of participatory management, but that only those officers in administrative positions believed that they were allowed an adequate level of participation. All other officers believed that they were not allowed adequate participation in decision making and strategic planning. Managers sometimes are given objectives that are counter to the expectations of officers. Such disagreements on policy usually center on law enforcement versus service roles. If there is a high degree of trust within the police organization, however, this may be only a minor problem. In the vast majority of cases, subordinates should be allowed to have some level of input into decisions. An open discussion of such matters generally brings about compliance and cooperation.

Police organizations must move toward the latter two styles of leadership. Approximately 80 percent of any police department's budget is devoted to salaries for personnel, and personnel represent an important resource in police agencies. These resources must be used to their maximum advantage. The consultative and participatory styles of leadership create a positive motivational atmosphere in which officers are more likely to be concerned about doing an excellent job in accomplishing objectives.

Downs's Bureaucratic Leadership Styles

Close examination of Likert's leadership styles would lead one to assume leadership is strictly a matter of authority and subordinate participation in decision making. Downs (1967) examined bureaucratic organizations and developed a typology of leadership based on a leader's effort and orientation within the organization. He identified four styles of leadership: (1) climbers, (2) conservers, (3) zealots, and (4) advocates. *Climbers* are ambitious and generally unethical people who use every opportunity to further their careers. They actively recruit sponsors to help themselves. They will take on extra duties in order to gain attention or approval from superiors, and they willingly sacrifice subordinates in order to make themselves look good. They look for every opportunity to promote themselves. Most police departments have a few climbers who constantly are involved in internal politics for their self-promotion.

Conservers essentially are bureaucrats who strive to maintain the status quo. They work themselves into a position within the organization, and they get comfortable by thoroughly understanding the tasks and policies associated with the position. They settle in and seldom seek promotion. They resist change and innovation and expend a great deal of energy ensuring that nothing changes. Conservers usually are older and become classic bureaucrats, ensuring that policies are followed to the letter regardless of circumstances.

Zealots, on the other hand, are organizational members with a mission. They generally have a narrow interest and a great deal of energy, which they focus on their special interest. They often neglect their duties as they focus almost exclusively on their crusade. They are so adamant about their area of interest that they tend to antagonize others. In the end, they tend to be unproductive leaders. In police organizations, zealots often find their way into specialized units that match their interests.

Finally, *advocates* are those leaders who care only about their sphere of influence—their particular unit. When dealing with outsiders, they look only at what is good for them and their unit and seldom compromise for the greater good. They are just as zealous as zealots, but rather than focusing on an issue, they focus on their domain. Advocates in police departments often refuse to cooperate with other units and are often at odds with members of other units in the department.

Downs's styles of leadership focus on how various types of leaders react in the organization. They really do not consider subordinate input or participation but center on leaders' idiosyncracies and personal agendas. Each type is plentiful in police departments, and each type presents a unique set of problems.

Station House Sergeants and Street Sergeants

To learn the differences in leadership style as a function of workplace, we consider an interesting study of a 1,000-officer police department by John Van Maanen (1984), who identified two contrasting types of police sergeants: "station house" and "street." *Station house sergeants* have been out of the "bag" (uniform) since before their promotion to sergeant and prefer to work inside in an office environment once they win their stripes. This preference is clearly indicated by the nickname of "Edwards, the Olympic torch who never goes out" given to one sergeant. Station house sergeants immerse themselves in the management culture of the police department, keeping busy with paperwork, planning, record keeping, press relations, and fine points of law. Their strong orientation to conformity also gave rise to nickname "by the book Brubaker."

In contrast, Van Maanen (1984) found that *street sergeants* were serving in the field when promoted; consequently, they had a distaste for office procedures and a strong action orientation as suggested by nicknames such as "Shooter McGee" and "Walker the Stalker." Moreover, their concern was not with conformity, but with "not letting the assholes take over the city."

Station house sergeants and street sergeants are thought of differently by those whom they supervise: Station house sergeants "stood behind their officers," whereas street sergeants "stood beside their officers." Station house sergeants might not be readily available to officers working in the field but can always be located when a signature is needed and are able to secure more favors for their subordinates. Street sergeants occasionally interfere with the autonomy of their subordinates by responding to and handling a call assigned to a subordinate.

Station house sergeants spend considerable time learning routines, procedures, and skills that will improve future promotional opportunities. Furthermore, they are making contacts with senior police commanders who can give them important assignments and possibly influence future promotions. In contrast, street sergeants may gain some favorable publicity and awards for their exploits, but they are also more likely to have citizen complaints against them, be investigated by internal affairs, or be sued. Consequently, street sergeants are regarded by their superiors as "good cops" but difficult people to supervise. In short, the action-oriented street sergeant may not go beyond a middle-manager's position in a line unit such as patrol or investigation.

WHEN LEADERS ADOPT A CUSTOMER FOCUS

The most successful organizations today are using a variety of systematic improvement methods to reengineer their organizations around a concept that has many names but is often termed *total quality management,* or TQM (Hoover, 1996). TQM is increasingly becoming a dominant practice in police departments, especially with the implementation of community policing. Essentially, TQM calls on the department to emphasize culture, customers, and counting. *Culture* refers to the department's adopting a culture that emphasizes service. Traditional policing focused on law enforcement or catching crooks, but research shows that this is only a small part of the job (Gaines, Kappeler, and Vaughn, 1999). Successful companies have a customer orientation, and it is reasonable that police departments should follow suit. Second, the police should consider citizens as *customers.* When citizens are considered customers, police will treat them better and strive harder to provide assistance and solve their problems. Finally, we should depart from the traditional police practice of *counting* when measuring productivity. Historically, we have measured success in the number of arrests, convictions, and citations issued. Police productivity is better measured by citizen satisfaction with the police, levels of fear of crime, and how well the police respond to community problems.

Entrepreneurial governments that have adopted the TQM concept are driven by their vision, values, and goals instead of their rules and regulations. They espouse participatory management, less bureaucracy, pushing organizational power and decision making downward, delegating authority, and encouraging problem solving at the lowest appropriate levels. In TQM, managers and supervisors listen to the voices of their subordinates, including dissenters, and are always open to ideas for improvement.

In *The Seven Habits of Highly Effective People,* Steven Covey (1989) provided a list of principles and advice on leadership, management, and organizational relationships that are important to a leader's effectiveness. As Covey explained:

> When one of our governing values is total quality, we will care not only about the quality of our products and services, but also about the quality of our lives and relationships. Total quality is a total philosophy. And it is sequential; if you don't have it personally, you won't get it organizationally.

The total quality, entrepreneurial spirit of government can be adopted to public safety. Following are some examples of how many of these principles can be implemented when police leaders begin to reinvent their organizations:

- *Tulsa, Oklahoma,* police studied arrest trends and school dropout statistics. They concluded that teenagers from a section of town with a major public housing development were creating most of the city's drug problems. They organized residents and together they prosecuted and evicted drug dealers; they created an antidrug education program and established job placement and mentoring programs; they set up a youth camp for teenagers; and they worked with the schools to develop an antitruancy program. (Osborne and Gaebler, 1992:50)

- *Sunnyvale, California,* developed performance measures for all municipal departments, defining the results it wanted. In each program area, the city articulated a set of goals, objectives, and performance indicators. For example, one objective was to keep the city "within the lowest 25 percent of Part I crimes [serious crime] for cities of comparable size, at a cost of $74.37 per capita." (Osborne and Gaebler, 1992:143–144)

- *Paulding County, Georgia,* built a 244-bed jail when it needed only 60 extra beds, so it could charge other jurisdictions $35 a night to handle their overflow. In the first year of business, the jail brought in $1.4 million, $200,000 more than its operating costs. (Osborne and Gaebler, 1992:197)

- *California* has some enterprising police departments that are earning money renting out motel rooms as weekend jails. They reserve blocks of rooms at cheap motels, pay someone to sit outside to ensure inmates stay in their rooms, and rent the rooms to convicted drunk drivers at $75 a night. (Osborne and Gaebler, 1992:197)

These examples clearly demonstrate what can happen when police leaders begin to think like entrepreneurs rather than like bureaucrats. Obviously, this is unlike conventional police work; a different mind set is required to think and act in this fashion. When we think outside the box, however, we sometimes are better able to solve our problems.

Another means of addressing customers' needs is community surveys. Today's police agencies must attempt to "feel the pulse" of their communities. Public opinion surveys provide vital information and feedback for assessing public perceptions of police performance, fear of crime, perceived problems in the community, and effectiveness of police communication with the public and can assist police leaders in making public policy decisions. Surveys can have citizens rate their police in areas such as concern, helpfulness, fairness, knowledge, quality of service, and professional conduct; how well they solved the problem; and whether they put the person at ease (Osborne and Gaebler, 1992:173). Surveys also help the police connect better with the community.

TEAM BUILDING

Why Teamwork?

Why do we think in terms of teams? Teamwork is vital to an organization for accomplishing its goals. It is also an important responsibility of the supervisor. Pollar (1997) notes that a team is a group of highly energetic people cooperatively working together to achieve common objectives. As such, teams build on the idea of synergy. *Synergy* occurs when the whole is greater than the sum of the parts. That is, when a team or group of officers work together, they are able to produce much more than when they work individually. Buckholz and Roth (1989) have identified eight characteristics of successful teams:

1. *Participatory Management.* Creating a situation in which everyone on the team feels free to contribute, and contributions are nonjudgmentally considered.

2. *Shared Responsibility.* All members of the team have a stake in team efforts and outcomes.

3. *Common Purpose.* All members of the team have an aligned vision regarding goals and objectives.

4. *Open Communications.* Members communicate openly and their information is valued by other members of the team.

5. *Future Focused.* Teams focus on accomplishments, not programs or duties. The team envisions how results will have a positive impact on the problem at hand.

6. *Goal Directed.* Team meetings and activities are focused on goals and results.

7. *Creativity.* Teams think outside the box. They look for the best solutions, not the normal responses.

8. *Timeliness of Response.* Teams identify and act on opportunities. They recognize that delays detract from results.

Building a Successful Team

Team building requires leadership. The team setting also requires a unique set of leadership skills. According to Hellriegel, Slocum, and Woodman (1983), effective team leaders display the following traits:

1. Focuses continuously on a goal

2. Participates in the group and at the same time observes the activities of the group as a detached leader

3. Acknowledges the need for assuming primary responsibility for controlling the relationships between the group and other units or individuals.

4. Facilitates group members in the assumption of leadership roles when the situation dictates or group needs change.

The team must perform a number of tasks when it is initially created. Most of these activities are diagnostic in nature. First, a team leader or facilitator is selected. The leader's primary responsibility is to ensure that the team achieves maximum results by identifying member roles and responsibilities. Second, the team should decide if it has the resources and capabilities to tackle an identified problem. In some cases, other officers with specialized expertise might be added to the team. For example, a crime analyst might be added to help clarify a crime problem. Third, team-building training is conducted to assist members in understanding their individual roles and the team's responsibilities. It is important for members to work together, but at the same time, each member must complete his or her individual responsibilities. Finally, once the team-building activities are completed, the team must identify objectives and plan and initiate activities to accomplish the objectives. The team leader ensures that the team remains on task and functions as a team. This is best accomplished by developing an action plan using input from all members of the team.

Teamwork is a strong motivational factor in policing. Team development transforms a group of independent people into an interdependent and productive entity. It feels good for the members to be a part of a winning team or a successful organization. Looking at Maslow's hierarchy of needs, the implementation of teams satisfies the belongingness and esteem needs. Thus, teams substantially contribute to motivation.

Policing is a field that is naturally composed of teams. Most police departments, as a result of specialization, create a number of teams. Patrol is organized into teams of officers that are supervised by a sergeant and assigned to different areas of town. The detective division is divided into teams of officers working fraud, robbery/homicide, juvenile, burglary, or auto theft. Other teams work gang, traffic, crime prevention, and training areas. Many specialized functions in police agencies involve teams of officers. Police managers and supervisors must attempt to ensure that these groups of officers function as teams, especially when they are engaged in problem solving.

WHY LEADERS FAIL

The previous discussion of theories and methods of leadership—some of which were developed several decades ago—is intended to help managers and supervisors avoid failure. In today's stop-and-go, ever dangerous, litigation-vulnerable world of

Supervisors are often responsible for coordinating the responses of patrol and specialized units, such as detectives and crime scene technicians at crime scenes.
Courtesy Washoe County, Nevada Sheriff's Office Photo Unit.

policing, the price paid for incompetent supervision is too high; there is little room for error. Moreover, it means that we must not depend on on-the-job-training but must develop our leaders before they are placed in leadership positions.

Some supervisors are too preachy, rigid, cold, uncaring, and vindictive, while others are too friendly, accommodating, or self-centered. Thus far, we have addressed how a supervisor, manager, or administrator should lead. However, it is also helpful to examine how a leader should *not* conduct business. The following are some types of "problem bosses":

1. *Ticket Punchers:* They maneuver daily to advance in status, power, and rank. Promotion is paramount, and they will do whatever is necessary to get ahead.

2. *Spotlighters:* They require attention and center stage, demanding recognition for all the positive results. When things go awry, they are quick to disappear. They rarely share the successes with others.

3. *Mega-Delegators:* These people seldom do real work and view them-selves as "participatory managers." They accomplish nothing, while everyone else is working hard.

4. *Micro Managers:* These bosses are either insecure or perfectionists or need to control every aspect of work; they seek feedback incessantly and require frequent reporting. They expend too much energy on details rather than getting the job done.

5. *One Best Style:* These managers believe that only one style of manag-ing guarantees success. In other words, if you mimic this person's style, you're a winner. They are too inflexible in too many situations.

6. *Control Takers:* These people crave power; force is foremost, control is critical, and being correct is imperative. They too often cannot dele-gate and do not allow their subordinates to grow with the job.

7. *The Phantoms:* These bosses are uncomfortable with social interaction, preferring to remain invisible or secreted away in their offices. They are uneasy empowering others. They are usually excellent test takers and thus are able to attain positions of command. (Whisenand and Fer-guson, 1996)

Finally, Steven Brown (1989) provided a list of 13 fatal errors that can erode a leader's effectiveness:

1. Refuse to accept personal accountability
2. Fail to develop people; operations should function successfully in your absence
3. Try to control results instead of activities
4. Join the wrong crowd
5. Manage everyone the same
6. Forget the importance of service
7. Concentrate on problems rather than objectives
8. Be a buddy, not a boss
9. Fail to set standards
10. Fail to train your people
11. Condone incompetence
12. Recognize only top performers
13. Try to manipulate people

A number of pitfalls are waiting for the police supervisor or manager. Being a good leader entails a great deal of hard work. The best leaders are those who are actively involved with their subordinates and the department. They have a vision of where they are going, and they adhere to a set of values to guide their actions.

——— Case Studies ———

The following two case studies provide some substantive issues for the reader to use for applying chapter information.

The "Rising Star" Who Falls Too Far

Detective Thurmond Thomas is a "rising star" in the Bently County Sheriff's Department, and at age 25 is the youngest officer there ever to be promoted to rank of detective. Recently married, Thomas is excited about his new assignment and is looking forward to the day-shift hours and weekends off. Thomas begins his new assignment with great desire, often volunteering for the less popular cases and working a lot of overtime. He is doing everything possible to make a good impression on his more experienced peers. Sgt. Wise takes a particular liking to Thomas and is making every effort to recognize his good work among the other detectives. He even suggests that Thomas consider being promoted at the soonest possible time and offers to coach him for the promotional exam. Everything appears to be going well for young Thomas. After a couple of months, however, Sgt. Wise begins to notice that Thomas is using a lot of sick time and has lost much of his enthusiasm for the job. Wise meets with Thomas to discuss the matter. Thomas explains that he is now uncomfortable in the detective division and does not fit in with the rest of the detectives. He adds that the others simply ignore him, never inviting him to lunch or coffee. Sgt. Wise decides that Thomas is simply lacking self-confidence due to his young age. He then discusses Thomas's concerns and his potential with the other detectives, in hopes of improving relations. Instead, matters only worsen, and now the lieutenant is directing Wise to investigate Thomas's sick days to determine if he is abusing his leave time.

1. What is your assessment of this situation?
2. Does Sgt. Wise correctly understand the nature of the problem?
3. How would you describe Thomas's problem, using the motivation theories discussed in the chapter?
4. What could Sgt. Wise have done differently?

Where to Begin When a Veteran Comes In

Officer Maria Sanchez has 17 years of experience, mostly as a detective in undercover narcotics and vice. She is a capable officer with numerous departmental commendations and awards for her work. As a result, Sanchez was selected to be a member of an elite multiagency vice and narcotics task force. On the first day of her new assignment, Sanchez met with her new supervisor, Sgt. Webster. He is from a neighboring agency and does not know Sanchez outside the selection interview process and review of her personnel file. Sgt. Webster was also recently assigned to the unit from patrol division where he gained the reputation of being somewhat of a perfectionist and detail person. Webster assumed responsibility for breaking in all new team members to ensure they knew exactly what, when, where, and how they should perform their tasks. Webster had developed a four-week orientation for all new members. After two weeks of basic orientation, including an elementary review of drug law, raid procedures, vice laws, and so on, Sanchez becomes extremely frustrated with Sgt. Webster and asks why she is not being allowed to participate in drug and vice raids with the rest of her team. She argues that she has worked with the task force on many occasions, is very familiar with operational procedures, and could demonstrate her abilities if Webster would only allow her to work with the rest of the team. Webster denies her request, saying she has to finish the orientation just the same as everyone else does. The next day, Sanchez submits a memo to the lieutenant in charge of the task force, requesting to be reassigned back to her agency. In the memo, Sanchez states that she believes Sgt. Webster is treating her differently from other people in the unit and does not have any respect for her past experience and work. She does not believe she can work under these conditions, in which she is "being treated like a child."

1. Could this problem have been avoided? If so, how?
2. What situational style of leadership was Sgt. Webster employing?
3. How would you assess the maturity level of Officer Sanchez?
4. Discuss what style of situational leadership would be more appropriate for this situation.

SUMMARY

This chapter has examined several management theories that are of interest to supervisors and managers, including what motivates employees, how managers are distinguished from leaders, theories of leadership, and quality leadership and team building. In addition to covering these theories, we pointed out several theories and approaches that have not succeeded. One can learn much from a failed approach.

It should be remembered that all of these elements and issues of management and supervision revolve around one very important feature of the workplace: people. Perhaps the major point being emphasized in this chapter is that managers and supervisors must know their people, and how to motivate them. To be effective in the labor-intensive field of policing, superior officers should first learn all they can about this most valuable asset, just as much as they must learn about agency policies and procedures and new technology. Effective leaders are made, not born; thus, they must also receive the requisite training and education for performing well. An educated approach is far better than simply marching the new leader off the plank, to either sink or swim.

ITEMS FOR REVIEW

1. There are a number of theories of motivation. How might these theories be applied in the police setting?

2. Contrast what is meant by "leader" versus "manager."

3. Describe situational leadership and how it applies to the police leader.

4. Review some of the ways in which a manager can increase his or her personal power.

5. Describe the idea of a team as it applies to law enforcement. How does one go about developing solid, productive teams?

6. Explain the concept of *equity* as it applies to motivating employees, and its importance for doing so.

7. Delineate several ways in which a leader can fail, and how failure can be avoided.

REFERENCES

Adams, J. S. (1963). Toward an understanding of inequity. *Journal of Abnormal Psychology* 67 (5):422–436.

Argyris, C. (1957). *Personality and organization.* New York: Harper & Bros.

Bennett, W. W., and Hess, K. (2001). *Management and supervision in law enforcement.* Belmont, CA: Wadsworth.

Bennis, W., and Nanus, B. (1985). *Leaders.* New York: Harper & Row.

Bernard, C. (1938). *The functions of the executive.* Cambridge, MA: Harvard University Press.

Blake, R. R., and Mouton, J. S. (1962). The developing revolution in management practices. *Journal of the American Society of Training Directors* 16:29–52.

Brown, S. B. (1989). *Fatal errors managers make: And how you can avoid them.* Police Leadership Report, The National Law Enforcement Leadership Institute, Safety Harbor, Florida, 1(3):6–7.

Buckholz, S., and Roth, T. (1989). *Creating the high-performance team.* New York: Wiley.

Burns, T., and Stalker, G. M. (1961). *The management of innovation.* London: Tavistock.

Certo, S. C. (1989). *Principles of modern management: Functions and systems,* 4th ed. Boston: Allyn & Bacon.

Covey, S. R. (1989). *The seven habits of highly effective people.* New York: Simon & Schuster.

Davis, R. C. (1940). *Industrial organization and management.* New York: Harper & Bros.

Downs, A. (1967). *Inside bureaucracy.* Boston: Little, Brown.

Favreau, D. F., and Gillespie, J. E. (1978). *Modern police administration.* Upper Saddle River, NJ: Prentice Hall.

Fieldler, F. (1965). Engineer the job to fit the manager. *Harvard Business Review* 43 (September/October):115–122.

Gaines, L. K., Kappeler, V. E., and Vaughn, J. (1999). *Policing in America.* Cincinnati: Anderson.

Greenberg, J., and Baron, R. (1995). *Behavior in organizations.* Upper Saddle River, NJ: Prentice Hall.

Hellriegel, D., Slocum, J. W., Jr., and Woodman, R. W. (1983). *Organizational behavior,* 3d ed. St. Paul, MN: West.

Hersey, P., and Blanchard, K. H. (1988). *Management of organizational behavior.* Upper Saddle River, NJ: Prentice Hall.

Herzberg, F. (1968). One more time: How do you motivate employees? *Harvard Business Review* (January/February):53–62.

Hoover, L. (1996). Translating total quality management from the private sector to policing. In L. Hoover, ed., *Quantifying quality in policing.* Washington, DC: PERF, pp. 1–22.

Katz, R. L. (1975). Skills of an effective administrator. *Harvard Business Review* 52:23.

Kotter, J. (1995). Leading change: Why transformation efforts fail. *Harvard Business Review* (March/April):59–67.

Kotter, J. (1977). Power, dependence, and effective management. *Harvard Business Review* (July/August):128–135.

Likert, R. (1961). *New patterns of management.* New York: McGraw-Hill.

Maslow, A. H. (1954). *Motivation and personality.* New York: Harper & Row.

McClelland, D. (1964). *The achieving society.* Princeton, NJ: Van Nostrand Reinhold.

Osborne, D., and Gaebler, T. (1992). *Reinventing government: How the entrepreneurial spirit is transforming the public sector.* Reading, MA: Addison-Wesley.

Plunkett, W. R. (1983). *Supervision: The direction of people at work.* Dubuque, IA: Wm. C. Brown.

Pollar, O. (1997). Sticking together. *Successful Meetings* (January):87–90.

Rippy, K. M. (1990). Effective followership. *The Police Chief* (September):45.

Sales, S. M. (1969). Supervisory style and productivity: Review and theory. In Larry Cummings and William E. Scott, eds., *Readings in organizational behavior and human performance.* Homewood, IL: Richard D. Irwin.

Stoner, J. A., and Freeman, R. E. (1992). *Management,* 5th ed. Upper Saddle River, NJ: Prentice Hall.

Swanson, C. R., and Territo, L. (1982). Police leadership and interpersonal communications styles. In J. Greene, ed., *Police and police work.* Beverly Hills: Sage.

Swanson, C. R., Territo, L., and Taylor, R. W. (2001). *Police administration,* 5th ed. Upper Saddle River, NJ: Prentice Hall.

Tannenbaum, R., and Weschler, I. R. (1961). *Leadership and organization: A behavioral science approach.* New York: McGraw-Hill.

Toch, H. (1997). The democratization of policing in the United States: 1895–1973. *Police Forum* 7(2):1–8.

Van Maanen, J. (1984). Making rank: Becoming an American police sergeant. *Urban Life* 13:155–176.

Vroom, V. H. (1964). *Work and motivation.* New York: Wiley.

Whisenand, P. M., and Ferguson, F. (1996). *The managing of police organizations.* Upper Saddle River, NJ: Prentice Hall.

Witte, J. H., Travis, L. F., and Langworthy, R. H. (1990). Participatory management in law enforcement: Police officer, supervisor, and administrator perceptions. *American Journal of Police* 9(4):1–24.

Woodward, J. (1965). *Industrial organization: Theory and practice.* London: Oxford University Press.

4

Communication and Negotiation

LEARNING OBJECTIVES

After reading this chapter, the student will:

- understand the communications process and the problems associated with it
- be able to communicate more effectively by applying the appropriate method to the situation
- use negotiations to effectively communicate ideas and information while gaining greater compliance to orders and directives
- understand the nature of organizational and group conflict
- be able to effectively mediate conflict when it occurs

The difference between the right word and the almost right word is the difference between lightning and lightning bug.

—Mark Twain

The right of every person "to be let alone" must be placed in the scales with the right of others to communicate.

—Chief Justice
Warren Burger

INTRODUCTION

When people think of police departments, they often think of patrols, investigations, speeding tickets, or arrests. These are police outputs or products of police efforts to control crime and provide citizens with services. Behind those outputs is a substantial amount of work, all of which is coordinated and conducted through communications. A police officer, regardless of rank, spends a significant portion of a workday communicating with citizens, other officers, or superiors. Essentially, police departments run on information and communications.

A companion process to communication is negotiation. A good supervisor must be skilled in negotiations. When we think of negotiations, we think of people attempting to work out a problem when there is appreciable disagreement. However, negotiation actually occurs in most communications. A police chief can issue an order, but it will not necessarily be followed unless it is accepted and understood. Negotiation skills legitimize the order, while communications skills transmit it clearly to subordinates. Therefore, to some extent, negotiation is the art of gaining compliance or selling people on an idea. How to successfully negotiate conflicts is addressed in this chapter.

The chapter opens with a general look at communication process; then, we consider barriers to effective communication and methods for improving communication in police agencies. Next, we examine the art of negotiating, including various approaches and tactics, and then turn to conflict—its nature, levels, and sources and how to cope with it. The chapter concludes with two case studies.

THE ACT OF COMMUNICATING

A Large Part of the Workday

Communication is a complex process. Indeed, communications, formal or informal, written or verbal, serve to link people and activities. We use a variety of technologies to communicate, including telephones, fax machines, the Internet, and police computers and radios. Yet, people seldom give much thought to how they communicate and the content of their communications. When there are errors in communication, or when information is not communicated effectively, a greater probability exists that those receiving the information will not fully grasp the meaning of the communication, and mistakes can result. Proper communication essentially serves to make a group of workers into a team and provides a means to coordinate people and work.

Several studies have examined the amount of communications in the police department. Mayo (1983) found that police executives spent about 70 percent of their time communicating, with the overwhelming majority of their communication occurring in meetings. A substantial amount of communication occurs at all levels of the organization. Supervisors communicate with a variety of people at all levels of the department. More and Wegener (1996) reported that about 55 percent of supervisors' communications is with subordinates. Approximately 26 percent of their communications is with superiors in the department, while only 4 percent is with other supervisors. Only 15 percent of a supervisor's communications is with the public. They also examined the tasks performed by sergeants and found that 51 percent of the tasks involved some form of communication. Their statistics indicate that sergeants spend most of their time working with and supervising subordinates.

Another study of supervisors found that they spent about 80 percent of their time communicating. The various types of communication in which they engaged are as follows: 45 percent listening, 30 percent talking, 16 percent reading, and 9 percent writing (Von der Embse, 1987). It appears that about 39 percent of the time supervisors are communicating to others, and 61 percent of the time someone is communicating to the supervisor. Supervisors spend more time receiving information than providing it. This study indicates that police supervisors are extensively involved in the communications process, and that they communicate with an array of people.

The Communication Process

Communication has been defined as "the process by which the sender—a person, group, or organization—transmits some type of information (the message) to another person, group, or organization (the receiver)" (Greenberg and Baron, 1995, p: 330). Lussier (1999) expands this definition by noting that communications occur with the intent to (1) influence, (2) inform, or (3) express feelings or opinions. Thus, the act of communicating is a complicated transaction between two or more parties that occurs with the intention of having an impact. In reality, communicating is a complicated process wrought with pitfalls that can lead to mistakes or ineffective communications. Figure 4–1 provides a detailed schematic for communicating and shows how complicated communications really are.

The process begins with the communicator or sender wishing to communicate an idea or information to another person(s) or organization. The first step in the communication process is that the sender must *encode* the idea or information—translate it into a form such as writing, language, or nonverbal communication. The encoding process can be difficult, especially if the sender is attempting to communicate a set of complex ideas. Although people may have little difficulty conceptualizing complex ideas, they sometimes have trouble putting them into the proper words or language so that others can understand the full meaning of their ideas. In other instances, the communicator may have difficulty in communicating. That is, some people are restricted by a limited vocabulary or their understanding of language.

Once a message has been encoded, the sender must select a communications *channel* through which a message is transmitted or sent to the recipients. The primary communications channels are formal and informal. Within these two channels, communications can be written, verbal, and nonverbal. *Formal communications* are the official transmission of information in the organization, and they generally follow the police department's chain of command or organizational chart. Formal communications generally are written in the form of letters, memoranda, or orders. *Informal communications* are usually oral and are used to convey a variety of official and unofficial information throughout the department. Formal and informal communication are discussed more later.

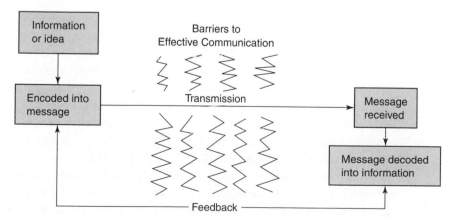

FIGURE 4–1 The Communications Process

When deciding on the channel to use, the communicator also selects a medium. *Medium* refers to the manner in which the message is sent. It may be written and sent in the form of a memorandum or policy, or it may be verbal at a meeting, on the telephone, or through a one-on-one conversation. It is important to select the proper medium when communicating. For example, if a lieutenant wants to discuss staffing problems with his or her sergeants, a face-to-face meeting would be more effective than a memorandum or a telephone call.

Once information is transmitted to a recipient, the recipient must *decode* the message, or conceptually translate the information into meaningful knowledge. When people receive new information, they typically give it meaning by comparing it with past experiences and knowledge, which can be either a help or a hindrance. The receiver may have difficulty internalizing its full implication or, in the worst case, may reject it entirely.

It is important that the receiver have the same conceptual impression of the information as that envisioned by the individual transmitting the message. If inconsistencies occur, then the desired information has not been fully internalized. One way of ensuring full internalization is *feedback:* the process whereby the sender initiates additional two-way communications to test the receiver's comprehension and understanding of the information communicated. Feedback serves to ensure that everyone received the correct information. The level of feedback should increase (1) as the content of messages becomes more complex, (2) when it is critical that receivers have the information, (3) when the information is drastically different from past information or operating procedures, and (4) when there are disruptions in the communications process itself. The supervisor has the responsibility for ensuring that information is properly exchanged.

Formal and Informal Communication

Formal and informal communications, discussed briefly earlier, can be written or verbal. Generally, however, formal communications are written, while informal communications are verbal. Written communications allow all participants to have a permanent record of the communication. This may be important at a future time when the people involved in the communications must refresh their recollection of the transaction. Also, as an official document, written communications have weight or authority requiring a measure of action or response. The problem with written communication is that it is sometimes difficult for people to reduce complex issues into writing, and there is no two-way communication or feedback to ensure that the message was fully comprehended.

Formal communications generally flow downward, although feedback and information about problems and issues are sometimes transmitted upward by subordinates. Katz and Kahn (1966) found that downward communications fall into one of five categories: (1) job instructions; (2) rationale or explanations about jobs; (3) procedures, practices, and policies; (4) feedback on individual performance; and (5) efforts to encourage a sense of mission and dedication toward departmental goals. Thus, official communications serve a variety of purposes for managers and supervisors. An example would be a patrol division captain who observes problems with offense reports being submitted late by officers; the captain then writes a memorandum to his lieutenants and sergeants, informing them that all such reports must be turned in to and reviewed by a supervisor by the end of the shift.

Informal communications are generally accomplished via conversations and informal notes. For example, a supervisor on a shift may leave a note for a supervisor on the following shift to have the officers check a residence because of reports of prowlers or suspicious persons. In this example, although the note is a form of informal communications, it is being used in an official capacity. By leaving a note, the supervisor is able to communicate rapidly and effectively without going through the chain of command. Instead of leaving a note, the supervisor could have waited for the next shift supervisor to tell him or her directly about the problem. This face-to-face conversation would have allowed the sergeant to fully explain what had happened and what actions the sergeant took. In essence, informal communications can be used for formal or informal

Establishing two-way communication with officers is essential for the supervisor.
Courtesy Washoe County, Nevada, Sheriff's Office Photo Unit.

purposes. They allow officers to communicate rapidly without going through the chain of command.

Informal communications typically consist of "interpersonal networking" (Schermerhorn, Hunt, and Osborn, 1994) and quasi-formal exchanges of information between co-workers. Such exchanges typically use verbal and nonverbal communications. Oftentimes, members of an organization find that formal communications are inadequate for accomplishing communications activities. When this occurs, people tend to use informal networks through which they contact others to obtain official information, or they work unofficially with others to solve problems. For example, officers will use informal communications to get information about a new commander and his or her priorities.

Informal communications essentially allow information to flow more freely and rapidly. In their review of excellent organizations, Peters and Waterman (1983) found that increased levels of informal communications were associated with organizational success. Indeed, managers and supervisors who can rapidly gain information or discuss problems with subordinates and managers throughout the police department have an important advantage.

Another type of informal communications are rumors, or the *grapevine,* so termed because it zigzags back and forth across organizations like a grapevine. There is probably *no* type of organization in our society that has more grapevine information than that found in police agencies. Departments even establish "rumor control" centers during major riots. Policing is a 24-hour per day, 7-day per week occupation, so rumors are easily carried from one shift to the next as officers discuss issues such as pay raises, assignments, new policies or procedures, and other matters that affect them at work or at home.

Although it may carry many falsehoods, cynicism, and employee malice, the grapevine has several potential benefits, including that it is fast; it operates mostly at the place of work; and it supplements regular, formal communication. It can be a tool for management to get a feel for employees' attitudes, to spread useful information, and to help employees vent their frustrations. Without a doubt, the grapevine is a force for supervisors to reckon with on a daily basis. Some officers initiate false information in the grapevine to cause dissension or disruptions in the formal organization. Efforts should be made to monitor the information being communicated informally in the work group and take measures to ensure that false information does not result in problems in work group performance.

BARRIERS TO EFFECTIVE COMMUNICATION

The act of communicating occurs under a variety of circumstances. For example, a lieutenant may be coordinating a crime scene where he or she must communicate to subordinates while maintaining the integrity of the scene, keeping witnesses separated, and providing assistance to injured persons. It is extremely difficult for the lieutenant to effectively communicate to all the sergeants, officers, and civilians in this situation. The lieutenant must ensure that everyone receives the appropriate orders or directions.

Many distractions can occur in any type of situation. Such distractions are commonly referred to as *noise,* which is anything that disrupts the communications process (Van Fleet and Peterson, 1994). The different types of noise that the supervisor should be aware of when communicating are discussed in the following sections.

Perceptual Problems

Perceptual problems occur when either the sender's or the receiver's perception of the other affects how the message is sent or received. One such perceptual problem is *status*. To a great extent, people judge the significance and accuracy of information by the status and ability of the sender. Information from an assistant chief will be received differently from information that is given by a lieutenant, even though both officers provide their receivers with accurate information. All information should be evaluated on its own merits. Another perceptual problem is *stereotyping:* Judgments are made about communications because of the sender's traits or qualities. For example, it is assumed that a police union leader and a police captain would likely interpret the same information differently, because of their relative orientations about the department. The information should be given due consideration, regardless of where it emanated from.

A third perceptual problem is the *value judgments* people make about information. If the information is consistent with old information or values, it generally is given more credibility. If it is not, receivers sometimes have difficulty accepting or internalizing it. Supervisors should take extra precautions when attempting to communicate new or radically different information.

A fourth perceptual problem is *semantic problems,* which refer to instances when the receiver improperly decodes a message because symbols or verbiage used by the sender is interpreted differently by the receiver. Certain words have different meanings to different people. Semantic problems can be overcome through the feedback process or by restating the same information several times. Semantic problems perhaps are the most difficult problems to detect in the communication process, especially when there is no feedback.

Physical Barriers

Physical barriers to communication are those attributes and activities in the immediate environment that interfere with or detract from the communications process. If police officers are spread over a wide area, it is more difficult to communicate effectively with them. It is distracting when a supervisor tries to counsel subordinates in an office while answering the telephone. Every effort

It is often a challenge for supervisors to motivate officers who are assigned to less prestigious functions, such as traffic control.
Courtesy NYPD Photo Unit.

should be made to ensure that communications are free of such barriers. When
barriers do exist, the sender should delay communicating or take special precautions to ensure that receivers obtain information correctly.

This discussion shows that communicating is a complicated process and
that the person communicating a message should give careful consideration to
how to convey the message. The following elements should be considered prior
to communicating:

1. The sender's purpose
2. The sender's and receiver's positions in the department, perceptions,
    and listening skills
3. The content of the message
4. Available methods for sending the message
5. Possible interpretations of the message and its content
6. The sender's desired results

IMPROVING COMMUNICATION IN POLICE AGENCIES

The act of communicating can be troublesome because of the many inherent problems that can occur. The most effective way to communicate is to be aware of potential pitfalls and take action to counteract them when they occur. The following section provides information that can be used to overcome communication problems.

Face-to-face communication is the most effective way of communicating because it can maximize the feedback between the sender and receiver. Supervisors should not only be open to feedback, but they must also solicit it to ensure that communications are received and understood.

Furthermore, many police departments are investing in computer network systems and in-car computers or terminals that facilitate the communications process. These systems also allow officers to communicate through electronic mail (e-mail), which can substantially enhance formal and informal communications throughout a police department. It allows officers to communicate at any time and encourages feedback through its messaging system. A problem with in-car computers is the inappropriate information that flows through the system. For example, the Christopher Commission (Christopher, 1991) examined the logs for the Los Angeles Police Department's in-car computers and found a number of racial slurs and derogatory comments. This points to a need to monitor this type of communications network.

Another method of enhancing communications is empathy. *Empathy* is the act of putting oneself in another's position. The communicator should be receiver oriented and consider how the message will affect the receiver. If a supervisor understands how information will affect the listener, then he or she can better organize and present the message so that it has a greater chance of being accepted by the listener. At the same time, the sender should participate in *active listening*—coaxing or assisting the other's communication. This is accomplished by asking questions, providing comments, and being especially attentive when information is being provided. When supervisors actively listen to subordinates, especially when they have just given them information about policies or directives, they actively engage the subordinates in feedback to ensure that they comprehend the information.

THE ART OF NEGOTIATING

Definition and Function

Negotiation is a form of communicating. The ability to effectively negotiate with others is an important characteristic, and it essentially consists of effectively communicating with other people. Negotiations play a key role when management and employees attempt to agree on a new contract or working conditions. In this instance, the two sides communicate until an agreement is reached. When the two sides communicate effectively, they are more likely to arrive at an agreement. Donnelly, Gibson, and Ivancevich (1995:433) defined negotiations as "the collaborative pursuit of joint gains and a collaborative effort to create value where none previously existed."

When a group of people discuss an issue, there likely will be conflict or disagreement. For example, officers often disagree with departmental policies regarding pursuit driving, arrest procedures, or dealing with citizens. Racial profiling is a primary example. Police agencies often examine officers' actions in terms of their effects on public relations and community support, while officers tend to emphasize their law enforcement role. Officers resent that their patrol stops and citations are being reviewed for racial profiling patterns. Communication and negotiations are sometimes necessary to ensure that policies and actions are properly balanced. Situational leadership, as discussed in the previous chapter, plays a key role in getting things done, and supervisors must learn to apply various leadership styles to different situations. This is a key part of negotiating.

One can easily see the need for negotiation skills when dealing with the public. For example, when a police officer encounters a domestic violence situation or a barroom fight, the situation is best handled when the officer can talk or negotiate the combatants into submission. Negotiation is an important tool that is used in a variety of situations.

Approaches to Negotiating

Effective negotiations occur when issues of substance are resolved and the working relationships among the negotiating parties are improved or at least not harmed (Schermerhorn, 1996). Because negotiations sometimes occur over a long period of time, it is critical that the parties attempt to maintain good working relationships. It is not in the interest of a particular side to decimate the other side, because they likely will meet again in a similar situation.

Three criteria are used to judge the effectiveness of negotiations: quality, cost, and harmony (Schermerhorn, 1996). First, *quality* refers to attempts by both sides to come to a win-win solution. In some cases, one side may be more interested in using the negotiations as a form of disruption. For example, when officers lodge complaints about minor issues and reject honest efforts to resolve them, they are probably attempting to be disruptive as opposed to pursuing legitimate concerns. Such actions are counterproductive and have substantial long-term costs to everyone involved.

Cost does not refer to the amount of money involved with negotiations, but rather to the time and energy spent negotiating. When two sides have a disagreement, it is in everyone's best interest to resolve it as soon as possible. When supervisors allow a problem to drag on and worsen, they can cause the unit to suffer in terms of lost effectiveness and reduced morale.

Finally, *harmony* refers to the feelings of personnel about the department and its members after the conflict or problem is resolved. If a supervisor orders subordinates to conform to a departmental policy or order without explaining its importance to the police, then work group harmony is damaged or lost. Furthermore, it may take a considerable amount of time for the supervisor to recapture the collegiality that was destroyed. To a great extent, negotiation involves selling ideas to gain acceptance and compliance.

The Prenegotiation Stage

Negotiation is a process that occurs in steps; the first is the prenegotiation stage. Negotiators must prepare themselves in advance. Three important elements comprise the prenegotiation stage. First, the negotiator must fully understand what is at issue. In some cases, this is rather simple, such as whether or not space is available in the training schedule for personnel to receive training. But when the issues are complex, as is often the case in collective bargaining, it may be a fairly difficult task to come to some understanding about what is at stake. The successful negotiator is able to ferret out the real issues when conflict occurs.

Second, it is important for the negotiator to be empathetic and understand the other side's position. In some cases, officers may be making demands that are totally out of the question, or they may not be feasible because of budget constraints or personnel limitations. In other cases, however, officers may be making demands as a result of a problem that adversely affects their ability to perform their assigned duties. For example, officers may complain about how beats are configured. Some officers may be overworked as a result of beat boundaries, while others have too little to do. Thus, it is important for the supervisor to become thoroughly familiar with officers' concerns before attempting to address them.

Third, the successful negotiator understands all the options before sitting down to negotiate. For example, if a sergeant is aware that officers are upset about a particular policy, then the sergeant should research it prior to discussing it. A new departmental policy may prohibit officers from eating meals outside their beats. For officers working early morning hours, this policy might pose a major problem, especially if there are no restaurants on their beat and their home is outside the beat area. The graveyard shift supervisor might need to independently study the situation and recommend a policy change to the chief executive.

Personal Factors Affecting Negotiations

Cohen (1980) examined successful negotiations and identified three important factors that identify a successful negotiator: power, time, and information. *Power* refers to the negotiator's ability to influence or have an impact on the other side. Power can be used in a positive or negative way. Rewards often are greater motivators than the threat of punishment. Further, power in negotiations does not necessarily refer to the power derived from one's position. Other sources of power include technical expertise or association with other powerful individuals in the department.

Time is also an important factor. The previous section discussed the importance of eliminating conflicts, because if they are drawn out, they can have a greater negative impact on the work unit. Sometimes it is best to extend negotiations, however. This allows tempers to cool. For example, if some officers are upset over a new policy, it is perhaps best to discuss it with them after they have had time to think about it. In some cases, the issue becomes less important over time. The good negotiator understands time and uses it to his or her advantage.

Finally, *information* is the most important tool when negotiating. When a person is knowledgeable about an issue, he or she is in a much better position to negotiate. Often knowledge disarms adversaries since a great deal of conflict often is the result of misunderstandings or misinformation.

Negotiation Tactics

A number of tactics are available to the negotiator. If all the information about the other side as well as possible options have been collected, the negotiator is better able to select a set of tactics that will result in a desired outcome. Donnelly et al. (1995) identified a number of tactics from which the negotiator can select:

1. *Good-guy/bad-guy team.* The good-guy and bad-guy ploy has long been used by the police when interrogating suspects. The bad guy tends to be a hard liner who refuses to give an inch. The good guy comes in later after the opponent has had time to reflect on the extreme position and makes several accommodations. This ploy helps negotiations move the other side toward the middle, especially when the other side is intransigent.

2. *The nibble.* The nibble occurs when a small concession is made in order to facilitate movement on the other side. A nibble often gives the negotiator the leverage to obtain a greater concession. The nibble usually is the first step in a series of concessions on both sides to come to an agreement.

3. *Joint problem solving.* Joint problem solving occurs when both sides recognize the need to identify an acceptable solution. If at all possible, this is the method that should be used; but in most circumstances, other tactics are required to get the parties to the point that they will engage in joint problem solving.

4. *Power of competition.* Competition with other units or agencies can be used to gain cooperation or compliance. Every unit commander in the police department constantly battles for additional personnel. The police executive can sometimes get these unit commanders to agree to perform additional tasks by providing new officers. The competition for additional officers often can lead to agreements about workload.

5. *Splitting the difference.* Splitting the difference occurs when both sides simultaneously move to a mutually acceptable position. Splitting differences can be effective only after each side has become thoroughly familiar with the other side's negotiating position.

6. *Lowballing.* Lowballing occurs when one side makes a ridiculously low offer in an effort to scare the other side into a negotiating position. Lowballing also disguises the real distance between the two sides. Lowballing is also used to try to get the other side to move substantially as a result of negotiating. The best reaction to lowballing is to hold one's position until the offering side reshapes its negotiating position. This line of reasoning frequently is not effective in police organizations.

Guidelines for Conducting Negotiations

Although every negotiation will proceed differently, some general guidelines may be helpful (Stoner and Freeman, 1992):

1. Have and understand your objectives. This includes the rationale for the objectives and their relative importance.

2. Do not hurry when negotiating. Information is far more important than time, and information is lost when negotiating is hastily done.

3. When there is doubt, consult others for the facts. It often is extremely difficult to break agreements that are the result of negotiations.

4. Ensure that you have access to supporting documentation and data as the negotiations become more formal.

5. Maintain some measure of flexibility in your position.

6. Attempt to discover the driving force behind the other side's request.

7. Do not become deadlocked over minutiae or some singular point.

8. Ensure that you allow room for your opponent to save face. Total defeat of an opponent leads to long-term resentment and future problems.

9. Focus on listening throughout the negotiating, and pay close attention to the other side.

10. Make sure that your emotions are controlled, regardless of how the negotiations proceed.

11. During the negotiations process, ensure that you listen and consider every word. Nail down statements into precise, understood language.

12. Try to understand your opponents.

These guidelines can assist the supervisor when negotiating with subordinates, peers, or superiors.

Negotiation by Police Managers and Supervisors

Police managers and supervisors must constantly negotiate with their subordinates and be able to ensure their maximum compliance with orders, directives, and assignments. In some cases, orders are clearly within the bounds of reason and the purview of the superior's authority. In these cases, the orders generally are unquestioned. In some cases, however, the superior may issue an order that is not understood or is outside the range of past practices, and the subordinate may come to question it. For example, while a sergeant can order an officer to perform certain tasks, it is generally more effective if a consensus is reached, and a consensus can normally be reached only through discussion and negotiation. A supervisor is better able to induce voluntary compliance when he or she is able to negotiate effectively. The exception would be emergencies or critical incidents, when the officer is expected to follow orders without delay.

Police supervisors also must often negotiate with their superiors and peers. They must argue their case when there are personnel shortages, when members of the unit are given too many responsibilities, or when the unit needs new equipment. Negotiations skills allow the manager or supervisor to better present his or her case and ultimately be more successful.

Conflict between units over assignments sometimes occurs, resulting in managers and supervisors having to negotiate with peers about working conditions. For example, officers engaged in community policing projects may work contrary to patrol or investigative operations. Detectives and patrol officers sometimes have disputes over cases and arrests. When such conflicts occur, they must be negotiated.

It becomes even more evident that negotiation is important when we consider the nature of police work. Police officers are often called on to engage in activities that are perceived as being less important or not as prestigious as other tasks. For example, most police officers would rather investigate a homicide or robbery than direct traffic after a high school football game. Directing traffic is not as interesting, nor will it reap the same amount of prestige or publicity that a successful homicide investigation might bring to the officer. Nonetheless, directing traffic is a vital function to be performed by the police department. Indeed, there are many more mundane tasks for officers than there are exciting ones. Yet, all of these tasks must be performed and be performed well. Without a doubt, the efforts of a supervisor with negotiations skills will increase the probability that officers will perform these tasks more effectively.

COPING WITH CONFLICT

Thus far, we have discussed communications and negotiations. This section examines conflict and conflict resolution. Communication and negotiations skills are necessary to avoid conflict. Regardless of the efforts put forth by managers and supervisors, however, conflict erupts. This section describes how best to deal with it.

The Nature of Organizational Conflict

Conflict is a natural phenomenon, occurring in all organizations. *Conflict* is a situation in which two or more people disagree over issues of organizational substance and experience some emotional antagonism with one another (Schermerhorn et al., 1994). Conflict has four key elements: (1) individuals or groups with opposing interests, (2) acknowledgment that the opposing viewpoints or interests exist, (3) the belief by parties that the other will attempt to deny them their goal or objective, and (4) one or both sides of the conflict have overtly attempted to thwart the other's goals and objectives (Greenberg and Baron, 1995). These elements require that overt action has occurred, but conflict may exist prior to that action. If the level of antagonism between the parties is substantial, then conflict will exist without any action by either of the parties.

Conflict should be viewed as a continuous process, occurring against a backdrop of relationships and events. Conflict is inevitable when there are people, relationships, and activities. Thus, conflict is not an isolated, short-term event, but rather it is something that managers and supervisors will encounter on a continuing basis. Conflict as a process also affects and involves a variety of people and activities within the organization. It tends to spread and cut across other activities. Finally, it can result from a variety of causes, ranging from personal to professional; personal conflict affects professional relationships just as professional conflict affects personal relationships (Thomas, 1992).

The nature of police work often leads to conflict. Few citizens are pleased when they encounter a police officer, regardless of the nature of the encounter. Such encounters often require intervention and negotiation by a supervisor. In other instances, the police supervisor is seen as the person in the middle who must mediate the impact of departmental policies on subordinate officers. Officers tend to expect supervisors to make policies realistic in their application, while managers expect supervisors to follow the letter of the law with regard to policies and procedures. Such differences of opinion often lead to conflict.

Levels of Conflict

Conflict can occur throughout an organization. For example, two precinct commanders may develop a conflict over resources. Both may need additional officers in order to properly staff their patrol beats. Specialized services such as the jail, community relations, or crime prevention often compete with patrol and criminal investigation for officers. At another level, conflict may develop between detectives and patrol officers when both are attempting to solve the same case. Two officers may engage in conflict when they request to work the same beat or shift. Managers and supervisors should be aware of the conflict swirling around them, since this conflict will likely have some impact on them or their units. With this in mind, conflict can occur at four levels within the agency:

Conflict can occur within organizations, such as when different divisions of the agency compete for personnel and other resources.
Courtesy San Bernardino, California, Sheriff's Office.

1. *Intrapersonal:* An individual has a conflict within him- or herself.

2. *Interpersonal:* Individuals have a conflict with others in the unit or department.

3. *Intergroup:* Work groups within the organization develop a conflict.

4. *Interorganizational:* Different organizations are at odds as the result of some issue or event.

Intrapersonal conflict occurs when the individual is not content or satisfied with what is occurring in his or her life. The conflict may be work related, such as dissatisfaction with an assignment or potential for promotion. It may also be related to the individual's personal life. An officer may be experiencing problems at home or in some other part of his or her life (police officer stress and wellness is discussed in Chapter 7). Such conflict generally manifests itself in withdrawal or aggression. When a supervisor observes changes in a subordinate's demeanor or personality, the change should be investigated and support provided to the officer. Attempts should be made to prevent the problem from affecting work or resulting in overly aggressive behavior when dealing with the public.

Interpersonal conflict occurs when members of the work group have personal disagreements and conflicts with one another. Whenever several people work together, conflict is inevitable. Again, the conflict can be the result of the job or can be personal in nature. For example, some officers may become agitated because they perceive that their work schedule or assignments are not equitable relative to others. They may become jealous or threatened by other officers' productivity. Personality conflicts may develop and must be addressed. Often such conflict will not be dealt with by supervisors, who hope that it will dissipate. In most cases, however, if not addressed, interpersonal conflict will only worsen and, ultimately, affect the productivity and collegiality of the work group.

Intergroup conflict occurs when officers in one unit have conflict with the officers in another unit. A good example of intergroup conflict occurred on the popular television show *NYPD Blue.* A homicide occurred on the street that separated two precincts. Detectives from one precinct moved the body to the other side of the street, forcing detectives from the other precinct to investigate the case. Needless to say, when the detectives who were investigating the case learned what the other detectives had done, a significant confrontation ensued. Work activities must be carefully monitored and any possible conflicts among work groups must be mediated. Sergeants must be prepared to intervene and mediate such disputes, and in some cases, it may require raising the issue with managers. Regardless, the conflict should not be allowed to manifest itself in aggressive, unprofessional acts. Decisive action is required.

Finally, *interorganizational* conflict occurs when there are problems between the police department and other organizations. Unfortunately, law enforcement is not always the united, amicable, cooperative "family" that out-siders perceive it to be. It is not at all uncommon for a county sheriff's office and a municipal police department in the county to have problems or conflict because of professional jealousy or for reasons relating to "turf protection." For example, the city police department may resent deputies performing undercover operations in the city without coordinating their efforts. Indeed, turf battles and refusal to communicate and cooperate between certain federal law enforcement agencies have been long-standing issues and are well known in police circles. These inter-departmental problems often are due to a rift between the respective agency administrators and do not directly involve lower-ranking supervisors or their respective responsibilities. Nevertheless, such disagreements ultimately can affect managers and supervisors, because when the actual conflict occurs, it occurs between line officers.

Conflict sometimes occurs between the judiciary and the police. A judge may require that officers not wear their weapons in court. Most police officers would be highly offended at such a requirement. Nonetheless, it is a requirement that must be followed. In this case, the supervisors must counsel officers about the possible impact of their not following the directive, which is being held in contempt of court or having cases dismissed, and emphasize that the object of going to court is to present evidence in the best possible manner. In other words, the officers must get beyond the order and attend to the business at hand. At another level, a supervisor must communicate officers' concerns up the chain of command to the chief of police, to intercede in the problem and possibly have the order rescinded.

Sources of Conflict in Police Organizations

Conflict can occur for a variety of reasons. Most often, it can be categorized as organizational or interpersonal. Greenberg and Baron (1995) have identified a number of causes of conflict, which are addressed in Figure 4–2.

Organizational Causes

One source of conflict is *competition over resources,* which occurs when units or sections within a police department compete for personnel, responsibilities, equip-ment, and other tangibles related to the job. Indeed, if supervisors are doing their job, they will constantly strive to obtain greater amounts of personnel or equip-ment. When resources become available, everyone generally attempts to garner as many of them as possible. Competition for resources inevitably leads to conflict, especially when the parties resort to political measures to obtain their objectives. For example, a commander may go to a member of the city council to lobby for a particular program, bypassing the normal staff decision-making process concern-ing resource allocation in the department. While not acceptable, this often occurs.

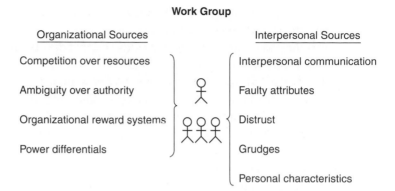

FIGURE 4–2   Causes of Conflict in Organizations

A second source of conflict is *ambiguity over authority,* which refers to instances when two units or supervisors believe they have authority over a situation or personnel. It is similar to a breach in the span of control, discussed in Chapter 1. As an example, detectives will allow patrol officers to do as much work as possible on low-profile cases but immediately take control of high-visibility cases such as sex crimes, homicides, or large drug arrests.

Third, *organizational reward systems* cause conflict. Organizational reward systems consist of tangible and intangible benefits. Tangible benefits include extra pay in the form of overtime or specialists' pay, new equipment, and new vehicles. Intangible benefits include prestige and media exposure. Detectives frequently receive vast amounts of publicity when they solve a major case, while other units, even though they may have been central to the investigation, receive little if any recognition. Because of the nature of their work, some units have more equipment; and some units, such as traffic, may be afforded substantial amounts of overtime. As perceptions of inequality increase as a result of a department's reward system, so will job dissatisfaction and conflict. It is almost impossible to have all rewards distributed evenly within a police agency, because of the nature of the work. Efforts should be made, however, to ensure equity in a department's reward system.

Fourth, conflict results when there is a *power differential* within the police department. A power differential refers to some members having more power than others and usually occurs as a result of "nonlegitimate" power. For example, the chief may have spent most of his or her career in the traffic unit and now favors that unit over others. Individuals in the organization, because of their assignment, past work record, or personal relationships, may have closer ties with the chief or other high-ranking commanders, affording them higher levels of power and access. Each of these instances can cause animosity and conflict within the police organization.

Problems of power differential occur at lower levels of an organization as well as across units. When those at the lower levels, such as officers or sergeants, believe that they have little input in decisions and that they are not appreciated by the department, they will feel frustration and be more likely to engage in conflict. For example, the planning unit may develop a new policy and not adequately consider its consequences on the officers it affects. Line officers may come to see the policy as a bureaucratic hindrance. Line personnel should be allowed input into the policy decision, and the policy's use and rationale should be fully explained to officers.

Interpersonal Causes

The *failure to properly communicate* is a common interpersonal cause of conflict. The information or message may not be complete, contain faulty information, or be communicated in such a way as to antagonize the receiver. Supervisors sometimes do not take the time to ensure that their message is complete or to obtain suitable feedback to ensure that their subordinates clearly understand the message. Managers sometimes fail to consider how a decision will affect officers and sergeants. In other cases, managers and supervisors may be curt or discourteous when communicating to subordinates. These examples show the importance of proper communications, and when effective communications are not used, subordinates may become frustrated, which ultimately leads to conflict.

A second interpersonal cause of organizational conflict is *faulty attributes*—the intentions or rationale for an action is misunderstood by someone who is directed to complete some task. In such cases, the assignment is seen as an act of malevolence rather than a legitimate request. For example, when a detective supervisor requests that a detective recontact some witnesses in a case, the detective may see the request as harassment, while the supervisor may believe that the detective's report contained insufficient information. Faulty communications often lead to faulty attributions in the workplace.

Third, *distrust* creates a great deal of conflict. For example, a substantial amount of distrust exists between some citizens and the police (Gaines, Kappeler, and Vaughn, 1999). At the organizational level, officers may distrust other officers or units within the department. Most officers, if not all, distrust officers assigned to the Internal Affairs Unit. Some officers may come to distrust officers working in the Domestic Violence Unit, because at some point a domestic violence unit may have complained because an officer did not make an arrest in a mandatory arrest situation. Officers may come to distrust superiors. An officer may come to distrust a sergeant because the sergeant fails to communicate adequately, to back the officer when there is a problem, to keep a promise about an assignment, or imposes disciplinary action when the officer believes that he or she made an honest mistake. Innumerable situations may result in officers coming to distrust one another. Unfortunately, these situations are seldom addressed and resolved, which leads to festering conflict.

Fourth, people develop and tend to hold *grudges* against others in the department. Grudges may be personal in nature—two officers attempt to date the same person or an officer sells another officer an automobile that turns out to require unforeseen repairs. Or, grudges can be professional in nature—an officer withholds information in a case so he or she can make the arrest, or one officer reports another officer's deviant or improper behavior to superiors. Grudges may occur for a variety of reasons. It is important to understand that they may last a number of years, and in some cases, officers never forgive the person toward whom they hold a grudge.

Finally, an officer's *personal characteristics* may lead to conflict. Personal characteristics refer to attributes such as curtness, inability to communicate clearly, a need to pry into others' business or affairs, or being unorganized and often failing to perform adequately. All sorts of people can be labeled as difficult or uncooperative. Generally, it is the nature of their personality that causes them to have difficulties with others. These people are frequently difficult to work with, and the reactions of others to them often antagonizes, rather than appeases, them.

Supervisors' and Managers' Roles in Conflict Resolution

Supervisors and managers can choose to deal with conflict using a variety of strategies. Good senior police managers will constantly monitor the supervisors and managers within their command. This entails meeting with and talking with all of them periodically. The effective manager will maintain good communications so that he or she will know what is transpiring within the unit. At the same time, the manager should openly discuss problems with supervisors. In essence, managers should hold supervisors accountable and direct them to resolve problems. As discussed in Chapter 2, supervisors sometimes avoid intervening in difficult situations. Good managers push supervisors into working with difficult situations.

There is no one way to deal with conflict because it manifests itself in many ways, and a different set of factors is always contributing to it. It is important, however, for the supervisor to be able to recognize conflict when it occurs and quickly take action. As noted earlier, negotiations skills play a key role in conflict resolution. Such skills are necessary to mediate between the combatants when conflict occurs. The goal of conflict resolution is to eliminate the causes of conflict and reduce the potential for additional conflict in the future.

Intervention in conflict essentially involves two supervisory skills: cooperativeness and assertiveness (Schermerhorn, 1996). *Cooperativeness* refers to a superior officer's attempts to cooperate with the conflicting parties and work toward a solution. *Assertiveness* is shown when the superior orders or directs combatants to behave in a certain manner, usually in accordance with departmental policies and procedures. Assertiveness does not attempt to alleviate the conflict, rather to remove its manifestations from the workplace.

Figure 4–3 shows the conflict management grid, which contains five means of addressing conflict along with corresponding levels of cooperativeness and assertiveness. Perhaps the most common reaction to conflict is *avoidance;* the superior refuses to recognize its existence and hopes that it simply will go away. Conflict is seldom resolved without intervention on a timely basis, however, and when it is left to its own designs, it will have a negative impact on the conflicting parties and their associates in the work group. Intervention in conflicts is generally difficult, personal, and uncomfortable and can be a highly emotional ordeal that can result in additional conflict between the negotiator and the parties involved. Thus, there is a natural tendency to avoid dealing with conflicts. This, of course, is a mistake since the problem likely will only worsen.

A second strategy for handling conflict is *accommodation,* or smoothing. Accommodation involves minimum intrusion on the part of the superior, who attempts to smooth over differences between those engaged in the conflict. Accommodation requires a high level of cooperativeness and a low level of assertiveness

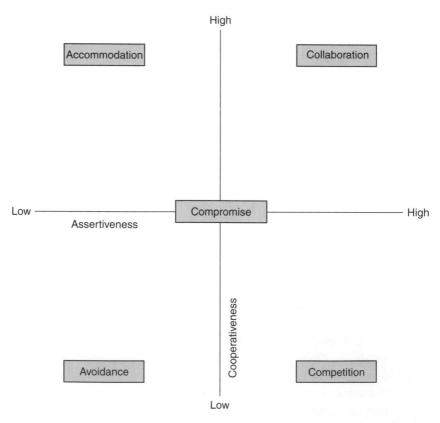

FIGURE 4–3   Conflict Management Grid

on the part of the superior. The superior does not attempt to assert his or her authority but tries to induce a higher level of cooperativeness. Actual differences are avoided so that harmony may be achieved. A sergeant involved in accommodation would attempt to work more closely with the officers engaged in the conflict. The sergeant would attempt to become more personable, engaging the officers in conversation about departmental and extradepartmental issues. Here, the sergeant would attempt to make the issues at the center of conflict a low priority.

A third conflict resolution strategy is *competition*. The superior intervenes and meets with the combatants, forcing them to present all the facts about the situation and then making a decision. The conflict becomes a competitive situation with a clear winner and loser. It involves a maximum degree of assertiveness with little or no cooperation on the part of the supervisor. Obviously, this strategy does not resolve the underlying cause of the conflict and may result in its reoccurring at a later time. It should be used only as a last resort.

An example of competition occurs when patrol officers and detectives dispute cases or arrests. On completing a preliminary investigation, patrol officers will generally turn the case over to detectives. When patrol officers make an arrest or are close to making an arrest in a high-profile case, however, they resent giving the case, and its inherent credit, to detectives. Thus, case assignment becomes a "winner take all" proposition unless other accommodations are made. Some departments have resolved this type of situation by allowing patrol officers to work with detectives throughout the follow-up investigation so that credit is shared. This arrangement also provides invaluable experience and training to patrol officers, which ultimately results in improved investigative skills.

A fourth strategy to resolve conflict is *compromise,* which involves a mix of cooperation and assertiveness. The intervening superior officer searches for a solution that satisfies all parties involved in the conflict. It is a process whereby everyone generally gains something, but at the same time it accommodates others. It is essentially a search for a middle ground. Sergeants frequently use compromise when they make the work schedule. They attempt to divide days off and hours worked so that everyone is accommodated to some extent. At the same time, few officers are totally happy with the arrangement.

Finally, conflict resolution can involve *collaboration*. Superior officers attempt to work through problems to fully address everyone's concerns. Sergeants should consult with or involve managers when attempting to solve problems. Managers often have to give their consent to solutions; therefore, it can be fruitful to have them involved in the beginning. Collaboration involves having all parties discuss the issues and look for solutions. Debate helps to clear any impediments and allows participants to understand the other side's issues. Once this occurs, people are more willing to work with one another toward a solution. Collaboration is akin to problem solving when the problem or cause of conflict is identified and removed or solved.

Whenever there is conflict, there likely will be winners and losers. Avoidance and accommodation generally result in lose-lose conflict resolution outcomes because the conflict is never really addressed, and no one really attains his or her objectives. If the conflict is allowed to continue, it will ultimately result in ill feelings that affect work relations for some time. Competition and compromise strategies generally result in win-lose outcomes, where one side wins and the other side loses. Again, this ending will have negative effects on at least one side of the conflict. Competition and compromise fail to address the root causes of conflict and even though a temporary solution can be found, the conflict will probably reoccur. Only collaboration attempts to seek solutions whereby all sides win. Collaboration attempts to impress on all the parties that it is mutually beneficial for a solution that is acceptable to everyone to be identified. Collaboration attempts to engage people in problem solving, and it encourages them to work out differences.

A supervisor may use all of these strategies when dealing with conflict. Obviously, collaboration results in the best outcome, but in some cases the situation and the people involved in the conflict may prohibit the use of a collaborative strategy. Jealousies and dislikes among the parties involved in the conflict may be too deeply ingrained. In that case, other resolution strategies must be used.

——— Case Studies ————————————————

Following are two case studies that will provide some insight into how communications can pose dilemmas for supervisors and managers.

Giving the "Bum's Rush" to City Problems

Urban City's downtown district recently witnessed a serious increase in panhandling, inebriated individuals, and various types of crime. The mayor and council voice concern about these problems and their impact on the coming summer tourist season. A day-long planning session is held involving city officials, the police chief, and business owners, and a comprehensive plan of action is developed. The chief of police delivered the plan to his command staff to be implemented. The downtown watch commander, Lt. Jennings, met with the supervisors and verbally explained that "the administration" is upset with the "bums" downtown and wants it cleaned up in two weeks. Sgt. Washington, the swing shift supervisor downtown, met with his team to convey the lieutenant's orders. The officers became upset and began to argue about how busy they already were. Washington quickly cut them off, stating the issue was not negotiable and that he expected them to "handle it as ordered." Two weeks later, Washington is pleased to see that the area is largely free of transients;

indeed, he and his team are praised by the lieutenant for their efforts. At a recent regional law enforcement executive's meeting, however, a neighboring county's sheriff complains to the chief that his deputies have noticed a major influx of transients in that county; furthermore, the transients are telling his deputies that they were dumped outside the city limits by Urban City officers. The chief is horrified and demands an investigation. When questioned, Washington's officers defend their actions, stating that "The sergeant told us to clean up the downtown; we simply followed orders . . . this is what the chief and mayor wanted."

1. Discuss how the communications process broke down in this case.
2. How could this situation have been avoided?
3. Did the officers simply do what the chief and mayor wanted?
4. Despite the breakdown of communications, what could Sergeant Washington have done to prevent these incidents from occurring?

The Case of "Superman" on Patrol

Officer "Spike" Jones recently transferred back to patrol division after three years in a street crimes unit, where he was involved with numerous high-risk arrests of dangerous offenders. He has built a reputation within the department as being a highly skilled tactical officer, he is team leader of the agency's special operations (SWAT) team, and he is also a trainer in special operations and tactics at the regional police academy. For these reasons, Jones's supervisor was pleased to have him assigned to the team, to impart his knowledge and experiences to the other officers. Indeed, when Jones first comes to the team, the supervisor praises his accomplishments in front of the other officers. Within a month, however, the supervisor begins to notice a wide rift developing between Jones and the rest of the team. Jones is overheard on several occasions discussing the menial work of patrol, saying it's not "real" police work. He is always trying to impress other officers with his experiences; he also says he cannot wait to get out of patrol and into another specialized, high-risk assignment. The team members complain to the supervisor that Jones does not fit in. After two months, this rift has grown much wider, and the supervisor is noticing that the other officers have begun to be slow in backing up Jones at calls. Upon questioning some of the team members, they tell the supervisor that "Superman Jones doesn't need our help anyway."

1. As the supervisor concerned, how would you mediate the conflict that is developing within your team?
2. What kinds of strategies can the supervisor employ to reduce or eliminate the rift that has developed within the team?

3. What does the supervisor need to do with the other team members? What kinds of compromises or adjustments do the team members need to make in order to include Jones as part of their team?

4. What does the supervisor need to do with Jones? What kinds of compromises or adjustments does Jones need to make in order to become a team member?

SUMMARY

This chapter has addressed the interpersonal dynamics surrounding organizational communication, negotiation, and conflict resolution. These three activities must be mastered if the supervisor is to effectively oversee and direct subordinates and activities. Leadership, to a great extent, involves superiors interacting with people, and these three activities form a foundation for effective interaction. They allow the superior officer to translate departmental goals and objectives into action.

Communication is the effective transmittal of information, ideas, and directives to others. In order to interact and ensure that departmental goals are fulfilled, a leader must possess good communications skills. Communications, formal or informal, written or verbal, serve to link people and activities. In reality, tasks are accomplished in police organizations through communications.

Likewise, negotiations play an important role in a supervisor's success. To a great extent, successful policing involves reaching a consensus about police goals and objectives. Not everyone agrees with what should be done or how it should be done, however. Negotiation skills are often used to make officers accept or see the importance of following departmental procedures.

Finally, conflict is a natural phenomenon and occurs in all organizations. A substantial amount of conflict is the result of poor communications skills; oftentimes, effective negotiation skills are called on to resolve conflict. The supervisor must understand that conflict is almost always present; it is the nature of organizations and work groups. Steps must be taken to resolve conflict when it exists. This chapter identified a number to ways to accomplish this.

ITEMS FOR REVIEW

1. Describe the communication process.
2. Define formal and informal communications.
3. Explain barriers to effective communications.
4. Describe how police supervisors communicate.
5. How do managers and supervisors negotiate? Review the tactics they use and the guidelines that apply to successful negotiation.

6. Define organizational conflict, its levels and sources.

7. Explain how managers and supervisors can engage in conflict resolution.

REFERENCES

Christopher, W. (1991). *Summary: Report of the independent commission on the Los Angeles Police Department.* Los Angeles: City of Los Angeles.

Cohen, H. (1980). *You can negotiate anything.* Toronto: Bantam Books.

Donnelly, J. H., Gibson, J. L., and Ivancevich, J. M. (1995). *Fundamentals of management,* 9th ed. Chicago: Irwin.

Gaines, L., Kappeler, V., and Vaughn, J. (1999). *Policing in America.* Cincinnati: Anderson.

Greenberg, J., and Baron, R. A. (1995). *Behavior in organizations,* 5th ed. Upper Saddle River, NJ: Prentice Hall.

Katz, D., and Kahn, R. (1966). *The social psychology of organizations.* New York: Wiley.

Lussier, R. (1999). *Human relations in organizations: Applications and skill building.* New York: McGraw-Hill.

Mayo, L. (1983). *Analysis of the role of the police chief executive.* Ann Arbor: University Microfilms.

More, H. W., and Wegener, W. F. (1996). *Effective police supervision,* 2d ed. Cincinnati: Anderson.

Peters, T. J., and Waterman, R. H. (1983). *In search of lessons from America's best-run companies.* New York: Warner Books.

Schermerhorn, J. R. (1996). *Management,* 5th ed. New York: Wiley.

Schermerhorn, J. R., Hunt, J. G., and Osborn, R. N. (1994). *Managing organizational behavior,* 5th ed. New York: Wiley.

Stoner, J. A., and Freeman, R. E. (1992). *Management,* 5th ed. Upper Saddle River, NJ: Prentice Hall.

Thomas, K. W. (1992). Conflict and negotiation processes in organizations. In M. Dunnette and L. Hough, eds., *Handbook of industrial and organizational psychology,* 2d ed., Vol. 3. Palo Alto: Consulting Psychologists Press, pp. 651–718.

Van Fleet, D. D., and Peterson, T. O. (1994). *Contemporary management,* 3rd ed. Boston: Houghton Mifflin.

Von der Embse, T. J. (1987). *Supervision: Managerial skills for a new era.* New York: Macmillan.

PART TWO

Supervising Human Resources

5

Training and Professional Development

---- ❖ ----

After reading this chapter, the student will:

- know the major types of training that exist in law enforcement
- know how police training is developed and delivered
- understand liability issues with training
- be able to distinguish between training for officers and training for those who have been promoted
- be familiar with the workings of a field training officer (FTO) program

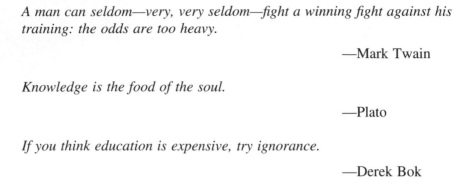

A man can seldom—very, very seldom—fight a winning fight against his training: the odds are too heavy.

—Mark Twain

Knowledge is the food of the soul.

—Plato

If you think education is expensive, try ignorance.

—Derek Bok

INTRODUCTION

Training is one of the most critical functions performed by today's police organizations. It can also be one of the most critical, because of liability and public trust and treatment issues. It is a primary responsibility of supervisors and managers. Our society's growing crime, economic, and legal problems challenge the police to acquire and maintain the knowledge, skills, and abilities necessary to cope with the ever-changing and challenging world. Proper training provides a vital link to employee performance appraisal, discussed in Chapter 6.

This chapter begins by discussing the rationales for and types of police training; following is an overview of the various methods available for instructing police officers, both during and after the basic academy phase. Means of assessing training needs are then reviewed, as well as materials that are useful in the endeavor. Then, we examine the important subject of professional development for supervisors and managers themselves. If these individuals are to instruct their subordinates, then it follows that they must in turn have the requisite teaching skills, training and education, and information to do so in a professional manner. A review of liability issues is presented next, and the chapter concludes with three case studies.

RATIONALE AND TYPES OF TRAINING

Training enables police departments to ensure that officers have the knowledge, skills, and abilities to perform the varied tasks that are part of law enforcement. Policing is a complicated job because citizens expect the police to respond to many requests for service as well as to combat crime and disorder. Training is a process whereby officers receive information about how to respond. Lussier (1999) distinguishes training from development by noting that training focuses on the current job and development is future oriented, preparing officers for other jobs in the organization.

For example, a department may provide patrol officers with training so that they can be more effective patrol officers. At the same time, some training should be devoted to preparing them to work in investigations, traffic, juvenile, domestic violence, and so on. They should also receive some preparatory work on being promoted to sergeant. Developmental activities ensure that a department has adequate human resources to staff all the positions in the department. Here, we use the term *training* to refer to both processes.

Training has two important aspects: technical and discretionary. *Technical* aspects refer to providing officers with information about the procedures and laws for doing the job. Many of these procedures are outlined in departmental policies, and the laws refer to statutes as well as case law. *Discretionary* aspects refer to the training officers receive about how to apply procedures and law and the ramifications should the procedures and law be applied inappropriately.

Perhaps a good example is firearms training. Police departments provide officers with technical training to ensure that they are capable of using a service revolver, shotgun, and other weapons that might be used in the line of duty. They also provide discretionary training whereby officers are taught when to use their weapons. Weapons cannot be used haphazardly because of the potential for loss of life and liability. In essence, police officers are not effective unless they possess both the technical and discretionary skills associated with the job.

CONTEMPORARY POLICE TRAINING: ROLES OF SUPERVISORS AND MANAGERS

The supervisor plays a key role in the training process. Sergeants must ensure that every officer under their command is capable of doing the job properly and must monitor and review officers' ability to do the job. When deficiencies are identified, some corrective action must be taken. This may include sending the officer to a training course or providing the officer with individual counseling and instruction. Newly appointed officers often receive individualized training.

Police managers also play a key role in training. Unit commanders are ultimately responsible for the operation of their units. They must ensure that all their subordinates have the capability to properly function. When deficiencies are identified, they must take some action, usually providing additional training. Also, the goals and objectives of individual units are always changing. Community policing has resulted in substantial change for a number of operational units. The manager must recognize that training is the key to assisting officers in adopting such change. True effectiveness can come only when officers are prepared to meet the challenges of the job.

One of the effects of having a well-trained unit is what Davis and Newstrom (1989) refer to as the *training multiplier effect*. They note that a large number of well-trained people create synergy in the work unit. Officers tend to cooperate and collaborate more and are more productive in pursuing goals and objectives. The training builds on itself as officers strive to improve. Training not only provides officers with the knowledge, skills, and ability to do the job, but it also is a motivator.

As a cautionary note, many police departments do not allocate the necessary resources to ensure that officers receive maximum or even adequate training. Few departments have the resources necessary to do the best job. As operational units vie for scarce resources in the department, training often is neglected with the intention that it will receive more resources as they become available. The prudent police administrator must understand that effective training is just as important as effective operational units, and units such as patrol, criminal investigation, or domestic violence will be only as effective as the training their officers receive.

Having provided an overview of the importance of training, we turn next to a discussion addressing the various training methods that are used by police departments. Later, we provide a discussion of how they are developed.

METHODS OF POLICE INSTRUCTION

Training is a critical function of police agencies in general, and supervisors specifically have a responsibility to ensure that their officers are well trained. Unit effectiveness is directly tied to training. This section addresses the training methods used in the police organization. They include basic or academy training, problem-based learning, field training officer (FTO) programs, roll call training, and in-service training.

Basic or Academy Training

Types and Methods

A new recruit's career begins with academy training, which is one of the largest investments in training for police departments. Academy training usually lasts three to six months and includes classroom instruction on a variety of topics. In the past, most larger agencies administered their own academies and utilized their own staff as instructors; however, this is not generally the case today. The high cost of administering and staffing an academy has led agencies to seek less expensive alternatives, such as regional training centers. These training centers have changed the environment of police academy training.

In many states, community colleges are the sites for a regional police academy. In Ohio, Minnesota, and California, a student can go to a community college and earn state law enforcement certification while earning an associate's degree. In other states, the community college provides the training and bestows some college credit on the officers while in the academy. The officers later can use the credit toward a degree. A number of positions in each class are reserved for people who are interested in becoming police officers but have not yet been hired. These students pay their own expenses and fees and receive a certificate of completion, but they are not guaranteed employment.

Other states have developed a system of regional academies that are not associated with colleges and that service all the departments in the region. These academies are self-sufficient and provide complete basic training, as well as specialized courses and in-service training. In some cases, people who are interested in becoming police officers but have not yet been hired are allowed to pay their way through the academy and receive certification. However, they are not guaranteed employment. The certification does make them attractive as prospective police officers since the department does not have the expense of training them.

A study by the U.S. Bureau of Justice Statistics (BJS) (1996) examined police training nationally. This study found that the average number of training hours required of new police recruits ranged from more than 865 hours in departments serving a population of 1 million or more to less than 300 hours in those agencies serving fewer than 2,500 residents. The average number of hours required for new officers is 425. Figure 5–1 shows a comparison of various hours of training required by state.

Basic training academies provide instruction on a wide range of topics, from skills training in the areas of firearms and first aid to discretionary areas such as police ethics, use of force, handling domestic violence calls, and relations with citizens. Figure 5–2 provides a breakdown of the topics and hours that are included in California's academy training. The hours associated with each block are minimum standards, and some departments provide additional training in some of the areas.

The topics included in Figure 5–2 are meant to provide recruits with the knowledge, skills, and ability to perform as police officers. When departments fail to train their officers adequately, the departments can be liable. In *City of Canton v. Harris* (1989), the U.S. Supreme Court ruled that departments were liable under Title 42 U.S. Code section 1983 when officers violated citizens rights as a result of a failure to train. Ross (2000) examined about 1,500 of these lawsuits and found the following areas in which the police have been challenged as the result of inadequate training: use of force, false arrest or detention, search and seizure, failure to protect, detainee suicide, use of emergency vehicles, and the provision of medical assistance. A number of studies found that the basic academy was inadequate in preparing officers for the job. Ness (1993) found this to be the case in Illinois, and Marion (1998) found similar issues in Ohio.

MINIMUM ACADEMY HOURS MANDATED, BY STATE

State	Minimum Hours
Alabama	480
Alaska	400
Arizona	440
Arkansas	280
California	560
Colorado	352
Connecticut	568
Delaware	498
District of Columbia	1120
Florida	520
Georgia	280
Hawaii	1000
Idaho	430
Illinois	400
Indiana	480
Iowa	400
Kansas	320
Kentucky	400
Louisiana	240
Maine	480
Maryland	400
Massachusetts	720
Michigan	440
Minnesota	350
Mississippi	360
Missouri	450
Montana	400
Nebraska	500
Nevada	480
New Hampshire	430
New Jersey	669
New Mexico	400
New York	445
North Carolina	432
North Dakota	360
Ohio	444
Oklahoma	300
Oregon	370
Pennsylvania	520
Rhode Island	640
South Carolina	343
South Dakota	320
Tennessee	340
Texas	400
Utah	440
Vermont	550
Virginia	400
Washington	440
West Virginia	498
Wisconsin	400
Wyoming	410

FIGURE 5–1   Comparison of Training Hours, by State
Source: Adapted from Pennsylvania P.O.S.T. Commission, Pennsylvania, 1992.

California Basic Academy Curriculum		
DOMAIN NUMBER	DOMAIN DESCRIPTION	MINIMUM HOURS
1.	Ethics and Professionalism	8
2.	Criminal Justice System	4
3.	Community Relations	12
4.	Victimology/Crisis Intervention	6
5.	Introduction to Law	6
6.	Crimes Against Property	10
7.	Crimes Against Persons	10
8.	General Criminal Statutes	4
9.	Crimes Against Children	6
10.	Sex Crimes	6
11.	Juvenile Laws	6
12.	Controlled Substances	12
13.	ABC Law	4
14.	Laws of Arrest	12
15.	Search and Seizure	12
16.	Concepts of Evidence	8
17.	Report Writing	40
18.	Vehicle Operations	24
19.	Use of Force	12
20.	Patrol Techniques	12
21.	Vehicle Pullovers	14
22.	Crimes in Progress	16
23.	Handling Disputes	12
24.	Domestic Violence	8
25.	Unusual Occurrences	4
26.	Missing Persons	4
27.	Traffic Enforcement	22
28.	Traffic Investigation	12
29.	Preliminary Investigations	42
30.	Custody	4
31.	Physical Fitness	40
32.	Weaponless Defense	60
33.	First Aid/CPR	21
34.	Firearms/Chemical Agents	72
35.	Information Systems	4
36.	Persons with Disabilities	6
37.	Gangs	8
38.	Crimes Against the Justice Process	4
39.	Weapon Violations	4
40.	Hazardous Materials	4
41.	Cultural Awareness	24
	[a]**Additional hours added** TOTALS	599

FIGURE 5–2   California POST Curriculum
Source: Adapted from California P.O.S.T.

In addition to providing officers with the necessary tools to be a police officer and to protect against liability, the basic academy serves to instill a commitment to law enforcement in officers. The academy is part of a socialization process whereby officers not only learn official information, but also learn unofficial boundaries and rules (Bayley and Bittner, 1997; Little, 1990). As Niederhoffer noted, "The cord binding the rookie to the civilian world is clipped at the police academy, where the beginner is taught fundamentals of the job" (1967:45).

Some issues must be examined when considering the basic academy. First, many such academies are operated as stress academies. That is, the tone of the instruction often mirrors that of a Marine Corps boot camp. Instructors using this tack believe they are teaching discipline and weeding out the weaker recruits. It should be understood that you cannot teach discipline in the academy; a recruit already possesses it or not as a result of past socialization and education. A recruit's discipline level can best be measured through the background investigation and psychological screening. Violanti (1993) examined high-stress training and found that recruits tend to use a variety of maladaptive responses to this training such as having difficulty making some decisions or needing close supervision. These

Training academies provide new officers with necessary skills.
Courtesy San Bernardino, California, Sheriff's Office.

responses inhibit the learning process and may also result in problems once the recruit is on the job. Post (1992) found that recruits actually learned better in non-stress academies.

Another critical area in the basic academy training is how the students respond to and accept the training. Several studies have asked recruits about the appropriateness of their training (did it adequately prepare them for the job?), and the results revealed that in many cases, the recruits felt inadequately prepared (Marion, 1998; Ness, 1993). Thus, it is important for trainers to ensure that training is relevant and adequately prepares officers for the job. One of the problems may be that recruits tend to view training on soft issues (e.g., family violence, report writing, first aid, discretion, or cultural diversity) less favorably than tactical areas (e.g., driving, firearms, or unarmed defense). This means that trainers must ensure that the training instills the importance of the soft issues.

Finally, training methods are an important consideration in basic academy training. Critics note that academies tend to overly depend on lectures and videos. These methods primarily use one-way communications whereby the instructor strictly imparts information. When this occurs, an important part of the learning process is neglected; instructors do not collect feedback to determine if the information is internalized, and recruits are not given the opportunity for class discussions to reinforce learning. One way to overcome this issue is to use more problem solving. For example, the Kentucky Department of Criminal Justice Training has been experimenting with giving recruits a written problem, a police policy manual, a set of statutes, and a criminal investigation text. Groups of recruits are then directed to determine what offense has occurred and what investigative actions should be taken. This type of problem solving has been found to be much more effective than traditional training methods.

State Certification

Once a recruit graduates from the academy, the state's commission or board of Peace Officers Standards and Training (POST) awards a basic certificate of completion. Over the years, POSTs have also developed intermediate, advanced, managerial, and executive certificates for police officers; these certificates, above the basic level, are generally categorized as "advanced" certificates. Each certificate requires a specified number of hours of training and/or higher education in various areas such as investigation, management, and operations.

The purpose of advanced certification programs is to enhance lifelong learning and career development for the officer. Over the years, advanced POST certification and higher education have become popular bargaining issues for police unions and associations. Some agencies offer as much as a 5 percent pay increase for an advanced certificate or a combination of advanced certificates and a four-year college degree. This system provides strong motivation for some officers to continue their education and training.

In some states, basic certification is tied to police discipline; that is, officers are required to have the certification in order to be a police officer. In some cases, if an officer's disciplinary infraction is substantial, the POST will revoke his or her certification. This means that the officer then is unable to obtain employment as an officer with any other department in the state.

The basic academy training has a number of implications for every level of the police department. Police commanders must ensure that new officers are prepared for the job. When new officers have problems, it generally falls on the sergeants to remedy any identified problems.

Problem-Based Learning

A teaching model that has been widely used to teach medical students and increasing numbers of postsecondary, secondary, and elementary school students is problem-based learning (PBL). PBL originated in the late 1970s when an Ontario, Canada, medical school faculty member found that students were entering examining rooms with vast amounts of knowledge but were unable to ask the right questions of the patients they were examining. Although knowledgeable in a textbook sense, the interns were often unable to *apply* their knowledge toward curing the patient's ailments (Hoover, Glensor, and Peak, 2002).

The similarities to policing are striking. Trainees need to learn much more than just the laws and agency procedures. They must understand how to use their knowledge judiciously and effectively when encountering different community problems. This training model incorporates layers of "learning circles" where officers not only learn facts, but they develop an understanding of their use and implication. Here problem solving and collaboration are promoted.

Field Training Officer Programs

Following the completion of a basic academy, most departments assign their new officers to a field training officer (FTO) program. The FTO program is located in the uniformed patrol division. The FTO program serves two primary functions. First, it has a training function. Some aspects of the job can only be learned through experience. These are demonstrated and taught by the FTOs. Second, the FTO program is an evaluation phase that determines if new officers have the ability to be police officers. This is, it is determined if the new officer can adequately apply the information he or she learned while in the academy. If not, the officer is terminated. A study of the Tallahassee, Florida, Police Department FTO program found that 20 percent of the new officers were terminated during the FTO program (Doerner and Patterson, 1992). Thus, the FTO program is actually a training and a selection device.

Most larger or progressive police agencies have adopted an FTO program based on the San Jose, California, Police Department model of 1968. Although this model has a number of shortcomings such as focusing on termination of officers and reducing departmental liability, it remains the mainstay of these types of programs. McCampbell (1997) has identified a number of advantages for implementing field training programs:

- Reductions in civil liability complaints
- Development of standardized training processes
- Improved documentation for new officers
- Reduction in Equal Employment Opportunity (EEO) complaints
- Improved training of new officers

A typical FTO program, as shown in Figure 5–3, is divided into three phases and ideally takes 52 weeks. Many departments have shortened the program to about 14 weeks, which limits the training. Most departments can ill afford having officers in training for such an extended period. Each phase is designed to help the recruit learn a particular set of tasks. The first three phases in the 14-week program are about four weeks' duration each, and the last phase consists of a final two-week evaluation. The trainee is normally assigned to different FTOs and different shifts during each of the first three phases. This provides the officer with maximum exposure and experience before returning to the original FTO for the final phase. If an officer does not do well during any of the three phases, he or she may be required to repeat the phase. The content of each phase of training is as follows:

Phase I is the introductory phase. The trainee is taught certain basic skills, including officer safety and other areas of potential liability to the organization and officer. This phase serves as an orientation for the new officers. An important element of this phase is the trainee's acceptance of training and willingness to learn from experienced officers. In other words, the new officer must have a positive attitude toward the job.

Phase II is a continuation of Phase I; however, the training becomes more intense. The trainee begins to apply his or her mastery of basic skills. The routine activities of report writing, traffic enforcement, and crime scene investigations become routine for the trainee during this phase. Therefore, the FTO will begin to share more workload and decision-making responsibilities with the trainee. Whereas Phase I consisted primarily of training, Phase II includes a larger measure of evaluation.

Phase III is the last phase of directly supervised formal training. It is characterized by advanced skills training and polishing those skills already learned. This is also an opportunity for the FTO to review those tasks

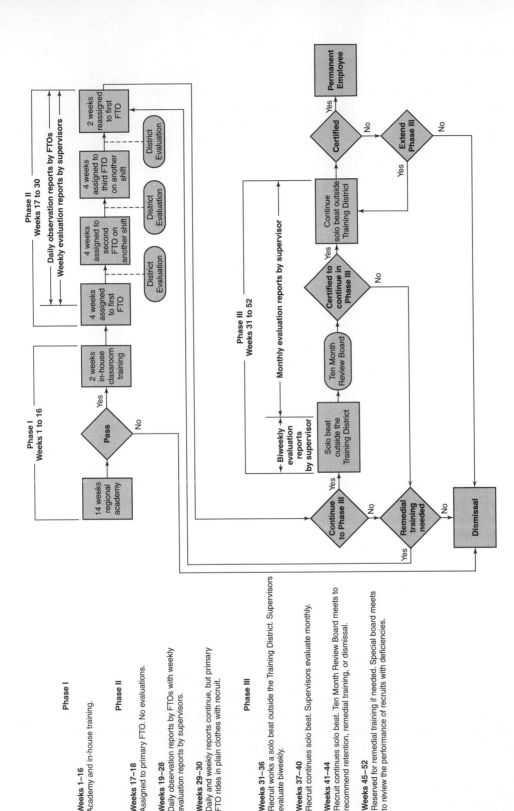

FIGURE 5–3 Schematic for FTO Program, from Campbell

Source: M. S. McCampbell, *Field Training for Police Agencies: State of the Art.* Washington, DC: U.S. Department of Justice, National Institute of Justice, 1997, pp. 4–6.

Phase I

Weeks 1–16
Academy and in-house training.

Phase II

Weeks 17–18
Assigned to primary FTO. No evaluations.

Weeks 19–28
Daily observation reports by FTOs with weekly evaluation reports by supervisors.

Weeks 29–30
Daily and weekly reports continue, but primary FTO rides in plain clothes with recruit.

Phase III

Weeks 31–36
Recruit works a solo beat outside the Training District. Supervisors evaluate biweekly.

Weeks 37–40
Recruit continues solo beat. Supervisors evaluate monthly.

Weeks 41–44
Recruit continues solo beat. Ten Month Review Board meets to recommend retention, remedial training, or dismissal.

Weeks 45–52
Reserved for remedial training if needed. Special board meets to review the performance of recruits with deficiencies.

previously accomplished and to ensure that the trainee is prepared for the final phase. By the completion of this phase, the trainee should be able to assume responsibilities in the most difficult situations, including shootings and robberies in progress, with little assistance from the FTO.

Phase IV is the final evaluation period. The trainee returns to the original FTO and assumes the role of primary officer while the FTO might wear civilian clothes and only observe. The purpose of this phase is to evaluate if the trainee is capable of functioning without the direct supervision of an FTO.

Field training programs are labor intensive and require a great deal of administration and management. FTOs complete a comprehensive daily observation report (DOR) form, as shown in Figure 5–4. The DOR is a permanent record of the trainee's progress and includes remedial efforts and identified problems. The form shown in Figure 5–4 is composed of five major performance areas: appearance, attitude, knowledge, performance, and relationships, which are divided into 30 rating categories. These categories address a range of skills necessary for an officer to become proficient. The FTO observes and evaluates the trainee in each applicable area during a shift, using a rating scale of 1 to 7. A narrative explanation is required in every area in which the trainee is rated below average (less than 2) or exceptional (more than 6).

The selection of good officers as FTOs is critical, as they have a long-term impact on the behavior and performance of new, and often impressionable, trainees. Criteria for FTOs should include their education, experience, police skills, and ability and interest in training. The role of the FTO is similar to that of a supervisor. Guidance, counseling, and remediation of minor mistakes are required daily.

Since the new officers in the FTO program eventually will be assigned to patrol, the patrol commander must ensure that they are prepared to function as patrol officers. On the other hand, the FTO program is a training program and as such usually is responsible to the training commander. These managers must work together to ensure that the program functions properly.

Patrol supervisors play a vital role in the FTO program. It is the sergeant's responsibility to ensure that the standards and objectives of the agency's field training program are met. The supervisor must pay close attention to the training activities of the FTO and seek periodic feedback on the new trainees as the FTO program progresses. In essence, the sergeant must supervise the FTOs and the new officers.

When assigned a trainee, sergeants should periodically observe the trainee's handling of calls. The supervisor should also ensure that necessary corrective actions are taken so that the trainee has every opportunity to complete the program or that the proper documentation exists in the case of a recommendation to terminate the trainee from employment. The sergeant should also observe the interaction between trainee and FTO to ensure that the FTO is properly doing his

DATE_____   DAILY OBSERVATION REPORT NO._____

_____   _____
TRAINEE'S LAST NAME FIRST (MI) NO.   FTO'S LAST NAME FIRST (MI) NO.

RATING INSTRUCTIONS: RATE OBSERVED BEHAVIOR WITH REFERENCE TO THE SCALE BELOW. COMMENT
ON THE MOST AND LEAST SATISFACTORY PERFORMANCE OF THE DAY. A SPECIFIC COMMENT IS REQUIRED
ON ALL RATINGS OF "2" OR LESS AND "6" AND ABOVE. CHECK "N.O." IF NOT OBSERVED. IF TRAINEE FAILS TO
RESPOND TO TRAINING. CHECK "N.R.T." BOX AND COMMENT.

WATCH WORKED_____
FTO PHASE_____
ASSIGNMENT_____

	NOT ACCEPTABLE BY FTO STANDARDS			ACCEPTABLE LEVEL	SUPERIOR BY FTO STANDARDS					
	1	2	3	<4>	5	6	7			

R.T.   N.O. N.R.T

                                                                APPEARANCE
[ ] [ ] 1.   1   2   3   4   5   6   7   [ ] [ ]   GENERAL APPEARANCE

                                                                ATTITUDE
[ ] [ ] 2.   1   2   3   4   5   6   7   [ ] [ ]   ACCEPTANCE OF FEEDBACK-FTO
[ ] [ ] 3.   1   2   3   4   5   6   7   [ ] [ ]   ATTITTUDE TOWARDS POLICE WORK

                                                                KNOWLEDGE
                                                           DEPARTMENT POLICIES AND PROCEDURES
                                                             REFLECTED IN:
[ ] [ ] 4.   1   2   3   4   5   6   7   [ ] [ ]   VERBAL/WRITTEN TESTING
[ ] [ ]   1   2   3   4   5   6   7   [ ] [ ]   FIELD PERFORMANCE
                                                           CRIMINAL STATUTES REFLECTED IN:
[ ] [ ] 5.   1   2   3   4   5   6   7   [ ] [ ]   VERBAL/WRITTEN TESTING
[ ] [ ]   1   2   3   4   5   6   7   [ ] [ ]   FIELD PERFORMANCE
                                                           MUNICIPAL ORDINANCES REFLECTED IN:
[ ] [ ] 6.   1   2   3   4   5   6   7   [ ] [ ]   VERBAL/WRITTEN TESTING
[ ] [ ]   1   2   3   4   5   6   7   [ ] [ ]   FIELD PERFORMANCE
                                                           TRAFFIC ORDINANCES REFLECTED IN:
[ ] [ ] 7.   1   2   3   4   5   6   7   [ ] [ ]   VERBAL/WRITTEN TESTING
[ ] [ ]   1   2   3   4   5   6   7   [ ] [ ]   FIELD PERFORMANCE

                                                                PERFORMANCE
[ ] [ ] 8.   1   2   3   4   5   6   7   [ ] [ ]   DRIVING SKILL: NORMAL CONDITIONS
[ ] [ ] 9.   1   2   3   4   5   6   7   [ ] [ ]   DRIVING SKILL: STRESS CONDITIONS
[ ] [ ] 10.   1   2   3   4   5   6   7   [ ] [ ]   ORIENTATION/RESPONSE TIME
[ ] [ ] 11.   1   2   3   4   5   6   7   [ ] [ ]   ROUTINE FORMS: COMPLETE/ACCURATE
                                                             REPORT WRITING
[ ] [ ] 12.   1   2   3   4   5   6   7   [ ] [ ]   ORGANIZATION/DETAILS
[ ] [ ] 13.   1   2   3   4   5   6   7   [ ] [ ]   GRAMMAR/SPELLING/NEATNESS
[ ] [ ] 14.   1   2   3   4   5   6   7   [ ] [ ]   APPROPRIATE TIME USED
[ ] [ ] 15.   1   2   3   4   5   6   7   [ ] [ ]   FIELD PERFORMANCE: NON-STRESS
[ ] [ ] 16.   1   2   3   4   5   6   7   [ ] [ ]   FIELD PERFORMANCE: STRESS
[ ] [ ] 17.   1   2   3   4   5   6   7   [ ] [ ]   INVESTIGATIVE SKILL
[ ] [ ] 18.   1   2   3   4   5   6   7   [ ] [ ]   INTERVIEW/INTERROGATION
[ ] [ ] 19.   1   2   3   4   5   6   7   [ ] [ ]   SELF-INITIATED FIELD ACTIVITY
[ ] [ ] 20.   1   2   3   4   5   6   7   [ ] [ ]   OFFICER SAFETY: GENERAL
[ ] [ ] 21.   1   2   3   4   5   6   7   [ ] [ ]   OFFICER SAFETY: SUSPECTS/PRISONERS
[ ] [ ] 22.   1   2   3   4   5   6   7   [ ] [ ]   VOICE COMMAND
[ ] [ ] 23.   1   2   3   4   5   6   7   [ ] [ ]   PHYSICAL SKILL
[ ] [ ] 24.   1   2   3   4   5   6   7   [ ] [ ]   PROBLEM SOLVING/DECISION MAKING
                                                             RADIO
[ ] [ ] 25.   1   2   3   4   5   6   7   [ ] [ ]   USE OF CODES/PROCEDURES
[ ] [ ] 26.   1   2   3   4   5   6   7   [ ] [ ]   LISTEN AND COMPREHEND
[ ] [ ] 27.   1   2   3   4   5   6   7   [ ] [ ]   ARTICULATION/TRANSMISSION

                                                                RELATIONSHIPS
[ ] [ ] 28.   1   2   3   4   5   6   7   [ ] [ ]   CITIZENS IN GENERAL
[ ] [ ] 29.   1   2   3   4   5   6   7   [ ] [ ]   ETHNIC GROUPS OTHER THAN OWN
[ ] [ ] 30.   1   2   3   4   5   6   7   [ ] [ ]   OTHER DEPARTMENT MEMBERS
                                                 _____MINUTES OF REMEDIAL TIME

FIGURE 5–4   Daily Observation Report

or her job and conduct periodic informal meetings with the FTOs and trainees to discuss the progress of training.

The sergeant will also be responsible for the collection, review, and approval of all DOR forms completed by the FTO. The forms are reviewed to ensure that they are consistent with program goals and guidelines. A weekly supervisory observation report (SOR) should also be completed. This is the sergeant's evaluation of the trainee's performance. Should the sergeant identify problems, they are discussed with the patrol watch commander.

Earlier, some problems with FTO programs were noted. Other concerns also have direct implications for sergeants and unit commanders. Doerner and Patterson (1992) found some issues involving gender and race. First, they found that women and minorities were underrepresented as FTOs. They also found that women trainees had a lower perception of their FTO than did males: "Female rookies find themselves uncomfortable with what they see as a harsh, unbending, military-like atmosphere" (p. 31). It seems that some departments and individual officers carry over the stress training that typifies many basic academies. This type of demeanor on the part of FTOs is not conducive to learning, nor is it a proper atmosphere in which to evaluate new officers.

Roll Call Training

Roll call occurs during the 15 to 30 minutes prior to the beginning of a tour of duty. This time is used by unit commanders to prepare officers for patrol. Roll call sessions usually begin with a sergeant assigning officers to their respective beats. Information about wanted and dangerous persons and major incidents on previous shifts is usually disseminated. Other matters may also be addressed, such as issuing officers court subpoenas, explaining new departmental policies and procedures, and discussing shift and beat-related matters.

Roll call meetings also afford an excellent opportunity for the department to update officers' knowledge and to present new ideas and techniques. For example, when the department changes a policy or adopts a new one, it is presented in roll call. Officers can then ask questions and clarify its meaning. Such two-way communication leads to a better understanding of the policy. It also allows the department to address issues, such as racial profiling. Roll call training provides an opportunity to clarify a department's policy regarding discretionary traffic stops and, it is hoped, reduce any problems of bias that occur in stops.

In-Service Training

Changes in departmental policies and procedures, court decisions, and operational strategies and techniques demand that training be an ongoing process throughout a police officer's career. It is simply unreasonable to expect that the knowledge gained during academy training or specialized training can serve an officer for an entire career. In-service training is the most commonly utilized method for maintaining and improving officer performance and competency and may also reduce the likelihood of citizen complaints and future litigation. In-service training is also used to recertify, refresh, or provide new information to officers in the most critical areas of their job, including weapons qualification, driving, defensive tactics, first aid, and changes in the law (Moore and Stephens, 1991).

Creating an effective in-service training program presents many challenges for the department. First, few departments have adequate funds to provide training beyond what is mandatory by law or for those issues that create the greatest public concern or liability. Scheduling training can also be a nightmare. In-service and specialized training often result in staffing shortages in areas where officers attending the training are assigned. For example, the legislature in California recently mandated that every police officer receive four hours of training on racial profiling within a two-year period. The San Bernardino Sheriff's Department has more then 1,400 deputies. It took a considerable amount of resources and planning to meet this legislative mandate within the two-year time frame. This training will also result in units having personnel shortages, which will be extremely problematic for sergeants and unit commanders. In other words, the work does not stop when officers go to training.

Labor agreements can also hinder training. Some police officer contracts may prohibit agencies from moving officers off an evening shift to train on day shift without compensation at an overtime rate. Agencies may also be required by contract to maintain certain established staffing levels, further complicating the task of ensuring that officers are properly trained.

Sergeants and unit commanders play a key role in in-service training. They try to ensure that their subordinates are assigned to in-service courses that will provide them with additional skills for their current assignment. Detective sergeants want to ensure that newly appointed detectives receive the proper training in criminal investigation. Also, when sergeants observe officers who have deficiencies or problems with some aspect of the job, it may be more effective to remedy the deficiency through training as opposed to disciplinary action.

ASSESSING TRAINING NEEDS

Training evolves from a logical and cyclical process. The training cycle contains five interrelated components: training needs assessment, establishing objectives, program development, delivering training, and conducting an assessment.

Training must be based on organizational goals and employee needs. The latter are determined by conducting surveys and interviews with officers, supervisors, citizens, and elected officials; reviewing lawsuits and citizen complaints; and looking at what other agencies are doing (Rossett, 1987). A training needs assessment is the foundation for developing a training curriculum. It ensures that the training will meet the needs of the organization and employees. The failure to conduct such a needs assessment may result in the training having no practical application in the minds and functions of the officers.

The most common method of validating training or determining training content is the *job analysis,* which consists of surveying all or a sample of officers to determine what they do on the job. The job analysis generates a list of tasks and the knowledge, skills, and abilities associated with each of the tasks. This information then is used to develop training objectives, the building blocks of a good training program.

Figure 5–5 shows the top 30 tasks performed by Lexington, Kentucky, police officers in order of importance as determined by a departmental job analysis.

Training objectives identify what the trainer hopes to accomplish during the course of a session. They should clearly define the nature of the training and its intended outcomes. In essence, objectives should address what the trainee is expected to learn. They relate directly to expected performance and generally serve as benchmarks for testing purposes.

After needs and objectives have been established, the training can be developed. This is when the trainer decides the "who, what, when, where, why, and how" of the course. The information is assembled and developed into a structured lesson plan that serves as a guide for the instructor to present the information. Time, available resources, costs, and type of audience are all factors requiring consideration in the development of training. At the same time, student learning materials should be developed. Too often training consists of the lecture method whereby information is provided to officers by an instructor. Officers should be provided source material that should be read prior to the lecture to maximize training. Too many training programs neglect providing this necessary source material.

After the training has been presented, an evaluation of its effectiveness should follow. Training that is currently successful and applicable may soon become outdated. The two most common methods of assessing training are examinations and student evaluations. The Federal Bureau of Investigation's Instructor Development Course recommends four steps to complete a total course assessment:

1. Evaluation reaction: How well did the trainee like the training?

2. Learning evaluation: What principal facts and techniques were learned?

3. Behavior evaluation: What job behavior resulted from the training program?

4. Results: What were the tangible results of the program (reduced costs, improved performance, reduced liability)?

LEXINGTON DIVISION OF POLICE OFFICER TASK LIST

PATROL DUTIES

1. Patrols to establish a presence, reduce opportunities for crime, detect crimes, and render service to citizens.
2. Searches for or observes for wanted persons, suspect vehicles, or evidence.
3. Responds to crimes in progress.

EQUIPMENT OPERATION

4. Maintains firearms proficiency.
5. Operates various police vehicles as assigned.

PUBLIC CONTACT

6. Responds to citizen requests for police service or assistance such as directions, stranded motorists, etc.
7. Deals with distressed individuals to calm them, explain police procedures, and obtain their cooperation.

HANDLING DISTURBANCES

8. Responds to special situations such as barricaded persons, hostages, riots, etc.
9. Responds to disorders in order to prevent physical injuries and damage and restore peace.
10. Intervenes in fights, separates participants and attempts to restore order.

TRAFFIC ENFORCEMENT

11. Handles traffic control at construction sites, other special events and projects, and accident scenes.
12. Observes motorists to detect violations, safely pulls over violators, and takes appropriate police action.

CRIME AND ACCIDENT INVESTIGATION

13. Interviews complainants, victims, suspects, and/or witnesses to gather information relating to the investigation or locating individuals.
14. As first responder at a crime/accident scene, radios for assistance, protects scene, detains witnesses, performs rescue operations as needed.
15. Searches for and collects evidence at a crime scene or accidents.
16. Speaks to informants to gather information and possible leads about recent crimes.
17. Searches premises or property with a search or arrest warrant or with consent of the owner.

APPREHENSION AND ARREST

18. Serves domestic violence papers, restraining orders, protective orders, etc.
19. Arrests suspected law violators, with or without a warrant, observing legal requirements.
20. Takes necessary precautions against blood-borne pathogens.
21. Uses force necessary to affect an arrest using physical force, OC spray, or baton.
22. Searches persons for stolen property, concealed weapons or illegal substances, observing legal requirements.
23. Fires weapon at suspect in line of duty.

COURT PREPARATION AND TESTIMONY

24. Meets with attorney to provide case facts, discuss evidence, prepare for testimony, etc.
25. Gathers and organizes all records, reports and information needed for grand jury or court presentation.
26. Testifies in court regarding the facts of the case as known first-hand, evidence collected, notes, actions taken, etc.

REPORTS, RECORDS, AND PAPERWORK

27. Writes reports in narrative form, describing activities, events, investigations, enforcement actions taken, etc.
28. Completes various departmental forms and paperwork.

TRAINING

29. Attends in-service training classes, workshops, and conferences.
30. Reads and remains abreast of department general orders, bulletins, policies, etc.

FIGURE 5–5 Top 30 Police Officers' Tasks, Lexington, Kentucky.

At first glance, we may think that the new officer's reaction to the training is not important. If he or she did not like or understand the training, however, there is a high probability that learning did not take place. It is important that officers enjoy and be involved in the training process. The question of evaluation reaction can be answered in a well-constructed evaluation form. A sample training evaluation form is shown in Figure 5–6.

Student examinations are used to measure learning. Most training programs have an examination at the end of the training. When training programs span several weeks, as they do at the basic academy, tests are administered weekly or at the end of each major block of instruction. Instructors too often rely on multiple-choice tests to measure learning. Such tests show only how well facts are memorized, and not whether material was actually learned. Multiple-choice tests should be supplemented with role-play exercises, simulations, and other testing in which the trainees actually use the material learned. For example, if veteran officers are being trained on the use of a new report, they should be given a case study and should complete a copy of the form at the end of the training.

Behavior is measured by sergeants and unit commanders and generally is documented by the administration of performance appraisals, which are addressed in the following chapter. That is, once the training was completed, did the trainee's behavior change to incorporate the training program's content?

Instructor:_____   Course:_____

In an effort to improve this course, we would appreciate your candid comments concerning the following items. Thank you for your cooperation.

1. How would you rate the content of this course in terms of its value to you?

Poor		Average		Excellent
1	2	3	4	5

2. Do you believe the course objectives were met by the instructor?

     Yes   No   Partially

     Comments:

3. What topical area covered was of most benefit to you?

4. Identify the weak areas of the course that either need to be strengthened or eliminated.

5. How would you rate the overall performance of the instructor?

Poor		Average		Excellent
1	2	3	4	5

6. Was the instructor prepared, with adequate material, and was a lesson plan used?

7. Can you offer any suggestions to help the instructor improve?

8. Please offer any other comments or suggestions you think will improve the quality of this course.

FIGURE 5–6   Sample Training Evaluation Form

Commanders must then ensure that sergeants reinforce the training as a result of the supervision process.

Finally, we must ensure that the results are what was intended. The officer may apply the principles learned in the training, but the outcomes do not match expectations. In this case, the training itself is deficient. It does not prepare officers for the situations they meet. As part of their evaluation of officers and activities, sergeants should look for such problems. When they are observed, they should be communicated to the training staff so that the training curriculum can be altered.

MATERIALS AND TEACHING AIDS

A variety of instructional materials is available to improve a training curriculum. Instructors and training staff should consider different training tools and materials to make the training more meaningful and lasting, such as the following:

> *Visual Aids.* The old adage "a picture is worth a thousand words" is true with training. Visual aids can greatly enhance a presentation and help re- duce the gap between speaker and listener. The most common and simplest types of visual aids are overheads, computer graphics, films, videotapes, chalkboards, and flipcharts.

> *Audio and Video Cassettes.* As training requirements continue to increase, police departments are finding it more and more difficult to free person- nel to attend mandated annual training because of scheduling concerns and the lack of personnel to cover shifts while officers attend training. Short videotapes and audiotapes are excellent methods of delivering training during roll call sessions. They also provide supervisors with the flexibility of assigning one officer at a time to review a videotape or listen to an audiotape during nonpeak hours of a shift or to take training videos home to review at their leisure. The Fair Labor Standards Act (FLSA) and employee contracts, however, may prohibit home checkout, or at least require the department to compensate employees for the time devoted for this purpose.

> *Video Simulation.* Interactive video simulation adds realism to police train- ing in a variety of areas, including driver's training, domestic violence, and firearms use. Several companies offer "shoot–don't-shoot" simulators that present scenarios involving night vehicle stops, drug deals, domestic violence incidents, armed robberies, and hostage situations. This realistic training often challenges officers to make a deadly force decision and adds stress and realism to the training. The instructor can change the scenario using the computer. The system evaluates the officer's decision to shoot,

shooting technique, and accuracy. Most systems offer a variety of realistic guns that shoot laser light at a 10- to 20-foot screen. The system's computer logs every shooting and compares each exercise with previous reaction times and decision making.

Computer-Assisted Training. Police recruits today are more comfortable and skilled with computer technology. Many courses are being adapted to the personal computer for instructional purposes. This affords students the opportunity to engage in learning at their own pace and the department the flexibility of providing training in a format that may have the least impact on scheduling. Such training can be conducted on stand-alone computers located at the police department, or it can be adopted for use on the Internet. When Internet courses are developed, officers can work on them in the office or at home. Computer-assisted instruction allows for the introduction of short video clips, and students can interact with an instructor and ask questions via e-mail.

Teleconferencing. The advancement and availability of communications satellite technology during the past few years have made teleconferencing more available to departments. Through interactive teleconferencing, colleges, universities, and governmental agencies can transmit a training session from one site to an unlimited number of sites across the country. Unlike videotapes, teleconferencing allows for two-way conversation between the presenter and viewers. Most important, it allows a variety of training opportunities with minimal cost and coordination. Videoconferencing allows for a department to provide simultaneous instruction at a number of training sites.

Television Programming. The Law Enforcement Television Network (LETN) is policing's answer to Cable Network News (CNN). LETN provides a 24-hour-a-day television schedule of programming on various police issues. Agencies pay a monthly fee for satellite connection. Programs can be taped and shown at the convenience of the agency and offer an excellent tool for agencies that cannot afford training and struggle with state-mandated requirements. LETN's format of short programs makes it well suited for roll call and in-service courses. It is important to note that supervisors should review all such outside training materials to ensure they do not present any liabilities. For example, methods for conducting high-risk vehicle stops and weaponless defense procedures may vary greatly between jurisdictions.

National Criminal Justice Research Service. This clearinghouse of publications and online reference service about a broad range of criminal justice issues can be found on the Internet at http://www.ncjrs.org/. This source has

Many of today's police recruits engage in computer-assisted training.
Courtesy Riverside, California, Police Department.

some of the most current information on police research and is used extensively by police agencies across the country.

National Law Enforcement and Corrections Technology Center. This center provides information about new equipment and technologies to federal, state, and local law enforcement and corrections officials and can be found on the Internet at http://www.nlectc.org/.

U.S. Department of Justice. This department has information about a wide range of research, training, and grants and can be found on the Internet at http://www.usdoj.gov/.

Community Policing Consortium. The consortium provides a compendium of information about community policing and problem solving training and funding under the crime bill and can be found on the Internet at http://www.communitypolicing.org/.

Bureau of Justice Statistics. The bureau's Web site includes a variety of information about criminal justice statistics and provides links to other research Web sites and can be found on the Internet at http://www.ojp.usdoj.gov/bjs/.

Law Enforcement Sites on the Web. This site lists all federal, state, and local agencies on the Web and can be found on the Internet at http://www.ih2000.net/ira/ira.htm.

COPNET. This site contains a myriad of information about police training, job opportunities, links to other agencies, and chat rooms on various subjects and can be found on the Internet at http://police.sas.ab.ca/.

SUPERVISORY AND MANAGEMENT PROFESSIONAL DEVELOPMENT

Requisite Skills

Once officers are promoted to a higher-level position, an entirely different world of policing emerges for them. Supervisors are the backbone of an organization. Promotion forces them into situations they may never have experienced. The dual demands of operations and administration are overwhelming at times and require an entirely new set of knowledge and skills to be successful. At the same time, when a sergeant is promoted to lieutenant, he or she assumes more responsibility in the administration of a unit. This also entails making many more decisions that ultimately affect the unit's operations.

The International Association of Chiefs of Police (IACP; 1985:81) noted that being promoted "represents probably the most critical and challenging adjustment for the employee who must, for the first time, supervise the performance of others in the agency." In other words, a promotion entails that the newly promoted officer perform an almost entirely new job. Unfortunately, most police departments do not provide newly promoted officers with the training that they need. Once promoted, they may receive some guidance from a superior officer, but it generally is assumed that they are ready to accept their new responsibilities as a result of having been on the job for a number of years.

Sandwith (1993) examined supervisory and management training needs. He noted that these needs went well beyond the technical aspects of the job. He identified five domains or areas in which promoted officers need competence. First, they need conceptual skills. They need to be able to grasp and understand the inner workings of their units (i.e., they need to see the larger picture). It also means that they must be able to translate goals and objectives into action. Second, they need leadership skills. Officers do not necessarily need to possess leadership skills. Once promoted, however, leadership is a necessity. Third, they must possess interpersonal skills. They must be able to effectively communicate to subordinates and others. Fourth, they must possess administrative skills. They must be able to plan, complete reports, and otherwise ensure that the unit and officers are functioning according to expectations. Finally, they need technical skills. Even though they are not functioning as officers, they must completely understand how the job is to be performed. Otherwise, they are not able to provide adequate supervision.

Although a specialized course on supervision will provide the new sergeant with professional management skills and knowledge, the application of new knowledge is often provided via a field training program similar to that discussed earlier for patrol officers. For example, some agencies require that new sergeants complete a structured field training program consisting of up to six or more weeks' duration before being assigned to supervise a team of officers. A shift lieutenant assumes the role of FTO and utilizes a critical task manual to evaluate the newly promoted supervisor's field performance. A number of supervisory dimensions are evaluated, including role identification, leadership, employee performance appraisal, discipline, employee relations, training, report review, and critical incident management. Then, on completion of the field training program, the sergeant is assigned to manage a team of officers in a uniformed patrol division. Figure 5–7 is an example of the training and critical incident sections of a critical task manual for supervisors.

Few departments have a program of this nature for anyone promoted above the rank of sergeant. Training at these higher levels consists of on-the-job training in which a superior officer makes assignments to the newly promoted lieutenant or captain and then monitors his or her progress. In fact, few national training programs are aimed at officers above the rank of sergeant.

Next, we discuss other related aspects of a supervisor's professional development in supervision and management: training, education, literature, and professional and civic organizations.

Training

One obvious route to supervisory professional development is training. Whenever possible, new supervisors should receive basic supervisory training when they are promoted or, at the latest, soon thereafter. This type of training typically lasts for a week or longer and generally is provided, or at least certified, in each state by the Peace Officer Standards and Training Commission or a similar entity. Larger police departments often conduct this training themselves for their own supervisors and sometimes make space available for personnel from other agencies.

Armstrong and Longnecker (1992) examined 144 police agencies, including the two largest in each state. They found that 78 percent of the agencies reported that they had an in-house training program for sergeants. The most common topics addressed in the training included

	Instructed by Trainer	Satisfactorily Understood
	Trainer's Initials/Date	Trainee Initials

Training: The supervisor will understand the responsibilities of being a trainer		
1. Understands the instructional role of the supervisor.		
2. Understands the elements of the agency's FTO program and supervisory responsibilities.		
3. Understands the need to plan, schedule, and conduct roll call training.		
4. Understands the need to evaluate the training subordinates received:		
a. To ensure it meets their needs.		
b. To ensure they are applying what they learned.		
5. Is aware of the training resources that are available within the agency.		
6. Understands the career development process and provides subordinates proper guidance.		
7. Understands the concepts of *vicarious liability* and *failure to train*.		
8. Critical Incident Management: The supervisor will demonstrate an understanding of the agency's procedures in managing critical incidents utilizing the Critical Incident Checklist:		
a. Bomb threats		
b. Barricaded suspect		
c. Command post operations		
d. Hazardous materials spills		
e. Use of SWAT/Hostage negotiations		
f. Multiagency operations		
g. Officer-involved shootings		
h. Other disasters		

UPON COMPLETION PLACE IN MASTER TRAINING FILE

FIGURE 5–7 Supervisor's Critical Task Guide

153

- Supervisory techniques   95%
- Use of the disciplinary process   92%
- Counseling techniques   80%
- Performance evaluation   79%
- Motivational strategies   73%
- Management theory   68%
- Handling employee grievances   64%
- EEO and affirmative action compliance   62%
- Personnel harassment policies   52%

In states that mandate annual in-service training for all police personnel, supervisory and management training should be geared toward developing skills in the domains just listed. Refresher courses, updates, and training in new subjects should all contribute to the supervisor's professional development. One noteworthy example is the Law Enforcement Management Institute of Texas (LEMIT). The core program within LEMIT is the Graduate Management Institute, or GMI, composed of a one-week and 3 two-week modules. The modules focus on developing writing and analytical skills (including computer skills) and on three substantive topics: business management, Texas government and politics, and police administration. Each module is scheduled several times per year and is held at various locations throughout the state. LEMIT also offers a variety of shorter executive issues seminars and special topics programs each year.

At the national level, several highly regarded institutions offer professional development courses appropriate for police supervisors and/or higher-ranking police executives. Among the best known of these are the Federal Bureau of Investigation's National Academy, the Police Executive Research Forum's Senior Management Institute for Police, the Southwestern Law Enforcement Institute's Command and Management College, and the long courses offered by the Northwestern University Traffic Institute and the Southern Police Institute. Shorter courses are also offered by the International Association of Chiefs of Police, the Federal Law Enforcement Training Center, and the Institute for Police Technology and Management.

Supervisors should also be aware of training opportunities outside the police industry. Local and state governments, the federal government, universities, private companies, and private vendors often offer generic supervision, management, and special topic training courses. The IACP offers a program called Operation Bootstrap that coordinates training with major industries and companies. Police supervisors and middle managers are sent to training programs that are normally reserved for corporation executives.

Higher Education

The purposes of higher education are broader and more general than those of police training, although the line gets harder and harder to draw as training becomes more sophisticated and education seeks to become more practical (Haley, 1992). Police managers and supervisors can benefit from education in many subjects beyond police administration or criminal justice: psychology, sociology, political science, public administration, history, business, and the humanities, to name just a few. Any education that broadens a supervisor's outlook and contributes to reading, writing, reasoning, and managing skills and their understanding of people, organizations, and society is likely to be beneficial to him or her individually and to the department.

Higher education seems an appropriate option to prepare rank-and-file officers, supervisors, and middle managers to effectively cope with the difficult demands of police work. Yet, higher education continues to be one of most controversial and debated issues among academics and police administrators alike. Many question its utility.

Increasing empirical evidence supports the need for higher education for police officers and supervisors. Studies have found that educated officers

- Have significantly fewer citizen complaints than their non–college-educated counterparts (Kappeler, Sapp, and Carter, 1992)
- Have better peer relationships and are likelier to take a leadership role in the organization (Weirman, 1978)
- Tend to be more flexible (Trojanowicz and Nicholson, 1976)
- Are less dogmatic and authoritarian (Dalley, 1975)
- Have lower absenteeism, take less time off, and are involved in fewer traffic accidents (Cascio, 1977)
- Have a greater ability to analyze situations and make judicious decisions and have a more desirable system of personal values consistent with the police function in a modern society (Sterling, 1974)
- Are less insubordinate (Lynch, 1987)

The emergence of community policing has also been used to argue for the need for higher education of police (Carter and Sapp, 1992). The knowledge and skills required of an officer under community policing to be an effective decision maker, service provider, communicator, and problem solver make college education even more critical.

Literature

One mark of professionals is that they keep up with developments in their fields, largely by reading professional literature. Police managers and supervisors should pursue this approach to professional development by keeping up with books, governmental publications, and periodicals pertinent to policing and police management. This is difficult to do, of course, since dozens of books on police topics and untold numbers of governmental documents are published every year, and police supervisors have many other demands on their time.

The most feasible approach involves two methods. The first is to register with the National Criminal Justice Reference Service (NCJRS), a no-cost federally funded service that notifies criminal justice professionals each month of pertinent new publications. Reading the monthly NCJRS bulletin is a quick means of identifying new publications of interest and determining how to obtain them (some are free). To register with NCJRS, call 1-800-851-3420 or 1-301-251-5500. It is easy to register and it really is free.

The other key method for keeping up with the literature is to rely on periodicals: newsletters, magazines, and journals. These periodicals come out several times a year and are generally more current than books and present information in a more condensed format. In addition, they frequently contain reviews of recently published books.

The police field now has a surprising number of periodicals. Some cater more to police practitioners while others aim at policymakers and police educators. Some of the better known police periodicals are briefly described next.

FBI Law Enforcement Bulletin: a magazine-style periodical published monthly by the FBI. Contains articles on various police-related issues, legal analyses, book reviews, and regular features. Readable and informative.

Law & Order: a privately published monthly magazine that contains extensive advertising, short articles describing contemporary police practices, and opinion pieces.

Law Enforcement News: a newspaper-style periodical published every two weeks by the John Jay College of Criminal Justice in New York City. Contains news items, short articles, and interviews with police officials. Useful for keeping up with current events in the police field.

Police Forum: a quarterly newsletter of the Police Section, Academy of Criminal Justice Sciences. Contains short articles and book reviews.

Subject to Debate: a quarterly newsletter of the Police Executive Research Forum. Contains short articles, organization news, legislative updates, and other regular features.

The Police Chief: a monthly magazine of the International Association of Chiefs of Police. Contains extensive advertising, legal notes, short articles describing contemporary police practices, organization news, and regular features such as open positions.

Police Quarterly: a journal of the Police Section of the Academy of Criminal Justice Sciences and the Police Executive Research Forum devoted to research in law enforcement.

Law Enforcement Technology: a monthly magazine published by Cygnus Business Media, Ft. Atkinson, Wisconsin, showing communications-, computer-, and police protection–related technologies that are available, as well as presenting case histories that demonstrate how those technologies may be applied to solving problems in policing.

Professional Organizations

Another mark of professionals is that they organize in order to share information and further their interests. No organizations focus exclusively on police supervision, as far as we know, but there are several prominent national organizations for police specialists and police managers. Regular or associate membership in these organizations would generally be open to police supervisors. Seven general-purpose professional organizations are briefly described next.

International Association of Chiefs of Police: the primary membership organization of police chief executives. Provides publications, training, consulting, and other membership services and holds a major annual conference.

International Association of Law Enforcement Planners: a membership organization catering to police planners, analysts, and middle managers. Provides a newsletter, credentials police planners, maintains a database of police programs, and holds an annual conference.

National Organization of Black Law Enforcement Executives: a membership organization that represents and gives a voice to African Americans in policing. Develops new programs and provides various membership services.

National Sheriffs Association: the primary membership organization for sheriffs, an often overlooked group of law enforcement executives. Provides publications, training, consulting, and other membership services and holds an annual conference.

Police Executive Research Forum: a membership organization for police chief executives of larger jurisdictions. Requires a college degree for membership. Conducts studies; develops new programs; provides publications, training, and consulting; and holds an annual meeting.

National Association of Field Training Officers: a membership organization composed of field training officers. Promotes the dissemination of information on FTO programs.

Police Section, Academy of Criminal Justice Sciences: the primary membership organization for faculty teaching criminal justice in colleges and universities. Provides a newsletter for its members and helps organize the police portion of the annual conference. Members include police and criminal justice practitioners and students in addition to teachers and researchers.

THE SUPERIOR OFFICER AS TRAINER

Superiors' or supervisors' primary function is to obtain results through people. They are judged on their ability to get their subordinates to accomplish their agency's mission, goals, and objectives. Training is an important tool for obtaining the desired results. As More and Wegener (1996:435) observed,

> Everything a supervisor does in directing the work force has some element of training in it; conversely, every training activity involves an element of supervision. Supervision and training are inherent in the sergeant's role. [He or she makes] an incalculable contribution to the growth and development of the department's human resources.

We also know that

> good teaching does not just happen—it is not accidental. It is a result of careful preparation. Success or failure in any instruction program is seldom due to the efforts of the learner alone. The major portion of the responsibility rests upon the individual instructor. (Barlow, 1951:iii)

Thus, much of the success and failure of an organization rests with the supervisor's ability to guide and train officers to perform their duties within the law and in accordance with departmental goals and objectives. An officer's attitude, performance, perceptions, motivation, stress, and job satisfaction are strongly influenced by his or her supervisor. Most of the training provided by managers and supervisors is informal and involves interacting daily with subordinates, conducting roll call training, and continuous counseling, advising, guiding, and coaching on proper police procedures and difficult field situations. The result of this close working relationship is a trust and respect that does not always exist between the ranks in the department.

The training of subordinates is not an easy task, and it cannot be assumed that every newly promoted supervisor will succeed as a trainer. But as supervisors gain experience and develop their interpersonal skills, they should find their training role much easier to perform. Any group of police officers will be composed of individuals with varying skills, knowledge, and abilities. In order to correctly assess their individual needs, the supervisor must first consider the officer's career background, previous training, educational level, and career aspirations.

It is also important to note that correcting an officer's behavior serves a training purpose. Discipline, when applied correctly, teaches the officer what is unacceptable behavior. Thus, training and discipline often accomplish the same objective—a change in employee behavior. For this reason, as discussed in Chapter 9, training is often a recommendation in the disciplinary process.

Several benefits result when the supervisor is involved in the training process (More and Wegener, 1996):

1. *Getting to know subordinates.* Training helps supervisors to understand their subordinates' needs, wants, and potential. This information can be factored into decisions concerning discipline, transfers, promotions, and pay raises.

2. *Promoting good human relations.* Through training, police officers gain self-confidence, pride, and a sense of security. The supervisor's actions give subordinates reasons to cooperate with their peers and the administration. Training helps establish unity of purpose, trust, and mutual respect.

3. *Feeling good about accomplishments.* Training subordinates to do a good job produces a good feeling and motivates the supervisor to put forth more effort.

4. *Furthering one's own career.* As subordinates grow in abilities, expertise, and reputation, so will the supervisor. As subordinates look better, feel better, and perform better, they enhance the supervisor's reputation.

5. *Gaining more time.* Training helps make people more confident and self-sufficient. As their performance improves, the supervisor spends less time correcting behaviors. This time can be invested in other supervisory functions, such as planning, organizing, and coordinating.

LIABILITY ISSUES

Chapter 8 discusses the broad issue of liability; thus, it is given only brief attention here. Federal and state laws hold agencies and their supervisors liable for acts of negligence. The importance of training from a liability perspective cannot be overemphasized. The failure to train officers and supervisors in this regard has resulted in costly litigation against departments; furthermore, the negligence of

The supervisor must be a trainer, coach, and mentor. Here, a supervisor trains S.W.A.T. officers in team movement.
Courtesy Reno, Nevada, Police Department.

police supervisors is currently one of the most frequently litigated areas of liability. The public's inclination to sue individual officers, supervisory personnel, and chiefs of police is quite strong. The courts have sent a clear message: Supervisors may be held accountable for the negligence and wrongful acts of their subordinates.

Supervisors are expected to keep their personnel properly informed and trained and to take necessary action to correct problems and prevent future harm. The failure to do so may result in a lawsuit for failing to act or properly train personnel. Thibault, Lynch, and McBride (1995) provide the following checklist to help agencies and supervisors guard against liability:

1. Do not allow untrained officers to perform any field police duties.
2. Official departmental policies should be reflected in training. Critical issues such as deadly force, pursuit driving, arrest procedures, and weaponless defense should be carefully outlined in the context of academy and updated in-service training courses.
3. All lesson plans, policies, training bulletins, and instructional techniques should be reviewed periodically and updated.

——— Case Studies ———————————————————

The following three case studies provide some substantive issues for the reader to use for applying information from this chapter on training.

In the Hot Seat: Developing a New Training Model

You are the shift commander, a lieutenant, on the evening shift of a medium-sized city police department. Your captain has become increasingly disheartened with the old field training officer (FTO) training program, as she does not believe that it best suits the needs for today's community policing era. You are initially charged with developing an outline for a new program that incorporates problem solving, using what you know about community policing and problem solving as well as existing training methods.

1. What would be some of the topics you would want to cover in this program?

2. How would you measure whether or not officers were learning how to solve problems?

3. How would you build in some hands-on learning experiences for the class members? What kinds of community problems would you include?

An FTO "Drives" Her Points Home

Six months has passed since the Arturo Hills Police Department lost its first officer to a traffic accident. A probationary officer was killed when his vehicle collided at an intersection with a passenger vehicle, also killing the female driver and her two young children. An investigation of the accident determined that the officer was responding to a business alarm and ran through a stop sign at 50 miles per hour. It was determined that the circumstances did *not* warrant the speed involved and concluded that the accident was avoidable. A lawsuit quickly ensues, and lawyers representing the family of the woman and her two children begin by reviewing the department's training files. They learn that 54 percent of the agency's accidents involved probationary officers, and that 90 percent of those employees were trained by the same field training officer (FTO): Nancy Banks. Banks is a veteran officer with 12 years of patrol experience; she is the department's pursuit driving instructor. She tells probationary officers assigned to her shift that she loves working nights because of its freedom from the administrative "brass hats" and the boring school and shoplifting calls that are so common on day shift. For Banks and her officers, stop signs and stop lights do not exist on the graveyard shift, because "only 'cops and crooks' are out." Banks is hard on the recruits, uses FTO information to terminate a greater proportion of new officers than her peers, and pushes their driving skills to the limit during in-progress calls. A few recruits have complained to the shift commander about the dangers involved with the driving style that she teaches and requires, but their concerns are ignored.

1. What lessons can be learned from this case?
2. Could the department have done anything differently in the administration of its FTO program to keep this situation from developing?
3. Should a supervisor have known about the potential problems and intervened? How?

The "Too Cool for School" Supervisor, or How to Conduct Training in Absentia

Sergeant Arnold Kazinsky has been with the state police for nearly 30 years. His reputation for being a no-nonsense, hard-nosed veteran is legendary, as are stories about the record number of citations he has written over the years. Kazinsky often yearns for a return to the days when troopers were hired and given a map, a citation book, and the keys to a cruiser and assigned to work by their sergeant. Kazinsky does not agree with the new, contemporary emphasis on trooper training and believes that the troopers' time can be better spent on the road instead of in the classroom. When state headquarters issues a series of officer safety videos to be shown at briefings, in typical fashion Kazinsky does not take the training seriously. He plays the videotapes during briefings as told but turns down the volume so low that it is almost impossible to hear them; furthermore, he does not distribute the accompanying handout materials for discussion and even leaves the room while the training video is playing, allowing the troopers freedom to banter among themselves at will. Meanwhile, Trooper Benjamin Scott, who has just completed the nine-month basic training academy, is assigned to work for Sgt. Kazinsky. Scott idolizes the legendary Kazinsky and wants to do his best to please his first supervisor. At briefing, even with the training video sound turned low, Scott strains to watch and hear the video intently, in hopes of picking up some new methods for doing his job better. That evening, Scott is dispatched to a suspicious person call at a highway truck stop. Scott uses a frisk technique he saw earlier that day on the briefing video, patting the suspect down with one hand while holding his shotgun in the other. The shotgun accidentally discharges, killing the suspect. Internal Affairs later discovers that the video was actually a demonstration on how *not* to frisk a suspect; the discussion during the video and handout materials made that fact clear, and a training staff member was supposed to be present to emphasize the point. Without any training or supervisory personnel making this clear to all who saw the video, the viewers did not get this major point.

1. Did Kazinsky err? If so, how? Is he civilly liable?
2. Do you feel Trooper Scott is blameworthy?
3. This chapter discussed different types of training. How can training create liability for supervisors?
4. How can training that is national in scope be in conflict with local ordinances or policies? What should an agency do to ensure that the wrong training information is not distributed to officers?

SUMMARY

This chapter has examined police training, which occupies a central position in contemporary police organizations. The changing nature of our society and its laws, coupled with increasing technology and diversity, places incredible demands on officers, supervisors, and managers to maintain the skills, knowledge, and abilities to perform their duties proficiently. Supervisors are in a unique position in an organization's structure to assess officers' training needs and to provide employees with the necessary instruction and guidance. Unit commanders have a need to ensure that officers are well trained; the effectiveness of the unit depends on it. We also noted that training is important for supervisors themselves; among the avenues of professional growth for police supervisors are training, education, literature, and professional and civic organizations that contribute to career development.

This chapter noted that training begins in the academy and continues through a variety of means including roll call, in-service, and specialized training formats. These formats allow for training in a variety of settings and circumstances. They allow a department substantial flexibility while ensuring that personnel are well trained. The failure to properly train or recognize the need for training can create tremendous liability for an organization. Liability alone requires that agencies take training seriously and obligate the necessary people and resources to organize, plan, and document all courses taught.

ITEMS FOR REVIEW

1. Explain the status and types of police training.
2. Describe what is meant by "field training officer" and "police training officer" programs.
3. What is the supervisor's role in police training?
4. Delineate the components of a police training program, and what instructional materials are needed.

5. Review what is involved in a supervisor's professional development program.

6. Describe the benefits that accrue to the supervisor who provides training.

7. Explain how supervisors may be liable for inadequate training of their subordinates.

REFERENCES

Armstrong, L., and Longnecker, C. (1992). Police management training: A national survey. *FBI Law Enforcement Bulletin* 61(1):18–22.

Barlow, M. (1951). Quoted in *Instructor's guide for roll call training*. Los Angeles, CA: Los Angeles Police Department.

Bayley, D., and Bittner, E. (1997). Learning the skills of policing. In R. Dunham and G. Alport, eds., *Critical issues in policing*. Prospect Heights, IL: Waveland, pp. 114–138.

Carter, D. L., and Sapp, A. D. (1992). College education and policing: Coming of age. *FBI Law Enforcement Bulletin* 1:8–14.

Cascio, W. F. (1977). Formal education and police officer performance. *Journal of Police Science and Administration* 5:89–96.

City of Canton v. Harris. 57 U.S.L.W. 4263 (1989).

Dalley, A. F. (1975). University and non-university graduated policemen: A study of police attitudes. *Journal of Police Science and Administration* 3:458–468.

Davis, K., and Newstrom, J. W. (1989). *Human behavior at work*. New York: McGraw-Hill.

Doerner, W., and Patterson, E. (1992). The influence of race and gender upon rookie evaluations of their field training officers. *American Journal of Police* 11(2):23–37.

Haley, K. N. (1992). Training. In G. W. Cordner and D. C. Hale, eds., *What works in policing? Operations and administration examined*. Cincinnati: Anderson, pp. 143–155.

Hoover, J., Glensor, R. W., and Peak, K. J. (2002, March 9). The next generation field training officer (FTO) program: A problem-based learning model. Paper presented at the annual conference of the Academy of Criminal Justice Sciences. Anaheim, CA.

International Association of Chiefs of Police (1985). *Police supervision*. Arlington, VA: Author, p. 130.

Kappeler, V. E., Sapp, A. D., and Carter, D. E. (1992). Police officer higher education, citizen complaints and departmental rule violations. *American Journal of Police* (November):37–54.

Little, R. (1990). The police academy: Toward a typology of modes of anticipatory occupational socialization among a sample of police recruits. *Police Journal* (April):159–167.

Lussier, R. N. (1999). *Human relations in organizations: Applications and skill building*. New York: McGraw-Hill.

Lynch, G. W. (1987). Cops and college. *America* (April 4):274–275.

Marion, N. (1998). Police academy training: Are we teaching recruits what they need to know? *Policing: An International Journal of Police Strategies & Management* 21(1):54–79.

McCampbell, M. S. (1997). Field training for police officers: State of the art. In R. Dunham and G. Alport, eds., *Critical issues in policing*. Prospect Heights, IL: Waveland, pp. 139–148.

Moore, M. H., and Stephens, D. W. (1991). *Beyond command and control: The strategic management of police departments*. Washington, DC: Police Executive Research Forum, pp. 85–87.

More, H. W., and Wegener, W. F. (1996). *Effective police supervision,* 2d ed. Cincinnati: Anderson.

Ness, J. J. (1993). The relevance of basic law enforcement training—does the curriculum prepare recruits for police work: A survey study. *Journal of Criminal Justice* 19:181–193.

Niederhoffer, A. (1967). *Behind the shield: The police in urban society*. New York: Doubleday.

Post, G. M. (1992). Police recruits: Training tomorrow's workforce. *FBI Law Enforcement Bulletin* 61(3):19–24.

Ross, D. L. (2000). Emerging trends in police failure to train properly. *Journal of Police Strategies and Management* 23(2):169–193.

Rossett, A. (1987). *Training needs assessment.* Upper Saddle River, NJ: Educational Tech. Publications.

Sandwith, P. (1993). A hierarchy of management training requirements: The competency domain model. *Public Personnel Management* 22(1):43–62.

Sterling, J. W. (1974). The college level entry requirement: A real or imagined cure-all? *The Police Chief* 8:28–31.

Thibault, E. T., Lynch, L. M., and McBride, R. B. (1995). *Proactive police management,* 3d ed. Upper Saddle River, NJ: Prentice Hall.

Trojanowicz, R., and Nicholson, T. (1976). A comparison of behavioral styles of college graduate police officers v. non–college going police officers. *The Police Chief* 43(August):58–59.

United States Department of Justice, Bureau of Justice Statistics. (1996). *Local police departments.* Executive Summary, Washington, DC: U.S. Department of Justice.

Violanti, J. M. (1993). What does high stress police training teach recruits? An analysis of coping. *Journal of Criminal Justice* 21:411–417.

Weirman, C. L. (1978). Variances of ability measurement scores obtained by college and non–college educated troopers. *The Police Chief* (May):34–36.

6

Evaluation Methods and Performance Appraisal

---❖---

LEARNING OBJECTIVES

After reading this chapter, the student will:

- understand both performance appraisal and productivity measurement, and how they can be used in a police department
- understand how community policing has affected the measurement of police productivity
- understand the different forms or scales that are used to collect performance appraisal information
- comprehend how performance targeting can increase a police officer's performance
- know how commanding officers are evaluated under New York City's COMP-STAT program

Excellence is to do a common thing in an uncommon way.

—Booker T. Washington

Excellent firms don't believe in excellence, only in constant improvement and constant change.

—Tom Peters

INTRODUCTION

As we have noted throughout this book, police supervisors have the important responsibility of ensuring that officers effectively perform tasks, diligently attend to responsibilities, generally work toward the department's goals and objectives, coordinate officers' activities, and ensure that these activities meet organizational expectations. Supervisors must also hold officers accountable by reviewing their activities and providing feedback to them when their activities are deficient. Along these same lines, they must provide officers support and positive feedback when applicable to maintain levels of motivation.

These are not easy tasks; many supervisors, both new and old, find the obligation to evaluate and appraise the performance of their subordinates to be quite daunting. But for most supervisors, this is a "make or break" component of management. One can hardly be called a leader if he or she does not fairly and accurately rate subordinates.

This chapter explores several issues surrounding police evaluation and appraisal. The chapter is divided into two primary sections: productivity measurement and performance appraisal. The productivity measurement section includes definitions of productivity, planning, and problem solving and addresses how police managers and first-line supervisors should collect information about subordinates' activities. Performance appraisal refers to the formal process police departments establish to measure officers' performance and provide them with feedback on their performance. Most departments perform this activity on an annual or semi-annual basis. This chapter section includes an overview of performance appraisal, rating forms, a view of how the performance of commanding officers is evaluated under the New York's COMPSTAT philosophy, improving rater performance, providing feedback, how subordinates can accomplish appraisals of supervisors, and performance targeting. The chapter concludes with two case studies.

PRODUCTIVITY MEASUREMENT

Productivity measurement is important because managers and supervisors must make judgments about the relative success of their subordinates and operational units. This generally entails comparing their productivity to some standard. In some cases, officers are compared to one another using averages; in other instances, they are compared to some universal departmental or unit standard. The latter method is inherently superior to the former for two reasons. First, if averages are used, half of the officers, regardless of productivity, will always be below the average. Second, the use of averages means that the work group, rather than supervisors or administrators, is setting productivity levels. This often occurs with traffic enforcement officers who tend to have work-group–established quotas that are lower than the number of citations that can be easily written in a given shift. Regardless of the method used, supervisors are faced with the prospect of developing productivity measures to accomplish this function.

A host of potential measures exist. Every activity a police officer performs can be measured. It is critical to focus on the *correct* measure, however, because officers pattern their behavior and activities using prescribed performance standards and expectations. For example, if a patrol sergeant emphasizes traffic citations, officers will tend to write more tickets and possibly neglect other activities. If the same sergeant fails to comment about or investigate officers' performance at domestic violence calls, officers may develop the attitude that such calls are unimportant and feel free to deal with them less judiciously. Thus, productivity measurement is important in molding police officer behavior and contributes heavily to overall departmental effectiveness.

What Is Productivity?

Productivity theoretically refers to how well the police provide services to citizens. It is the relationship between the resources used by a police department and the amount or level of services provided (Kuper, 1975). The National Commission on Productivity (1973:1) has defined productivity as "the return for a given unit of input." These definitions point to four general concerns when attempting to measure productivity: efficiency, effectiveness, equity, and accountability (Gaines, Southerland, and Angell, 1991). We briefly discuss each concern.

Efficiency refers to the accomplishment of a given task with a minimum expenditure of resources. Constituents want to minimize costs while maximizing outputs (desired outcomes such as services, arrests, or stolen property recovered by the police). The various strategies to accomplish a given task must be considered and the ones that not only achieve desired objectives but also do so at the lowest cost should be implemented. For example, should detectives or patrol officers be assigned to teams? How many patrol units should be dispatched to calls? Can the department take some citizen reports by telephone?

The calculation of efficiency measures is no easy task; costs of activities are generally computed by examining the number of personnel, amount of equipment and staff support, and the amount of noncapital supplies (such as gasoline, paper, and electricity consumed by the program). The cost of outputs, on the other hand, is either difficult or impossible to compute; for example, how can we determine how many accidents or deaths were prevented by setting up a drunk-driving check lane? Nonetheless, the police should strive to increase organizational efficiency.

Managers maximize efficiency through program planning, while supervisors can increase efficiency through proper assignment and supervision. The commander of the criminal investigation unit must examine the volume of reported crimes and then decide how to allocate detectives. These decisions require the commander to ensure that functions or units within the detective division are staffed at the proper level. Too many detectives in an area will result in wasted personnel. On the other hand, too few detectives results in a lowered clearance rate. Once allocation decisions are made, supervisors must ensure that detectives handle cases properly and expediently.

Effectiveness refers to how well the task is performed, regardless of cost, as a result of program activities: Were program goals met? The calculation of measures of effectiveness requires the identification of goals and goal achievement strategies. If objectives were not completely met, how close did the program come to doing so? For example, a police supervisor might decide to implement a problem-solving initiative in an area with low-income housing that has had high numbers of calls for service (CFS) during the past six months. A goal might be set to reduce the number of CFS by 25 percent in the next two months. Strategies to achieve this objective might include increased patrol, increased citizen contacts, crime prevention activities, neighborhood cleanups, and so on. If officers are given an assignment or dispatched to a call, did they satisfactorily resolve the situation? If officers must repeatedly return to family disturbance calls, it may indicate that they are taking inappropriate measures on the first occasion. Supervisors must use follow-up calls and activities to ensure that officers make every effort possible to adequately manage situations.

Equity refers to the quality of police services delivered to various groups in the community (Hepburn, 1981). All citizens' problems should receive the same level of concern. This is accomplished through operational planning. Equity in police services frequently becomes a political focal point. Citizens are concerned with the number of patrol units in their area, the probability of being victimized, and the response time of the police. If police services in their area are perceived to be consistent with those of other areas, citizens are more likely to have a positive image of the police.

To a large extent, equity is at the root of the current racial-profiling controversy in policing. For years, the police did little in many minority neighborhoods. Minorities often received fewer or inferior services and viewed this as an inequitable situation (Gaines and Kappeler, 2003). As a result of community policing and problem solving, the police today are attacking crime, drug, and disorder problems in many minority communities. The end result is that more minorities are being stopped and questioned by the police. This can result in a perception of inequity since minorities are stopped at higher rates than nonminority citizens.

Finally, **accountability** refers to whether or not resources are used for proper purposes and infers that the police are public servants and, consequently, should provide services that meet public concerns and needs (Gaines and Kappeler, 2003). Police officers too often see their role as that of "crime fighters" and want to subjugate other responsibilities. Research indicates, however, that the public consistently requests the police to be more involved in peacekeeping and service activities than in law enforcement activities (Gaines and Kappeler, 2003). Managers and supervisors must ensure that officers understand their role in society and meet these citizen expectations.

MEASURING ACCOUNTABILITY CITYWIDE: COLORADO SPRINGS

The Colorado Springs, Colorado, Police Department recently implemented a new organizational performance evaluation system called the Police Accountability and Service Standards (PASS), which is a measurement system to evaluate police services and determine whether or not the agency is working effectively and efficiently. The four main goals of PASS are to (1) provide a method of accountability to the city for providing a high level of service and maintaining a secure community, (2) establish priorities of the community's needs, (3) assess the agency's ability to provide services for those needs, and (4) identify resources spent and needed to accomplish agency goals. PASS analyzes six categories of service standards: response times, clearance rates, neighborhood policing, citizen satisfaction with police services, vice and narcotics activity, and officer deployment. PASS attempts to identify the best practices in the agency, while addressing those practices that are not performing up to standard. Outcome measures were developed for each category of service standard, to explain why the department was or was not able to meet the individual standards.

Source: Information provided by the Colorado Springs Police Department; see also "Beyond the Numbers: How Law Enforcement Agencies Can Create Learning Environments and Measurement Systems," *The Police Chief,* April 2002, pp. 164–173.

Traditional Views

The police historically have been more concerned with efficiency than effectiveness, equity, or accountability. Police managers and supervisors have been primarily concerned with the number of activities generated by officers or units. Such measures include number of citations issued, number of arrests, percentage of cases cleared by arrest, number of citizen complaints about police services and conduct, conviction rates, and amount of stolen property recovered. These conventional measures, collected by most agencies for the FBI's Uniform Crime Reports (UCR), have been used as the primary source of officer performance criteria; however, they do not indicate that the department, unit, or officers are striving to achieve specified goals and objectives or that they are achieving them. Police officers may write large numbers of traffic citations, but if they are written at locations where there are few accidents or for violations other than those that contribute to accidents at specific locations, the officers' efforts will not contribute to the objective of reducing the number of traffic accidents.

Spelman (1988) compared traditional police productivity measures to bean counting. Police managers or supervisors too often focus on the number of activities, rather than what the activities are supposed to accomplish. Police activities should

Number of reports, citations, and arrests by officers are traditional performance measures still in use by many police agencies.
Courtesy Reno, Nevada, Police Department.

be directed toward some problem or goal. The police are productive when they solve some problem or accomplish a desired goal. (Note how commanders are now being evaluated in New York City Police Department, as an outgrowth of the city's COMPSTAT strategy, discussed later.)

Patrol, the backbone of any police department, has been examined in a variety of ways to generate productivity measures. Mastrofski (1984) discussed measuring patrol productivity in terms of individual officers' knowledge of their patrol area. Knowledge of the patrol beat is of critical importance and a prerequisite to effective policing (Rubinstein, 1973; Van Maanen, 1974). Unfortunately, police departments seldom measure what officers know about the area or people they police. Thus, no organizational reason exists for officers to attempt to learn their beats. Officers without adequate knowledge of their beats tend to be reactive and deal superficially with calls and problems.

Others have proposed more traditional methods for increasing patrol productivity. The National Commission on Productivity (1973) considered the availability of patrol to be the most critical factor. The commission advocated increasing the number of officers assigned to patrol, use of special tactical units to assist with directed patrol activities, flexible scheduling, and simplification of administrative chores. The thrust of the commission was to reemphasize patrol over specialized units; to maximize officer time spent on patrol; and to focus on the deterrence of crime, apprehension of criminal offenders, and the provision of noncrime services. The commission viewed efficiency as the first step to improving police patrol.

Others have taken productivity a step further and conceptualized it in terms of outputs (Hatry, 1975; Hirsch and Riccio, 1974). These researchers advocated results such as the number of arrests surviving the first judicial screening relative to the number of patrol hours for each arrest, convictions relative to arrests, number of patrol officers relative to the total number of sworn personnel in the department, patrol response time, and amount of sick time taken in relation to the number of available officers. These researchers attempted to not only examine critical patrol areas, but also to place them in a context that would allow for comparisons over time and across departments. For example, number of felony convictions divided by the number of felony arrests provides information well beyond what just the number of arrests provides. It describes the "quality" of investigations and cases. When examined for individual officers, it identifies officers who are not proficient in investigations and court presentations.

Research indicates that officers vary in their outputs. Walsh (1985) examined the arrests for one precinct in New York City in 1980 and found varying rates of felony arrests across patrol officers. He found that 63 officers did not make a felony arrest during the year; 59 officers had 1 to 8 arrests; 19 officers had 9 to 20 felony arrests; and 15 officers had 25 to 69 felony arrests. Walsh's data demonstrates the importance of productivity monitoring. Every critical area of police work can be examined similarly.

Planning and Problem Solving

The previous section addressed some of the traditional views of productivity measurement, especially as applied to police patrol. They focus on internal uses and considerations but fail to link them to external needs and outcomes. Longmire (1992) has referred to this problem as the "activity trap." An activity trap is an easily quantifiable activity, and police managers remain content to measure the activity as opposed to examining the effects of the activity on problems. Measurement of police activities must go beyond efficiency and focus on effectiveness, accountability, and equity. Police supervisors and managers must think beyond bean counting—measuring police productivity by counting activities.

If a police agency is to be productive, a large percentage of its officers' activities must relate to solving some community problem or helping citizens. Police departments have attempted to accomplish this objective through *planning,* which may be defined as "an orderly, systematic, and continuous process of bringing anticipations of the future to bear on present decisions" (Law Enforcement Assistance Administration, 1975). Planning is also, roughly stated, deciding what the police agency should be doing; it is the linking of current activities to future conditions. It is decision making regarding operational activities based on anticipated contingencies (Gaines et al., 1991).

As may be seen in Figure 6–1, top-level administrators monitor and evaluate the environment or community and identify police department goals; mid-level managers then break these goals down into unit-level objectives and develop programs to accomplish the objectives; and finally, supervisors are charged with ensuring that officers perform according to operational plans and achieve the desired objectives. The planning process becomes the link between internal measures or productivity and external needs.

FIGURE 6–1 The Planning Process

This planning model has a number of problems. First, police departments have difficulty identifying overall goals for the department and as such often resort to general statements that provide little direction for lower-level managers and supervisors (Hoover, 1993). Second, when goals are identified, it becomes difficult to make adjustments when the environment changes. This inflexibility results in discrepancies between services being provided by the department and actual community need. Third, lower-level managers and supervisors often have little input into the system. They are not involved in designing work activities or performance measures; furthermore, they are provided little opportunity to criticize or make adjustments in organizational activities that are not working properly.

Formal planning has been abandoned in some departments in favor of management systems that focus on productivity and therefore attempt to correct some of these problems. Swanson, Territo, and Taylor (1998) advocated the use of total performance management (TPM) in policing. TPM consists of three principles:

1. The collection of data from customers and employees to provide information about both positive and negative aspects of performances, along with data about productivity

2. Playing back the data in summarized forms to both managers and employees

3. Development of action plans by managers and employees to build on strengths and eliminate or reduce weaknesses

With TPM, action planning is vested at lower levels of the police department, which allows officers and supervisors to provide feedback into the planning process. Also, since TMP involves obtaining data from citizens, it allows the department to understand and respond to community problems more rapidly. TPM constructs a management structure that is conducive to productivity. It is a bottom-up planning process whereby planning originates and is conducted at lower levels of the organization.

Another similar organizational form that enhances police productivity is community oriented policing and problem solving (COPPS), which is discussed in detail in Chapter 13. Essentially, COPPS focuses on concerns in the community. Problem solving is the primary tactic used in this strategy, with the police department attempting to identify a problem and then developing a plan to solve it. Each problem is handled differently, depending on the nature of the problem, and the police department works with other units of government or private agencies in deploying solutions.

The evaluative criteria employed in the traditional policing model, such as crime rates, clearance rates, and response times, have been problematic when applied to the professional model itself and are even less appropriate for the COPPS model. Geller and Swanger (1995) argue for a marriage between the quality and quantity of performance criteria, noting "who cares how many coffee beans we have got if the java tastes nasty!" These measures also fail to gauge the effect of crime prevention efforts. Under a COPPS philosophy, the department must change its criteria for determining the quality of officer performance. Following are some of the criteria that might be used in this appraisal:

- Identifying and solving local crime and disorder problems through a police-community consultation process
- Increasing reporting rates for both traditional crime categories and non-traditional crime and disorder problems
- Reducing the number of repeat calls for service from the same addresses
- Improving the satisfaction with police services by public users of those services, particularly with victims of crime
- Increasing the job satisfaction of police officers
- Increasing the reporting of information of local crime and disorder problems by community residents and increasing the knowledge of the community and its problems by local beat officers
- Decreasing the fear of personal victimization (Peak and Glensor, 2002:328–329)

Productivity is an important issue in policing. Too often, managers and supervisors fail to measure and take steps to improve productivity. When this occurs, the department is usually stagnant and not effective in meeting the needs of the community. Every manager and supervisor in the police organization should constantly evaluate productivity so that they know where they need to be and what changes must be made to get there.

PERFORMANCE APPRAISAL

According to Mathis and Jackson (1997), *performance appraisal* is "the process of evaluating how well employees do their jobs compared with a set of standards and communicating that information to those employees" (p. 343). Thus, in order for a department to have an effective performance evaluation system, it must have (1) performance standards, (2) a method of measuring performance, and (3) a way to provide officers with feedback relative to their performance. Departments have used a variety of names to refer to the performance appraisal process: performance evaluation, activity audit, employee rating, or performance review. Generally, performance appraisal is a formal process whereby supervisors examine subordinates' performance, rate their performance, and provide them with feedback about their behavior. It is a formal process because departments generally evaluate all officers at the same time using the same rating form and system.

A department's formal performance appraisal process should co-exist with and be parallel to supervisors' constantly and informally evaluating their subordinates' behavior and performance. The informal process allows supervisors to collect information for the performance appraisal, and it allows them to take action and change subordinates' behavior that does not comply with the department's expectations. A captain should monitor the activities of his or her lieutenants and sergeants just as sergeants should constantly oversee the activities of their officers. Neither the formal process nor the informal process should supplant the other.

Rationale and Purposes

Police departments generally identify three reasons for a formalized performance appraisal:

1. To standardize the nature of the personnel decision-making process so that the rights of the job incumbent are fully represented
2. To assure the public that the agency representatives are fully qualified to carry out their assigned duties
3. To give the job incumbent necessary behavior modification information to maintain behaviors that are appropriate (Landy and Goodin, 1974:167)

Performance appraisal, in essence, is an accountability and control process. It is a system for ensuring accountability because the results can be used to evaluate individual officers and units within the police department, or the department as a whole. Administrators are able to make a number of comparisons by examining the results of performance appraisals. It is a control process because the results can be used by managers to direct and change subordinates' behavior. Supervisors can counsel individual officers who do not perform at expected levels and managers can discuss results with supervisors and unit commanders when unit productivity does not reach expected levels.

More specifically, the performance appraisal serves a number of organizational purposes: formalized feedback to employees, recruitment and selection, training, field training officer evaluation, horizontal job changes, promotions, compensation management, and discipline. We briefly discuss each of these uses.

Formalized Feedback to Employees. Superior officers, regardless of rank, should constantly provide their subordinates with feedback about their performance. This activity is the very essence of supervision. The quality and quantity of this feedback varies tremendously even within a given police department. Some supervisors will closely supervise their subordinates and constantly counsel them about their performance, while other supervisors may

Superior officers, regardless of rank, should constantly provide officers with feedback. *Courtesy Riverside, California, Police Department.*

only discuss performance occasionally with their subordinates. The department should provide the structure—a minimum agenda—to guide the evaluation and the resulting feedback session. Also, the department should establish a policy that dictates the time and frequency of appraisals. A formal feedback session for subordinates is the most important purpose for performance appraisals, although formal feedback sessions should be supplemented with informal counseling.

Recruitment and Selection. As a formal process, performance appraisal provides a structure whereby supervisors can collectively have input into recruitment and selection criteria. Personnel specialists should examine performance appraisals to identify personnel weaknesses or deficiencies. As problems are identified, they should be used to target pools of people for recruitment and to refine selection tests and criteria.

Training. The performance appraisal process should identify deficiencies or problems with officers' performance, especially those officers who recently graduated from the basic training academy. In some instances, these deficiencies are the result of improper training or the lack of training. The training staff should review the results of each annual performance evaluation to identify training deficiencies. Adjustments can then be made in the recruit or basic training program or provide veteran officers with in-service training programs.

Field Training Officer (FTO) Evaluation. As discussed in Chapter 5 (along with the newly developed PTO program), most police departments have a FTO program for their new officers, which represents a special type of performance appraisal. The program is designed to allow the department to determine whether or not officers should be retained. These field training evaluations are extremely important, because if the officer is retained after the probationary period, he or she can be dismissed only by showing cause. This creates a situation in which departments are forced to retain officers who are mediocre or who constantly cause minor problems. Below average or problem-causing officers should be dismissed during the probationary period. These evaluations can also serve to provide feedback to the training process.

Horizontal Job Changes. An accurate performance appraisal system will document officers' strengths and weaknesses. Many police departments have specialized units, such as traffic, criminal investigation, or planning, that require officers to have a variety of skills and different levels of job knowledge. Commanders of these units can review performance appraisal information to identify those officers who possess the best skills and productivity levels for these units. The performance appraisal can provide invaluable information when making decisions about transfers across units.

Promotions. The performance appraisal is one of the most common measures used in the promotion process. A survey by the International Association of Chiefs of Police (IACP) and the Police Foundation (PF) showed that 32 percent of the departments surveyed used performance evaluations in their promotion system (IACP and PF, 1973). Only written tests and oral boards were used more frequently. The performance appraisal allows the department to consider officers' past behavior when making promotional decisions. Generally, past behavior is the best predictor of future behavior. When performance is used for promotions, police departments should use promotability ratings (Cederblom, 1991). The difference between promotability ratings and performance appraisals is that promotability ratings concentrate on job dimensions that are important for the next level supervisory position while performance appraisals focus on important job behaviors for the current position. Officers should be evaluated on their performance relative to the new position rather than on how well they perform in the old position.

Compensation Management. A number of departments base annual salary increments on the performance appraisal. Officers in the Lexington, Kentucky, Police Department must have a minimum of 70 percent on their annual performance appraisal in order to receive their annual increment. Other departments provide merit raises for officers who receive high rankings. For example, the 10 officers who receive the highest performance appraisal scores for the department might receive an extra 5 percent merit raise. Performance appraisals are used extensively in determining raises for police officers.

Discipline. In some instances, the performance appraisal can be used as a basis to discipline officers. This is especially applicable when an officer fails to meet departmental expectations but does not do anything that violates policies or lies outside the bounds of acceptable behavior. Performance that is consistently below average or otherwise deficient can be documented on the performance appraisal form. If an officer fails to correct the behavior and receives several such deficient evaluations, the department might take disciplinary action. The performance appraisal formally documents unacceptable behavior and provides a record of the feedback to the officer.

Overview of Performance Appraisals

One of the problems with performance appraisals is that police managers attempt to use them for multiple purposes. The purpose of the ratings generally affects how supervisors rate their subordinates. For example, supervisors tend to be more lenient when ratings are used for promotions as compared to when they are used strictly for counseling. Consequently, when a department attempts to use a single set of ratings for multiple purposes, it tends to distort the ratings and create a variety of problems. Given the fact that performance appraisal is such a critical part of supervision, police departments should consider developing a variety of rating schemes.

It should also be understood that performance appraisal is not an event but functions as a process. Even though the performance appraisal may be administered only once or twice a year within a given department, a great deal of activity precedes it and occurs after its administration. Adequate attention must be given to these details if the performance appraisal process is to effectively accomplish its objectives.

When developing or implementing a performance appraisal system, great care should be taken to ensure that the system meets the needs of the department. Four overarching criteria should be considered for the successful implementation of a performance appraisal system: (1) relevancy, (2) sensitivity, (3) reliability, and (4) acceptability (Cascio, 1982). In terms of *relevancy,* the system must force supervisors to make judgments about subordinates' performance on critical or important work behaviors. If an activity is not important, it should not be measured or included on the performance appraisal. In terms of *sensitivity,* the system should distinguish and separate workers by the quality and quantity of their work.

In essence, there must be variability in the ratings. A system that fails to classify or identify the gradations separating employees is of little utility to the department or to individual employees. *Reliability* infers that the ratings should accurately measure subordinates' performance. Subordinates must be able to have confidence in their scores. Finally, the system should possess *acceptability* for the organization and those personnel who are being rated. Acceptability refers to how the results are used. If the results are used incorrectly, the system will not be acceptable to employees. An unacceptable system can result in internal turmoil and conflict.

Defining Rating Criteria

Defining rating criteria is a three-step process. First, the job is studied in an attempt to identify what should be measured by the performance appraisal system. This includes reviewing job descriptions, job-task analysis information, and other job-related information, such as departmental policies and procedures, to identify the critical and most important activities associated with the position. This process ultimately should provide a listing of job activities and measures of their relative importance. Hence, the most important job components can be identified for measurement.

Second, once this is accomplished, performance standards must be established. That is, at what level must subordinates perform these tasks or activities for their behavior to be deemed unacceptable, acceptable, or above average? When rating subordinates' work behavior, supervisors must have fairly specific standards to guide their decision making. Furthermore, subordinates must be made aware of standards so that they can evaluate their own work. These performance standards must then be captured on the performance appraisal rating form, the third step in the process.

Performance standards are usually articulated by using some form of the critical incident method (Henderson, 1984). The critical incidents or important tasks as identified by the job analysis are reviewed by supervisors and incumbent officers, who are asked to describe the worst, average, and best examples of how each task has been performed by fellow officers. These examples are then studied and condensed into short descriptions for inclusion in the rating system.

Job criteria and performance standards must be articulated within the performance appraisal system. That is, the department must develop rating forms and guidelines that are provided to everyone prior to their usage. Every officer must be trained on the system prior to implementing it. Police administrators cannot expect subordinates to perform at acceptable levels unless the subordinates have been informed of the standards (Figure 6–2).

When Bradley and Pursley (1987) developed a performance appraisal system for the North Little Rock, Arkansas, Police Department, they identified 202

```
┌─────────────────────────────────────────────────────────────────────────┐
│    Job          ---------->      Performance      ---------->   Evaluation │
│  Elements                         Standards                       Criteria │
└─────────────────────────────────────────────────────────────────────────┘
```

FIGURE 6–2   Defining the Rating Criteria

unique tasks that were critical or frequently performed by the officers. They also identified 23 skills, knowledge, and abilities (SKAs) that were necessary to perform the tasks. The 23 SKAs were then grouped into eight general categories: job knowledge, decision making, dependability, initiative, equipment use, communication, demeanor, and relations with others. The performance appraisal system was then developed around these eight dimensions.

A system does not necessarily have to concentrate on SKAs. The Ohio Highway Patrol implemented a performance rating system that focused on critical job tasks (Rosinger et al., 1982). Sergeants rated officers on "stopping vehicles for violations," "detecting intoxicated drivers," and "securing accident scenes."

Finally, it should be noted that performance appraisal ratings represent unique measures of officer performance. Falkenberg, Gaines, and Cordner (1991) investigated the constructs or dimensions used in performance appraisals. They found that the measurements were distinctive from other psychological dimensions or scores on management tests. They concluded that performance appraisals provided productivity information that could not be obtained through other means.

Choosing Among Rating Forms

Managers have a variety of rating forms from which to choose when developing a performance appraisal system. Each form has its strengths and weaknesses. The purposes of the performance appraisal should dictate the type of form used by a department. The following sections examine the various forms.

Graphic Rating Form

Perhaps the simplest rating form, the graphic rating form, is that shown in Figure 6–3. The graphic rating form lists the job dimensions to be rated and provides a space for the rater to select a numerical rating. When using the rating form in Figure 6–3, the supervisor would merely place an "X" or a check mark in the box that best describes the officer's performance. For example, if the officer's performance in public relations skills was "good," it would be so noted. The supervisor would make this determination by considering the officer's behavior as well as citizen input (both complaints and commendations).

A variation on the graphic rating form is the numerical rating form. The only difference between these two forms is that the descriptive adjectives at the

DIMENSION	UNSATISFACTORY	FAIR	GOOD	SUPERIOR	EXCEPTIONAL
Relationship with Others					
Quantity and Quality of Work					
Communications Skills					
Attendance and Punctuality					
Public Relations Skills					

FIGURE 6–3   Graphic Rating Form for Rating Police Officers

top of the form in Figure 6–3 are replaced by numbers, generally ranging from 0 to 10 or 50 to 100. When a numerical rating form is used, the rater is allowed to provide a numerical score, which allows the rater a wider range of possible scores. For example, the rating "fair" may be replaced by a range of 61 to 70. The rater can then give the officer a score within this range.

The foremost difficulty with graphic rating forms is that they lack reliability. Police departments generally have several people involved in rating. Sergeants from each shift or unit are responsible for rating their officers. The difficulty arises in interpreting the descriptive adjectives or numbers used in the scale. For example, one supervisor may rate a subordinate good on a dimension, while another supervisor will rate the same employee superior. As the number of supervisors involved in the rating process increases, so does the number of errors or inconsistencies. The problem is that each supervisor has associated different meanings with the adjectives. The form does not provide the raters with information to assist in giving the ratings a meaning.

Behaviorally Anchored Rating Scale

Another variation of the graphic rating scale is the Behaviorally Anchored Rating Scale (BARS; Bradley and Pursley, 1987). The BARS attempts to provide the rater with more information about performance standards and, therefore, to lead to more accurate and reliable ratings. Figure 6–4 provides an example of a BARS for rating officers' handling of domestic violence situations. Notice that in addition to a numerical rating scale and an adjective rating scale, the form includes weighted descriptions of police officer behavior or performance when handling these situations. The form contains "fixed standard" information. When rating a subordinate, the supervisor attempts to select the description that best fits how the officer typically handles family disturbances. The primary advantage of BARS is that the descriptions assist the supervisor in making better ratings and to be more consistent when rating several subordinates.

DIMENSION: HANDLING DOMESTIC VIOLENCE SITUATIONS		
Extremely good	+ 7	Uses good judgment in determining proper action. Always considers what performance is best for the victim. Will also attempt to discover a workable solution for the aggressor. Will consider actions for the short term as well as the long term.
Good performance	+ 6	Generally uses good judgment in determining proper action. Always considers what is best for the victim but does not necessarily take action that considers the aggressor or a long-term solution.
Slightly good performance	+ 5	Responds to calls. Generally collects information that is helpful in deciding what action to take. Sometimes considers both the victim and the perpetrator. Usually makes the correct decision.
Adequate performance	+ 4	Responds to calls. Attempts to collect information that is helpful in deciding what action to take. Attempts to help the victim but usually does not consider the perpetrator. Sometimes makes the correct decision.
Slightly poor	+ 3	Responds to the calls and takes information from the complainant and other witnesses. Usually will only do the minimum necessary action. Not interested in problem solving at all.
Poor performance	+ 2	Only interested in answering the call and takes the action that is the most expedient for the officer. Always does the absolute minimum. Sometimes takes action that escalates the situation.
Unacceptable	+ 1	Responds to calls because he or she has to. Sometimes becomes embroiled in the conflicts and too frequently leaves the situation worse than before police intervention.

FIGURE 6–4 Behaviorally Anchored Rating Scale

Mixed Standard Scale

The mixed standard scale (Blanz and Ghiselli, 1972; Rosinger et al., 1982) is a variation of the BARS. The mixed standard technique involves developing a number of ordered statements, similar to the ones used in the BARS. The statements then are randomly ordered and the supervisor is asked to review each statement and indicate if the officer's performance is better than (+), about the same as (0), or not as good (−) as the performance described in the statement. An officer's score is tabulated by adding the pluses, zeros, and minuses.

The mixed standard technique has a number of advantages. First, like the BARS, it provides raters with more information with which to make better ratings. Second, it is constructed and administered in a fashion that forces raters to give more time and consideration to each rating. Raters must consider each statement individually when conducting a performance appraisal. Finally, it provides a mechanism for administrators to verify the consistency of each rater's ratings. This is accomplished by reviewing the statements and scores associated with each rating dimension.

For example, consider the following two statements: (1) "Uses good judgment in determining proper action. Always considers what is best for the victim. Will also attempt to discover a workable solution for the aggressor. Will consider actions for the short term as well as the long term." (2) "Generally uses good judgment in determining proper action. Always considers what is best for the victim but does not necessarily take action that considers the aggressor or a long-term solution." If the statements in Figure 6–4 were used and a supervisor rated an officer a plus for the first statement and then rated the officer a zero on the second statement, there would be an inconsistency.

Inconsistencies can be checked by administrators and too many inconsistencies indicate that the rater did not exercise due care in assigning the ratings. This evaluation component in the mixed standard technique allows for more reliable ratings.

Forced Choice Evaluation Method

The Forced Choice Evaluation Method (FCEM) was developed in an effort to force raters to evaluate their subordinates in the blind. That is, when using the FCEM system, raters do not know whether they are rating subordinates high, low, or somewhere in the middle. This method was developed to eliminate or at least reduce rater biases and other rater errors that commonly occur in ratings.

The FCEM incorporates a series of items consisting of four statements, such as those found in Figure 6–5. The rater is asked to select the two statements that best describe the officer being rated. Two of the statements in Figure 6–5 are more important and have more weight than the other two. If the rater selects one or both of the "important" statements, the officer being rated receives points. If the "important" statements are not selected, the officer does not receive any points.

EXAMPLE OF THE FORCED CHOICE
EVALUATION METHOD

Select two of the following statements that best describe the officer being rated.

1. The officer always does a comprehensive job of completing his or her reports, and they seldom have any mistakes.

2. The officer gets along with his or her fellow officers and superiors.

3. The officer ensures that departmental equipment in his or her control is well cared for.

4. The officer writes a substantial number of traffic citations each month and always is a leader in productivity.

FIGURE 6–5   Forced Choice Evaluation Method

The statements used in the FCEM are taken from a job analysis, which identifies the most important and frequently performed tasks for a given job or position. Important or critical tasks are paired with less important task statements. The less important task statements may appear to be important to the casual observer, but they are not rated highly as a result of the job analysis. This method essentially forces raters to describe officers using predetermined statements. The raters are not told which statements are weighted. If an officer's performance does not match or associate with the critical statements, he or she does not receive points.

These performance appraisal forms and techniques are the ones most commonly used in law enforcement. There are innumerable other forms and systems. Police managers are constantly experimenting with different forms, and police departments tend to borrow systems from other police agencies. Walsh (1990) found that 79 percent of the 122 police agencies he surveyed used forms that were obtained from some other department. Regardless, research tends to indicate that it really does not matter what form or system is used; the outcome is usually the same (Giffin, 1989; Guion and Gibson, 1988).

APPRAISAL IN ACTION: COMMANDING OFFICERS UNDER NEW YORK CITY'S COMPSTAT PROGRAM

The New York City Police Department's (NYPD) COMPSTAT (for "computer statistics") program emerged in the mid-1990s as a computerized tool for tracking the most serious crimes in New York City. Initial COMPSTAT meetings found the NYPD executive and command staff analyzing statistics from the most serious crimes and plotting them electronically to determine patterns and trends—and to hold commanders accountable for reducing crime in their areas.

Since then, the program has taken over the NYPD, becoming a business management tool. Originally focusing on seven major crime categories, COMPSTAT now records information on more than 700 "performance indicators," also tracking such relatively minor crimes as prostitution, panhandling, excessive noise, public drinking, and a multitude of other minor violations. Indeed, nothing is outside the scope of COMPSTAT: Officials keep track of officer overtime, citizen complaints, and even building maintenance and how quickly a police vehicle is returned to the streets after being serviced (McKay, 2002).

Four principles govern COMPSTAT: timely and accurate intelligence, rapid deployment, effective tactics, and relentless follow-up and assessment. The assessments contain information gathered and mapped electronically; several maps can be overlapped to form layers of statistical information that can be projected onto video screens. A dense pattern of dots, or hot spots, on a map suggests a spree of criminal activity and means someone is going to be held accountable for the causes and solutions (McKay, 2002).

EXHIBIT 6-1 _____

ASSESSING NYPD COMMANDER PERFORMANCE

NYPD's COMPSTAT program has become an agency-wide philosophy that guides much of what the organization does, and it has been expanded to include accountability over and appraisal of many non–crime-fighting facets of the department. Another unique feature of the rapidly spreading reach of COMPSTAT is the manner in which the organization's commanders are evaluated. Statistics are gathered for generating a profile of commanding officers and assessing their performance. Commander Profile Reports scrutinize the commander's performance on a variety of management variables, including the commander's appointment date, years in rank, and the amount of education and specialized training he or she received. In addition, each profile contains noncrime statistics such as the amount of overtime generated by members of his or her command, the number of department vehicle accidents, absence rates, and the number of civilian complaints.

Adapted from Jim McKay (2002). COMPSTAT for the 21st century. *Government Technology* (July):30, 32.

COMPSTAT also includes a statistical profile of NYPD's commanding officers, as explained in Exhibit 6–1.

COMMUNITY POLICING AND PERFORMANCE APPRAISALS

Although a majority of the police agencies in the United States have adopted community policing, a remaining problem has been to get officers and units at the lower levels of the police department to adopt the strategy (Trojanowicz, Kappeler, and Gaines, 2002). One way to facilitate acceptance is to adopt community policing activities into the performance appraisal system. This helps to identify the important aspects or activities associated with the strategy, and it provides a mechanism for rewarding officers who excel in community policing activities. Oettmeier and Wycoff (1997) noted that the Houston, Texas, Police Department used the performance appraisal to solidify that department's community policing efforts. Figure 6–6 shows some of the criteria Houston used. Note that the performance objectives provide substantial guidance to officers in performing community policing.

IMPROVING RATER PERFORMANCE

Perhaps the most notable problem associated with performance appraisals is raters' ability to accurately evaluate subordinates. DeNisi, Cafferty, and Meglino (1984) described the rating process as a complicated operation whereby supervisors need to constantly collect, encode, store, and retrieve information for rating purposes.

Community Policing Performance Dimensions for the Houston Police Department

Tasks/Activities

Activities are listed beneath the tasks they are intended to accomplish.
Several activities could be used to accomplish a number of different tasks.

1. Learn characteristics of area, residents, businesses
   a. Study beat books
   b. Analyze crime and calls-for-service data
   c. Drive, walk area and make notes
   d. Talk with community representatives
   e. Conduct area surveys
   f. Maintain area/suspect logs
   g. Read area papers (e.g., "shopper" papers)
   h. Discuss area with citizens when answering calls
   i. Talk with private security personnel in area
   j. Talk with area business owners/managers

2. Become acquainted with leaders in area
   a. Attend community meetings, including service club meetings
   b. Ask questions in survey about who formal and informal area leaders are
   c. Ask area leaders for names of other leaders

3. Make residents aware of who officer is and what s/he is trying to accomplish in area
   a. Initiate citizen contacts
   b. Distribute business cards
   c. Discuss purpose at community meeting
   d. Discuss purpose when answering calls
   e. Write article for local paper
   f. Contact home-bound elderly
   g. Encourage citizens to contact officer directly

4. Identify area problems
   a. Attend community meetings
   b. Analyze crime and calls-for-service data
   c. Contact citizens and businesses
   d. Conduct business and residential surveys
   e. Ask about other problems when answering calls

5. Communicate with supervisors, other officers and citizens about the nature of the area and its problems
   a. Maintain beat bulletin board in station
   b. Leave notes in boxes of other officers
   c. Discuss area with supervisor

6. Investigate/do research to determine sources of problems
   a. Talk to people involved
   b. Analyze crime data
   c. Observe situation if possible (stakeout)

7. Plan ways of dealing with problem
   a. Analyze resources
   b. Discuss with supervisor, other officers
   c. Write Patrol Management Plan, review with supervisor

8. Provide citizens information about ways they can handle problems (educate/empower)
   a. Distribute crime prevention information
   b. Provide names and number of other responsible agencies; tell citizens how to approach these agencies

9. Help citizens develop appropriate expectations about what police can do and teach them how to interact effectively with police
   a. Attend community meetings/make presentations
   b. Present school programs
   c. Write article for area paper
   d. Hold discussions with community leaders

10. Develop resources for responding to problem
   a. Talk with other officers, detectives, supervisors
   b. Talk with other agencies or individuals who could help

11. Implement problem solution
   a. Take whatever actions are called for

12. Assess effectiveness of solution
   a. Use data, feedback from persons who experienced the problem, and/or personal observation to determine whether problem has been solved

13. Keep citizens informed
   a. Officers tell citizens what steps have been taken to address a problem and with what results
   b. Detectives tell citizens what is happening with their cases

FIGURE 6–6   Performance Dimensions for the Houston Police Department
Source: Oettmeier, T., and Wycoff, M. *Personnel Performance Evaluations in the Community Policing Context.* Washington, DC: Community Policing Consortium, 1997.

Many personnel experts, however, believe that this process results in more problems than the form or system utilized. The following sections expound on rating problems and possible solutions.

Rater Errors

Rater errors refer to problems that potentially occur anytime superiors rate subordinates. Errors occur for a variety of reasons, and they must be controlled if the department is to have an effective performance appraisal system. The following is a discussion of some of the most common rater errors.

Halo Effect.   The halo effect occurs when a rater evaluates a subordinate high or low on all rating dimensions because of one dimension. For example, a sergeant may believe that patrol officers should write a generous number of traffic citations. Officers who tend to write more citations receive higher ratings in all categories, while those who do not write above average numbers of tickets receive only average or below average ratings. In this example, the sergeant allows the number of citations written by officers to cloud his or her judgment about other rating dimensions.

Recency Problem.   Recency problem refers to when a recent negative or positive event unduly affects an officer's ratings. An officer may make a traffic stop that results in the seizure of several pounds of cocaine and the arrest of several mid-level drug dealers immediately prior to the end of the rating period. The sergeant doing the ratings may give this arrest undue weight and rate the officer high. It may not matter that the arrest was the only felony arrest made by the officer during the rating period, and that the officer's performance overall was less than average. Ratings should represent the average performance during the total rating period.

Rater Bias.   Rater bias refers to raters' values or prejudices distorting their ratings. People have all sorts of biases that can affect ratings: religious, racial, gender, appearance, existence of a disability, prior employment history, or membership in civic clubs and organizations. Biases can help or detract from an officer's ratings. Biases are one of the most difficult rater errors to overcome.

Constant Error Problem.   Some raters are too strict, others may be too lenient, while still others tend to rate everyone in the middle. For example, a new sergeant may rate all his subordinates lower in order to show improvement in the next rating period. These rating patterns affect the outcome of combining the ratings for several different raters. When ratings are combined, some officers have a distinct advantage or disadvantage over others.

Unclear Standards. Unclear standards is a problem when there is little agreement about the rating dimensions or associated standards. For example, sergeants may be asked to rate their subordinates on productivity. One sergeant may define productivity one way, while another may define it differently. Varying interpretations of rating dimensions substantially affect ratings. If sergeants' ratings are to be consistent, they must have a clear, corresponding understanding of the standards being used.

These five errors represent the most common rating errors. Raters can make a number of other mistakes. For example, raters tend to value officers who are more like themselves or dislike those who are different. This can apply to a person's appearance, background, education, hobbies, and so on. First impressions by new officers may also have an undue impact on subsequent ratings. Finally, officers who previously had high-profile assignments may have an advantage over other officers because of their being perceived as better. Innumerable factors that have nothing to do with officers' performance can affect their performance appraisal ratings.

Rater Training

One of the most important methods for controlling rater error is rater training. Too often, supervisors are given performance appraisal forms and expected to accurately complete them. Research indicates that the rating process is extremely complicated (DeNisi et al., 1984) and that rater training is one of the better administrative mechanisms for improving ratings. Bernardin and Buckley (1981) identified three key performance appraisal areas that require training: enhanced observational skills, a common frame of reference for raters, and the ability to be critical.

Enhanced Observational Skills. As noted earlier, the rating process involves several steps: collecting information, encoding the information into a meaningful form, storing the information, and finally, retrieving the information for rating purposes. Raters must be taught to gather and store pertinent information in a fashion that enhances the rating process.

When faced with the prospect of having to complete performance appraisal forms for their subordinates, supervisors often hurriedly ponder past activities, make judgments about those activities, and prepare to complete the required forms. This haste generally results in consideration of only partial data and leads to errors such as the halo effect or recency.

Raters can be trained to collect and store information for the rating process. Supervisors should be taught to observe and critically analyze subordinates' performance. The key here is to focus on critical job events. They should also be trained to keep diaries of subordinates' behavior and activities throughout the rating period. In an effort to ensure that all pertinent information is considered, raters should retain both positive and negative information, regardless of its magnitude. A few exceptional examples of work behavior should not counterbalance an otherwise below average performance period. Likewise, one or two mistakes should not overly blemish a productive work period.

Common Frame of Reference.　　In an effort to reduce the error of unclear standards, training should be provided to all raters to ensure that they clearly understand, accept, and adhere to the rating standards. Raters must use a common frame of reference when completing performance appraisals. For example, if sergeants are rating subordinates on interpersonal relationships, each sergeant involved should have the same understanding of what interpersonal relationships mean. If variation occurs among the sergeants, some officers will be treated unfairly, departmental morale will be affected, and the intended purposes of the performance appraisals will not be fulfilled. Behavioral anchors such as those found on a BARS are helpful in eliminating this problem, but a training program that exposes all raters to thorough and complete discussion of the rating dimensions, their meanings, and expected behavior will substantially reduce rater error. A training program can provide raters with video-recorded examples or vignettes of critical incidents of the job. Supervisors' ratings can be analyzed and discussed in a classroom atmosphere to foster more accurate ratings.

Critical Appraisal of Subordinates.　　As mentioned earlier, one of the major problems associated with performance appraisals is that raters oftentimes are too lenient and rate all or most of their subordinates too high. They fail to critically appraise subordinates' activity and behavior and reflect that appraisal in their ratings. This occurs for a number of reasons. It is a natural behavioral reaction since almost everyone attempts to avoid confrontations. Supervisors may fail to properly supervise subordinates and believe that they could not adequately explain or defend lower ratings. Raters may evaluate everyone high because low ratings may cast a doubt on the rater's ability to supervise. Another reason is that supervisors may not properly understand departmental expectations and therefore cannot accurately distinguish a poor performance from a good one.

A training program can emphasize the standards used to evaluate officers, and it can be used to underscore the importance of making accurate ratings that distinguish good, average, and below average performers. Training can indoctrinate raters on how ratings are used and the importance of making distinctions in ratings. In the end, training is one of the most important mechanisms that a department can use to enhance the accuracy of ratings.

It is important that officers are evaluated on their individual assignments. A footbeat officer
would not necessarily be evaluated on the exact same criteria as one who is assigned to
detectives, traffic, or training.
Courtesy NYPD Photo Unit.

DIFFERENT APPROACHES TO APPRAISAL

Using Peer and Self-Evaluations

For the most part, performance appraisals have been viewed as a management
prerogative in policing. That is, performance appraisals have been used almost
exclusively by management to evaluate subordinates. Few departments have
experimented with or used peer evaluations (Gaines and Falkenberg, 1992; Love,
1981a, 1981b) or subordinate evaluations of superiors (McEvoy, 1987).

Peer evaluations refer to officers completing performance appraisal forms
for the other officers within their work group. One supposed benefit of peer evaluations is that as the result of closer working relationships, officers possess more
information about their colleagues than do supervisors and can consequently
make better appraisals. It is questionable as to whether or not officers have more

knowledge about their peers than do their supervisors, but they unquestionably have different information. The circumstances in which police work is conducted among peers is probably quite different from the interactions among police officers and their supervisors. The inclusion of this information in the performance appraisal process could be beneficial.

Love (1981a, 1981b) noted that the primary concerns with peer evaluations are reliability, validity, friendship bias, and negative user reactions. Love's research indicated that peer evaluations were just as reliable and valid as performance appraisals. Furthermore, he did not find that friendship bias affected ratings. When placed in a position of rating peers, officers would attempt to consider only those aspects of a peer's performance that related to the rating dimensions. Finally, they, like many supervisors, found performance rating to be a negative experience.

Gaines and Falkenberg (1992) investigated peer evaluations in an attempt to determine what they measured. They examined the relationships among peer ratings and a number of psychological dimensions, management qualities, and departmental performance appraisals. No consistent relationships were identified. They concluded that peer evaluations represent unique measures of performance, which provide information that otherwise is not included in performance appraisals.

Finally, self-evaluations must also be considered (Kakar, 1998). It may be beneficial to a department to have officers complete self-evaluations to identify their own strengths and deficiencies. Supervisors could compare the department's performance appraisal with the individual's self-evaluation to identify areas of agreement, blind spots, and areas of over evaluation. The self-evaluation could also serve as an excellent catalyst when discussing performance with subordinates.

The extent to which agencies are using peer, subordinate, or self-evaluations is not known. Police managers should be open minded and use the type of rating system that best meets the needs of the department.

Subordinate Appraisal of Supervisors

McEvoy (1987) investigated subordinate appraisals of managers, with the following findings:

1. Subordinate appraisals frequently have been used for management development rather than evaluation purposes, but anecdotal reports of their use for both purposes are generally positive.

2. Managers report that subordinate feedback is helpful in improving their performance.

3. A substantial amount of "halo" exists in subordinate appraisals of their managers as they tend to rate superiors on only one dimension rather than differentiating the multiple dimensions that are commonly used on the rating forms.

4. A modest positive correlation exists between ratings by subordinates and ratings of the same individuals by superior officers, indicating some level of validity or agreement.

McEvoy's research revealed that subordinate ratings were effective in predicting manager success. He compared the results of subordinate appraisals to the results of an assessment center and found that subordinate appraisals more effectively predicted future performance appraisal scores. He also found that regardless of the number of dimensions used in such ratings, subordinates tended to rate superiors on one universal dimension.

PROVIDING APPRAISAL FEEDBACK

A critical component of the performance appraisal process is subordinate feedback. Substantial efforts should be exerted to ensure that this purpose is effectively achieved. The previous sections addressed a number of mechanical aspects of performance appraisal, including how to prepare raters for rating. It is just as important for supervisors to prepare for feedback sessions. There are a number of steps in this process:

1. Prior to a feedback session, supervisors should refresh their memories regarding the ratee's productivity record. Departmental printouts and other productivity records should be reviewed. This information should be discussed as a supplement to the performance appraisal itself.

2. Supervisors should know what they are going to say or the major points they will cover before the interview. Furthermore, the supervisor should ensure that the feedback session does not become sidetracked; the officer's performance should remain the focal point at all times. These interviews should be planned or mapped out prior to the interview. Supervisors should even rehearse interviews when possible.

3. Both positives and negatives should be discussed. Positive reinforcement of good work habits is just as important as eliminating negative ones.

4. Force the ratee to discuss his or her performance. This can be accomplished by asking questions or requesting the ratee to comment about his or her performance. This helps the subordinate to realistically evaluate his or her behavior.

5. Force the ratee to develop a performance plan. If an officer is substantially below expectations, require the officer to present a plan explaining how he or she will improve his or her performance. The plan can be verbal or written, but it is critical that a plan be presented. The plan can be used in subsequent counseling sessions should they be necessary.

6. Leave the subordinate with a clear understanding of what is expected. This can be accomplished by providing the officer with goals and objectives, discussing other officers' performance, and reinforcing overall departmental goals. Regardless of method used, subordinates must have clear ideas of what is expected of them if they are to be good employees.

No matter what methods a department uses to evaluate police officer performance, the system will be only as good as the feedback sessions that supervisors provide subordinates. Unfortunately, many supervisors take this responsibility too lightly and do only a mediocre job during the performance appraisal feedback session. Police managers must ensure that effective feedback sessions are conducted by supervisors.

EFFECTIVENESS OF PERFORMANCE APPRAISALS

What Works? Reasons for Ineffectiveness

The performance appraisal is an important supervisory tool. Theoretically, it should assist in increasing productivity and contribute to a police department's overall performance. Sometimes it is not effectively used, and the police department fails to reap its benefits. Walsh (1990) surveyed 122 police sergeants from several small and medium-size police departments and found that 87 percent reported that the performance evaluation was of little utility to them. That is, it was not helpful in their job as supervisors. The most common reasons given as to why performance appraisals were ineffective were

1. The performance criteria are subjective.
2. The systems lack managerial control. This creates rater inconsistency and favoritism.
3. Supervisors have little input into the process but are its major users.
4. The forms are filed and mean nothing.
5. Management is not concerned about performance, just making sure that things run smoothly.
6. Supervisor's performance assessments are changed by administrators who have not observed the officer perform on a daily basis. (p. 101)

Walsh's findings clearly indicate that police departments must pay more attention to how their performance appraisal systems function. The problems voiced by the supervisors in Walsh's study are the result of deficiencies or problems that were addressed earlier. Such problems also indicate that departments are failing to use the information produced through performance appraisals. Police managers must put forth the effort to ensure that performance appraisals are functioning as envisioned by the department.

Performance Targeting

Halachmi (1993) recognized these same deficiencies and believes that police departments should abandon traditional performance appraisals and adopt performance targeting. *Performance targeting* occurs when the subordinate and the supervisor jointly identify performance goals for the subordinate and how they are to be achieved. Such an arrangement provides the subordinate with superior direction, and it creates an obligation on the part of the supervisor to work with the subordinate to ensure that the subordinate has the resources to accomplish assigned goals.

Performance targeting can be used at all levels within the chain of command. It is a modified form of management by objectives (MBO), in which a superior officer identifies objectives for the next subordinate level. This ensures that activities throughout the department are ultimately tied to the department's primary goals. Thus, a patrol captain could use a modified form of COMSTAT and identify priorities for each of his or her patrol squads. The patrol supervisors would then work with their officers to ensure that the objectives were met. The officers would then be evaluated on how well they contributed to accomplishing these objectives, rather than on global standards that usually are used on performance appraisals.

The Bainbridge, Ohio, Police Department implemented a modified performance targeting system (Kramer, 1998). The department identified a number of performance dimensions for which officers are evaluated. Unit commanders could select from the list for an individual officer or for an entire unit. Only important dimensions for a specific job were selected. The system gave the department a measure of flexibility allowing managers to have a focused evaluation. This allowed supervisors to select performance areas and provide officers with better direction.

⎯⎯ Case Studies ⎯⎯⎯⎯⎯⎯⎯⎯⎯⎯⎯⎯⎯⎯⎯⎯⎯⎯⎯

Following are two case studies that enable the reader to consider some of the substantive issues involved with appraising officer performance and to consider some possible solutions.

Knowing Your People, or Searching for Hidden Meanings

You are a supervisor in Bay City, recently transferred from the robbery/homicide section of detectives to day shift patrol. You begin your new assignment by reviewing crime reports and calls for service data for the area and meeting with each of your officers to discuss their view of the area's problems and their work productivity. The south area of the district is divided geographically into five beats, consisting of single-family homes, small commercial businesses, and several large apartment complexes. Approximately 50,000 citizens live in the area; most are middle-class white and Hispanic people who reside and work in the area. Crime analysis data reveals that the most prevalent crime problems are daytime burglaries and thefts of property from the apartment complexes, juvenile drinking, and vandalism. The vandalism is not gang related and is mostly spray paint tagging of schools and businesses. There are three main thoroughfares through the area, but traffic accidents are low in comparison with the rest of the city. After reviewing three of your officers' past performance evaluations, you determine that Officer Stengel leads the patrol division in felony arrests. Her follow-up investigations have led to the identification of two groups of daytime burglars who were truants from the local school. A review of other performance areas shows similar good effort. Officer Robbins has just completed his probationary period. Troubled by the vandalism, he began working with the city attorney and local business owners on an ordinance that would ban the sale of spray paint to juveniles. Robbins makes every effort to work on this project between calls for service, but some of his fellow officers have complained about having to handle some of his calls. Officer Franklin has 10 years' experience and would like to work a motorcycle traffic assignment. Selections will be made in six months. In an effort to demonstrate his interest in that assignment, Franklin currently leads the department in the number of citations written. He also leads the department in citizen complaints of rude behavior, but only 2 of 10 complaints in the past three months were sustained. Assume that you are about to engage in an annual performance appraisal for each officer.

1. Discuss your observations of each officer's performance.
2. Do you have any concerns about any of the behaviors demonstrated by any of the officers?
3. Do the officers satisfactorily address the district's problems?
4. Are there any other issues that may require your attention? If so, how would you handle those issues?
5. Which performance appraisal system (among those described in this chapter) would you opt to use?

Seeing the World (and Subordinates) Through Rose-Colored Glasses

Sgt. Wilcox is a 10-year veteran, having worked mostly in the fraud section of detectives. She is recently assigned to day shift patrol division and assumes responsibilities for a team of mostly experienced and capable officers. Wilcox believes in a participative management style and therefore thinks that her officers should be involved in setting their work goals and objectives and should participate in the performance evaluation process. Wilcox meets with her team and outlines her approach to performance evaluations. Believing that this should be a positive experience for all, she instructs her officers to keep an individual log of their more notable achievements during the performance period. At the end of the rating period, Wilcox uses their top five accomplishments as a basis for their annual evaluation. When the first rating period is completed, Wilcox is pleased to find that her officers received some of the highest performance ratings in the department. However, she recently learns from her lieutenant that other supervisors are voicing criticisms of her evaluation methods. She is now confused about her evaluation method.

1. What, if any, do you perceive to be the good aspects of Wilcox's personal method of evaluation?
2. What problems might arise from Sgt. Wilcox's rating system?
3. What rater errors are being committed, if any; what might be the basis for the peer supervisors' criticisms?

SUMMARY

This chapter has addressed two important issues in police management, productivity measurement and performance appraisals. First-line supervisors are primarily responsible for a department's productivity. They supervise line personnel and must ensure that officers are not only productive, but that their activities have a demonstrable effect on community problems. Managers and commanders, on the other hand, must assist in the development of programs and strategies that result in officers being able to accomplish goals and objectives. Thus, productivity is best accomplished through a team effort with management, supervisors, and officers working to provide services to the community.

One way departments manage productivity is through performance evaluations. Performance evaluations are formalized feedback sessions at which supervisors advise their subordinates about the quantity and quality of their activity. One of the purposes of the performance appraisal is to use it as a supervisory tool to direct officers' behavior. Moreover, performance appraisals should be used throughout the chain of command or anywhere there is a superior-subordinate relationship.

Performance appraisals also serve a variety of other departmental functions. When they are used for more than one function, the process becomes complicated and stated objectives may not easily be accomplished. The critical aspect about performance appraisals is that they represent a system, and as such every aspect of the system from developing rating forms to training supervisors to rate and provide feedback to officers must be managed properly. If any one link in the system is defective, the total system will be damaged.

ITEMS FOR REVIEW

1. Define productivity measurement, and why it is so important for supervisory personnel.

2. Explain how efficiency, effectiveness, equity, and accountability are of concern when attempting to measure productivity.

3. Describe how evaluation criteria employed in the traditional policing model, such as crime rates, clearance rates, and response times, have been problematic when applied to the community oriented policing and problem solving strategy.

4. Define performance appraisal and describe its purposes and uses.

5. Describe the various rating forms that supervisors may employ in a performance appraisal system, as well as some of the strengths and weaknesses of each.

6. Delineate some of the problems and errors that exist when raters attempt to evaluate subordinates.

7. Explain some of the advantages, disadvantages, and problems of having subordinates rate their supervisors.

REFERENCES

Bernardin, H. J., and Buckley, M. R. (1981). Strategies in rater training. *Academy of Management Review* 6(2):205–212.

Blanz, F., and Ghiselli, E. E. (1972). The mixed standard scale: A new rating system. *Personnel Psychology* 25:185–199.

Bradley, D. E., and Pursley, R. D. (1987). Behaviorally anchored rating scales for patrol officer performance appraisal: Development and evaluation. *Journal of Police Science and Administration* 15(2):37–44.

Cascio, W. F. (1982). Scientific, legal, and operational imperatives of workable performance appraisal systems. *Public Personnel Management Journal* 11(4):367–375.

Cederblom, D. (1991). Promotability ratings: An underused promotion method for public safety organizations. *Public Personnel Management Journal* 20(1):27–34.

DeNisi, A., Cafferty, T. P., and Meglino, B. M. (1984). A cognitive view of the performance appraisal process: A model and research propositions. *Organizational Behavior and Human Performance* 33:360–396.

Falkenberg, S., Gaines, L. K., and Cordner, G. W. (1991). An examination of the constructs underlying police performance appraisals. *Journal of Criminal Justice* 19:351–359.

Flanagan, J. C. (1949). A new approach to evaluating personnel. *Personnel* (January/February):42.

Gaines, L., and Falkenberg, S. (1992). Anatomy of peer evaluations: What do they measure? *Justice Professional* 6(1):39–46.

Gaines, L., and Kappeler, V. (2003). *Policing in America,* 3d ed. Cincinnati: Anderson.

Gaines, L. K., Southerland, M. D., and Angell, J. E. (1991). *Police administration*. New York: McGraw-Hill.

Geller, W. A., and Swanger, G. (1995). *Managing innovation in policing: The untapped potential of the middle manager.* Washington, DC: Police Executive Research Forum.

Giffin, M. E. (1989). Personnel research on testing, selection and performance appraisal. *Public Personnel Management* 18(2):127–137.

Guion, R. M., and Gibson, W. M. (1988). Personnel selection and placement. *Annual Review of Psychology* 39:349–374.

Halachmi, A. (1993). From performance appraisal to performance targeting. *Public Personnel Management* 22(2):323–344.

Hatry, H. P. (1975). Wrestling with police crime control productivity measurement. In J. Wolfe and J. Heaphy, eds., *Readings on productivity in policing.* Washington, DC: Police Foundation, pp. 86–128.

Henderson, R. I. (1984). *Performance appraisal.* Reston, VA: Reston.

Hepburn, J. R. (1981). Crime control, due process, and measurement of police performance. *Journal of Police Science and Administration* 9(1):88–98.

Hirsch, G. B., and Riccio, L. J. (1974). Measuring and improving the productivity of police patrol. *Journal of Police Science and Administration* 2(2):169–184.

Hoover, L. T. (1993). Police mission: An era of debate. In L. Hoover, ed., *Police management: Issues and perspectives.* Washington, DC: Police Executive Research Forum, pp. 1–30.

International Association of Chiefs of Police and the Police Foundation (1973). *Police personnel practices in state and local governments.* Washington, DC: Police Foundation.

Kakar, S. (1998). Self-evaluations of police performance: An analysis of the relationship between police officers' education level and job performance. *Policing: International Journal of Police Strategies and Management* 21(4):632–646.

Kramer, M. (1998). Designing an individual performance evaluation system. *FBI Law Enforcement Bulletin* 67(3):20–27.

Kuper, G. H. (1975). Productivity: A national concern. In J. Wolfle and J. Heaphy, eds., *Readings on productivity in policing.* Washington, DC: Police Foundation, pp. 1–10.

Lab, S. P. (1984). Police productivity: The other eighty percent. *Journal of Police Science and Administration* 12(3):297–302.

Landy, F., and Goodin, C. (1974). Performance appraisal. In O. Stahl and R. Staufenberger, eds., *Police personnel administration.* North Scituate, MA: Duxbury, pp. 180–181.

Law Enforcement Assistance Administration (1975). *Criminal justice planning workbook.* Washington, DC: Author.

Longmire, D. R. (1992). Activity trap. In L. Hoover, ed., *Police management: Issues and perspectives.* Washington, DC: Police Executive Research Forum, pp. 117–136.

Love, K. G. (1981a). Accurate evaluation of police officer performance through the judgment of fellow officers: Fact or fiction? *Journal of Police Science and Administration* 9(2):143–149.

Love, K. G. (1981b). Comparison of peer assessment methods: Reliability, validity, friendship bias, and user reaction. *Journal of Applied Psychology* 66(4):451–457.

Mastrofski, S. (1984). Police knowledge of the patrol beat as a performance measure. In G. Whitaker, ed., *Understanding police agency performance.* Washington, DC: National Institute of Justice, pp. 55–76.

Mathis, R., and Jackson, J. (1997). *Human resource management.* St. Paul: West.

McEvoy, G. M. (1987). Using subordinate appraisals of managers to predict performance and promotions: One agency's experience. *Journal of Police Science and Administration* 15(2):118–124.

McKay, J. (2002). COMPSTAT for the 21st century. *Government Technology* (July):30, 32.

National Commission on Productivity (1973). *Opportunities for improving productivity in police services.* Washington, DC: Author.

Oettmeier, T., and Wycoff, M. (1997). *Personnel performance evaluations in the community policing context.* Washington, DC: Community Policing Consortium.

Peak, K. J., and Glensor, R. W. (2002). *Community policing and problem solving: Strategies and practices,* 3d ed. Upper Saddle River, NJ: Prentice Hall.

Rosinger, G., Myers, L. B., Levy, G., Loar, M., Mohrman, S. A., and Stock, J. R. (1982). Development of a behaviorally based performance appraisal system. *Personnel Psychology* 35:75–88.

Rubinstein, J. (1973). *City police.* New York: Farrar, Straus and Giroux.

Spelman, W. (1988). *Beyond bean counting: New approaches for managing crime data.* Washington, DC: Police Executive Research Forum.

Swanson, C. R., Territo, L., and Taylor, R. W. (1998). *Police administration: Structure, processes, and behavior.* New York: Macmillan.

Trojanowicz, R., Kappeler, V., and Gaines, L. (2002). *Community policing.* Cincinnati: Anderson.

Van Maanen, J. (1974). Working the street: A developmental view of police behavior. In H. Jacob, ed., *The potential for reform of criminal justice.* Criminal Justice System Annals, Vol. 3. Beverly Hills: Sage, pp. 83–130.

Walsh, W. F. (1990). Performance evaluation in small and medium police departments: A supervisory perspective. *American Journal of Police* 9(4):93–109.

Walsh, W. F. (1985). Patrol officer arrest rates: A study of the social organization of police work. *Justice Quarterly* 2(3):271–290.

Wilson, J. Q. (1968). *Varieties of police behavior.* Cambridge, MA: Harvard University Press.

7

Stress, Wellness, and Employee Assistance Programs

---❖---

LEARNING OBJECTIVES

After reading this chapter, the student will:
- know the primary stressors for police officers, supervisors, and managers, and their impact over the course of a career
- be able to list ways in which police officers may reduce stress levels, and the responsibility of supervisors and managers in this endeavor
- know the meaning of health and wellness
- know how employee assistance programs operate and can enhance police officer health

There are two ways of meeting difficulties: you alter the difficulties or you alter yourself meeting them.

—Phyllis Bottome

Health is a state of complete physical, mental and social well being, and not merely absence of disease or infirmity.

—Heave

INTRODUCTION

There is a side of policing, and its supervision and management, that we would prefer to ignore: the stress that is induced by the job. Indeed, Sir W. S. Gilbert observed that "When constabulary duty's to be done, the policeman's lot is not a happy one" (quoted in Bartlett, 1992:529). Furthermore, William A. Westley (1970:3) observed that "The policeman's world is spawned of degradation, corruption and insecurity. He walks alone, a pedestrian in Hell."

The people police deal with today are often heavily armed and arrogant. Being a cop has been described as a "stop-and-go nightmare" (Witkin, Gest, and Friedman, 1990:32). The job of policing has never been easy, but the danger, frustration, and family disruption of the past have been made worse by the drug war and violent criminals who have more contempt for the police than ever before. Furthermore, as will be seen later, compounding this situation is that the officer's own organizational policies and practices often generate more stress than the streets.

Therefore, police supervisors, managers, and administrators have become increasingly concerned about the health and welfare of their employees and must ensure that employees are mentally and physically prepared for the challenges of the workplace. This chapter focuses on the supervisor's role in recognizing and dealing with stress.

The chapter begins with a definition of stress and the patterns of its effects over a career. Following that is a discussion of the major stressors that are specific to police work, from both inside and outside the organization. The effects of stress on the individual officer as well as the agency are then examined, including ways of coping with it. Employee wellness programs are reviewed, including a discussion of employee assistance programs. After an overview of how police supervisors and managers can assist in stress recognition and treatment, the chapter concludes with two case studies.

UNDERSTANDING POLICE STRESS

Dimensions and Process

Police work is different from any other occupation in our society. Our police system is society's primary mechanism for controlling aberrant and illegal behavior. As such, society vests police officers with a substantial amount of authority—a level of authority possessed by no other occupation—including the right to employ deadly force or to deny someone his or her freedom.

This work environment can and does have adverse effects on police officers. It creates stress, which may be defined as a force that is external in nature that causes both physical and emotional strain upon the body. The late Hans Selye, who is known as "the father of stress research," defined stress as a nonspecific response of a body to demands placed on it. Succinctly, stressors are situations or occurrences outside of ourselves that we allow to turn inward and cause problems.

Stress has two dimensions. First, it can be positive or negative. Positive stress is referred to as *eustress,* while negative stress is called *distress.* When people think about stress, they usually focus on negative stress and negative situations; however, positive events in our lives can create stress. For example, an officer's promotion to sergeant is a positive experience, but at the same time, it creates stress. The officer has to react and adjust to the new position. The promotion, although positive for the officer's career, is somewhat psychologically disruptive.

Second, stress has a magnitude dimension. Using a list of 144 stressful events, Sewell (1983) surveyed 250 police officers in a Federal Bureau of Investigation (FBI) National Academy class and found the three most stressful events reported by officers were violent death of a partner in the line of duty, dismissal from the force, and the taking of a life in the line of duty. Although few police contacts are of this magnitude, police officers are confronted with a variety of situations daily, and each stressful situation affects the officer differently. Table 7–1 provides a listing of the top 25 most stressful situations.

Traumatic stress is the result of an extremely stressful event, such as a line-of-duty shooting or a hostage situation. This stress is immediate and has a significant and profound impact on the officer. On the other hand is *chronic stress,* which generally represents the accumulation of the effects of numerous stressful events over time. Each can adversely affect a police officer and result in physical, emotional, and psychological problems. Traumatic stress may subside over time, but chronic stress for many police officers is ever-present.

Selye (1981) formulated the general adaptive syndrome (GAS) to describe the stress process. GAS consists of three stages: (1) alarm, (2) resistance, and (3) exhaustion. The alarm stage occurs when the stressful event happens and the individual becomes aware of the event. Psychological and physiological reactions follow. A variety of psychological reactions can surface, including fear, anxiety,

TABLE 7–1 Twenty-five Most Stressful Law Enforcement Critical Life Events

1. Violent death of a partner in the line of duty
2. Dismissal from the force
3. Taking a life in the line of duty
4. Shooting someone in the line of duty
5. Suicide of an officer who is a close friend
6. Violent death of another officer in the line of duty
7. Murder committed by a police officer
8. Duty-related violent injury (shooting)
9. Violent job-related injury to another officer
10. Suspension
11. Passed over for promotion
12. Pursuit of an armed suspect
13. Answering a call to a scene involving violent nonaccidental death of a child
14. Assignment away from family for a long period of time
15. Personal involvement in a shooting incident
16. Reduction in pay
17. Observing an act of police corruption
18. Accepting a bribe
19. Participating in an act of police corruption
20. Hostage situation resulting from aborted criminal action
21. Response to a scene involving the accidental death of a child
22. Promotion of inexperienced/incompetent officer over you
23. Internal affairs investigation against you
24. Barricaded suspect
25. Hostage situation resulting from a domestic disturbance

Source: J. Sewell. 1981. Police stress. *FBI Law Enforcement Bulletin* 50(4):7–11.

depression, apprehension, or aggressiveness. Physiological reactions include an increase in heart rate and a release of adrenaline into the bloodstream. If the threat subsides, the individual ultimately returns to a normal state.

Resistance is the process whereby the individual attempts to cope or co-exist with the stress. The threat remains, but the individual continues to muster the strength to endure and contend with the situation. Resistance is characterized by continued psychological and physiological changes or adaptations in the individual. Exhaustion is the point at which the individual is no longer able to effectively cope with the stressful situation. If the stressful event continues, the individual experiences physical, emotional, or psychological problems. Physiological responses can be as severe as a heart attack. Emotional responses include withdrawal, lack of motivation, and anxiety. Psychologically, an individual may reach the point that he or she cannot properly function at work or home. For example, an officer may be unable to nurture his or her children or withdraw from all social responsibilities such as church, children's education, or interaction with family members.

No human being can exist in a continuous state of alarm. The body strives to maintain its normal state, homeostasis, and to adapt to the alarm, but it can actually develop a disease in the process. The effects of stress on an individual officer are discussed next.

Patterns During a Career

A limited amount of research has examined stress patterns in police departments. Dietrich (1989) and Violanti (1983) attempted to articulate police officer stress patterns based on years of service and identified several stages of stress, which are based on Niederhoffer's (1967) four stages of police career development as shown in Figure 7–1. The first five years of a police officer's career can be described as a period of alienation and alarm. Officers essentially experience a reality shock; they discover that the job is substantially different from what they first imagined. As a result of the many negative situations in which they intervene, officers come to view citizens as the enemy. Police officers generally have a negative outlook on life during this phase of their career.

The second phase may be characterized as the disenchantment phase. Violanti postulated that this phase generally lasts from years 6 through 13. Officers become extremely disappointed, emotionally detached, and bitter about the job during this period. To a great extent, they withdraw during these years as a result of not being able to reconcile the realities of police work with their perception of "how the world ought to be." These feelings often spill over into family life causing additional stress. This is the peak period for police officer stress.

It appears that police officers get back on track during years 14 through 20. During this period, they become more interested in their families and outside activities. They may engage in hobbies and second jobs to satisfy their interests. It is a period when police work begins to become secondary. That is, during this phase officers come to realize that their jobs are not their lives and there are other, more important aspects to life. Their negativism tends to subside during this phase, and they are less bitter and cynical about the job and citizens they

Author	Stages			
Niederhoffer (1967) and Violanti (1983)	Alarm stage (0–5 yrs.)	Disenchantment stage (6–13 yrs.)	Personalization stage (14–20 yrs.)	Introspection stage (20+ yrs.)
Dietrich (1989)	Alienation from nonpolice world (0–5 yrs.)	Emotional shutdown (5–10 yrs.)	Emotional unsureness (10–15 yrs.)	Namelessness (15–20 yrs.)	Maintaining the status quo (20–35 yrs.)

FIGURE 7–1 Stress Patterns by Years of Service

serve. They often become more helpful and engaging when they respond to calls or become involved in other job-related activities. They come to realize that police work is nothing more than a job.

Finally, as their career approaches 20 years, police officers become introspective about their jobs. That is, they typically do their jobs and avoid worrying about job-related problems such as failing to get promoted, not being able to meet citizen expectations, or the demands of their superiors. They tend to take life in stride, realizing that the job is only a small part of life. They tend to focus even more on their families and their own personal needs.

These stress phases have two implications for supervisors. First, it should be noted that supervisors themselves are not immune from this stress paradigm. They frequently develop stress symptoms that affect their own performance. Supervisors must remain focused and exert every effort possible to ensure that they and their subordinates work toward departmental goals and objectives. Second, supervisors must be able to recognize the symptoms and stages of stress and help officers deal with them. Supervisors must provide social support, training,

The authoritarian nature of police organizations creates stress for supervisors as well as for officers. Here, a sergeant receives directions from a captain.
Courtesy Lexington, Kentucky, Police Department.

counseling, and, when necessary, outside intervention to reduce the debilitating effects of stress on officers.

SOURCES OF POLICE STRESS

Police officers can experience job stress as the result of a wide range of problems and situations. Next, we examine four sources of stress: (1) organizational and administrative practices, (2) the criminal justice system, (3) the public, and (4) stress intrinsic to police work itself.

Organizational Sources

A primary source of stress is the police organization itself. One survey of police officers in eight medium-sized departments found that organizationally based problems were the most stressful problems for police officers (Crank and Caldero, 1991). Police departments typically are bureaucratic, authoritarian organizations (Franz and Jones, 1987; Harrison and Pelletier, 1987; Langworthy, 1992). This situation creates a substantial amount of stress for officers. Police agencies are unique in their operation and consequently place a number of restrictions on how police officers conduct their daily activities.

A police department's authoritarian nature creates stress for individual officers in at least four ways. First, police departments follow strict rules and regulations that are dictated by top management. Line officers and first-line supervisors seldom have direct input into their formulation, resulting in officers feeling powerless and alienated about the decisions that directly affect their jobs. Second, these rules dictate how officers specifically perform many of their duties and responsibilities. They are created to provide officers with guidance and direction. Police officers, however, sometimes view them as mechanisms used by management to restrict their freedom and discretion or to punish them. Officers also view rules as protection for the department when officers make incorrect decisions or errors. In these instances, departments sometimes use rules to avoid liability when officers' actions are challenged in civil actions.

Kirschman (1997) and Lord, Gray, and Pond (1991) identified a number of other organizational stressors, which include inadequate training, volume of paperwork required of officers, limited opportunities for advancement, shift work, understaffing, and the amount of work or calls assigned to officers. Indeed, a number of problems confront the modern police department. Unfortunately, many departments do not have the resources to resolve them.

It is also necessary to discuss some of the problems faced by female police officers. Policing is a male-dominated occupation, and female officers do not have the same standing in a number of police agencies. Studies tend to indicate that the primary source of stress for female officers is sexual harassment and treatment different from that which males receive in the workplace. Women officers report that they are given different assignments, are the object of jokes (especially those with a sexual orientation), are propositioned by male officers, and generally are victimized by gender stereotyping in the department (Haarr and Morash, 1999). Many such behaviors are prohibited by sexual harassment statutes, and any other behaviors of this nature are totally unprofessional. Supervisors must ensure that female officers are treated equally in the workplace and are not sexually harassed—from both humanitarian and legal standpoints.

One of the key factors relating to organizational stress is the size of the department. Morash and Haarr (1991) found that officers in larger departments tended to experience more stress than officers in smaller departments. Some researchers suggest that the personal relationships that develop in smaller departments help mediate organizational stress (Brooks and Piquero, 1998). Police managers must understand that as a department grows and becomes more complex, officers are often subjected to greater levels of stress.

The Criminal Justice System

The criminal justice system itself can be a source of stress when officers have difficulty interacting with other components of the system or complying with the decisions made and actions taken by other criminal justice agencies. Each component of the criminal justice system affects the other components. For example, judges have openly displayed hostile attitudes toward the police, or prosecutors have not displayed proper respect to officers, arbitrarily dismissing cases, having them appear in court during regularly scheduled days off, and advocating rulings restricting police procedures (Brooks and Piquero, 1998). Another example occurs when parole officers do an inadequate job of supervising parolees, which results in their being involved in an inordinate amount of crime. The courts have the most direct impact on police officers and probably are the greatest source of stress from the criminal justice system.

Police supervisors have an obligation to ensure that police officers understand and appreciate their role within the criminal justice system, and, for their mental health, they need to let go of the case following their arrest of the subject and not be fazed by the plea bargaining (or acquittals) that might ensue.

At the same time, police managers must continually monitor the activities of other criminal justice agencies and, when problems are identified, take action to reduce or eliminate the problem. In 2001, the San Bernardino, California, Police Department noticed that the California Department of Corrections was "dumping" parolees in the city. Consequently, the city had a disproportionately high number of parolees. The police department worked with the city attorney to force the Department of Corrections to limit the number of parolees released in the city. This eventually resulted in less crime problems for the police.

The Public

Most citizens recognize that the police perform an important function in our society. In addition to combating criminal activities, the police provide many important services that otherwise would not be available. When police officers perform these services, however, they become involved in conflicts or negative situations. They arrest citizens; they write tickets; and they give citizens orders when intervening in domestic violence or disorder situations. Often, to resolve problems, they make half of the participants happy but the other half are unhappy.

The problem is that police officers develop unrealistic or inaccurate ideas about citizens as a result of their negative encounters (Albrecht and Green, 1977). For example, Crank and Caldero quoted one officer as saying, "Anytime you deal with the public they have certain images, stereotypes, and expectations of you. . . . Most people aren't happy to see the police, as it is usually some sort of negative contact" (1991:345). Skolnick (1994) noted that police officers often view all citizens as "symbolic assailants" who are not only unfriendly, but are also potentially dangerous.

In order to reduce police stress in this area, supervisors must ensure that officers keep their relationship with citizens in proper perspective. This is achieved by open, straightforward discussions of public attitudes and encounters with citizens.

Stressors Intrinsic to Police Work

Police work is fraught with situations that pose physical danger to officers. Anytime officers confront a felon, especially if drugs are involved, there is the potential for physical violence. Domestic violence, felonies in progress, and fight calls often require officers to physically confront suspects. It would seem that police work itself, since it includes dealing with dangerous police activities and dangerous people, would be the most stressful part of police work. Certainly traumatic incidents such as the bombing of the World Trade Center in New York and the Federal Building in Oklahoma City, plane crashes, and natural disasters can require long-term follow-up support for law enforcement personnel. The Federal Bureau of Investigation has created a Critical Incident Stress Management Program to provide immediate interventions and long-term treatment of trauma, which is a model for other law enforcement agencies to follow (McNally and Solomon, 1999). With another new program, tactical officers traumatized by the death or severe injury of a colleague are now able to talk about their stress with someone who might best understand—other Special Weapons and Tactics officers—through a new initiative launched by the National Tactical Officers Association and its Critical Incident Response Team; it is the first stress management program to be provided free of charge to tactical officers anywhere in the country ("Tactical officers get help," 2002).

Painful sights on the ocean floor
overcome police divers.
Courtesy NYPD Photo Unit.

Another major job-related stressor involves undercover work. The glamorous depiction of undercover officers in books, movies, and other media does not adequately portray the stress that is caused by the overall nature of the work—the isolation, danger, relationships with suspects, loss of personal identity, protracted periods of removal from family and friends, and fear of discovery (Band and Sheehan, 1999).

Research, however, tends to indicate that the actual work of policing may not be excessively stressful for officers. As noted earlier, Crank and Caldero (1991) found that organizationally induced stress was a far greater problem. Police officers understand that the job has some dangers, but they do not see them as overwhelming problems.

Regardless, the supervisor's role is to ensure that police officers view their jobs and responsibilities realistically. Police officers cannot be complacent when confronting potentially hazardous situations, for example, by using poor defensive posture when talking with a subject who is standing near the officer or sitting in his or her vehicle, which substantially increases the probability of physical injury. First-line supervisors must ensure that officers follow established policies and procedures. These orders are developed to provide as much protection to officers as possible. Commanders have a responsibility to ensure that the department's policies ensure maximum safety for officers. Also, as a result of performing command inspections and direct observations of subordinates performing field duties, they should ensure that policies are followed and that they accomplish the desired results.

DEALING WITH STRESS

The preceding sections defined stress, its sources, and some of its resultant problems. Given that stress is a significant problem in policing, departments must endeavor to reduce and, where possible, eliminate stress. As such, a number of actions may be taken to accomplish this objective. Prior to discussing these actions, however, the effects of stress on the officer and the agency must be examined.

Potential Officer Afflictions

It has been estimated that at any point in time, 15 percent of a department's officers will be in a burnout phase. These officers account for 70 to 80 percent of all the complaints against their department, including physical abuse, verbal abuse, and misuse of firearms. If officers do not relieve the pressure, they eventually may suffer heart attacks, nervous breakdowns, back problems, headaches, psychosomatic illnesses, and alcoholism (Daviss, 1982). They may also manifest excessive weight gain or loss; combativeness or irritability; excessive perspiration; excessive use of sick leave; excessive use of alcohol, tobacco, or drugs; marital or family disorders; inability to complete an assignment; loss of interest in work, hobbies, and people in general; more than the usual number of "accidents," including vehicular and other types; and shooting incidents (Fishkin, 1988). An extreme reaction to stress is suicide. Police are at a higher risk for committing suicide because of their access to firearms, continuous exposure to human misery, shift work, social strain and marital difficulties, physical illness, and alcohol addiction. Police are eight times more likely to commit suicide than to be killed in a homicide and three times more likely to kill themselves than to die in job-related accidents ("What's killing America's cops?" 1996; see also Vila, 2000).

As noted earlier, no human being can exist in a continuous state of alarm. Often, however, the problem of stress is exacerbated by the reluctance of police to admit they have problems. They often avoid seeking professional psychological help, fearing that they will be placed on limited duty or be labeled "psychos" by their peers. As they start to acknowledge the problem, many police departments are attempting to improve their recruit screening and provide better counseling programs.

It is imperative that officers learn to manage their stress before it causes deep physical and/or emotional harm. One means is to view the mind as a "mental bucket" and strive to keep it full through hobbies or activities that provide relaxation. Exercise, proper nutrition, and positive lifestyle choices (such as not smoking, and moderation with alcohol) are also essential for good health.

Stress can have a number of effects on police officers. First, officers can experience *emotional exhaustion*. When officers are stressed in the workplace, they can become emotionally exhausted, and this usually takes its toll in the home. Officers who are emotionally exhausted often withdraw or do not have the energy to cope with problems at home. They tend to isolate themselves from their families. This further compounds the stress problem because problems in the home contribute to the level of chronic stress in the workplace.

Officers under a great deal of stress tend to experience a *hardening of their emotions*. Officers tend to detach and isolate themselves emotionally from the job and their families. It becomes more difficult for the officer to express basic emotions such as love, joy, excitement with accomplishments of their children, or basic involvement in many family functions. The officer appears to be uncaring and impersonal. In some cases, this hardening of emotions leads to sexual problems such as an inability to be intimate or infidelity. These emotional responses to stress further contribute to the officer's chronic stress.

Police officers who are experiencing enhanced levels of stress tend to *be overprotective of their families*. They become overly concerned with the actions and whereabouts of family members. They tend to view all other citizens as "symbolic assailants" who have the potential to harm family members. This overprotectiveness leads to increased levels of conflict within the family as the officers tend to restrict the activities of other members of the family to an unacceptable degree.

Another stress-induced problem is *negative public image*. Stressed police officers have a tendency to view everyone negatively. For example, an officer may respond to an assault call and do little to solve the case. The officer's actions are the result of his or her feeling that the victim likely got what he or she deserved. When officers have a pronounced negative image of the public, they tend to exert little effort to do the job correctly.

Any of these symptoms can manifest themselves in the stressed police officer. When an officer is suffering from acute levels of stress for a long period, usually more than one of these symptoms will emerge. The supervisor must be ever diligent and observe officers' emotional and overt behaviors in an effort to diagnose stress problems as early as possible. Once an officer with stress problems has been identified, the supervisor must take action to reduce the problem. Some of the tools to reduce stress are addressed in later sections.

Negative Effects on the Agency

A study by the National Institute of Justice interviewed nearly 100 stress-management program directors, police administrators, mental health providers, union and association officials, officers and their families, and civilians. The respondents agreed that the negative effects of stress on individuals typically harm agencies as well as officers, leading to

- Reduced morale
- Public relations problems
- Labor-management friction
- Civil suits stemming from stress-related shortcomings in personnel performance
- Tardiness and absenteeism
- Increased turnover due to leaves of absence and early retirements
- Added expenses of training and hiring new recruits, as well as paying overtime, when the agency is short staffed due to turnover (Finn, 1997)

Social Support Systems

Social support refers to communications and actions that lead individuals to believe that they are cared for, important, and an integral part of a network of mutual obligations. Social support can be emotional in nature—people let others know that they care for them—and instrumental—the providing of assistance, such as money or doing another's work. Social support buffers or moderates the conditions of work, thus making it less stressful (Kaufmann and Beehr, 1989). Social support can be an important factor in mediating stress in policing.

Supervisors and managers must increase their ability to provide support services to officers—not only in traumatic situations, but also on a daily basis. Officers constantly need support and encouragement. Graf (1986) has identified several strategies to increase organizational support for officers. First, departments should attempt to reduce officer cynicism, which is most pronounced during the first 10 years of an officer's career. This is done through direct intervention by supervisors to correct behavior and change officer attitudes. It also involves supervisors becoming involved in a wider range of officer problems. Supervisors should be supportive but also ensure that officers' behavior is within acceptable boundaries.

Second, departments should provide counseling services. Psychologists and other professionals should be available to counsel officers who are experiencing problems. Some problems can be effectively dealt with only by professionals. At the same time, psychologists should not be used to supplant supervisors' efforts and responsibilities. Some counseling services are discussed later. It should be remembered, however, that police officers generally are resistant to using any kind of counseling services. Shearer (1993) surmises that they fear losing the respect of their fellow officers if they seek such services, or they fear that their use of counseling services may jeopardize their fitness for duty or potential for promotion. Regardless, supervisors and commanders must make efforts to ensure that these services are available and are used by officers. They must also ensure that no negative consequences ensure when officers do voluntarily use such services.

It cannot be overemphasized that the supervisor is the key to reducing police officer stress. A police department can have the best programs and training available, but their effectiveness depends on the supervisor to encourage officers to use them. The supervisor must take action to prevent job stress in the first place, and if this fails, the supervisor must diagnose the problem and ensure that the proper solution is applied. Supervisors must constantly evaluate their personnel and encourage officers to be involved in stress reduction programs.

EMPLOYEE WELLNESS PROGRAMS

When we contemplate health, we not only consider disease, but we also assess diet, mental outlook, and social integration and skills. This approach has come to be known as *wellness,* which means that individuals will adopt a lifestyle that will help them achieve their highest level of well-being. This does not mean that everyone must achieve perfect wellness, but everyone should constantly be aware of the implications of his or her actions and strive for a more healthy lifestyle that includes physical exercise, a good diet, moderate or no consumption of alcohol or drugs, avoidance of tobacco products, and the use of a seatbelt when in a vehicle.

Five important dimensions are subsumed within wellness (Anspaugh, Hamrick, and Rosato, 1991). In order to move toward optimal health or wellness, individuals must improve their lifestyle in each of the following areas:

1. *Spiritual.* Spirituality refers to the belief in some force or belief system, such as religion, science, nature, or a higher power. It includes the individual's ethics, values, and morals. It provides direction and enables people to discover and act out their basic purposes in life.

2. *Social.* Social skills are extremely important in life. People must have the ability to interact with others in their environment, and they must have the ability to form intimate relationships with significant others. Individuals must be socially mature to the point that they are tolerant of ideas and opinions that are different from their own.

3. *Emotional.* An individual is emotionally healthy when he or she is able to express feelings and to understand the feelings and emotions of others. One must be able to control stress and deal with people and situations under adverse conditions.

4. *Intellectual.* People must be able to continuously learn and use newly acquired information. This is a necessary component for coping with the job, environment, and life in general. People who fail to absorb new information have difficulty keeping up with our ever-changing society.

5. *Physical.* The physical dimension implies that individuals not only maintain an adequate level of physical ability to perform the job, but that they also strive to achieve physical well-being. This ability is measured in terms of cardiovascular capacity, body fat, and nutrition. It also means that individuals will avoid tobacco products and drugs and other substances and activities that adversely affect their health.

Each of these dimensions is important to a healthy life. An overcommitment to one area and the neglect of other areas will not result in any appreciable improvement in a person's life or wellness. Individuals must examine their lives with respect to each of these dimensions.

EMPLOYEE ASSISTANCE PROGRAMS

Historically, police departments hired or sought the volunteer services of ministers and priests to serve as department chaplains. The use of chaplains was seen as the primary tool with which to deal with human problems. Later, formal programs were developed to deal with alcohol problems among police officers. For example, the Chicago Police Officers' Fellowship began in 1955 to work with officer alcoholism, the New York City Alcohol Program was started in 1966, and Boston assigned a full-time officer to a departmental alcohol program in 1959.

It was not until the 1970s and 1980s, when increasing numbers of departments began to implement employee assistance programs (EAPs) that employee assistance was recognized as an important human resource tool. In addition to alcohol rehabilitation programs, some departments hired psychologists or counselors. The psychologists not only worked with the alcohol dependent officers, but they also worked with officers who were suffering from stress or had been involved in critical events such as shootings. Finally, the drug epidemic of the 1990s created a need for drug counseling. A number of departments started drug testing and counseling programs that were housed within EAPs.

Police officers experience a number of problems that can necessitate their use of an EAP, including drug and alcohol abuse and marital problems. Police agencies need a comprehensive wellness program to assist officers in coping with stress, but if that fails or is absent, an EAP should be available to assist officers who experience significant amounts of stress or whose health is jeopardized by stress. This is especially true when job stress results in drinking problems, substance abuse, psychological problems such as depression, or family management problems.

Advocates of EAPs note that such programs help the organization and managers. EAPs help employees who are responsible for disrupting the organization and will reduce the amount of time managers must spend dealing with problem employees. The primary function of an EAP is to reduce employee absenteeism, accidents, terminations, and compensation claims and enhance the organization's overall productivity.

Even though police supervisors are generally charged with intervening in employee problems, EAPs can play an important role in intervention. EAPs should regularly educate supervisors on how to identify problem employees and encourage them to respond. Supervisors too often cover for the troubled employee or attempt to handle the situation themselves. In most cases, formal intervention by an EAP is much more effective and beneficial to the employee and the agency, especially if done early.

Alcohol Abuse and Counseling

Excessive drinking and alcoholism remain a problem in policing, as demonstrated by the following incidents taken from newspaper reports:

- A Baton Rouge police supervisor was suspended without pay following a traffic accident. The supervisor crashed his unmarked police vehicle into a ditch. A subsequent breath test found the officer had a 0.23 percent alcohol level where the legal limit is 0.10.
- A sheriff from De Queen, Arkansas, remained on the job after being fined $750.00 and having his license suspended after pleading no contest to a drunk driving charge.
- A Ritzville, Washington, police chief was given a work release sentence stemming from a conviction for robbery. The lenient sentence was attributed to the chief's history of alcoholism.

Police officers are a close-knit group who work and relax together, often in isolation from other people. When they unwind, they generally use alcohol. When officers' drinking becomes excessive, other officers and frequently supervisors and the department cover up for them. In the end, however, covering up drinking problems postpones officers' seeking or being required to obtain assistance. When drinking behavior remains untreated, it quite often leads to legal and departmental problems.

Officers with drinking problems usually have identifiable symptoms that can serve to alert the supervisor. They tend to deny that they have a drinking problem; they often drink alone; they cannot control the amount of alcohol they consume; they crave alcohol; they have an increased tolerance to its effects; they have memory blackouts; and they develop a physical dependence on alcohol. Officers with drinking problems also tend to use more sick time and have other personal problems as a result of their drinking. Obviously, supervisors who encounter such problems among their subordinates must see that they obtain professional assistance.

Drug Abuse and Counseling

Drug abuse can also be present among officers, although it is not known if it is a significant problem. What is known, however, is that drug testing reduces the incidence of drug usage among police officers. If officers know they are going to be tested, they are less likely to use drugs. A number of departments require officers in selected assignments such as narcotics or special response teams to submit to drug testing, and some departments require officers being transferred to such units to be tested.

If an officer is found to be using illegal drugs, the police department is faced with a difficult decision: What should be done with the employee? There are a number of arguments for immediate termination. First, the police officer has committed a crime. Second, the officer has associated with known criminals when obtaining the illegal drugs. And third, the officer's drug use poses a liability problem for the police department.

Immediate termination is counter to a humane view of police personnel administration, however. It should be realized that job stress may be the primary contributing factor to the drug usage. Second, the department has a significant investment in each of its officers, and a termination decision should not be taken lightly. Finally, problem officers can be salvaged and returned to work as productive officers. Thus, termination, although an acceptable choice for officers with chronic drug problems, may not be the best solution for officers who had not previously caused the department any problems or had not otherwise been in trouble. Factors considered in making this decision include the severity of the offense (type and amount of drug used and whether or not the officer went beyond mere usage), prior drug and disciplinary problems, and the probability of the officer's being rehabilitated.

IN BRIEF: HOW SUPERVISORS AND MANAGERS CAN HELP

Stress is obviously a significant problem. The manner in which the supervisor or manager acknowledges and responds to officers' stress creates the norm to which other officers will later react. It is recommended that supervisors and managers

The death of a fellow officer is one of the most traumatic experiences that officers will face during their career.
Courtesy Washoe County, Nevada, Sheriff's Office.

consider the following practices for helping patrol officers deal with their stress (adapted from Anderson, Swenson, and Clay, 1995):

- *Use listening skills.* They should check to be sure they are accurately hearing the facts and tuning into the right emotions.
- *Read people, including their body language and what is not expressed.*
- *Be supportive.* Supervisors should actively let the officers know they want to help and are available.
- *Reward good work.* Everyone strives to be recognized when they excel.
- *Use discipline fairly.* For discipline to work, it must be applied predictably and appropriately, across officers, and across time.
- *Encourage the development of support groups.* Officers will learn to give and receive support, express themselves, develop strong team discussions, and increase trust.
- *Reflect on your own style and relationships.* Supervisors develop new values, priorities, and styles of relating and should periodically reflect on what is important, how the job is changing, and the kinds of relationships and ideas about professionalism that are being imparted.

The federal government took official notice of the problem of police stress when the National Institute of Justice awarded grants to eight police agencies and organizations for developing effective stress-reduction programs ("Stressed out?", 1997).

___ Case Studies ___

The following two case studies provide the reader with some insights concerning how quickly stress can be generated and its effect on police officers; also included are some of the difficult decisions that supervisors, managers, and administrators have to make regarding stressful situations involving their subordinates.

Near Shootout at K-9 Corral

The headlines read "Near Shootout at K-9 Corral." The department is stunned by the events of Sunday evening. During a weekly training session, K-9 Officer Tom Watson pointed his duty weapon at Officer Jack Connolly and threatened to shoot him during an argument. Fortunately, no one was injured, but Watson is under investigation for assault. Officer Watson's friends are not surprised. Since joining the K-9 Unit three months ago, he has been the subject of intense teasing, especially by Connolly, who liked to imitate Watson's stuttered speech. Watson is very sensitive about his speech and attended three years of therapy at the local university before gaining enough confidence to take the police officer test. Lately, Connolly's teasing has become more personal—he has imitated Watson's stutter over the police radio. When other officers and dispatchers began to join in, Watson asked Sgt. Aldous to speak with Connolly. Aldous explained that all new guys got teased and warned him not to make the situation worse by complaining. For the next two weeks, Watson called in sick on the six days that he and Connolly would have worked together. Just prior to the incident, Watson's fiancé had broken up with him (telling Watson she had a new love interest), he had learned that he owed a significant amount of money in back taxes to the government, and he was bitten on the hand by another K-9 handler's dog during practice exercises. When Connolly initiated his teasing on the day in question, Watson burst into a rage of vulgarities and threats, drew his service revolver, and pointed it at Connolly; other officers tackled and disarmed Watson.

1. What were some of the issues and precipitating factors leading to this incident?

2. Were there any warning signs? If so, what were they?

3. Could this incident have been avoided? If so, how?

4. What were Sgt. Aldous's responsibilities in this matter? Did he meet those responsibilities?

An Agency at the End of Its ROP

Hill City is a relatively small community of about 80,000 population, whose police department has developed an aggressive Repeat Offender Program (ROP). Its eight hand-picked and specially trained officers engage in forced entries into apartments and houses, serving search warrants on the "worst of the worst" wanted felons. Their work is dangerous and physical, thus all of ROP's officers are in top physical condition. The supervisor overseeing the ROP team, Sgt. Lyle, was a drill instructor in the military prior to joining the force. He has developed an impressive training regimen for the ROP officers. They usually work out on their own time at least once a week, have high esprit de corps, and pride themselves on never losing a suspect or a physical confrontation. They often go out partying together to "blow off steam." They generally consider themselves to be elite and "head and shoulders above the rest." One day, while the team was attempting to serve a robbery warrant at a local motel, the suspect escaped through a rear window and led three ROP officers on a foot pursuit. After running extremely hard for about six blocks, the officers became exhausted and were unable to maintain their chase.

The following week, the same suspect robbed a fast-food establishment, and during his escape he killed a clerk and seriously wounded a police officer. Irate because the ROP team failed to catch the suspect earlier, many Hill City patrol officers begin to criticize the ROP team—whose members they consider to be overly exalted prima donnas—with one officer stating to a newspaper reporter that the entire team should be disciplined and that ROP should be disbanded. In one instance, a fight nearly ensued between two officers. The situation has now reached a boiling point, causing nearly all officers to take one side or another, fomenting a lot of stress and turmoil within the small agency, and causing officer call-ins for sick leave and requests for vacation time off to spike as never before. Sensing the urgency of the situation, and that his agency is being torn apart both from within and without, the chief asks all administrators (two deputy chiefs) and middle managers (four lieutenants) for input to deal with the public and the press, reduce the internal strife, and determine if any procedural or training issues require the department's attention. He further asks his six supervisors to provide input concerning means of reducing or ending the high level of hostility among patrol officers.

1. Should Sgt. Lyle shoulder any responsibility for the suspect situation and its aftermath (dissension within the department)? What kinds of inquiries might you make to determine whether or not this is the case?

2. Given that this seems to have become an agency-wide stress problem, what might the deputy chiefs, lieutenants, and sergeants recommend to the chief?

3. Should the ROP team be disbanded or continued under different supervision, training, and methods of operation?

SUMMARY

This chapter has addressed police officer stress, wellness, and employee assistance programs. These three areas represent critical issues in police supervision and management. Police departments must plan for meeting the needs of their human resources just as they plan for the purchase of capital equipment or for operations.

This chapter demonstrated that the supervisor and manager play a key role in employee stress reduction and wellness. Supervisors must constantly evaluate their subordinates, make judgments about their stress and wellness, and, when necessary, encourage officers to seek help. This is a key function of supervision.

Managers, on the other hand, must provide support to the supervisors. They must also ensure that departmental resources are available to combat the stress problem and to provide assistance to officers who have become debilitated as a result of stress. First-line supervisors can work with officers to reduce stress, but managers are the ones who must supply the resources and tools to accomplish the mission.

ITEMS FOR REVIEW

1. Explain the dimensions and processes of stress.
2. Describe the typical stress pattern by years of police service.
3. Examine the four general areas of police work that contribute to stress.
4. Explain how police personnel may attempt to manage their stress levels.
5. Describe the kinds of measures supervisors can undertake to assist officers in dealing with their stress.
6. Explain the function of an employee assistance program.

REFERENCES

Albrecht, S., and Green, M. (1977). Attitudes toward the police and larger attitude complex and implications for police-community relationships. *Criminology* 15:67–86.

Anderson, W., Swenson, D., and Clay, D. (1995). *Stress management for law enforcement officers.* Upper Saddle River, NJ: Prentice Hall.

Anspaugh, D. J., Hamrick, M. H., and Rosato, R. D. (1991). *Wellness: Concepts and applications.* St. Louis: Mosby.

Band, S. R., and Sheehan, D. C. (1999). Managing undercover stress: The supervisor's role. *FBI Law Enforcement Bulletin* (February):1–6.

Bartlett, J., ed. (1992). *Familiar quotations,* 16th ed. Boston, MA: Little, Brown.

Brooks, L., and Piquero, N. (1998). Police stress: Does department size matter? *Policing: An International Journal of Police Strategies and Management* 21(1):600–617.

Crank, J. P., and Caldero, M. (1991). The production of occupational stress in medium-sized police agencies: A survey of line officers in eight municipal departments. *Journal of Criminal Justice* 19:339–349.

Daviss, B. (1982). Burnout. *Police Magazine* (May):24–27.

Dietrich, J. F. (1989). Helping subordinates face stress. *Police Chief* 56(11):44–47.

Finn, P. (1997). Reducing stress: An organization-centered approach. *FBI Law Enforcement Bulletin* (August):22–28.

Fishkin, G. L. (1988). *Police burnout: Signs, symptoms and solutions.* Gardena, CA: Harcourt Brace Jovanovich.

Franz, V., and Jones, D. (1987). Perceptions of organizational performance in suburban police departments: A critique of the military model. *Journal of Police Science and Administration* 15(2):153–161.

Graf, F. A. (1986). The relationship between social support and occupational stress among police officers. *Journal of Police Science and Administration* 14(3):178–186.

Haarr, R., and Morash, M. (1999). Gender, race and strategies of coping with occupational stress in policing. *Justice Quarterly,* 16(2):303–306.

Harrison, E. F., and Pelletier, M. A. (1987). Perceptions of bureaucratization, role performance, and organizational effectiveness in a metropolitan police department. *Journal of Police Science and Administration* 15(4):262–270.

Kaufmann, G. M., and Beehr, T. A. (1989). Occupational stressors, individual strains, and social supports among police officers. *Human Relations* 42(2):185–197.

Kirschman, E. (1997). I love a cop: What police families need to know. New York: Guilford Press.

Langworthy, R. H. (1992). Organizational structure. In G. W. Cordner and D. C. Hale, eds., *What works in policing?* Cincinnati: Anderson, pp. 87–105.

Lord, V., Gray, D., and Pond, S. (1991). The police stress inventory: Does it measure stress? *Journal of Criminal Justice,* 19:139–149.

McNally, V. J., and Solomon, R. M. (1999). The FBI's critical incident stress management program. *FBI Law Enforcement Bulletin* (February):20–25.

Morash, M., and Haarr, R. (1991). Gender, workplace problems, and stress in policing. Paper presented at the annual meeting of the Academy of Criminal Justice Sciences, Nashville, TN.

North, J. (Feb. 3, 1993). KC police fight fat along with crime. *Kansas City Star,* p. B–1.

Selye, H. (1981). *Stress without distress.* Philadelphia: Lippincott.

Sewell, J. D. (1983). The development of a critical life events scale for law enforcement. *Journal of Police Science and Administration* 11(1):109–116.

Shearer, R. (1993). Police officer stress: New approaches for handling tension. *Police Chief* (August):96–99.

Skolnick, J. (1994). *Justice without trial: Law enforcement in a democratic society.* New York: Wiley.

Stressed out? Help may be on the way. (1997). *Law Enforcement News* (January 31):5.

Tactical officers get help from those who've been there. (2002). *Law Enforcement News* (April 15):1.

Vila, B. (2000). *Tired cops: The importance of managing police fatique.* Washington, DC: Police Executive Research Forum.

Violanti, J. M. (1983). Stress patterns in police work: A longitudinal study. *Journal of Police Science and Administration* 11(2):211–216.

Westley, W. A. (1970). *Violence and the police.* Cambridge, MA: The MIT Press.

What's killing America's cops? (1996). *Law Enforcement News* (November 15):1.

Witkin, G., Gest, T., and Friedman, D. (1990). Cops under fire. *U.S. News and World Report* (December 3):32–44.

8

Ethics, Inappropriate Behaviors, and Liability

❖

LEARNING OBJECTIVES

After reading this chapter, the student will:

- have a basic understanding of ethics and its relationship to policing
- know the kinds of improper or illegal officer behaviors that supervisors and managers must address
- understand why physical abuse and excessive force are particularly delicate issues for police leaders
- be able to explain why training and policy guidelines are important for a police agency in its effort to reduce or prevent ethical problems, misbehaviors, and liability
- be knowledgeable about how supervisors can be liable if they are negligent in their supervision of officers

We should therefore examine whether we should act in this way or not, as not only now, but at all times.

—Plato

We are discussing no small matter, but how we ought to live.

—Socrates, in *Plato's Republic*

INTRODUCTION

Police supervision and management are mostly about people and activities; in the end, the primary responsibilities of police leaders involve monitoring subordinates' activities to ensure that they act correctly relative to their tasks and duties, and that their responsibilities are conducted in an acceptable and effective manner.

Therefore, at its root this chapter is concerned with what constitutes "correct" behavior on the part of subordinates. Individuals and organizations have standards of conduct. In order to understand organizations, it is important to comprehend these standards and their etiology.

First, we frame the question of ethics with two opening scenarios—the first being an extreme illustration, perhaps, but one that demonstrates an ethical issue in which the police can become involved. Next, we discuss ethics generally, including its philosophical underpinnings and types, and then move to the matter of ethical problems specific to policing. Following that is a review of inappropriate police behaviors as they relate to ethical conduct (including lying and deception, gratuities and corruption, use of force, verbal and psychological abuse, and sexual harassment and misbehavior). Then, the liability of police supervisors is addressed in terms of holding them and their subordinates accountable for their actions. The chapter concludes with two case studies.

The overall intention of this book is to define and illuminate the roles of both first-line supervisors (sergeants) and mid-level managers (lieutenants and captains). It will be seen, however, that this chapter focuses primarily on supervisory personnel because of their far more direct role in overseeing the patrol officers, whose large numbers lead to the greatest concern about and incidence of ethical problems and improper or illegal practices.

LAYING THE FOUNDATIONS OF ETHICS: TWO OPENING SCENARIOS

Does the End Justify the Means?

It might be beneficial to begin this chapter with a hypothetical scenario: Assume that the police have multiple leads that implicate Smith as a pedophile, but they have failed in every attempt to obtain a warrant to search Smith's car and home where evidence might be present. Officer Jones feels frustrated and, early one morning, takes his baton and breaks a rear taillight on Smith's car. The next day he stops Smith for operating his vehicle with a broken taillight; he impounds and inventories the vehicle and finds evidence leading to Smith's conviction on 25 counts of child molestation and possession of pornography. Jones receives accolades for the apprehension.

You and the Oral Interview

During oral interviews for police positions, applicants are often placed in hypothetical situations to test their ethical beliefs and character. For example, assume that you are a police officer who is, say, clearing a retail office supplies store that was found to have an unlocked door during the early morning hours. On leaving the building, you observe another officer, Brown, remove a $100 writing pen from a display case and place it in his uniform pocket. What would you do?

This kind of question commonly befuddles applicants for police positions. "How am I *supposed* to answer? Do they want to hire someone who will rat on their fellow officer? Should I protect the officer? Overlook the matter? Or merely tell Brown never to do it again?" Unfortunately, applicants are often more preoccupied with a self-debate concerning how they "should" respond than with a true introspective assessment of where they stand on the question.

What Does the Oral Board Want to Hear?

How does a values-laden police agency believe that the applicant should respond to these two scenarios? First, bear in mind that criminal justice agencies do not wish to hire someone who has ethical shortcomings. It is simply too potentially dangerous and expensive—from both litigation and morality standpoints—to take the chance of bringing someone who is corrupt into an agency (possibly for many years). It probably would not take too many such individuals to cause the entire organization to become pathological. This is the justification for such questioning and for thorough background investigations of applicants.

Was Officer Jones's act regarding the taillight legal? Should his actions, even if improper or illegal, be condoned for "serving the greater public good"? Did Jones use the law properly? How close is he to "planting evidence" on an innocent citizen just because he doesn't like him? Assume that a supervisor observed Jones breaking the taillight; what action(s), if any, should follow?

Before responding to a scenario concerning Officer Brown's theft, the applicant should also consider the following issues: Is this likely to be the first time that Brown has stolen something? Don't the police arrest and jail people for this same kind of behavior? If the police were to overlook this act, how much *should* the officer be allowed to steal before determining that it's wrong (this is a tongue-in-check, rhetorical query!)?

In short, police administrators should *never* want an applicant to respond or imply that it is proper for an officer to steal. Furthermore, it would be incorrect for an applicant to believe that police do not want to hear someone "rat out" another officer. People should never acknowledge that stealing or other such activities are to be overlooked.

We invite the reader to keep these scenarios and questions in mind as we discuss ethics and ethical dilemmas.

ETHICS, GENERALLY

Philosophical Foundations

The term *ethics* is rooted in the ancient Greek idea of character. Ethics involves doing what is right or correct and is generally used to refer to how people should behave in a professional capacity. Many people would argue, however, that there should be no difference between one's professional and personal lives. Ethical rules of conduct essentially should transcend everything a person does.

A central problem with understanding ethics is that there is always the question as to "whose ethics" or "which right." This becomes evident with controversies such as the death penalty, abortion, use of deadly force, or gun control. How individuals view a particular controversy largely depends on their values, character, or ethics. Both sides on controversies such as these believe they are morally right. These issues demonstrate that in order to understand behavior, the most basic values must be examined and understood.

Another area for examination is *deontological* ethics, which does not consider consequences but instead examines one's duty to act. The word *deontology* comes from two Greek roots, *deos* meaning duty, and *logos* meaning study. Thus, deontology means the study of duty. When police officers observe a violation of law, they have a duty to act. Officers frequently use this as an excuse when they issue traffic citations that, on their face, have little utility and do not produce a beneficial result for society as a whole. When an officer writes a traffic citation for a prohibited left turn at two o'clock in the morning when no traffic is around, the officer is fulfilling a departmental duty to enforce the law. From a utilitarian standpoint (which judges an action by its consequences), however, little if any good was served. Here, duty prevailed over good consequences.

Immanuel Kant, an eighteenth-century philosopher, expanded the ethics of duty by including the idea of "good will." People's actions must be guided by good intent. In the previous example, the officer who wrote the traffic citation for an improper left turn would be acting unethically if the ticket was a response to a quota or to some irrelevant cause. On the other hand, if the citation was issued because the officer truly believed that it would result in some good, he or she would have been performing an ethical action.

Some people have expanded this argument even further. Kania (1988) argued that police officers should be allowed to freely accept gratuities because such actions would constitute the building blocks of positive social relationships between the police and the public. In this case, duty is used to justify what under normal circumstances would be considered to be unethical. Conversely, if the officers take the gratuity for self-gratification rather than to form positive community relationships, then the action would be considered unethical by many.

Types of Ethics

Ethics usually involves standards of fair and honest conduct, and what we call the conscience, the ability to recognize right from wrong, and actions that are good and proper. There are absolute ethics and relative ethics. **Absolute** ethics issues have only two sides; something is either good or bad, black or white. The original interest in police ethics focused on unethical behaviors such as bribery, extortion, excessive force, and perjury, which were always considered wrong.

Issues of **relative** ethics are more complicated and can have a multitude of sides with varying shades of gray. What is considered ethical behavior by one person may be deemed highly unethical by someone else. Not all police ethical issues are clear cut, and communities *do* seem willing at times to tolerate extralegal behavior if there is a greater public good, especially in dealing with problems such as gangs and the homeless. This willingness on the part of the community can be conveyed to the police. Ethical relativism can be said to form an essential part of the community policing movement, discussed more fully next.

If a community accepts relative ethics, it may send the wrong message to the police: that there are few boundaries placed on police behavior, and that, at times, "anything goes" in their fight against crime. As Kleinig (1996:55) pointed out, giving false testimony to ensure that a public menace is "put away" or the illegal wiretapping of an organized crime figure's telephone might sometimes be viewed as "necessary" and "justified" though wrong. Another example is that many police believe they are compelled to skirt along the edges of the law—or even violate it—in order to arrest drug traffickers. The ethical problem here is that even if the action could be justified as morally proper, it remains illegal. But for many persons, the protection of society overrides other concerns. As a Philadelphia police officer put it, "When you're shoveling society's garbage, you gotta be indulged a little bit" (U.S. Department of Justice 1997:62).

This viewpoint is known as the "principle of double effect." It holds that when an act is committed to achieve a good end (such as an illegal search) and an inevitable but intended effect is negative (the person who is searched eventually goes to prison), then the act might still be justified. There has been a long-standing debate concerning how to balance the rights of individuals against the community's interest in calm and order.

These special ethical areas can become problematic and controversial, especially when police officers use deadly force or lie and deceive people in their work. Police could justify a whole range of activities that others may term *unethical* simply because the consequences resulted in the greatest good for the greatest number—the *utilitarian* approach. If the ends justified the means, perjury would be ethical when committed to prevent a serial killer from being set free to prey on society. In our democratic society, however, the means are just as important as, if not more important than, the desired end.

The community cannot tolerate unethical behavior of its officers, but it *will* seemingly tolerate extralegal behavior if there is a greater public good, especially with today's gang and homeless problems. One example occurs in New York City, where the police department has practiced community policing for a long while and is now enjoying the popular support of many citizens for "taking back the streets," given a 56 percent reduction in murders from 1990 to 1997 (Reibstein, 1997:64). But the department is also being castigated for its use of what many perceive to be heavy-handed police tactics. Many citizens believe they have paid a price for crime reduction. From 1994 to 1996, complaints of police abuse rose by more than 50 percent. Even George Kelling, co-author of the now famous "broken windows" theory, stated that "There's an enormous potential for abuse" (Reibstein, 1997:68). He criticized the NYPD for encouraging officers to demand identification from residents or to conduct neighborhood drug sweeps, indiscriminately stopping and frisking people and too often using excessive force.

It is no less important today than in the past for police officers and supervisors to appreciate and come to grips with police ethics. Indeed, ethical issues in policing have been affected by three critical factors (O'Malley, 1997): (1) the growing level of temptation stemming from the illicit drug trade; (2) the potentially compromising nature of the police organizational culture—a culture that exalts loyalty over integrity, with a "code of silence" that protects unethical, corrupt officers; and (3) the challenges posed by decentralization (flattening the organization and pushing decision making downward) through the advent of community oriented policing and problem solving (COPPS). The latter concept is characterized by more frequent and closer contacts with the public, resulting in the minds of many observers in less accountability and, by extension, more opportunities for corruption.

Imprisoned Officer Michael Dowd is highlighted during an NYPD internal affairs workshop. *Courtesy NYPD Photo Unit.*

Although perhaps small in comparison with the number of federal, state, and local police officers, incidents of criminal police behavior, corruption, brutality, or misuse of authority do occur and are given wide media coverage when discovered. These accounts might lead one to believe that American policing is experiencing an ethical and moral crisis. Is there a significant problem in police ethics? That is a relative question; it is clear, however, that some police officers are not fulfilling the ethical requirements of the job.

CHALLENGES FOR POLICE LEADERS

Codes of Ethics and Conduct

Fair and Pilcher (1991) argued that one of the primary purposes of ethics is to guide police decision making. Codes of ethics provide more comprehensive guidelines than law and police operational procedures and answer questions that may otherwise go unanswered. When in doubt, police officers should be able to consider the ethical consequences of their actions or potential actions to evaluate how they should act or proceed. It is impossible for a police department to formulate procedures that address every possible situation an officer may encounter. Therefore, other behavioral guidelines must be in place to assist officers when making operational decisions.

LAW ENFORCEMENT CODE OF ETHICS

All law enforcement officers must be fully aware of the ethical responsibilities of their position and must strive constantly to live up to the highest possible standards of professional policing.

The International Association of Chiefs of Police believes it is important that police officers have clear advice and counsel available to assist them in performing their duties consistent with these standards, and has adopted the following ethical mandates as guidelines to meet these ends.

PRIMARY RESPONSIBILITIES OF A POLICE OFFICER

A police officer acts as an official representative of government, and is required and trusted to work within the law. The officer's powers and duties are conferred by statute. The fundamental duties of a police officer include serving the community, safeguarding lives and property, protecting the innocent, keeping the peace, and ensuring the rights of all to liberty, equality and justice.

PERFORMANCE OF THE DUTIES OF A POLICE OFFICER

A police officer shall perform all duties impartially, without favor or affection or ill will and without regard to status, sex, race, religion, political belief or aspiration. All citizens will be treated equally with courtesy, consideration and dignity.

Officers will never allow personal feelings, animosities, or friendships to influence official conduct. Laws will be enforced appropriately and courteously and, in carrying out their responsibilities, officers will strive to obtain maximum cooperation from the public. They will conduct themselves in appearance and deportment in such a manner as to inspire confidence and respect for the position of public trust they hold.

DISCRETION

A police officer will use responsibly the discretion vested in the position and exercise it within the law. The principle of reasonableness will guide the officer's determinations and the officer will consider all surrounding circumstances in determining whether any legal action shall be taken.

Consistent and wise use of discretion, based on professional policing competence, will do much to preserve good relationships and retain the confidence of the public. There can be difficulty in choosing between conflicting courses of action. It is important to remember that a timely word of advice rather than arrest—which may be correct in appropriate circumstances—can be a more effective means of achieving a desired end.

USE OF FORCE

A police officer will never employ unnecessary force or violence and will use only such force in the discharge of duty as is reasonable in all circumstances.

Force should be used only with the greatest restraint and only after discussion, negotiation, and persuasion have been found to be inappropriate or ineffective. While the use of force is occasionally unavoidable, every police officer will refrain from applying the unnecessary infliction of pain or suffering and will never engage in cruel, degrading, or inhuman treatment of any person.

CONFIDENTIALITY

Whatever a police officer sees, hears, or learns of, which is of a confidential nature, will be kept secret unless the performance of duty or legal provision requires otherwise.

Members of the public have a right to security and privacy, and information obtained about them must not be improperly divulged.

INTEGRITY

A police officer will not engage in acts of corruption or bribery, nor will an officer condone such acts by other police officers.

The public demands that the integrity of police officers be above reproach. Police officers must, therefore, avoid any conduct that might compromise integrity and thus undercut the public confidence in a law enforcement agency. Officers will refuse to accept any gifts, presents, subscriptions, favors, gratuities, or promises that could be interpreted as seeking to cause the officer to refrain from performing official responsibilities honestly and within the law. Police officers must not receive private or special advantage from their official status. Respect from the public cannot be bought; it can only be earned and cultivated.

COOPERATION WITH OTHER OFFICERS AND AGENCIES

Police officers will cooperate with all legally authorized agencies and their representatives in the pursuit of justice.

An officer or agency may be one among many organizations that may provide law enforcement services to a jurisdiction. It is imperative that a police officer assist colleagues fully and completely with respect and consideration at all times.

PERSONAL/PROFESSIONAL CAPABILITIES

Police officers will be responsible for their own standard of professional performance and will take every reasonable opportunity to enhance and improve their level of knowledge and competence.

Through study and experience, a police officer can acquire the high level of knowledge and competence that is essential for the efficient and effective performance of duty. The acquisition of knowledge is a never-ending process of personal and professional development that should be pursued constantly.

PRIVATE LIFE

Police officers will behave in a manner that does not bring discredit to their agencies or themselves.

A police officer's character and conduct while off duty must always be exemplary, thus maintaining a position of respect in the community in which he or she lives and serves. The officer's personal behavior must be beyond reproach.

Source: Adopted by the Executive Committee of the International Association of Chiefs of Police on October 17, 1989. Used with permission.

FIGURE 8–1 Code of Ethics (IACP)
The International Association of Chiefs of Police

Some police officers, however, take the attitude that if a particular behavior is not prohibited by law or policy, then it is permissible. Conversely, if actions are not mandated, they merely represent an option. Such an attitude points to a general failure of police ethics. Their actions should be guided by what is "right" for the situation and individuals involved, not what is required or prohibited.

Police supervisors and managers obviously play a key role in police ethics. Not only must they enforce and uphold ethical standards, they must also set an example and see that officers are instructed in the ethical conduct of police business.

Toward this end, law enforcement has adopted a Code of Ethics, which is shown in Figure 8–1. In 1989, the International Association of Chiefs of Police replaced the Code of Ethics with a Police Code of Conduct, shown in Figure 8–2. This code is broader and incorporates value statements that express more contemporary police administrative concerns. The Code of Ethics and the Police

Police Code of Conduct

All law enforcement officers must be fully aware of the ethical responsibilities of their position and must strive constantly to live up to the highest possible standards of professional policing.

The International Association of Chiefs of Police believes it important that police officers have clear advice and counsel available to assist them in performing their duties consistent with these standards, and has adopted the following ethical mandates as guidelines to meet these ends.

Primary Responsibilities of a Police Officer

A police officer acts as an official representative of government who is required and trusted to work within the law. The officer's powers and duties are conferred by statute. The fundamental duties of a police officer include serving the community, safeguarding lives and property, protecting the innocent, keeping the peace and ensuring the rights of all to liberty, equality and justice.

Performance of the Duties of a Police Officer

A police officer shall perform all duties impartially, without favor or affection or ill will and without regard to status, sex, race, religion, political belief or aspiration. All citizens will be treated equally with courtesy, consideration and dignity.

Officers will never allow personal feelings, animosities or friendships to influence official conduct. Laws will be enforced appropriately and courteously and, in carrying out their responsibilities, officers will strive to obtain maximum cooperation from the public. They will conduct themselves in appearance and deportment in such a manner as to inspire confidence and respect for the position of public trust they hold.

Discretion

A police officer will use responsibly the discretion vested in his position and exercise it within the law. The principle of reasonableness will guide the officer's determinations, and the officer will consider all surrounding circumstances in determining whether any legal action shall be taken.

Consistent and wise use of discretion, based on professional policing competence, will do much to preserve good relationships and retain the confidence of the public. There can be difficulty in choosing between conflicting courses of action. It is important to remember that a timely word of advice rather than arrest—which may be correct in appropriate circumstances—can be a more effective means of achieving a desired end.

Use of Force

A police officer will never employ unnecessary force or violence and will use only such force in the discharge of duty as is reasonable in all circumstances.

The use of force should be used only with the greatest restraint and only after discussion, negotiation and persuasion have been found to be inappropriate or ineffective. While the use of force is occasionally unavoidable, every police office will refrain from unnecessary infliction of pain or suffering and will never engage in cruel, degrading or inhuman treatment of any person.

Confidentiality

Whatever a police officer sees, hears or learns that is of a confidential nature will be kept secret unless the performance of duty or legal provision requires otherwise.

Members of the public have a right to security and privacy, and information obtained about them must not be improperly divulged.

Integrity

A police officer will not engage in acts of corruption or bribery, nor will an officer condone such acts by other police officers.

The public demands that the integrity of police officers be above reproach. Police officers must, therefore, avoid any conduct that might compromise integrity and thus undercut the public confidence in a law enforcement agency. Officers will refuse to accept any gifts, presents, subscriptions, favors, gratuities or promises that could be interpreted as seeking to cause the officer to refrain from performing official responsibilities honestly and within the law. Police officers must not receive private or special advantage from their official status. Respect from the public cannot be bought; it can only be earned and cultivated.

Cooperation with Other Police Officers and Agencies

Police officers will cooperate with all legally authorized agencies and their representatives in the pursuit of justice.

An officer or agency may be one among many organizations that may provide law enforcement services to a jurisdiction. It is imperative that a police officer assist colleagues fully and completely with respect and consideration at all times.

Personal-Professional Capabilities

Police officers will be responsible for their own standard of professional performance and will take every reasonable opportunity to enhance and improve their level of knowledge and competence.

Through study and experience, a police officer can acquire the high level of knowledge and competence that is essential for the efficient and effective performance of duty. The acquisition of knowledge is a never-ending process of personal and professional development that should be pursued constantly.

Private Life

Police officers will behave in a manner that does not bring discredit to their agencies or themselves.

A police officer's character and conduct while off duty must always be exemplary, thus maintaining a position of respect in the community in which he or she lives and serves. The officer's personal behavior must be beyond reproach.

FIGURE 8–2 Police Code of Conduct
The International Association of Chiefs of Police

Code of Conduct are taught in most training academies and made available to officers in many departments. They provide the trappings of professionalism but may actually exert little control over police officer behavior. Generally, state statutes and departmental policy, which are more specific and less theoretical, govern police behavior.

THE VITAL ROLE OF SUPERVISORS AND MANAGERS

Some experts in the field of police ethics lay problems involving officers' ethics and their lapses in good conduct squarely at the feet of their supervisors. Edward Tully (1998:7) has stated the following:

> Show me a law enforcement agency with a serious problem of officer misconduct and I will show you a department staffed with too many sergeants not doing their job. [Leaders must] recognize the vital and influential role sergeants play within a police organization. They should be selected with care, given as much supervisory training as possible, and included in the decisionmaking process. Sergeants are the custodians of the police culture, the leaders and informal disciplinarians of the department, and the individual most officers look to for advice.

Perhaps a more tempered view of the daunting task confronting supervisors in reducing or preventing ethical lapses by officers is offered by Vicchio (1997:8–9); he believes that it is nearly impossible to prevent unethical officers from misbehaving if they are so inclined:

> No supervision of police officers can keep bad cops from doing bad things. There are simply too many police officers and too few supervisors. There will never be enough supervision to catch everyone.

Vicchio (1997:9) added another caveat—another complicating factor: Even in communities where there seems to be calm with respect to police behaviors, there may actually be trouble lurking beneath the surface:

> In departments where corruption appears to be low and citizen complaints are minimal, we assume that the officers are people of integrity. Sometimes this is a faulty assumption, particularly if the motivation to do the right thing comes from fear of punishment.

Tully (1998:3), however, did underscore the vast amount of temptation that confronts today's officers and what the police organization, society in general, and the individual officer must do toward combating it:

> Socrates, Mother Teresa, or other revered individuals in our society never had to face the constant stream of ethical problems of a busy cop on the beat. One of the roles of [police leaders] is to create an environment that will help the officer resist the temptations that may lead to misconduct, corruption, or abuse of power. The executive cannot construct a work environment that will completely insulate the officers from the forces which lead to misconduct. Help is needed from the labor associations, and support is needed from the executive, legislative, and judicial branches of government. The ultimate responsibility for an officer's ethical and moral welfare rests squarely with the officer.

We further discuss the supervisor's and manager's roles later in the chapter.

INAPPROPRIATE POLICE BEHAVIORS

Most of the efforts to control police behavior are rooted in statutes and departmental orders and policies. These written directives stipulate inappropriate behavior and, in some cases, the behavior or actions that are expected in specific situations. As we noted previously, written directives cannot address every contingency and officers must often use their discretion. These discretionary decisions should be guided by ethics and values. When there is an ethics or policy failure, the resulting behavior is generally considered to be illegal or inappropriate.

It should be noted that in many cases, no clear line separates acceptable behavior from that which is unacceptable. Instead, the two are separated by an expansive gray area referred to as relative ethics, discussed earlier. Some observers have referred to illegal police behavior as a "slippery slope": Officers tread on solid or legal grounds but at some point slip beyond the acceptable into illegal or unacceptable behavior. These slippery slopes serve as a point of analysis for the behaviors addressed in this section, which discusses areas in which officers can get into trouble: (1) lying and deception, (2) acceptance of gratuities and corruption, (3) improper use of force, (4) verbal and psychological abuse, (5) violations of civil rights, and (6) improper sexual relationships.

Officer Lying and Deception

Police officers lie or deceive for different purposes and under varying circumstances. In some cases, their misrepresentations are accepted and considered to be an integral part of a criminal investigation, while in other cases they are not accepted and are viewed as violations of law. Barker and Carter (1994, 1990) examined police lying and perjury and developed a taxonomy that centered on accepted lying and deviant lying. *Accepted lying* includes police activities to apprehend or entrap suspects. This type of lying is generally considered to be trickery. *Deviant lying,* on the other hand, refers to occasions when officers commit perjury to convict suspects or are deceptive about some activity that is illegal or unacceptable to the department or public in general.

Accepted Lying. Deception has long been used by the police to ensnare violators and suspects. For many years, it was the principal method used by detectives and police officers to secure confessions and convictions (Kuykendall, 1986). It is allowed by the law, and to a great extent, it is expected by the public. Marx (1982:170) identified three methods that the police use to trick a suspect: (1) offering the illegal action as a part of a larger socially acceptable and legal goal; (2) disguising the illegal action so that the suspect does not know the action is illegal; and (3) morally weakening the suspect so that the suspect voluntarily becomes involved.

The courts have long accepted deception as an investigative tool. In *Illinois v. Perkins* (1990), the U.S. Supreme Court ruled that police undercover agents who are posing as inmates are not required to administer the *Miranda* warning to incarcerated inmates when investigating crimes. The Court essentially separated trickery from coercion. Coercion is strictly prohibited, but trickery by police officers is unquestionably acceptable. Lying, although acceptable by the courts and the public in certain circumstances, does result in an ethical dilemma. It is a dirty means to accomplish a good end; the police use untruths to gain the truth relative to some event.

Another problem with deception is entrapment. *Entrapment* occurs when the idea of a crime begins with the police rather than the suspect, and the police facilitate the commission of a criminal act. The courts examine the offender's predisposition to commit the crime. If no predisposition exists, then the police have engaged in entrapment. Should police undercover officers be allowed to give drugs to suspects so that the suspects can be apprehended for possession? Should suspects be encouraged by undercover police officers to burglarize a business so that the suspects can be arrested? There are numerous instances in which police officers facilitate criminal activity to arrest persons suspected of other criminal activity.

Deviant Lying. In their taxonomy of police lying, Barker and Carter (1994) identified two types of deviant lying: lying that serves legitimate purposes and lying that conceals or promotes crimes or illegitimate ends.

Lying that serves legitimate goals occurs when officers lie to secure a conviction, obtain a search warrant, or conceal police omissions during an investigation. While studying police deviance in one city, Barker (1994) found that officers believed that almost one-fourth of the police force would commit perjury in order to secure a conviction in court or to obtain a search warrant. Lying becomes an effective, routine way to sidestep legal impediments. When left unabated by police supervisors, managers, and administrators, lying can become organizationally accepted as an effective means to nullify legal entanglements and other obstacles that stand in the way of convictions. Examples include officers misrepresenting the fact that they used the services of confidential informants to secure search warrants, concealing that an interrogator went too far and coerced a confession, or perjuring themselves to gain a conviction.

Lying to conceal or promote police criminality is, without a doubt, the most distressing form of police deception. Examples of this form of lying range from officers' lying to conceal their using excessive force when arresting a suspect to obscuring the commission of a criminal act. Barker and Carter (1990) and Skolnick (1982) reported that the practice is commonplace in some departments. They reasoned that the police culture approves and, in some cases, promotes it. Clearly, a police agency is in serious trouble when this type of behavior occurs.

The supervisor is primarily responsible for controlling police officer behavior. Too often supervisors look the other way. It is easier to allow the behavior to occur than to confront it. Deception and lying must be dealt with, however. First, supervisors must fully understand what is acceptable and what is not acceptable behavior; a line must be drawn. Second, this information must be communicated to officers on a regular basis. Third, supervisors must inquire into and actively supervise officers' cases. If supervisors inquire into and investigate the extent of deception and lying by individual officers, officers are less likely to engage in unacceptable deception. Finally, when problems are identified, supervisors must take immediate disciplinary action. If supervisors promote deception by failing to respond to it, they are only worsening the problem.

Gratuities and Corruption

Gratuities are commonly accepted by police officers as a part of their job. Restaurants frequently give officers free or half-price meals and drinks; bars and liquor stores give officers drinks or discounts for their alcoholic beverages; and a number of other businesses routinely give officers discounts for services or merchandise. Many police officers and departments accept these gratuities as a part of the job. Other departments prohibit such gifts and discounts but seldom attempt to enforce any relevant policy or regulation. Finally, some departments attempt to ensure that officers do not accept free or discounted services or merchandise and routinely enforce policies or regulations against such behavior.

There are two basic arguments against police acceptance of gratuities. First is the slippery slope argument, discussed earlier, which proposes that gratuities are the first step in police corruption. Once gratuities are received, police officers' ethics are subverted and officers are open to additional breaches of their integrity. Also, officers who accept minor gifts or gratuities are then obligated to provide the donors with some special service or accommodation. Second, some propose that receiving a gratuity is wrong since officers are receiving rewards for services that, as a result of their employment, they are obligated to provide. That is, officers have no legitimate right to accept compensation in the form of a gratuity.

As noted earlier, Kania (1988) attempted to categorically justify police officers' acceptance of gratuities. He argued that shopkeepers and restaurant owners often feel an indebtedness toward the police, and gratuities provide an avenue of repayment. Gratuities, Kania argued, result in social cohesion between the police and business owners. He also maintained that the acceptance of gratuities does not necessarily lead to the solicitation of additional gratuities and gifts or corruption. Plainly, officers are able to differentiate what is appropriate and develop their own ethical standards and adhere to them.

Kania may be correct in asserting that gratuities are harmless and even beneficial in some cases, but the evidence seems to suggest that this occurs only in sparse instances. Indeed, studies have shown the dysfunctional and corrupting influence gratuities can have on law enforcement. Perhaps the most notorious and disgraceful example can be found in the *Knapp Commission Report on Police Corruption* in New York City (1972). The commission found that a large number of officers were not only accepting gratuities, but that the active solicitation of gratuities and gifts was institutionalized within the department. The commission found that officers actively and routinely solicited free meals from restaurants and hotels, free drinks from bars and clubs, Christmas payments, free merchandise and other gifts, and tips for various services rendered. If the gifts and gratuities were not forthcoming, the police often issued summonses or otherwise harassed the shopkeeper or business owner.

The commission characterized a majority of the officers as "grass-eaters," while others were described as "meat-eaters." Grass-eaters are officers who freely accept gratuities and sometimes solicit minor payments and gifts. Meat-eaters, on the other hand, spent a significant portion of the workday aggressively seeking out situations that could be exploited for financial gain. These officers were corrupt and were involved in thefts, drugs, gambling, prostitution, and other criminal activities.

At least in some cases, it seems that gratuities may be a first step toward corruption. Gratuities do indeed provide a slippery slope on which officers can easily slide into corruption. The problem is that many officers fail to understand when and where to draw the line. Once a police department decides on a policy, it should ensure that all officers are familiar with the policy. Supervisors and managers must fully understand the department's policy regarding gratuities and emphatically enforce it; once a department draws the line distinguishing what is acceptable, it is responsible for ensuring that the following measures are taken.

First, as a consequence of their direct oversight of their subordinates, supervisors should inquire about activities and continually stress the department's policies. Second, supervisors should periodically check with business owners, restaurant managers, and liquor establishments in an effort to gauge police practices with regard to those establishments. The supervisor should communicate the department's policies to business owners and ask their cooperation when dealing with individual officers. They should also ask that business owners contact them when officers solicit gifts or gratuities. Finally, supervisors should aggressively investigate any evidence or indication that officers may be violating the department's policies. These actions are necessary to ensure that officers' actions regarding gratuities do not get out of hand.

It is difficult to specifically recognize when an officer has become corrupt. Part of the problem lies in defining corruption. Goldstein (1977:188) defined it as "acts involving the misuse of authority by a police officer in a manner designed to produce personal gain for himself or for others." The primary components are misuse of authority and personal gain. Using this definition, it would appear that efforts by police officers to solicit gratuities and gifts would be considered corruption. Such acts involve both the misuse of authority and personal gain. Only unsolicited gratuities would presumably fall outside the scope of this definition, since any form of solicitation would involve at a minimum a tacit misuse or misrepresentation of police authority.

Sherman (1982) developed a typology to describe police corruption: (1) rotten apples and rotten pockets, (2) pervasive unorganized corruption, and (3) pervasive organized corruption. *Rotten apples and rotten pockets* refer to situations in which a few officers are involved in corrupt activities, some of whom cooperate with one another to further their corrupt ventures. An officer may steal money during a drug raid or several officers may shake down a business owner who consistently violates an ordinance or law. *Pervasive unorganized corruption* occurs when a majority of a department's officers are corrupt, but little organization or collaboration exists. For example, a number of different officers may be shaking down bar owners and merchants, but they do it independently without coordinating their activities among themselves or with superiors. Finally, *pervasive organized corruption* involves large numbers of officers working together on a variety of corrupt activities. It entails a structure in which some officers are reporting to and taking commands from other officers who are masterminding the activities. Police commanders and supervisors generally are involved when pervasive organized corruption exists.

Supervisors are a department's first line of defense against corruption. For pervasive organized corruption to exist, rotten apples and rotten pockets had to exist first. If supervisors can prevent, or at least control, the corruption associated with rotten apples and rotten pockets, it is unlikely that more severe forms of corruption will emerge. Supervisors should review their subordinates' arrest activities, make law enforcement assignments targeting potential corruptive business establishments to ensure that enforcement activities occur, and monitor the activities of cliques that form in the work group. In essence, supervisors must proactively investigate and denigrate potential corruptive activities.

Improper Use of Authority and Force

As noted earlier, citizens bestow a substantial amount of authority on police officers. A central problem in police supervision occurs when officers improperly use this authority. Improper use of authority can range from being disrespectful to the inappropriate use of deadly force. To this end, Carter (1994) has attempted to provide a typology of abuse of authority by police officers. His categories include (1) physical abuse and excessive force, (2) verbal and psychological abuse, and (3) legal abuse and violations of civil rights.

Physical Abuse and Excessive Force

Physical abuse and excessive force can occur when the police use either deadly or nondeadly force. The use of excessive physical force often results in substantial public scrutiny. Indeed, such instances of improper use of their authority and excessive force have received national attention. Perhaps the most well-known incident was the Rodney King case in 1991, involving the Los Angeles Police Department. This incident had profound national effects on policing and how citizens view law enforcement. Local incidents may not receive national media coverage, but they oftentimes have the same dramatic, chilling effects in a community. All police officers are judged by the actions of one or a few officers.

Regardless of the type of force used, it must be used by police officers in a legally accepted manner. Police officers are allowed to use only that force necessary to effect an arrest. Thus, the amount of force that a police officer uses is dependent on the amount of resistance demonstrated by the person being arrested. This concept is taught to police officers in training academies through a use-of-force continuum, which includes actions ranging from verbal commands to deadly force. Figure 8–3 contains the use-of-force continuum.

The use-of-force continuum attempts to illustrate how officers respond to suspects' actions. For example, if a suspect attempts to physically assault an officer using his fists, an officer may be justified in using a police baton, pepper spray, or some other less-than-lethal means to ward off the attack and subdue the suspect. On the other hand, if the suspect is brandishing a knife, the officer may be justified in using a firearm. In addition to an officer's being justified in using that force which is necessary to effect the arrest, the officer must also respect the suspect's life. It may be reasonable and prudent for an officer to retreat and seek

Levels of Resistance	Levels of Control of Force
Suspect's Actions	*Officer's Response*
Psychological Intimidation 　Nonverbal clues that indicate a 　　subject's attitude, appearance, physical 　　readiness	Officer Presence 　Verbal direction
Verbal Noncompliance 　Verbal responses indicating an attitude 　　of unwillingness	Officer Presence 　Verbal direction 　Telling suspect what you want him or 　　her to do
Passive Resistance 　Physical actions that do not prevent 　　officer's attempt to control, dead 　　weight, active passiveness	Officer Presence 　Verbal direction 　Soft, empty-hand techniques 　Wrist locks, pressure point control
Defensive Resistance 　Physical actions that prevent officer's 　　control without attempting to harm the 　　officer	Officer Presence 　Verbal direction 　Soft, empty-hand techniques 　Strikes with hands, feet, knee, elbow in 　　response to defensive resistance; this 　　level of control should only be used 　　after lesser force has proved ineffective 　　in controlling the suspect and applied 　　only to nonvital areas.
Active Aggression 　Physical assault on the officer	Officer Presence 　Verbal direction 　Soft, empty-hand techniques 　Hard, empty-hand techniques 　Soft and hard intermediate weapons. 　Soft shall include radial arm locks, arm 　　bars, etc. Hard shall include strikes 　　with baton to nonvital areas.
Aggravated Active Aggression	Any of the above and deadly force
Deadly Force Encounters	Firearms, strikes to the head and other 　vital areas with impact weapons.

FIGURE 8–3 Use of Force Continuum

assistance from other officers or to contain the situation and wait for the suspect to surrender.

Deadly Force

Deadly force is an extension of excessive physical force. Deadly force, however, is more problematic because of its outcome and the fact that it generally leads to considerable scrutiny by the public and authorities; and it can also result in rioting by citizens.

When a police officer deliberately kills someone, a determination is made as to whether or not the homicide was justified to prevent imminent death or serious bodily injury to the officer or another person. According to a 2001 federal report on justifiable homicides by police (Brown and Langan, 2001), from 1976 to 1998, 8,578 felons were justifiably killed by police in the United States; the largest number of such killings in one year was 459 (in 1994), and the smallest number was 296 (in 1987). On average, 373 felons are lawfully killed by police each year. What is *not* reported (or available), however, is the number of so-called "bad" shootings, for which the subsequent investigation ruled that the police officer did not kill a citizen with justification.

It is difficult to detail the police decision-making process involved in using deadly force. Two issues appear to be used fairly consistently as justifications for using deadly force, however. First, as the Christopher Commission (1991) found in Los Angeles while investigating the Rodney King incident, police officers often believe that there are no effective mid-range force alternatives or tactics. In other words, officers believe that once significant resistance and danger are exhibited by a suspect, their only alternative is to use deadly force. This situation can be corrected by training and ensuring that officers adhere to the use-of-force continuum (shown in Figure 8–3).

Second, Fyfe (1986) opined that officers used the split-second syndrome to justify shootings, especially when bad shootings occur. The split-second syndrome essentially implies that officers must make deadly force decisions in a matter of a precious few seconds. Fyfe noted that the syndrome makes three assumptions. First, no two shootings are alike; therefore, it is virtually impossible to establish principles that can be used to diagnose potential shooting situations. Second, because of the stress and time limitations, it should be expected that police officers will make errors. The circumstances, stress, and time limitations should justify police actions, and any criticism of police officers is unwarranted, especially by nonpolice personnel who do not understand police procedures or do not have an appreciation of the problems encountered by officers. Third, any evaluation of police decision making should be based on the perceived exigencies. If a citizen has or is perceived to have committed an act justifying deadly force, any subsequent shooting by the police should be deemed necessary or permissible.

Fyfe further asserted that adherence to the split-second syndrome can lead to unnecessary violence. In many shooting instances, police officers have the time to analyze the situation and make reactive decisions. Police officers can avoid split-second decision situations by taking actions before the situation escalates. When there are fight calls or calls involving weapons, officers should deploy tactics or obtain assistance that reduces the need for deadly force.

Police supervisors have the primary responsibility for ensuring that officers respond to various calls correctly. Supervisors should counsel officers when they become lax and make sure they use proper procedures when approaching a suspect or answering a call. If officers follow procedures, the need to make split-second decisions about using deadly force will diminish.

Verbal and Psychological Abuse

Police officers sometimes abuse citizens by berating or belittling them. They antagonize citizens knowing that as police officers they are wrapped in the shroud of authority, and that citizens must take the abuse. One of the most common methods used by police officers to verbally abuse citizens is profanity. Research indicates that profanity is used for a variety of reasons: as a source of power to control others (Selnow, 1985), as a weapon to degrade or insult others (Paletz and Harris, 1975), as a method of alienating others (Selnow, 1985), as a method of labeling others (Warshay and Warshay, 1978), and as a way of defying authority (Paletz and Harris, 1975). Unfortunately, profanity has become a part of the police culture and many officers' everyday speech. When profanity is used liberally in the work setting, it increases the likelihood that it will be used inappropriately.

Profane language tends to polarize a situation. A citizen will either passively submit or respond aggressively, in either case causing the citizen to distrust and dislike the police. When police officers use profanity, especially in an aggressive manner, the focus shifts from the problem to the officer's language; and when it is used aggressively, profanity can easily create greater physical risks to the officer. Furthermore, even if the officer intended to resolve the situation, it may no longer be possible because of the harm caused by the language. And, because it can incite situations, profanity also increases the potential for liability and citizens' complaints; therefore, it also heightens the possibility of the officer's facing administrative action.

For all these reasons, the use of profanity by the police toward citizens is not justified, wise, or advised. Supervisors should discourage its use and review every instance in which an officer used profanity with a citizen.

Legal Abuse and Violations of Civil Rights

Legal abuse and civil rights violations consist of police actions that violate a citizen's constitutional or statutory rights. This abuse usually involves false arrest, false imprisonment, and harassment. For example, a police officer may knowingly make an unlawful search, charge the suspect with a crime, and then lie about the nature of the search. Another example occurs when police officers hassle a criminal to gain information or hassle a business owner to obtain some monetary gain.

Supervisors and managers play a key role in preventing legal abuse and violations of citizens' civil rights. Supervisors frequently back up officers when responding to calls and observe situations that lead to an arrest. They should ensure that officers' decisions to arrest are based on probable cause, not some lesser standard. They should also review arrest reports and question officers when arrests are not observed to ensure that the arrests meet the probable cause standard.

This is critical since research has long indicated that officers frequently base their decisions to arrest on factors such as a suspect's demeanor (Smith and Visher, 1981), socioeconomic status (Black and Reiss, 1967; Friedrich, 1977), race (Brooks, 1986; Smith and Visher, 1981), age (Brooks, 1986; Friedrich, 1977), relationship between the suspect and victim (Friedrich, 1977; Smith and Visher, 1981), and the preference of the complainant (Brooks, 1986; Smith and Visher, 1981). When police officers allow such factors to substitute for probable cause, they are abusing their authority. Officers should provide the same level of services to all citizens, and they should use consistent decision-making criteria when making an arrest that exclude race, gender, or social standing.

The homeless often claim to be victims of police abuse and harassment.

Improper Sexual Relations

Although no accurate data exists, it seems that a significant number of officers engage in improper sexual relationships. While studying deviance in a southern city, Barker (1994) found that the officers believed that about one-third of the department engaged in improper sexual relationships while on duty. This in itself is problematic, because officers who participate in this activity are not only showing poor judgment in doing so, they may also be compromising their ability to objectively enforce the law. Although many of the liaisons could be deemed romantic encounters, some of them may very well be associated with illicit activities.

Sapp (1994) noted that because of their authority, police officers have a number of opportunities to sexually harass citizens. They have the authority to stop and talk with citizens, and in many cases, they can limit their freedom. They also perform work activities while unsupervised and in relative isolation. Although the majority of police officers may never sexually harass other citizens, a significant number do.

There are many examples of police officers' sexual activities that have become public and have created an embarrassment for the department, such as the following (Sapp, 1994):

- Two Spokane, Washington, police officers pleaded guilty to charges that they employed underage female prostitutes.
- The Spartanburg, South Carolina, Police Department investigated allegations that as many as 20 police officers engaged in sexual activities with prostitutes. Two officers resigned as a result of the investigation.
- A Tennessee sheriff was charged with attempted rape and sexual battery after he visited a female job applicant at her home.
- A Connecticut police department had to remove cellular telephones from its vehicles because officers were using them to call numbers that provided sexually explicit conversations with females.

Activities of this nature undermine the effectiveness of a police department in two ways. First, they create a public relations nightmare. Sexual deviance cases involving the police become known, and citizens lose respect for their police, tend to be less cooperative, and are less likely to support them politically. Second, they undermine the operational effectiveness of a department. When these problems occur, officers tend to believe they are immune from disciplinary controls and can do their jobs as they please.

Supervisors and managers must closely scrutinize subordinates' activities to prevent or reduce the incidence of sexual misconduct. If they fail to investigate or pursue allegations of sexual misconduct, in essence they are condoning it. This only leads to additional and possibly more outrageous conduct on the part of some of the officers. Supervisors may not be able to completely eliminate such behavior, but through thoughtful supervision, they can minimize it.

Sexual Harassment

Another form of sexual misconduct that involves ethical conduct is sexual harassment, which is defined as

> Unwelcomed sexual advances, requests for sexual favors, and other verbal or physical conduct of a sexual nature constitute sexual harassment when (1) submission to such conduct is made either explicitly or implicitly a term or condition of an individual's employment; (2) submission to or rejection of such conduct by an individual is used as the basis for employment decisions affecting such individual; or (3) such conduct has the purpose or effect of unreasonably interfering with an individual's work performance or creating an intimidating, hostile, or offensive working environment. [29 C.F.R. 1604.11(a)]

There are two forms of sexual harassment, both of which are relevant to supervision and management (Higginbotham, 1988). First, is *quid pro quo,* which occurs when a sexual act is a condition of employment. For example, someone in a position of leadership may offer a subordinate a high rating needed for promotion if the subordinate provides sexual favors. Second is the *hostile environment,* in which employees are harassed because of their gender.

Widespread evidence exists that sexual harassment still permeates even the most professional police agencies. Even more troubling is a survey that indicates that 34 percent of police agencies have no written sexual harassment policy, and less than a quarter said they would promptly investigate a filed complaint (Lindemann and Kadue, 1997). Eighty-five percent of sexual harassment victims are female, and juries have become increasingly more sympathetic toward them; large costs have resulted relating to litigation and court-awarded damages in addition to the more than $400 million annual cost resulting from absenteeism, lower productivity, increased health care costs, poor morale, and employee turnover that are related to this problem (Carlan and Byxbe, 2000).

Considering the high stakes involved, police organizations must take affirmative and effective steps to prevent sexual harassment by providing training on the subject, expressing strong disapproval, developing appropriate sanctions, informing employees of their right to raise the issue, and intervening quickly when it occurs. Although these measures may be costly, in the end these costs will be offset by savings in legal fees, compensatory judgments, and punitive awards (Carlan and Byxbe, 2000).

Supervisors and managers must also be vigilant of other, related sexual harassment behaviors that their officers can perform; seven such behaviors have been identified (Sapp, 1994):

1. *Nonsexual Contacts That Are Sexually Motivated.* An officer will stop another citizen without legal justification to obtain information or get a closer look at the citizen.

2. *Voyeuristic Contacts.* Police officers attempt to observe partially clad or nude citizens. They observe apartment buildings or college dormitories. In other cases, they roust citizens parked on lovers' lanes.

3. *Contacts with Crime Victims.* Crime victims generally are emotionally distraught or upset and particularly vulnerable to sexual overtures from officers. In these instances, officers may make several return visits and calls with the intention of seducing the victim.

4. *Contacts with Offenders.* In these cases, officers may conduct body searches, frisks, and patdown searches. In some cases, officers may demand sexual favors. Offenders' complaints of sexual harassment will not be investigated by a department without corroborating evidence, which seldom exists.

5. *Contacts with Juvenile Offenders.* In some cases, officers have exhibited some of the same behaviors with juveniles that they have with adults, such as patdowns, frisks, and sexual favors. There have also been cases in which officers assigned as juvenile or school liaison officers have taken advantage of their assignment to seduce juveniles.

6. *Sexual Shakedowns.* Police officers demand sexual services from prostitutes, homosexuals, and others engaged in criminal activity as a form of protection.

7. *Citizen-Initiated Sexual Contacts.* Some citizens are attracted to police officers and attempt to seduce them. They may be attracted to the uniform, authority, or the prospect of a "safe" sexual encounter. In other cases, the citizen may be lonely or may want a "break" when caught violating the law.

DEPARTMENTAL GUIDELINES

The foregoing discussion about inappropriate behaviors effectively makes the point that police leaders need to ask themselves if there are clear rules regarding officer behavior and if officers know those rules. If so, are the officers adhering to them? Are they getting their meals free, against departmental policy? Are they treating all citizens courteously? These questions involve the fundamental principles of ethical policing in a democracy.

Indeed, it might well be argued that the *primary* function of police leaders is to ensure compliance with the department's rules and regulations. In many cases, a department will promulgate written guidelines to prevent inappropriate police behavior from occurring. In other cases, regulations provide guidelines on how certain tasks can be best performed. Regardless of rationale, written guidelines represent instructions that all officers must follow, and supervisors and managers must ensure that officers follow them.

Police officers often view written guidelines as impositions on their discretion. Officers generally do not like policies that restrict how they apply force or when they can engage in a hot pursuit. If officers are allowed to act without restrictions, however, behavioral, organizational, and community problems can occur. As emphasized earlier in this chapter, supervisors must actively monitor their subordinates. Passive or reactionary supervision results in supervision after a problem occurs. Supervisors should attempt to eliminate problems before they happen and ensure that police officers do their jobs correctly.

CIVIL LIABILITY AND POLICE SUPERVISION

Supervision is about behavior, for it is the direct responsibility of supervisors to monitor and regulate officers' behavior and when necessary, to take disciplinary action to ensure that negligent or illegal behavior does not recur in the future. This section explores some of the legal consequences when police supervisors fail to control officers' behavior.

In the years following the Civil War and in reaction to the states' inability to control the Ku Klux Klan's lawlessness, Congress enacted the Ku Klux Klan Act of 1871. This was later codified as Title 42, U.S. Code Section 1983. Its statutory language is as follows:

> Every person who, under color of any statute, ordinance, regulation, custom, or usage of any State or Territory, subjects, or causes to be subjected, any citizen of the United States or any other person within the jurisdiction thereof to the deprivation of any rights, privileges, or immunities secured by the Constitution and laws, shall be liable to the party injured in an action at law, suit in equity, or other proper proceeding for redress.

This legislation is intended to provide civil rights protection to all persons protected under the act, when a defendant acts "under color of law" (misuses power of office). It is also meant to provide an avenue to the federal courts for relief of alleged civil rights violations.

Several factors have contributed to a surge in Section 1983 actions. First, some lawyers believe that a better caliber of judges and juries can be found in the federal forum. Federal judges, who are appointed for life, can be less concerned about the political ramifications of their decisions than the locally elected judges. Furthermore, federal rules of pleading and evidence are uniform, and federal procedures of discovery are more liberal. Just as important, Section 1988 of the Civil Rights Act in 1976 allowed attorney's fees to the "prevailing party" over and above the award for compensatory and punitive damages. This provision in the law did as much to spur the use of Section 1983 as any other factor.

Supervisors must be mindful that a certain level of liability is attached to the job when they fail to supervise correctly. They should also remember that plaintiffs generally attempt to include as many officers, supervisors, and administrators in the lawsuit as possible to enhance the probability that the award will be greater and the defendants will have the ability to pay it. This is commonly referred to as the "deep pockets" approach.

Supervisors may incur liability for what their subordinates do. Supervisors have direct and vicarious liability. *Direct liability* is incurred for the actions of supervisors themselves, while *vicarious* or *indirect liability* refers to when supervisors are held liable for the actions of their subordinates. For direct liability to exist the supervisor must actively participate in the act. Supervisors may incur direct liability in the following ways (del Carmen, 1989):

1.   They authorize the act. They give officers permission to do something that ultimately results in liability.

2.   They are present when an act for which liability results occurs. They stand by and watch an act occur and fail to take corrective action.

3.   They ratify the act. Once the act is completed, they fail to admonish or take corrective action when it comes to their attention.

One of the most commonly litigated areas of liability is negligence. *Simple negligence* occurs when a supervisor fails to provide the degree of care and vigilance required for a situation, while *gross negligence* is a deliberate indifference to life or property. Generally, the courts require gross negligence to hold a supervisor liable.

As a result of case law, there are currently five areas in which supervisors have been found liable as a result of negligence: (1) negligent assignment, (2) negligent failure to supervise, (3) negligent failure to direct, (4) negligent entrustment, and (5) negligent failure to investigate or discipline (del Carmen, 1991:227). These areas of liability fall squarely with the supervisor and are discussed next.

Negligent assignment occurs when the supervisor assigns a task to a subordinate without first determining that the subordinate is properly trained or capable of performing the required work. Negligent assignment also occurs when a supervisor determines that an employee is not qualified for a position but fails to relieve the employee of the assignment.

An example of negligent assignment would be a supervisor who allows a subordinate to assume the duties of a police officer without receiving firearms training. If the officer then inappropriately shoots a citizen, the supervisor as well as the officer would be liable. A second example would be an officer who has had several complaints of sexual harassment and supervisors fail to reassign the officer to a position within the department that eliminates the opportunity for

sexual harassment. Even if disciplinary action was taken, supervisors must eliminate any opportunity for the act to recur. Supervisors must pay particular
attention to their subordinates' behavior and make assignments to ensure that
problems do not occur.

Negligent failure to supervise occurs when the supervisor fails to properly
oversee subordinates' activities. The court in *Lenard v. Argento* (1983) held that
at a minimum a plaintiff must demonstrate that the supervisory official authorized
(implicitly or explicitly), approved, or knowingly acquiesced in the illegal conduct. For example, if a supervisor knows that an officer on a number of occasions
has used more force than was necessary to effect an arrest and fails to take corrective action, the supervisor can be held liable for failure to supervise in a subsequent action. Thus, anytime a supervisor becomes aware of a problem, action
must be taken to rectify the problem. The courts have also examined individual
cases. In *Grandstaff v. City of Borger* (1985), police officials were held liable for
failing to take supervisory action after officers mistakenly opened fire and shot an
innocent bystander who was attempting to help the officers. The court reasoned
that the department's failure to reprimand, discipline, or fire officers constituted
a failure to supervise. Supervisors' failure to act is an abdication of authority, and
the courts consider this to be negligent supervision.

Negligent failure to direct occurs when supervisors fail to advise subordinates of the specific requirements and limits of the job. For example, if a police
department fails to provide officers with the limits of when they can use deadly
force and officers subsequently use deadly force inappropriately, the responsible
supervisors can be held liable. Negligent failure to direct has specific application
relative to departmental policies and procedures. If a department does not have a
policy dealing with a sensitive area and officers subsequently act inappropriately,
the department will be found negligent for failure to direct. Supervisors must be
knowledgeable about departmental policies and be able to properly advise officers about their content.

Negligent entrustment occurs when supervisors entrust officers with equipment and facilities and fail to properly supervise the officers' care and use of the
equipment, and subsequently the officers commit an act using the equipment that
leads to a violation of a citizen's federally protected rights. The government in
these cases must show that the officer in question was incompetent and the
supervisor knew of the incompetence. A supervisor's defense in negligent
entrustment is that the employee was competent to use the equipment and was
properly supervised.

Supervisors must investigate complaints and work activities and take proper
disciplinary actions when required. Clearly, police departments must have adequate disciplinary procedures and they must function to protect the rights of citizens. If a supervisor or department covers up or is inattentive to complaints of
police misconduct, the department and supervisor are liable. Too often supervisors

attempt to stall, discourage, or disregard complainants when they attempt to protest police officer actions. Such actions can ultimately lead to *negligent failure to investigate or discipline charges.*

Obviously, a department's and supervisor's defense in such cases is to establish a record of strong disciplinary procedures within the agency. This is accomplished through strong actions and documentation. Plaintiffs, on the other hand, will attempt to show that either no action or inadequate action took place.

▬▬ Case Studies ▬▬▬▬▬▬▬▬▬▬▬▬▬▬▬

The following two case studies demonstrate some of the ethical dilemmas in which supervisors and managers may find themselves.

Getting the Job Done

Gothamville is a midwestern city with a high crime rate and poor relations between the police and the public. The new reform mayor and police chief campaigned on a platform of cleaning up crime in the streets and ineffectiveness of government. They launched a commission to investigate what was termed a "litany of problems" within the police department. The investigation found that officers routinely lied about the probable cause for their arrests and searches, falsified search warrant applications, and basically violated rules of collecting and preserving evidence. They were also known to protect each other under a "shroud of secrecy" and to commit perjury in front of grand juries and at trials. These problems were found to be systemic throughout the agency; however, greed and corruption were not the motivating factors behind officers' giving perjured testimony. Officers believed that their false testimony and other such activities were the only means by which they could put persons they believed guilty behind bars. Worse yet, the study also found that prosecutors routinely tolerated or at least tacitly approved of such conduct. The study also found that many police officers did not consider giving false testimony to be a form of corruption, which they believed implies personal profit. Instead, they viewed testifying as just another way to "get the job done."

1. Do you believe that the officers' means of lying about the basis for their arrests and searches justified the end result of making arrests?
2. What about the prosecutors' tolerance of the officers' unethical behavior? To what ethical standards should the prosecutor's office be held?
3. As a supervisor, when these kinds of behaviors come to light, what punishment, if any, do you think is warranted for the persons involved?
4. What actions, if any, could a supervisor take to oversee officers' activities to prevent and detect such behaviors?

Redneck Causes Escalation to Black and Blue

Officer Burns is known to have extreme difficulty in relating to persons of color and others who are socially different from himself. Burns admits to his sergeant that he grew up in a prejudiced home environment and that he has little sympathy or understanding for people "who cause all the damn trouble." The officer never received any sensitivity or diversity training at the academy or within the department. The supervisor fails to understand the weight of the problem and has very little patience with Burns. So, believing it will correct the matter, the supervisor decides to assign Burns to a minority section of town so he will improve his ability to relate to diverse groups. Within a week, Burns responds to a disturbance at a housing project where residents are partying noisily and a fight is in progress. Burns immediately becomes upset, yelling at the residents to quiet down; they fail to respond, so Burns draws his baton and begins poking residents and ordering them to comply with his directions. The crowd immediately turns against Burns, who then has to call for backup assistance. After the other officers arrive, a fight ensues between residents and officers, and several officers and residents are injured and numerous arrests are made. The following day the neighborhood council meets with the mayor, demanding that Burns be fired and threatening a lawsuit.

1. Is there any liability or negligence present in this situation? If so, what kind?
2. Could the supervisor have dealt with Burns's lack of sensitivity in a better manner? If so, how?

SUMMARY

This chapter has examined police behavior from an ethical and legal standpoint. Ethics form the foundation for police officer behavior. It is important that officers understand ethics and the role ethics plays in their profession. Officers and departments must come to grips with the ethical boundaries of police work to ensure that the boundaries are not violated.

In terms of behavior, we discussed officer lying and deception, gratuities and corruption, use of force, verbal and legal abuse, and improper sexual relations. Police officers often fail to perform expected duties and responsibilities, while in other situations they become involved in corrupt or deviant activities. Police supervisors, in a number of these cases, must shoulder responsibility for failure to properly supervise their subordinates. Supervisors are the primary control mechanism in any police department, and they must ensure that officers perform to acceptable standards in all of these areas. Supervisors can accomplish this objective by understanding the morals and values of policing and applying them to their subordinates.

Finally, as a result of their position, supervisors need to assume a degree of liability. Civil actions against supervisors are the method society uses to hold them accountable for failing to properly oversee their subordinates.

ITEMS FOR REVIEW

1. Define ethics, and provide examples of what is meant by relative as well as absolute ethics.

2. Describe the vital role of police leaders, especially first-line supervisors, in preventing and addressing problems of patrol officer ethics.

3. Briefly review the several areas in which officers frequently get into ethical and legal difficulty through inappropriate behavior.

4. Explain the two types of liability that police supervisors may incur, as well as the five areas of liability.

5. Describe the nature and use of 42 U.S. Code Section 1983.

REFERENCES

Barker, T. (1994). An empirical study of police deviance other than corruption. In T. Barker and D. Carter, eds., *Police deviance*. Cincinnati: Anderson, pp. 123–138.

Barker, T., and Carter, D. (1994). Typology of police deviance. In T. Barker and D. Carter, eds., *Police deviance*. Cincinnati: Anderson, pp. 3–12.

Barker, T., and Carter, D. (1990). "Fluffing up the evidence and covering your ass": Some conceptual notes on police lying. *Deviant Behavior* 11:61–73.

Black, D., and Reiss, A. (1970). Police control of juveniles. *American Sociological Review* 35:63–77.

Brooks, L. W. (1986). Determinants of police orientations and their impact on police discretionary behavior. Unpublished Ph.D. dissertation. Institute of Criminal Justice & Criminology, University of Maryland.

Brown, J. M., and Langan, P. A. (2001, March). *Policing and homicide, 1976–1998: Justifiable homicide by police, police officers murdered by felons*. Washington, DC: U.S. Department of Justice, Bureau of Justice Statistics.

Carlan, P. E., and Byxbe, F. R. (2000). Managing sexual harassment liability: A guide for police administrators. *The Police Chief* (October):124–129.

Carter, D. (1994). Theoretical dimensions in the abuse of authority. In T. Barker and D. Carter, eds., *Police deviance*. Cincinnati: Anderson, pp. 269–290.

Christopher Commission (1991). *Report of the independent commission on the Los Angeles police department*. Los Angeles: City of Los Angeles.

del Carmen, R. V. (1991). *Civil liabilities in American policing*. Englewood Cliffs, NJ: Brady.

del Carmen, R. V. (1989). Civil liabilities of police supervisors. *American Journal of Police* 8(1):107–136.

Fair, F. K., and Pilcher, W. D. (1991). Morality on the line: The role of ethics in police decision-making. *American Journal of Police* 10(2):23–38.

Friedrich, R. J. (1977). The impact of organizational, individual, and situational factors on police behavior. Ph.D. dissertation. Department of Political Science, University of Michigan.

Fyfe, J. (1986). *Police personnel practices*. Washington, DC: International City Management Association.

Goldstein, H. (1977). *Policing a free society*. Cambridge, MA: Ballinger.

Grandstaff v. City of Borger, 767 F.2d 161 (5th Cir. 1985).

Higginbotham, J. (1988). Sexual harassment in the police station. *FBI Law Enforcement Bulletin* 9:22–29.

Illinois v. Perkins, 110 S.Ct. 2394 (1990).

Kania, R. (1988). Police acceptance of gratuities. *Criminal Justice Ethics* 7(2):37–49.

Kleinig, J. 1996. *The ethics of policing*. New York: Cambridge University Press.

Knapp Commission Report on Police Corruption (1972). New York: George Braziller.

Kuykendall, J. 1986. The municipal police detective: An historical analysis. *Criminology* 24(1): 175–201.

Lenard v. Argento, 699 F.2d 874 (7th Cir. 1983).

Lindemann, B., and Kadue, D. D. (1997). *Sexual harassment in employment law*. Washington, DC: Bureau of National Affairs.

Marx, G. T. (1982). Who really gets stung? Some issues raised by the new police undercover work. *Crime & Delinquency* (28):165–193.

O'Malley, T. J. (1997). Managing for ethics: A mandate for administrators. *FBI Law Enforcement Bulletin* (April):20–25.

Paletz, D. L., and Harris, W. F. (1975). Four-letter threats to authority. *Journal of Politics* 37:955–979.

Reibstein, L. (1997). NYPD black and blue. *Newsweek* (May 26):64–68.

Sapp, A. D. (1994). Sexual misconduct by police officers. In T. Barker and D. Carter, eds., *Police deviance*. Cincinnati: Anderson, pp. 187–200.

Selnow, G. W. (1985). Sex differences in uses and perceptions of profanity. *Sex Roles* 12:303–312.

Sherman, L. (1982). Learning police ethics. *Criminal Justice Ethics* 1(1):10–19.

Skolnick, J. L. (1982). Deception by police. *Criminal Justice Ethics* 1(2):27–32.

Smith, D. A., and Visher, C. (1981). Street-level justice: Situational determinants of police arrest decisions. *Social Problems* 29:167–178.

Tully, E. (1998). Misconduct, corruption, abuse of power: What can the chief do? *Beretta USA Leadership Bulletin*. www.berettabulletin.com (14 January 1998).

U.S. Department of Justice, National Institute of Justice, Office of Community Oriented Policing Services (1997). *Police integrity: Public service with honor*. Washington, DC: U.S. Government Printing Office.

Vicchio, S. J. (1997). Ethics and police integrity. *FBI Law Enforcement Bulletin* (July):8–12.

Warshay, D. W., and Warshay, L. H. (1978). Obscenity and male hegemony. Paper presented at the annual meeting of the International Sociological Association, Detroit, Michigan.

9

Officers' Rights, Discipline, and Appeals

❖

LEARNING OBJECTIVES

After reading this chapter, the student will:

- understand police officers' rights and limitations, according to legislative enactments and court decisions
- know the various forms of disciplinary action that can be taken by police leaders against officers, and how complaints against the police can be investigated in a fair manner
- understand how early warning systems may be employed by police leadership toward identifying and treating problem officers
- be able to explain racial profiling, and what police leaders are doing to cope with it
- be knowledgeable about how police agencies can be deemed negligent and even liable for the actions of their officers

The price of greatness is responsibility.

—Winston Churchill

No man is fit to command another that cannot command himself.

—William Penn

Discipline must be maintained.

—Charles Dickens

INTRODUCTION

Chapter 8 discussed ethics and inappropriate police behaviors, some of which may result in individual police supervisors or managers being found liable. This chapter essentially extends that discussion, by examining officer rights and discipline. These aspects of policing are especially delicate and important aspects of supervision and management; if they are ignored or handled improperly, they can foster serious internal and external problems, increased liability, and a loss of public respect and trust.

The police, more than most segments of government, are under the close scrutiny of the public. Therefore, it is important that police agencies develop sound disciplinary policies and ensure that supervisors and managers are properly trained to intervene in problems early. These leaders must also have a good working knowledge of departmental rules and regulations, as well as the resources available for dealing with disciplinary issues.

This chapter begins with an overview of police officers' rights and limitations under the U.S. Constitution and federal court decisions. We then look at the traditional problems surrounding the discipline of police officers and the need for a sound disciplinary system. Next is a look at the various forms of complaints, how they are investigated, and the kinds of outcomes and punishments that may result. Then, the means by which officers may grieve and appeal disciplinary measures are reviewed, and the early warning system concept for identifying problem officers is examined. After a brief assessment of the problem of racial profiling, the chapter continues with a discussion of legal considerations. Two case studies close the chapter.

OFFICERS' RIGHTS AND LIMITATIONS

Although they may be compelled to give up certain rights in connection with an investigation of on-duty misbehavior or illegal acts, police officers generally are afforded the same rights, privileges, and immunities outlined in the U.S. Constitution for all citizens. These rights are the basis for legislation such as the Peace Officers Bill of Rights (discussed next), labor agreements, and civil service and departmental rules and regulations that guide an agency's disciplinary process.

Next, we briefly discuss the rights and then the limitations that might be placed on the actions of police employees by virtue of their employment; a higher standard of behavior undoubtedly exists because of their occupation.

Peace Officers Bill of Rights

Beginning in the 1990s, police officers have insisted on greater procedural safeguards to protect them against what they perceive as arbitrary infringement on their rights. These demands have been reflected in statutes enacted in many states, generally known as the "Peace Officers Bill of Rights." These statutes confer on an employee a property interest (i.e., their job is to be viewed as their property) in his or her position and mandate due process rights for peace officers who are the subject of internal investigations that could lead to disciplinary action. These statutes identify the type of information that must be provided to the accused officer, the officer's responsibility to cooperate during the investigation, the officer's rights to representation during the process, and the rules and procedures concerning the collection of certain types of evidence. Following are some common provisions of state Peace Officers Bill of Rights legislation:

Written notice. The department must provide the officer with written notice of the nature of the investigation, summary of alleged misconduct, and name of investigating officer.

Right to representation. The officer may have an attorney or a representative of his or her choosing present during any phase of questioning or hearing.

Polygraph examination. The officer may refuse to take a polygraph examination unless the complainant submits to an examination and is determined to be telling the truth. In this case, the officer may be ordered to take a polygraph examination or be subject to disciplinary action.

It is imperative that supervisors and managers become thoroughly familiar with statutes, contract provisions, and existing rules between employer or employee, so that procedural due process requirements can be met, particularly in disciplinary cases when an employee's property interest might be affected.

Free Speech

Although the right of freedom of speech is one of the most fundamental of all rights of Americans, the Supreme Court indicated in *Pickering v. Board of Education* (1968:568) that "the State has interests as an employer in regulating the speech of its employees that differ significantly from those it possesses in connection with regulation of the speech of the citizenry in general." Thus, the state may impose restrictions on its employees that it would not be able to impose on the citizenry at large. These restrictions must be reasonable, however.

A police regulation may be found to be an unreasonable infringement on the free speech interests of officers if overly broad. A Chicago Police Department rule prohibiting "any activity, conversation, deliberation, or discussion which is derogatory to the Department" is a good example of one that is unreasonable as such a rule obviously prohibits all criticism of the agency by its officers, even in private conversation (*Muller v. Conlisk*, 1970:901).

A related area is political activity. As with free speech, governmental agencies may restrict the political behavior of their employees to prevent employees from being pressured by their superiors to support certain political candidates or engage in political activities, under threat of loss of employment or other adverse action. The federal government and many states have such statutes.

A police officer may also be protected because of his or her political affiliations. An example is a case involving the Sheriff's Department in Cook County, Illinois, where a newly elected sheriff, a Democrat, fired the chief deputy of the process division and a bailiff of the juvenile court because they were Republicans. The Supreme Court ruled that it was a violation of the employees' First Amendment rights to discharge them from non-policymaking positions solely on the basis of their political party affiliation (*Connick v. Myers*, 1983; *Jones v. Dodson*, 1984).

The First Amendment's reach also includes appearance. For example, the Supreme Court upheld the constitutionality of a regulation of the Suffolk County, New York, Police Department that established several grooming standards regarding hair, sideburn, and moustache length for its male officers to make officers readily recognizable to the public and to maintain the esprit de corps within the department (*Kelley v. Johnston*, 1976).

Searches and Seizures

The Fourth Amendment to the U.S. Constitution protects the right of the people to be secure in their persons, houses, papers, and effects against unreasonable searches and seizures. In an important case in 1967, the Supreme Court held that the amendment also protected individuals' reasonable expectations of privacy, not just property interests (*Katz v. United States*, 1967).

The Fourth Amendment usually applies to police officers when they are at home or off duty in the same manner that it applies to all citizens. Because of the nature of their work, however, police officers can be compelled to cooperate with investigations of their behavior when ordinary citizens would not. Examples include searches of equipment and lockers provided by the department to the officers. The officers have no expectation of privacy that affords or merits protection (*People v. Tidwell,* 1971). Lower courts, however, have established limitations on searches of employees themselves. The rights of prison authorities to search their employees arose in a 1985 Iowa case, in which employees were forced to sign a consent form allowing such searches as a condition of hire; the court disagreed with such a broad policy, ruling that the consent form did not constitute a blanket waiver of all Fourth Amendment rights (*McDonell v. Hunter,* 1985).

Police officers may also be forced to appear in a lineup, a clear "seizure" of their person. Lineups normally require probable cause, but a federal appeals court upheld a police commissioner's ordering 62 officers to appear in a lineup during an investigation of police brutality, holding that "the governmental interest in the particular intrusion [should be weighed] against the offense to personal dignity and integrity." Again, the court cited the nature of the work, noting that police officers do "not have the full privacy and liberty from police officials that [they] would otherwise enjoy" (*Biehunik v. Felicetta,* 1971:230).

Self-Incrimination

The Supreme Court has also addressed questions concerning the Fifth Amendment as it applies to police officers who are under investigation. In *Garrity v. New Jersey* (1967), a police officer was ordered by the attorney general to answer questions or be discharged. The officer testified that information obtained as a result of his answers was later used to convict him of criminal charges. The Supreme Court held that the information obtained from the officer could not be used against him at his criminal trial, because the Fifth Amendment forbids the use of coerced confessions.

It is proper to fire a police officer who refuses to answer questions that are related directly to the performance of his or her duties, provided that the officer has been informed that any answers may not be used later in a criminal proceeding. Although there is some diversity of opinion among lower courts on the question of whether or not an officer may be compelled to submit to a polygraph examination, the majority of courts that have considered the question have held that an officer can be required to take the examination (*Gabrilowitz v. Newman,* 1978).

Religious Practices

Criminal justice work often requires that personnel are available and on duty 24 hours per day, 7 days a week. Although it is not always convenient or pleasant, such shift configurations require that many criminal justice employees work weekends, nights, and holidays. It is generally assumed that one who takes such a position agrees to work such hours and abide by other conditions of the job (i.e., carrying a weapon, as in a policing position); it is usually the personnel with the least seniority on the job who must work the most undesirable shifts. There are occasions, however, when one's religious beliefs are in direct conflict with the requirements of the job, such as conflicts between one's work assignment and attendance at religious services or periods of religious observance. In these situations, the employee may be forced to choose between the job and his or her religious beliefs.

Title VII of the Civil Rights Act of 1964 prohibits religious discrimination in employment. Thus, Title VII requires reasonable accommodation of religious beliefs, but not to the extent that the employee has complete freedom of religious expression (*United States v. City of Albuquerque,* 1976; see also *Trans World Airlines v. Hardison,* 1977).

Sexual Misconduct

Although we discussed sexual misconduct in Chapter 8, it deserves further mention here. To be blunt, criminal justice employees have ample opportunity to become engaged in affairs, incidents, trysts, dalliances, or other behavior that is clearly sexual in nature. In addition, a number of police "groupies" do in fact chase police officers and others in uniform.

Instances of sexual impropriety in police work can range from casual flirting while on the job to becoming romantically involved with a foreign agent whose principal aim is to learn delicate matters of national security. And there have been all manner of incidents between those extremes, including the discipline of female police officers who posed nude in magazines.

Clearly, this is a delicate area, one in which discipline can be and has been meted out as police supervisors and executives attempt to maintain high standards of officer conduct. It has also resulted in litigation, as some officers believe that their right to privacy has been invaded.

Residency Requirements

Many governmental agencies specify that all or certain members in their employ must live within the geographical limits of their employing jurisdiction. In other words, employees must reside within the county or city of employment. Such residency requirements have been justified by employing agencies, particularly in criminal justice, on the grounds that employees should become familiar with and be visible in the jurisdiction of employment and that they should reside where they are paid by the taxpayers to work. Perhaps the strongest rationale given by employing agencies is that criminal justice employees must live within a certain proximity of their work in order to respond quickly in the event of an emergency.

Moonlighting

The courts have traditionally supported police agencies placing limitations on the amount and kinds of outside work their employees can perform (*Brenckle v. Township of Shaler*, 1972; *Cox v. McNamara*, 1972; *Flood v. Kennedy*, 1963; *Hopwood v. City of Paducah*, 1968). Police restrictions on moonlighting range from a complete ban on outside employment to permission to engage in certain forms of work, such as investments, private security, or teaching police science courses. The rationale for agency limitations is that "outside employment seriously interferes with keeping the [police and fire] departments fit and ready for action at all times" (Williams, 1975:4).

Misuse of Firearms

Police agencies typically attempt to restrain the use of firearms through written policies and frequent training of a "shoot/don't shoot" nature. Still, a broad range of potential and actual problems remain with respect to the use and possible misuse of firearms, as the following shows.

Police agencies generally have policies regulating the use of handguns and other firearms by their officers, both on and off duty. The courts have held that such regulations need only be reasonable and that the burden rests with the disciplined police officer to show that the regulation was arbitrary and unreasonable (*Lally v. Department of Police*, 1974).

Police firearms regulations tend to address three basic issues: (1) requirements for the safeguarding of the weapon, (2) guidelines for carrying the weapon while off duty, and (3) limitations on when the weapon may be fired.

Courts and juries are dealing more harshly with police officers who misuse their firearms. The current tendency is to "look behind" police shootings in order to determine if the officer acted negligently or the employing agency negligently trained and supervised the officer or employee. Courts have awarded damages against police officers and/or their employers for other acts involving misuse of firearms, such as when an officer shot a person while intoxicated and off duty in a bar (*Marusa v. District of Columbia*, 1973); an officer accidentally killed an arrestee with a shotgun while handcuffing him (*Sager v. City of Woodlawn Park*, 1982); an unstable officer shot his wife five times and then committed suicide with an off-duty weapon the department required him to carry (*Bonsignore v. City of New York*, 1981); and an officer accidentally shot and killed an innocent bystander while pursuing another man at nighttime (the officer had received no instruction on shooting at a moving target, night shooting, or shooting in residential areas) (*Popow v. City of Margate*, 1979).

An officer's personal weapon will be tested thoroughly following any incident where it was discharged.
Courtesy NYPD Photo Unit.

Alcohol and Drug Testing in the Workplace

Alcoholism and drug abuse problems have taken on a life of their own in contemporary policing; employees must be increasingly wary of the tendency to succumb to these problems, while supervisors and managers must be able to recognize and attempt to seek counseling and treatment for officers with these companion problems.

It is obvious, given the extant law of most jurisdictions and the nature of their work, that criminal justice employees must not be "walking time bombs," but must be able to perform their work with a "clear head," unbefuddled by alcohol or drugs (*Hester v. Milledgeville,* 1984; *Krolick v. Lowery,* 1969). Police departments often specify in their manual of policy and procedures that no alcoholic beverages will be consumed within a specified period prior to reporting for duty. Such regulations have been upheld uniformly as rational because of the hazards of the work. Enforcing such regulations will occasionally result in criminal justice employees being ordered to submit to drug or alcohol tests.

In March 1989, the U.S. Supreme Court issued a major decision on drug testing of public employees in the workplace in *National Treasury Employees Union v. Von Raab,* which upheld drug testing when there was no indication of a drug problem in the workplace and held that although only a few employees test positive, drug use is such a serious problem that the program could continue. It stated that the Customs Service had a compelling interest in having a "physically fit" employee with "unimpeachable integrity and judgment" (*National Treasury Employees Union v. Von Raab,* 1989:38).

DISCIPLINARY POLICIES AND PRACTICES

A Tradition of Problems

Throughout its history, policing has experienced allegations of misconduct and corruption. In the late 1800s, New York police sergeant Alexander "Clubber" Williams epitomized police brutality, as he spoke openly of using his nightstick to knock a man unconscious, batter him to pieces, or even kill him. Williams supposedly coined the term *tenderloin* when he commented, "I've had nothing but chuck steaks for a long time, and now I'm going to have me a little tenderloin" (Morris, 1951:112). Williams was referring to opportunities for graft in an area of downtown New York that was the heart of vice and nightlife, often referred to as Satan's Circus. This was Williams's beat, where his reputation for brutality and corruption became legendary (Inciardi, 1996).

Although police corruption and brutality are no longer openly tolerated, a number of events throughout history have demonstrated that the problem still exists and requires the attention of police officials. Incidents such as the beating of Rodney King by officers in the presence of supervisors, the controversy surrounding the testimony of former Los Angeles police detective Mark Fuhrman during the O. J. Simpson trial, as well as major corruption scandals in the New York, Philadelphia, and New Orleans police departments have led many people to believe that police misbehavior today is worse than during the riotous 1960s (MacNamara, 1995). This perception about corruption is supported by the Mollen Commission's 1994 report on the New York City Police Department, which suggested that a worsening pattern of corruption existed then and at higher levels in the organization than was the case 20 years earlier (Gaffigan and McDonald, 1997). It is apparent why the issue of police misconduct is at the forefront of the policing agenda.

Officer misconduct and violations of departmental policy are the two principal areas that involve discipline (McLaughlin and Bing, 1987). Officer misconduct includes acts that harm the public, such as corruption, harassment, brutality, and civil rights violations. Violations of policy may involve a broad range of issues, including substance abuse and insubordination or minor violations of dress and punctuality.

The Need for Policies and Guidelines

Police agencies must pay close attention to any signs of police misconduct and respond quickly. It is therefore important that agencies enact policies to guide supervisors and managers on the handling of disciplinary issues. Policies provide an overall plan that helps to translate agency philosophy into practice. Policies guide employee behavior and conduct by setting acceptable and realistic parameters of control. The following are important requisites of a disciplinary policy (Iannone and Iannone, 2001:207–210):

> *Certainty*. Certainty of punishment is perhaps the greatest deterrent to misconduct. The fear of losing peers' respect, however, may outweigh the fear of punishment. The fear of punishment may be a helpful tool for police leadership to gain conformity from some employees.
>
> *Swiftness*. Punishment should be swift as well as certain. Any delays in investigations of punishment create unnecessary anxiety for the accused employee and a perception among officers of weakness and indecisiveness.
>
> *Fairness and impartiality*. When considering punishment, supervisors and managers should set all personal feelings and emotions aside. A system of discipline that considers the seriousness of the offense, aggravating and mitigating circumstances, and the officer's career record helps to ensure that consistency is met (Barker and Carter, 1994). Officers expect to be treated fairly, honestly, and respectfully during the course of the investigation. Another important consideration is to employ "justice tempered with mercy." For example, an officer who decides to go fishing and intentionally misses a court date should be punished more severely than an officer who inadvertently notes the wrong time on a calendar and misses court.
>
> *Consistency*. Similar misconduct should result in similar punishment; however, the aggravating or mitigating circumstances of each case coupled with an employee's past performance should also be considered when reviewing disciplinary alternatives. Overly severe or lenient punishment may create the opposite reaction from employees than what was intended.

Sencio (1992) noted that an effective policy ensures that

- Citizens are afforded the opportunity to lodge complaints and obtain information regarding the progress of the investigation.
- An impartial and objective investigation is carried out to obtain facts and support to refute the allegation.

- The rights of employees are not violated and they are protected from false, unjust, or vindictive accusations.
- The agency is protected from unsuitable employees and unwarranted criticism, while morale and competence are maintained.
- The community enjoys confidence in the police force and receives quality police service.

WHEN TROUBLE HAPPENS: THE NATURE AND INVESTIGATION OF COMPLAINTS

Complaint Origin

A personnel complaint is an allegation of misconduct or illegal behavior against an employee by anyone inside or outside the organization. Internal complaints arise within the organization and may involve supervisors who observe officer misconduct, officers who complain about supervisors, supervisors who complain about other supervisors or middle managers, civilian personnel who complain about officers, and so on. External complaints originate from sources outside the organization and usually involve the public.

Supervisors may receive complaints from primary, secondary, and anonymous sources. A *primary* source is the victim. A *secondary* source is a party other than the victim, such as an attorney, school counselor, or parent of a juvenile. An anonymous source is unknown, and the complaint may be delivered to the police station via a telephone call or unsigned letter.

Every complaint, regardless of the source, must be accepted and investigated in accordance with established policies and procedures. Some complaints, however, may be disposed of without the formality of an investigation. In some cases, the accused employee's actions clearly may be within departmental policy, and a simple communication to that effect to the citizen by a supervisor would resolve the matter. Such may be the case of a citizen who is offended that officers would handcuff an elderly shoplifting suspect. Other complaints may be so trivial that further inquiry or investigation is not necessary. For example, a citizen's call to the watch commander with a general complaint that too many police officers are employed by the city is not an issue that would be handled within a disciplinary process.

Anonymous complaints are the most difficult to investigate because there is no opportunity to obtain further information or question the complainant about the allegation. Anonymous complaints are additionally troublesome for the supervisor because of the potentially negative impact they may have on the employee's morale. Officers may view these types of complaints as unjust and frivolous and question why the department gives them any attention whatsoever. Supervisors and managers must help officers understand that complaints, regardless of their source, cannot be ignored or disregarded, and that disciplinary processes are designed to protect both the officer and organization, as well as preserve the public's trust.

Police leaders should also be aware that the most bizarre of accusations may prove true. In one western city, an anonymous complaint was received alleging that a marked city police vehicle was observed in another city 120 miles away and across state lines during the early morning hours. It was discovered that officers working in the rural outskirts of the city were making bets on how far they could travel and return during the course of a shift. Photos of officers in uniform standing next to their vehicle and the city limits sign of the city in question were discovered and used as evidence against the officers during their disciplinary hearing.

Types and Receipt

Supervisors and managers may handle complaints informally or formally. The seriousness of the allegation and preference of the complainant usually dictate whether a complaint will be investigated in a formal or informal manner. A formal complaint involves a written, signed, and/or tape-recorded statement of the allegation, and the complainant requests to be informed of the investigation's disposition. Figure 9–1 provides an example of a complaint form used to initiate a personnel investigation.

An informal complaint is an allegation of minor misconduct made for informational purposes that can usually be resolved without the need for more formal processes. If a citizen calls the watch commander to complain about the rude behavior of a dispatcher but does not wish to make a formal complaint, the supervisor may simply discuss the incident with the dispatcher and resolve it through informal counseling as long as more serious problems are not discovered and the dispatcher does not have a history of similar complaints.

These examples are typical of the majority of complaints handled by supervisors. Few complaints involve serious acts of physical violence, excessive force, or corruption. Wagner and Decker (1997) found that the majority of complaints against officers fall under the general categories of verbal abuse, discourtesy, harassment, improper attitude, and ethnic slurs. These comprise the issues that supervisors contend with on a daily basis.

The process for receiving a complaint should be clearly delineated by departmental policy and procedures. Generally, a complaint will be made at a police facility and referred to a senior officer in charge to determine its seriousness and need for immediate intervention. Complaints will usually be accepted from any person who feels injured or aggrieved. Complaints may be made through a variety of means, including in person, by mail, or over the telephone. Technology has increased the capacity of police agencies to provide citizens with

```
*************************************************************************************
                                                        Control Number: _____

Date & Time Reported     Location of Interview     Interview
_____    _____       ____Verbal ____Written ____Taped
_____
Type of complaint:         ____Force ____Procedural ____Conduct
                           ____Other (Specify)
_____
Source of complaint:       ____In Person ____Mail ____Telephone
                           ____Other (Specify)
_____
Complaint Originally       ____Supervisor  ____On Duty Watch Commander  ____Chief
Received by:               ____IAU         ____Other (Specify)
_____
Notifications made:        ____Division Commander       ____Chief of Police
Received by:               ____On-Call Command Personnel
                           ____Watch Commander          ____Other (Specify)
_____
Copy of formal personnel complaint report given to complainant?    ____Yes ____No
_____
*************************************************************************************
Complainant's name:                       Address:
_____     _____Zip_____
Residence Phone:                          Business Phone:
_____              _____
DOB:              Race:                    Sex:              Occupation:
_____        _____               _____        _____
*************************************************************************************
Location of Occurrence:                   Date & Time of Occurrence:
_____              _____
Member(s) Involved:                       Member(s) Involved:
(1)_____               (2)_____
(3)_____               (4)_____
Witness(es) Involved:                     Witness(es) Involved:
(1)_____               (2)_____
(3)_____               (4)_____
*************************************************************************************
(1)_____  Complainant wishes to make a formal statement and has requested an investigation
           into the matter with a report back to him/her on the findings and actions.
(2)_____  Complainant wishes to advise the Police Department of a problem, understand that
           some type of action will be taken, but does not request a report back to him/her on
           the findings and actions.
*************************************************************************************
                             CITIZEN ADVISEMENTS
(1)  If you have not yet provided the department with a signed written statement or a tape-
     recorded statement, one may be required in order to pursue the investigation of this matter.
(2)  The complainant(s) and/or witness(es) may be required to take a polygraph examination in
     order to determine the credibility concerning the allegations made.
(3)  Should the allegations prove to be false, the complainant(s) and/or witness(es) may be
     liable for criminal and/or civil prosecution.


           _____     _____
             Signature of Complainant              Date & Time

_____
Signature of Member Receiving Complaint
```

FIGURE 9–1 Police Department Formal Personnel Complaint Report

easier access. Some departments have begun to include complaint forms on their Web page on the Internet.

The manner in which an agency receives citizens' complaints can say much about the agency's philosophy and rigor in this regard. Diop Kanau, executive director of the Police Complaint Center, a nonprofit organization that assists victims of police misconduct, believes that the police often intend to investigate the complainant instead of the officer. In one-third of the agencies he studied, complainants had to take a polygraph test if they wanted to file a complaint, and in another agency of fewer than 30 officers, the police insist on getting the date of birth from any caller reporting a crime. "This is preposterous," Kanau opined. "They're running a warrant check on the caller; they're assuming you must've had a run in with a cop, and they can use any information they get to undermine your credibility" (quoted in Pedersen, 2001:140).

The Supervisor's Role in Internal Affairs Investigations

Internal affairs investigations represent a significant part of both the police supervisor's and the manager's job. In the day-to-day ebb and flow of policing, however, it is most often the first-line supervisors who shoulder the responsibility for conducting investigations into both minor and major complaints. Their function is to determine the facts, even though the accused may be police employees and the supervisors are investigating their own. Next, we discuss the general role and guidelines for the supervisor who is conducting complaint investigations (Arnold, 1998).

First, some preliminary work must be done. After being assigned an investigation, supervisors need to review all pieces of evidence: documents, statements, and photographs submitted by the complainant. Next, they should obtain any supporting documentation the department may have, such as a copy of the crime or arrest report or a printout of the call for service or radio transmission.

Interviews of all the parties involved then occur. There is a specific order in which this should be done: witnesses first, so that supervisors can develop questions for the complainant and the subject officer, whom they will interview later. Witness interviews should be tape-recorded, and prior to every interview, supervisors should prepare a list of questions and then, prior to asking the questions, explain the purpose of the interview and give the witnesses an opportunity to provide a narrative statement. Then, the supervisors can follow up with specific questions and be confrontational (when the evidence or other witnesses have provided facts to the contrary) or challenging (if the witnesses' responses to confrontational questions are not believable) (Arnold, 1998).

After interviewing witnesses, supervisors should have a solid understanding of the case and prepare a list of questions to ask the complainant. This interview should also be tape-recorded, and the complainant should be allowed to enter a statement, give his or her side of the story, and provide independent recollection of dates, times, and descriptions. Following this, supervisors should ask specific questions regarding the incident and if the complainant has information unavailable when the complaint is filed, such as the names of witnesses.

With regard to subject officer interviews, supervisors must review their applicable state statutes or confer with their legal advisors regarding peace officers' rights while under investigation. It must then be determined if the officer wants to have an attorney or representative present. As with other interviews, supervisors should prepare a list of specific questions beforehand and tape-record the interview. The officer should be informed of the nature of the investigation and then be allowed to provide a narrative statement about the incident. After taking the statement, supervisors should ask the officer specific questions, such as "What did you do?" "What did you say?" "Did you say _____ to the complainant?" Posing questions in this manner (instead of, say, "Do you recall . . . ?" or "Have you ever . . . ?") is a better means of obtaining concrete details. If the officer's statements contradict the evidence, supervisors must ask confrontational questions in a professional manner; while this may be unpleasant, supervisors have a professional duty to determine the facts (Arnold, 1998).

An investigative report must then be written that contains all the relevant facts of the case. The format of this report should follow agency protocol. Some agencies include a *complaint synopsis* (for example, "The complainant alleges Officer Smith was rude and used profanity in front of her") and *synopsis of the investigation* sections ("The investigation revealed that Officer Smith was, in fact, rude and used profanity in the presence of the complainant"). Many report forms also call for supervisors to include their own opinions and conclusions ("I conclude that Officer Smith violated policy by leaving work one hour early on the date in question") (Arnold, 1998).

The recommendations section should state the suggested determination of the complaint: sustained, not sustained, unfounded, or exonerated (possible determinations and recommendations are discussed more thoroughly next). Some agencies have a set "schedule" listing specific disciplinary actions for particular violations.

Investigative reports are reviewed by managers and executives and may resurface in a later grievance hearing or a possible civil suit. Therefore, the reports must be detailed, accurate, thorough, and unbiased.

Determination and Disposition

Once an investigation is completed, the supervisor or Internal Affairs Unit (IAU) officer must make a determination as to the culpability of the accused employee. Each allegation should receive a separate adjudication. Following are the categories of dispositions that are commonly used:

Unfounded. The alleged act(s) did not occur.

The internal affairs office is the locus of investigations for allegations of police misconduct. Here an internal affairs supervisor interviews an officer.

Exonerated. The act occurred, but it is lawful, proper, justified, and/or in accordance with departmental policies, procedures, and rules and regulations.

Not sustained. There is insufficient evidence to prove or disprove the allegations made.

Misconduct not based on the complaint. Sustainable misconduct was determined but is not part of the original complaint. For example, a supervisor investigating an allegation of excessive force against an officer may find the force used was within departmental policy, but that the officer made an unlawful arrest.

Closed. An investigation may be halted if the complainant fails to cooperate or it is determined that the action does not fall within the administrative jurisdiction of the police agency.

Sustained. The act did occur and it was a violation of departmental rules and procedures. Sustained allegations include misconduct that falls within the broad outlines of the original allegation(s).

Once a determination of culpability has been made, the complainant should be notified of the department's findings. Details of the investigation or recommended punishment will not be included in the correspondence. As shown in

Figure 9–2, the complainant will normally receive only information concerning the outcome of the complaint, including a short explanation of the finding along with an invitation to call the agency if further information is needed.

Level and Nature of Action

When an investigation against an employee is sustained, the sanctions and level of discipline must be decided. Management must be careful when recommending and imposing discipline because of its impact on the overall morale of the agency's employees. If the recommended discipline is viewed by employees as too lenient, it may send the wrong message that the misconduct was insignificant. On the other hand, discipline that is viewed as too harsh may have a demoralizing effect on the officer(s) involved and other agency employees and result in

---

Police Department
3300 Main Street
Downtown Plaza
Anywhere, USA 99999
June 20, 2003

Mr. John Doe
2200 Main Avenue
Anywhere, U.S.A.

Re: Internal Affairs #000666-98
    Case Closure

Dear Mr. Doe:

Our investigation into your allegations against Officer Smith has been completed. It has been determined that your complaint is SUSTAINED and the appropriate disciplinary action has been taken.

Our department appreciates your bringing this matter to our attention. It is our position that when a problem is identified, it should be corrected as soon as possible. It is our goal to be responsive to the concerns expressed by citizens so as to provide more efficient and effective services.

Your information regarding this incident was helpful and of value in our efforts to attain that goal. Should you have any further questions about this matter, please contact Sergeant Jane Alexander, Internal Affairs, at 555-9999.

Sincerely,

I. M. Boss
Lieutenant
Internal Affairs Unit

FIGURE 9–2   Citizen's Notification of Discipline Letter

allegations that the leadership is unfair. This alone can have significant impact on the esprit de corps or morale of the agency.

We have discussed the importance of having a disciplinary process that is viewed by employees as fair and consistent, meaning that similar violations receive similar punishments. It is also important that discipline is progressive and more serious sanctions are invoked when repeated violations occur. For example, a third substantiated violation of rude behavior may result in a recommendation for a one-day suspension without pay, whereas a first offense may be resolved through documented oral counseling or a letter of reprimand. Listed next are disciplinary actions commonly used by agencies in order of their severity:

Counseling. This is usually a conversation between the supervisor and employee about a specific aspect of the employee's performance or conduct; it is warranted when an employee has committed a relatively minor infraction or the nature of the offense is such that oral counseling is all that is necessary. For example, an officer who is usually punctual but arrives at briefing 10 minutes late two days in a row may require nothing more than a reminder and warning to correct the problem.

Documented Oral Counseling. This is usually the first step in a progressive disciplinary process and is intended to address relatively minor infractions. It is provided when no previous reprimands or more severe disciplinary action of the same or similar nature have occurred.

Letter of Reprimand. This is a formal written notice regarding significant misconduct, more serious performance violations, or repeated offenses. It is usually the second step in the disciplinary process and is intended to provide the employee and agency with a written record of the violation of behavior; it identifies what specific corrective action must be taken to avoid subsequent more serious disciplinary steps.

Suspension. This is a severe disciplinary action that results in an employee's being relieved of duty, often without pay. It is usually administered when an employee commits a serious violation of established rules or after a written reprimand has been given and no change in behavior or performance has resulted.

Demotion. In this situation, an employee is placed in a position of lower responsibility and pay. It is normally used when an otherwise good employee is unable to meet the standards required for the higher position or the employee has committed a serious act requiring that he or she be removed from a position of management or supervision.

Transfer. Many agencies use the disciplinary transfer to deal with problem officers; officers can be transferred to a different location or assignment, and this action is often seen as an effective disciplinary tool.

Termination. This is the most severe disciplinary action that can be taken. It usually occurs when previous serious discipline has been imposed and inadequate or no improvement in behavior or performance has occurred. It may also be used when an employee commits an offense so serious that continued employment would be inappropriate.

An employee's disciplinary record is not a permanent record. The time period for maintaining and purging disciplinary records is often specified by state administrative code. In some jurisdictions, the maintenance of IAU files is a matter of confidentiality, making any violation an unlawful act. Therefore, the maintenance and security of IAU files is often assigned to the IAU supervisor.

GRIEVANCES AND APPEALS

Notwithstanding all of the limitations on their rights and freedoms, police officers still may complain and grieve contractual or other matters that upset or concern them.

Formally Processing Grievances

The purpose of grievance procedures is to establish a fair and expeditious process for handling employee disputes that are not disciplinary in nature. Grievance procedures often involve collective bargaining issues, conditions of employment, or employer-employee relations. Grievances may cover a broad range of issues, including salaries, overtime, leave, hours of work, allowances, retirement, opportunity for advancement, performance evaluations, workplace conditions, tenure, disciplinary actions, supervisory methods, and administrative practices. Grievance procedures are often established as part of the collective bargaining process.

The preferred method for settling officers' grievances is through informal discussion. The employee explains his or her grievance to the immediate supervisor. An important aspect of supervision involves allowing employees to vent their frustrations, because most complaints can be handled through informal discussions. Those complaints that cannot be dealt with informally are usually handled through a more formal grievance process, as described next. A formal grievance begins with the employee submitting the grievance in writing to the immediate supervisor, as illustrated in Figure 9–3.

The process for formally handling grievances will vary among agencies and may involve several levels of action. Following is an example of how a grievance may proceed:

Level I: A grievance is submitted in writing to a supervisor. The supervisor will be given five days to respond to the employee's grievance. If the employee is dissatisfied, the grievance moves to the next level.

```
┌─────────────────────────────────────────────────────────────────────────┐
│                          Police Department                                │
│                       Formal Grievance Form                               │
│  Grievance #_____                                                 │
│                                                                           │
│  Employee Name: _____ Work Phone: _____  │
│  Department Assigned: _____ │
│  Date of Occurrence: _____ │
│  Location of Occurrence: _____ │
│                                                                           │
│  Name of:  1.  Department Head: _____ │
│            2.  Division Head: _____ │
│            3.  Immediate Supervisor: _____ │
│                                                                           │
│  Statement of Grievance: _____ │
│  _____ │
│  _____ │
│  _____ │
│                                                                           │
│  Witnesses: _____ │
│  _____ │
│  _____ │
│                                                                           │
│  What article(s) and or section(s) of the labor agreement of rules and    │
│  regulations do you believe                                               │
│  have been violated?_____ │
│  _____ │
│  _____ │
│  _____ │
│                                                                           │
│  What remedy are you requesting? _____ │
│  _____ │
│  _____ │
│                                                                           │
│                                                                           │
│  _____       _____                       │
│  Employee Signature      Signature of Labor Representative                 │
└─────────────────────────────────────────────────────────────────────────┘
```

FIGURE 9–3 Employee Grievance Form

Level II: At this level, the grievance proceeds to the chief of police, who will be given a specified time (usually five days) to render a decision.

Level III: If the employee is not satisfied with the chief's decision, the grievance may proceed to the city or county manager, as is appropriate. The manager will usually meet with the employee and/or representatives from the bargaining association and attempt to resolve the matter. An additional 5 to 10 days is usually allowed for the manager to render a decision.

Level IV: If the grievance is still not resolved, either party may request that the matter be submitted to arbitration. Arbitration involves a neutral, outside person, often selected from a list of arbitrators from the Federal Mediation and Conciliation Service. An arbitrator will conduct a hearing, listen to both parties, and usually reach a decision within 20 to 30 days. The decision of the arbitrator can be final and binding. This does not prohibit the employee from appealing the decision to a state court.

The actions of supervisors in dealing with grievances are vital to their successful resolution. Failure to act on grievances quickly may result in serious morale problems within an agency. Snow (1990) offered some helpful advice for supervisors when dealing with employee grievances:

Give employees your attention. Grievances are important to officers and must be dealt with quickly so that officers do not think that their concerns are being ignored.

Let officers vent. Do not interrupt officers while they are expressing their grievances. Let them fully explain their concerns and never let them think that you have already made a decision.

Search for the facts. Separate facts from rumors and half-truths. Search for the underlying causes of problems—those small issues that are often symptoms of a larger hidden problem.

Seek the advice of peers. Talk to other supervisors or experienced officers who may have dealt with similar issues and find out what their solutions were.

Do not trivialize grievances. Grievances are often emotional and volatile issues and should be treated with dignity and respect, regardless of their veracity.

Explain your decision. Take the time to explain the logic and reasoning of your decision with the employee. Even if an officer does not agree with a decision, he or she may accept it based on your explanation and reasoning.

End on a positive note. Often, an officer only wants someone to talk to and listen to the complaint. Supervisors should attempt to conclude interviews on a positive note and with some resolution in mind.

Appealing Disciplinary Measures

The process for employees to appeal recommended disciplinary measures is frequently outlined in civil service rules and regulations, labor agreements, and departmental policies and procedures. Appeals processes normally follow an officer's chain of command. For example, if an officer disagrees with a supervisor's recommendation for discipline, the first step of an appeal may involve a hearing before the division commander, usually of the rank of captain or deputy chief. The accused employee may be allowed labor representation or an attorney to assist in asking questions of the investigating supervisor, clarifying issues, and presenting new or mitigating evidence. The division commander would have five days to review the recommendation and respond in writing to the employee.

If the employee is still not satisfied, an appeals hearing before the chief of police or sheriff would be granted. This is usually the final step in appeals within the agency, and the chief or sheriff would communicate a decision to the employee in writing within 5 to 10 days. Depending on labor agreements and civil service rules and regulations, some agencies extend their appeals of discipline beyond the department. Employees may be able to bring their issue before the civil service commission or city or county manager for a final review. In the most extenuating circumstances, employees may also have the right to an independent arbitrator's review of discipline. The arbitrator's decision is usually binding.

RESPONDING TO PROBLEM OFFICERS: THE EARLY WARNING SYSTEM

Purposes and Functions

It has become a truism among police leadership that 10 percent of their officers cause 90 percent of the problems. Indeed, some research has indicated that as little as 2 percent of all officers are responsible for 50 percent of all citizen complaints. Problem officers are well known to their leaders, their peers, and to the residents of the areas in which they work (Walker, Alpert, and Kenney, 2001:1).

The early identification of and intervention with employee misconduct or performance problems are vital to preventing ongoing and repeated incidents. In an *early warning system* (EWS), a department intervenes before such an officer is in a situation that warrants formal disciplinary action. The system is a databased police management tool designed to identify officers whose behavior is problematic and to provide a form of intervention to correct that performance. The system alerts the department to these individuals and warns the officers while providing counseling or training to help them change their problematic behavior. EWS should not be viewed as an alarm clock, however; it is not a mechanical device that automatically sounds an alarm. Rather, it is an extremely complex, high-maintenance administrative operation that requires close and ongoing human attention.

Nearly 4 of every 10 (39 percent) of all municipal and county law enforcement agencies that serve populations greater than 50,000 people either have an EWS in place or are planning to implement one. Most (67 percent) require three complaints in a given time frame (normally a 12-month period) to identify a problem officer. Furthermore, in most systems (62 percent), the initial intervention consists of a review by the officer's immediate supervisor. Almost half (45 percent) involve other command officers in counseling the officer. And nearly all agencies with an EWS monitor an officer's performance after the initial intervention (Walker et al., 2001).

These systems may be divided into two types. The first and most often used is based on external citizen complaints against officers. The second type of system tracks officers' use of force, which is broadly defined and may include defensive tactics, batons, oleo capsicum (pepper) spray, Tasers, and so on. By reviewing and approving use-of-force reports, the supervisor must make a judgment concerning whether the officer is acting within departmental policies and regulations. Figure 9–4 provides an example of a use-of-force form.

The use of an EWS appears to have a dramatic effect on reducing citizen complaints and other indicators of problematic police performance. Recently in Minneapolis, citizen complaints against officers dropped by 67 percent one year after the intervention; in New Orleans, that number dropped by 62 percent (Walker et al., 2001). These systems also have a significant effect on police supervisors, initiating their responsibility to monitor officers who have been identified by the program.

Benefits and Potential Drawbacks

No disciplinary system is perfect, but developing a system to identify potential problems early offers many benefits. An EWS has potential drawbacks, however. The overall success of any system depends on how employees perceive its benefits and drawbacks. Reiter (1993) identified the benefits of an EWS:

1. An employee's career may be salvaged before the problem gets too serious.

2. It forces supervisors, particularly in field operations, to become actively involved in employee development.

3. It may provide necessary progressive discipline steps to support termination of an employee who fails to respond to remediation and other supervisory techniques.

4. The agency can gain valuable information that can be used to develop positive changes in training, equipment, tactics, and policy.

5. Properly documented action in this system may defend the agency against a "custom and practice" allegation in a civil suit (i.e., that certain inappropriate behaviors of officers were routine, customary, and practiced often).

6. A workable and articulated system may encourage greater community confidence in the agency's ability to control and manage itself.

There may be several potential drawbacks to the use of an EWS, however, such as the following (Reiter, 1993):

1. The use of an EWS could have an adverse impact on an individual employee's career, particularly if used inappropriately by supervisors or managers.

Date:
Type of Incident:
Location of Occurrence:

Officer Involved: Badge Number:
Area/Div Assigned: State Compensation Claim Filed   Y/N_____
Injuries/Officer: ___None   ___Treat/rel   ___Hospitalized   ___Fatal
Other Officers Involved: ___ Yes   ___ No   Number___

Subject #1
Name (Last, First, MI)
Sex, Race, DOB:
Level of Resistance: ___ None   ___ Physical   ___ Firearm   ___ Other Weapon
Injuries to Subject: ___Y/N
If Yes: ___Treated/Released   ___Hospitalized   ___Fatal
Type of Force Used: ___ Physical   ___ Capstun   ___ K-9   ___Firearm   ___ Carotid
___ Other (specify):
Charges:

Subject #2
Name (Last, First, MI):
Sex, Race, DOB:
Level of Resistance: ___ None   ___ Physical   ___ Firearm   ___ Other Weapon
Injuries to Subject: ___ Y/N
If Yes: ___ Treated/Released   ___ Hospitalized   ___ Fatal
Type of Force Used: ___ Physical   ___ Capstun   ___ K-9   ___ Firearm   ___ Carotid
___ Other (specify):
Charges:

Witnesses
#1 Name (Last, First, MI):
Address & Phone:

#2 Name (Last, First, MI):
Address & Phone:

#3 Name (Last, First, MI):
Address & Phone:

Supervisor:
Further Investigation Required   ___No Further Investigation Required
Date: Signature:

Shift Lieutenant:
Further Investigation Required   ___No Further Investigation Required
Date: Signature:

Division Commander:
Further Investigation Required   ___No Further Investigation Required
Date: Signature:

FIGURE 9–4   Supervisor's Use of Force Form

2. The system could restrict some employees' field performance if they developed an attitude that "no action is safe action."

3. Some supervisors may simply go through the motions of their role and not truly become involved and supportive of the system.

4. If the police agency does create and implement such a system and then fails to use it, the agency could be harmed by failure to identify a problem employee.

5. This system could be used by a plaintiff's attorney to accumulate resource information that might be helpful in a subsequent civil lawsuit.

On balance, it would seem that the benefits of an EWS outweigh the potential drawbacks. This system provides police leaders with vital information for early identification of and intervention with employee problems and may also protect the agency against litigation.

Developing a Preventive Policy

A carefully constructed policy on disciplinary matters can serve as a blueprint for the development of effective procedures. The Police Executive Research Forum (PERF) developed a model policy on how to handle officer misconduct. The purpose of establishing an internal affairs process is threefold: It engenders the trust and confidence of the public, helps supervisors and managers identify problems and areas that need increased direction or training, and helps protect the rights and due process of citizens and officers. Following are the essential components of PERF's (1981:2) model policy:

> *Prevention of Misconduct:* Agencies should make every effort to eliminate any organizational conditions that may foster, permit, or encourage improper behavior by their employees. Preventing misconduct should be an agency's primary means of reducing and controlling it.

> *Recruitment and Selection:* Testing that includes written psychological exams and interviews may ensure that the highest quality individuals are hired and protect against the selection of those who may be unsuited for the difficult tasks of police work.

> *Training:* Ethics training should be included as a major component of recruit training and revisited periodically in in-service classes. Departments should develop systems to ensure that rules, procedures, and outcomes of disciplinary processes are communicated to officers.

> *Written Directives Manual:* Every officer should receive a complete manual of departmental general orders, procedures, and training bulletins. Particular attention should be paid to sections dealing with misconduct and officers' responsibility and accountability to protect the civil rights of all citizens.

Supervisory Responsibility: Properly training supervisors is critical to ensuring that officers' performance conforms with departmental policies and procedures. Emphasis should be placed on methods of identifying problems early, counseling and intervention strategies, training needs, and providing professional referral for more serious problems.

Data Collection and Analysis: It is mandatory that records are kept of all internal affairs actions. General information should be communicated throughout the agency for training purposes. An EWS will assist agencies in early intervention and prevention of problems.

A "HOT BUTTON" ISSUE: RACIAL PROFILING

A contemporary, volatile issue in which police find themselves open to criticism and even disciplinary action involves racial profiling. This issue has driven a deep wedge between the police and minorities, many of whom claim to be victims of this practice. Indeed, a New Jersey state police superintendent was fired by that state's governor in March 1999 for statements concerning racial profiling that were perceived as racially insensitive.

Many people remain convinced that the justice system unfairly draws minorities into its web, and that police methods are at the forefront of this practice. Racial profiling—also known as "driving while black or brown" (DWBB)—occurs when a police officer acts on a personal bias and stops a vehicle simply because the driver is of a certain race (Neubauer, 1999:62).

Anecdotal evidence of racial profiling has been accumulating for years, and now many people and groups (such as the American Civil Liberties Union) believe that all "pretext" traffic stops are wrong, because the chance that racism and racial profiling will creep into such stops is high.

For their part, many police executives defend such tactics as an effective way to focus their limited resources on likely lawbreakers; they argue that profiling is based not on *prejudice* but on *probabilities*—the statistical reality that young minority men are disproportionately likely to commit crimes. As explained by Bernard Parks, an African American and former police chief of Los Angeles,

> We have an issue of violent crime against jewelry salespeople. The predominant suspects are Colombians. We don't find Mexican-Americans, or blacks, or other immigrants. It's a collection of several hundred Colombians who commit this crime. If you see six in a car in front of the Jewelry Mart, and they're waiting and watching people with briefcases, should we play the percentages and follow them? It's common sense. (quoted in Kennedy, 1999:31)

Still, it is difficult for the police to combat the public's perception that traffic stops of minorities simply on the basis of race are widespread and prejudicial in nature.

The best defense for the police may be summarized in two words: *collect data* (see, for example, Aether Systems, 2001; Garrett, 2001; Oliver and Zatcoff, 2001). Collecting traffic stop data helps chiefs and commanders determine whether officers are stopping or searching a disproportionate number of minorities and enables them to act on this information in a timely fashion (Garrett, 2001:103). In 1999, Connecticut was the first state to require all its municipal police agencies and the state police to collect race data for every police-initiated traffic stop (Cox, 2001); by mid-2001, at least 34 states either had enacted laws that included data collection or were considering data-collection legislation, and Congress is considering federal racial-profiling legislation. It is anticipated that eventually all states will require the tracking of race data for all contacts. Technology that is available to the police, including mobile data computers and wireless handheld devices, is being adapted for this purpose (Aether Systems, 2001).

Figure 9–5 shows a race data traffic stop form for the state of Connecticut.

The International Association of Chiefs of Police recently issued a comprehensive policy statement on biased policing and data collection. The association "believes that any form of police action that is based solely on the race, gender, ethnicity, age, or socioeconomic level of an individual is both unethical and illegal,"

State of Connecticut
Traffic Stops Statistics

Department — ORI:_____   Town:_____

Date:____/____/____   Time:_____:_____   Age:_____

Gender: Male Female Unknown

Race: W - White   Ethnicity: H - Hispanic
(Circle One)   B - Black   (Circle One)   N - Not Hispanic
               I - Indian Amer./Alaskan Native   U - Unknown
               A - Asian/Pacific Islander
               U - Unknown

Stop Nature: I - Investigation, Criminal   Statute:_____

Vehicle Search:
(Circle One)   Y - Yes
               N - No
               V - Violation, Motor Vehicle
               E - Equipment, Motor Vehicle
Disposition: U - Uniform Arrest Report   Event Number:_____
(Circle One)   M - Misdemeanor Summons   (as defined by your department)
               I - Infraction Ticket
               V - Verbal Warning
               W - Written Warning
               N - No Disposition

FIGURE 9–5   Connecticut Traffic Stops Statistics Form

but that data-collection programs "must ensure that data is being collected and analyzed in an impartial and methodologically sound fashion" (Voegtlin, 2001:8).

LEGAL CONSIDERATIONS

Negligent failure to discipline is an area that involves both policy and supervisory liability. What are the consequences of an agency's failure to develop an adequate policy and a system to investigate and prosecute violations by officers? Is an agency required to develop a system for receiving and handling citizen complaints against an officer? Generally, case law has held that liability exists if the plaintiff is able to prove that the disciplinary process was so lacking that officers believed no consequences would result from their actions. The bases of this belief include numbers of citizen complaints, how discipline is handled, and the department's failure to take action in matters that needed intervention.

In *Parish v. Luckie* (1992), the plaintiff claimed that she was victim of a false arrest and rape by a member of the police department. The court found that the department had a history of ignoring and covering up complaints of physical and sexual abuse by officers. The officer in question also had a history of violent conduct. The chief would only investigate complaints against officers that were in writing and improperly applied the standard of "beyond a reasonable doubt" to determine whether or not the case was sustained.

An example of a supervisor's failure to address problems is *Gutierrez-Rodriguez v. Cargegena* (1989). Puerto Rican drug agents came on the plaintiff and his girlfriend in a parked car. The agents approached the vehicle in civilian clothes and with weapons drawn. The plaintiff, seeing them approaching, started his car and attempted to drive away. Without warning or notice that they were police officers, the officers began firing at the car, striking the plaintiff in the back and permanently paralyzing him. The plaintiff sued the squad, the supervisor, and the police chief under Section 1983. The court found evidence of numerous complaints against the supervisor (13 separate citizen complaints filed against him in three years). The court awarded a $4.5 million judgment.

Liability may also be established in the department's past practices. In *Bordanaro v. McLeod* (1989), the court found that the agency had a widespread practice of unconstitutional warrantless entries and that the chief had knowledge or should have known that the practice was occurring. The court observed that when a large number of officers are conducting themselves in a like manner, that alone is evidence of an established practice by the department.

In *Ramos v. City of Chicago* (1989), however, the plaintiff alleged that he was beaten by police without provocation and that his beating was the result of an institutionalized practice by the Chicago Police Department, but the court did not find the city liable. The court concluded that six unrelated incidents of police brutality over a 10-year period in a police department of more than 10,000 officers failed to prove that a policy or custom existed that condoned brutality. This case is important in that it considered the size of the department and its location in its decision.

──── Case Studies ────

Following are two case studies, which will challenge the reader to look at disciplinary issues and determine what, if any, supervisory style changes or punitive measures are appropriate for the circumstances.

Making Enemies Fast: The "Misunderstood" Disciplinarian

Sgt. Jerold Jones does not understand why his officers appeal all of his disciplinary recommendations. He takes matters of discipline seriously; it commonly takes him three to four weeks to investigate minor matters—three to four times longer than other supervisors. Jones believes that by doing so, he shows great concern for his officers and, in fact, does not even question the officers about their behavior until the investigation is nearly complete and he has interviewed everyone involved in the matter. Jones decides to speak to his officers about the matter. He is surprised when they tell him that they do not trust him. Indeed, they fail to understand why so much time is needed for him to investigate the minor incidents. They believe that he is being secretive and is always looking for ways to find fault with their performance. Jones argues that his recommendations are consistent with those of other sergeants and provides some examples of similar cases that were handled by various supervisors. Apparently unconvinced by Jones's argument, the next day an officer appeals one of Jones's disciplinary recommendations concerning a minor traffic accident.

1. Are the officers' allegations of Sgt. Jones's unfairness valid?
2. What requisites of sound disciplinary policy may Jones not understand that may be leading to the officers' appeals?
3. Under the circumstances, should Jones simply ignore the officers' complaints? Are their perceptions that important?

Downtown Sonny Brown

Officer Sonny Brown works the transport wagon downtown and has worked this assignment on day shift for several years. Because of his length of service in this assignment, he has earned the nickname "Downtown" Brown. He loves "hooking and booking" drunks and takes great pride in keeping the streets safe and clean. Local business owners appreciate his efforts, even once honoring him as the Chamber of Commerce "Officer of the Year." Sgt. Carol Jackson is recently promoted and receives her first patrol assignment to the downtown district. As it has been a while since she worked patrol, she decides to ride with Brown for a couple of days to learn about the district and its problems. She is pleased at the warm reception Brown receives from business merchants but quickly becomes concerned about some of his heavy-handed methods of dealing with drunks. When questioned about his tactics, Brown replies, "This ain't administration, Sarge, it's the streets, and our job is to sweep 'em clean." Jackson speaks with Brown's former supervisor, who said he had received several verbal complaints against Brown from citizens, but none could be substantiated. Apparently no one was interested in the word of a drunk against a popular officer. Two days later, Sgt. Jackson is called to the county jail to meet with a booking officer, Hamstead, who wants to talk with her about a drunk who was booked a few hours earlier by Brown. Another prisoner has confided to Hamstead that the drunk was complaining that Brown had injured him by kicking him off a park bench and pushing him down a hill to the transport wagon. The drunk, complaining of pain in his side, was then taken to the hospital and treated for three broken ribs. When asked later about the incident, the drunk refused to cooperate and simply told Hamstead, "I fell down."

1. How should Sgt. Jackson handle this matter?
2. What are her options? Her responsibilities?
3. What types of disciplinary policy changes should the department consider to prevent these situations from occurring?

SUMMARY

This chapter has demonstrated the importance of police agencies' developing and implementing sound disciplinary policies and practices. Policies and training are needed for supervisors and managers to identify and respond to employee misconduct or performance problems at an early stage. Policies also ensure that discipline is administered in a consistent and equitable manner throughout the organization. Prompt, complete, and full investigations of alleged misconduct coupled with the appropriate level of discipline may minimize or even eliminate potential civil liability.

The public's trust and respect are precious commodities and can be quickly lost with the disregard or improper handling of allegations of misconduct. The public expects that police agencies will make every effort to identify and correct problems and respond to citizens' complaints in a judicious manner.

ITEMS FOR REVIEW

1. Delineate the rights that police officers possess, as well as areas in which they have limitations placed on their behavior and activity, according to court decisions and legislation.

2. Review the various forms of disciplinary actions that may be taken against police officers.

3. Explain the basic procedure to be followed by supervisors when performing an internal affairs investigation.

4. Describe the benefits of having an early warning system (EWS) to identify problem officers.

5. Provide four examples of negligent supervision of police officers that have resulted in liability.

6. Define racial profiling, why it is problematic for both society and the police, and what police leaders may do to cope with it.

REFERENCES

Aether Systems, Mobile Government Division (2001). Special report II: Overcoming the perception of racial profiling. *Law and Order* (April):94–101.

Arnold, J. (1998). Internal affairs investigation: The supervisor's role. *FBI Law Enforcement Bulletin* (January):11–16.

Barker, T., and Carter, D. L. (1994). *Police deviance*. Cincinnati: Anderson.

Biehunik v. Felicetta, 441 F.2d 228 (1971).

Bonsignore v. City of New York, 521 F.Supp. 394 (1981).

Bordanaro v. McLeod, 871 F.2d 1151 (1989).

Brenckle v. Township of Shaler, 281 A.2d 920 (Pa. 1972).

Connick v. Myers, 461 U.S. 138 (1983).

Cox, S. M. (2001). Racial profiling: Refuting concerns about collecting race data on traffic stops. *Law and Order* (October):61–65.

Cox v. McNamara, 493 P.2d 54 (Ore. 1972).

Flood v. Kennedy, 239 N.Y.S.2d 665 (1963).

Gabrilowitz v. Newman, 582 F.2d 100 (1st Cir. 1978).

Gaffigan, S. J., and McDonald, P. P. (1997). *Police integrity: Public service with honor.* Washington, DC: U.S. Department of Justice.

Garrett, R. L. (2001). Changing behavior begins with data. *Law Enforcement Technology* (April):100–108.

Garrity v. New Jersey, 385 U.S. 483 (1967).

Gutierrez-Rodriguez v. Cargegena, 882 F.2d 553 (1st Cir., 1989).

Hester v. Milledgeville, 598 F.Supp. 1456, 1457 (M.D.Ga. 1984).

Hopwood v. City of Paducah, 424 S.W.2d 134 (Ky. 1968).

Iannone, N. F., and Iannone, M. P. (2001). *Supervision of police personnel* (6th ed.) Upper Saddle River, NJ: Prentice Hall.

Inciardi, J. A. (1996). *Criminal Justice,* 5th ed. Orlando, FL: Harcourt Brace.

Jones v. Dodson, 727 F.2d 1329 (4th Cir. 1984).

Katz v. United States, 389 U.S. 347 (1967).

Kelley v. Johnston, 425 U.S. 238 (1976).

Kennedy, R. (1999). Suspect policy. *The New Republic* (September 13):30–35.

Krolick v. Lowery, 302 N.Y.S.2d. 109 (1969), p.115.

Lally v. Department of Police, 306 So.2d 65 (La. 1974).

MacNamara, J. (1995, November). Panel discussion on ethics and integrity. California Peace Officers' Association Meeting, Napa, CA.

Marusa v. District of Columbia, 484 F.2d 828 (1973).

McDonell v. Hunter, 611 F.Supp. 1122 (S.D. Iowa, 1985), affd. as mod., 809 F.2d 1302 (8th Cir., 1987).

McLaughlin, V., and Bing, R. (1987). Law enforcement personnel selection. *Journal of Police Science and Administration* 15:271–276.

Morris, L. (1951). *Incredible New York.* New York: Bonanza.

Muller v. Conlisk, 429 F.2d 901 (7th Cir. 1970).

National Treasury Employees Union v. Von Raab, 489 U.S. 656 (1989).

Neubauer, R. (1999). Quoted in Keith W. Strandberg, Racial profiling. *Law Enforcement Technology* (June):62.

Oliver, J. A., and Zatcoff, A. R. (2001). Lessons learned: Collecting data on officer traffic stops. *The Police Chief* (July):23–29.

Parish v. Luckie, 963 F.2d 201 (1992).

Pedersen, D. (2001). Rising above corruption: How to put integrity at the forefront in your department. *Law and Order* (October):136–142.

People v. Tidwell, 266 N.E.2d 787 (Ill. 1971).

Pickering v. Board of Education, 391 U.S. 563 (1968).

Police Executive Research Forum (1981). *Police handling of officer misconduct: A model policy statement.* Washington, DC: Author.

Popow v. City of Margate, 476 F.Supp. 1237 (1979).

Ramos v. City of Chicago, 707 F.Supp. 345 (1989).

Reiter, L. (1993). *Law enforcement administrative investigations: A manual guide.* Tallahassee, FL: Lou Reiter and Associates.

Sager v. City of Woodlawn Park, 543 F.Supp. 282 (D. Colo., 1982).

Sencio, W. J. (1992). Complaint processing: Policy considerations. *The Police Chief* 7:45–48.

Snow, R. L. (1990). A right to complain: Grievance procedures for small departments. *Law and Order* 5:39–41.

Trans World Airlines v. Hardison, 97 S.Ct. 2264 (1977).

United States v. City of Albuquerque, 12 EPD 11, 244 (10th Cir. 1976).

Voegtlin, G. (2001). Biased-based policing and data collection. *The Police Chief* (October):8.

Wagner, A. E., and Decker, S. H. (1997). Evaluating citizen complaints against the police. In R. G. Dunham and G. P. Alpert, eds., *Critical issues in policing: Contemporary readings.* Prospect Heights, IL: Waveland.

Walker, S., Alpert, G. A., and Kenney, D. J. (2001, July). Early warning systems: Responding to the problem police officer. Washington, DC: U.S. Department of Justice, National Institute of Justice Research in Brief.

Williams, R. N. (1975). *Legal aspects of discipline by police administrators.* Traffic Institute Publication 2705. Evanston, IL: Northwestern University.

PART THREE

Supervising Police Work

10

Deploying and Scheduling Personnel

❖

After reading this chapter, the student will:

- understand how to calculate the number of officers required to meet calls for service and to be available for other functions
- know how to deploy officers by time and location
- be knowledgeable about prioritizing calls for service, and alternative responses to calls
- comprehend the major differences between the 8-hour and 10-hour duty schedules, as well as other compressed work schedules
- be informed about the unique nature of officer deployment under community policing
- understand problems concerning overtime work

We need a sense of value of time—that is, of the best way to divide one's time into one's activities.

—Arnold Bennet

INTRODUCTION

The scheduling and deployment of patrol officers are primary concerns for police administrators, middle managers, and supervisors alike, all of whom struggle on a daily basis with balancing the needs of officers with those of the department and the community. For these practitioners, ensuring 24-hour, 7-days-per-week shift coverage is a complex task. This chapter examines the issues surrounding the scheduling and deploying of police officers to satisfy departmental service delivery objectives.

A somewhat unique view is taken in terms of how this chapter's personnel deployment and scheduling material is presented. First, these matters are approached from primarily a *qualitative* point of view, rather than one that is highly quantitative. This chapter does provide some basic quantitative information, such as simple formulas and calculations for determining adequate numbers of personnel for every day, around the clock. It is assumed, however, that the complex aspects of deployment and scheduling can be accomplished or are greatly aided by computer software (discussed in the section on patrol planning), in-service training sessions, and available literature. Furthermore, once a police agency's executives adopt and implement a particular staffing pattern, that pattern is not likely to change often; therefore, supervisors and managers do not have to spend every duty day studying staffing schedules.

But what *does* change is the *philosophical,* or qualitative, aspect of personnel deployment and scheduling. As will be seen, the current adoption of the community oriented policing and problem solving strategy by more and more police departments across the country has fostered the need for greater examination, flexibility, and modification of personnel deployment. Once the COPPS philosophy is adopted, the task falls to the supervisor to see that personnel are deployed in keeping with the needs of that strategy and are given the necessary time to engage in COPPS activities.

This chapter begins with a look at the need for patrol planning and then examines methods of determining resource allocation needs, including calculating patrol force size. We then review some methods for performing a workload analysis and then consider several alternative patrol responses. Next is a look at some of the basic types and elements of compressed shift schedules, such as the 4–10 plan, and a comparison of permanent and rotating shifts; this section also includes a review of relevant federal legislation. We then discuss deployment strategies, including the deployment demands of the COPPS initiative. The chapter continues with a consideration of overtime and brief mention of the influence of unions on scheduling and deploying officers. Two case studies conclude the chapter.

PATROL PLANNING

The largest, most costly, and most visible function in a police agency is patrol. Yet patrol receives the least amount of planning or analysis. As an example, patrol beats are all too often created by convenient streets, railroad tracks, rivers, and so forth, rather than by thoughtful planning and analysis of officer workload by geographical area. Few police agencies pay regular attention to evaluating and adjusting patrol plans to meet service demands. Instead, patrol is often the first division for which a police administration seeks to reduce personnel in order to enhance specialized units or to create new programs. This practice often leaves the patrol division in need of personnel and often results in morale problems and unnecessary delays in responding to calls for service (CFS). The unfortunate consequence of this situation is that supervisors are left to manage the demands of patrol by reacting to crises rather than by thoughtful planning.

Planning is an important, powerful tool for helping police managers cope with the backlash of shrinking budgets and accompanying personnel cutbacks that have plagued police agencies since the 1970s. Patrol planning enables managers to properly assess service demands so that resources may be appropriately allocated across shifts and proportionate to workload. Computer software can design various combinations of shift patterns; print staffing reports for up to a year; provide quick access to all employee information, such as seniority date, shift preferences, and phone number; see an entire month's shifts at a glance; and quickly edit assignments. Several private corporations now produce and advertise such software in professional trade magazines, such as *The Police Chief,* published by the International Association of Chiefs of Police, and *Law and Order* magazine. Administrators and supervisors who want to maximize their resources would do well to consider investing in such software.

A lack of proper patrol planning may be attributed to several factors. First, few police agencies have planning units, so planning (aside from that involving the budget) is usually nonexistent. The lack of data also presents a problem. Few police agencies have sufficient data for analyzing their CFS, time spent on calls by officers, time that officers are available for CFS and other work, the number of units assigned, and so on. Even when this data exists, few agencies have the trained staff to conduct in-depth analyses. The natural resistance to new ideas by

The NYPD utilizes the COMPSTAT (computer statistics) process, meeting monthly to review crime trends, plan tactics, and allocate resources. *Courtesy NYPD Police Unit.*

some people may also create barriers to change. Many agencies are tradition bound and resist any new approaches to change patrol practices.

The primary purpose of patrol planning is to keep supervisors and managers apprised of how resources are being utilized. This enables them to make informed decisions about departmental operations and also to develop future plans. A patrol plan should be based on an analysis of data concerning the tasks that officers perform during their shifts of duty. These plans should also be flexible and constantly reviewed to meet the changing needs and goals of an organization.

RESOURCE ALLOCATION

Another important part of police leadership lies in how to best allocate resources, especially when new resources are difficult to obtain and the police are being asked to do more with less. Next, we examine the early research concerning how the patrol function should be allocated, and then we look at some methods for determining how many officers are required to do the job.

Early Research

One of the earliest studies of patrol allocation was conducted in Trenton, New Jersey. In 1959, the Trenton Police Department contracted with the International Association of Chiefs of Police to conduct a study to determine how many uniformed officers were needed to patrol the city's streets and neighborhoods. CFS were evaluated by location, time of day, and day of week. Incidents were also weighted to account for the longer time necessary to process more serious offenses. The study resulted in a plan that deployed personnel in proportion to workload variations.

This study marked the beginning of allocation studies and replaced the traditional equal distribution of personnel that was often used in the past. Under a *flat system,* an equal number of officers are distributed across shifts, days of week, and location. Flat systems fail to take into consideration variations in workload and are prone to creating disproportionate demands on officers.

By 1975, various mathematical models were used for determining the appropriate allocation of personnel to patrol functions. Then, by the late 1970s, a number of computer-based allocation schemes were developed to improve the efficiency and effectiveness of patrol allocation plans (e.g., Gay, Schell, and Schack, 1977). From these studies, more comprehensive workload factors were developed for determining allocation needs, based on dispatch information (Levine and McEwen, 1985:21). These factors include the following:

- Total numbers of CFS
- Officer-initiated activities
- Administrative activities
- Number of CFS by hour, shift, beat, and reporting area
- Average dispatch delay (in minutes)
- Average travel time (in minutes)
- Average on-scene time (in minutes)
- Average service time (in minutes)
- Average number of backup patrol units per call
- Probability that all units are busy
- Average number of free units

Determining Patrol Force Size

The collection and analysis of data are the foundation of proper patrol deployment. Unfortunately, as mentioned earlier, many police agencies do not adhere to such rational and scientific approaches. Three crude methods are used by police departments to determine resource needs (Roberg and Kuykendall, 1995:284):

Intuitive. This is basically educated guesswork based on the experience and judgment of police managers. It is probably the most commonly used method for small agencies when the number of incidents and officers available is so low that more analytical analysis may not be necessary for determining when and where officers should be deployed.

Workload. This requires comprehensive information, including standards of expected performance, community expectations, and the prioritization of police activities. Although rarely used by an entire police agency, it is most often used for determining resource needs for patrol or specific programs, such as crime prevention.

Comparative. Often the most common method used by police agencies, the comparative method is based on a comparison of agencies by number of officers per 1,000 residents. Data is available in the *Uniform Crime Reports* (UCR), published annually by the Federal Bureau of Investigation. The U.S. Department of Justice (2001:291) data reveals a national average of 2.4 full-time, sworn police officers per 1,000 residents in the United States; the range is 1.8 officers in communities with populations of 25,000 to 99,999 residents to 3.7 officers in cities with 250,000 or more residents; suburban and rural counties averaged 2.6 officers.

Another method for determining allocation needs is to set an objective related to the amount of time an agency wants officers to be committed to CFS and available for other functions. There is no established guideline, but agencies often set an objective that would restrict officers' time that is committed to CFS at 30 to 40 percent of total time available per shift. Gay et al. (1977) found that officers spend approximately 23 percent of their patrol time on administrative matters, 23 percent on calls for assistance, 40 percent on preventive patrol, and 14 percent on directed patrol. Levine and McEwen (1985:35) provided the following guide for agencies when determining allocation needs using this formula:

Step 1. Set an objective for patrol performance (e.g., 30 to 40 percent committed to CFS).

Step 2. Select a time period to be analyzed.

Step 3. Determine CFS workload for this time period.

Step 4. Calculate the number of units needed based on the workload and the selected objective.

Step 5. Calculate the number of on-duty officers needed per shift.

Step 6. Multiply by the relief factor (defined later) to obtain the total number of officers needed.

Table 10–1 uses these steps and shows the basic data for calculating the number of patrol officers needed in a city's patrol force. Assume that after discussion of how busy patrol units should be, and given that the agency is engaged in COPPS strategy, the following objective is determined: "There should be sufficient units on duty so that the average unit utilization on CFS will not exceed 30 percent." Assume further that a mix of 70 percent one-officer and 30 percent

TABLE 10–1 An Example of Data for Determining Patrol Force Size

	Midnights	Days	Evenings
1. Workload Data			
Calls for service	1,027	1,614	2,059
Average time (minutes)	32 min.	28	33
Assists	225	273	463
Average time (minutes)	22 min.	20	18
Traffic accidents	109	129	150
Average time (minutes)	63 min.	58	60
2. Hours of work for entire 4-week period	745	969	1,421
Average hours of work per shift	26.6	34.6	50.8
3. Units needed for 30%	11	14	21
4. Number of 1-officer units	8	10	15
Number of 2-officer units	4	4	6
5. Number of officers needed per shift	14	18	27
6. Total number of officers needed (relief factor = 2.2)	31	40	59

Source: U.S. Department of Justice, National Institute of Justice, *Patrol Deployment* (Washington, DC: U.S. Government Printing Office, 1985), p. 34.

two-officer units will be established for each shift. The data was collected during a four-week (28-day) period.

The first section of Table 10–1 shows the *total* number of calls for service, assists, and traffic accidents by shift for the four weeks, along with the average times for these activities for each shift. With these activities and average times, the total amount of work for the patrol force amounts to about 745 hours for the midnight to 8 A.M. shift; 969 hours for the 8 A.M. to 4 P.M. shift; and 1,421 hours for the 4 P.M. to midnight shift. Since a 28-day period was being studied, the average work *per shift* amounted to 26.6 hours, 34.6 hours, and 50.8 hours, respectively. (As an example, for midnight to 8 A.M., $1,027 \times 32 = 32,864$; $225 \times 22 = 4,950$; $109 \times 63 = 6,867$, for a grand total of 44,681 minutes or 745 hours of work; 745 hours of work divided by 28 shifts = 26.6 hours of work per shift.)

To calculate the number of patrol units needed to meet the desired objective—average unit utilization on CFS will not exceed 30 percent—we use the following formula:

Average Hours of Work Per Shift = Number of Units Needed
(Shift Length) (Unit Utilization)

Again, using the midnight shift as an example, the calculation would be as follows:

26.6 hours = 11.08 units
(8 hours) (30%)

The answer must be rounded to 11 units since fractions of units are not possible. Similar calculations for the day and evening shifts give results of 15 units and 21 units, respectively. Table 10–1 shows the officers needed for these shifts under the decision of a 70 percent/30 percent split between one-officer/two-officer units.

The final line in Table 10–1 multiplies the number of officers needed by the department's relief factor of 2.2 (to cover officers' absences due to days off, sick leave, vacations, training, and so on) to give a total of 35 officers for the midnight shift, 42 officers for the day shift, and 59 officers for the evening shift. A total of 136 officers would be required to meet the objective of an average 30 percent unit utilization. If an objective other than unit utilization had been selected, the same steps would have been followed to determine the number of units needed, but the calculations would have been different.

The selection of a 30 percent unit utilization objective is subject to criticism; remember that there is no universal rule to guide the choice of a percentage. A department should consider the "big picture" of patrol resource allocation; certainly, the existence of a COPPS philosophy should be weighted into this decision.

Finally, the use of a relief factor of 2.2 in the previous example and in Table 10–1 is also subject to debate. Another commonly accepted relief factor for determining the number of police officers that is needed to staff a shift annually is 1.66. Indeed, a common calculation that uses the 1.66 relief factor is that 5 officers are required to a position for an entire year: 3 (shifts) $\times$ 1.66 (officers) = 4.97 or 5 officers.

Other Allocation Issues

Traditional approaches to determining patrol allocation needs are vested in the belief that, whenever possible, patrol resources should be distributed in proportion to workload by day of week, time of day, and location. These workload analysis factors are discussed in more detail later. The rationale for this approach rests with the concern that nonproportional staffing may result in varying levels of service. It may also create morale problems for those officers who must handle a disproportionate share of the workload.

More recent patrol deployment formulations take into account a broad range of workload analysis data and other factors, including average time to travel to incidents due to geographic barriers (such as thoroughfares, freeways, bridges, and mountains), may have a significant impact on response times and should be considered when designing beats and car plans, discussed later in this chapter.

WORKLOAD ANALYSIS

Basic Approaches

A workload analysis produces essential data about patrol operations. The primary objective of a workload analysis is to provide supervisors with information concerning patterns of service demands for the purpose of determining allocation needs and developing efficient and effective shift schedules and deployment schemes.

A workload analysis provides information to assist with the temporal (short-term) and geographic allocation of personnel. Temporal allocation can be attained by calculating the percentage of the total workload occurring during each shift per day and then assigning a comparable percentage of available officers to shifts. The same process can be used for distributing personnel in each area. Table 10–2 shows an example of two plans for allocation of patrol resources.

Option one in Table 10–2 is the traditional approach to deployment used by many agencies, with equal staffing on all three shifts. Under option two (assuming that 20 officers are sufficient for the evening shift), the department reduces the total number of officers required by matching allocations to CFS demands. The savings are obvious. As an added bonus, the surplus of officers can be either transferred to an understaffed section of the department or redeployed as a special operations unit for enhancing crime prevention and directed patrol activities (Levine, 1982).

Deployment by Time and Location

Two of the most important factors in allocating personnel are location and time. The location of problems helps police in dividing the community into geographic beats or divisions of approximately equal workload. By analyzing the varying times of incidents, appropriate shifts can be determined. Mobility and geographic barriers are also important factors when considering allocation

TABLE 10–2 Two Plans for Allocating Patrol Resources

| | | *Deployment Options* | |
	Percentage of Total Calls for Service by Shift	Option One Equal Staffing	Option Two Efficiency[a]
Shift			
Midnight	20%	20	9
Day	35%	20	16
Evening	45%	20	20
Total personnel deployed[b]		60	45

[a]The efficiency option assumes that the 20 officers assigned to the Evening Shift are sufficient to respond to all calls for service and provide adequate preventive patrol during the peak demand period.

[b]This total reflects only the number of officers deployed and not the total complement actually needed, because the relief factor was not considered.

Source: Adapted from U.S. Department of Justice, National Institute of Law Enforcement and Criminal Justice, *Improving Patrol Productivity,* Volume I: *Routine Patrol* by Gay et al. (Washington, DC: U.S. Government Printing Office, July 1977), pp. 26–29.

needs. Table 10–3 shows how personnel workload can be determined by CFS per shift by calculating the percentage of the total workload occurring during each shift per day and then assigning a comparable percentage of the available officers to the shifts. Personnel can be distributed geographically using a similar process. That is, the first step is to determine the workload in each district or sector, then calculate the portion of the shift's workload handled in each area, and finally assign personnel accordingly.

Table 10–4 shows an example of CFS demands for each hour of the day, and Table 10–5 is a sample of CFS workload demands by day of the week broken down into 168 hours.

TABLE 10–3   Sample Distribution of Personnel by Hourly Workload

Hours by Shift	Calls for Service	Percent of Total Hourly Workload	Percent of Manpower Assigned
0700–0759	58	2.11	Day Shift
0800–0859	77	2.80	
0900–0959	90	3.28	29.27
1000–1059	100	3.64	
1100–1159	107	3.90	
1200–1259	117	4.26	
1300–1359	123	4.48	
1400–1459	132	4.80	
1500–1559	158	5.75	Evening Shift
1600–1659	153	5.57	
1700–1759	165	6.01	47.03
1800–1859	172	6.26	
1900–1959	161	5.86	
2000–2059	164	5.97	
2100–2159	164	5.97	
2200–2259	155	5.64	
2300–2359	159	5.79	Midnight Shift
2400–0059	118	4.30	
0100–0159	101	3.68	23.68
0200–0259	90	3.28	
0300–0359	60	2.18	
0400–0459	45	1.64	
0500–0559	37	1.35	
0600–0659	40	1.46	
Total	2,746	99.98*	99.98*

*Total does not equal 100% because of rounding.
Source: U.S. Department of Justice, National Institute of Justice, *Patrol Deployment* (Washington, DC: U.S. Government Printing Office, 1985), p. 29.

TABLE 10–4 Sample 24-Hour Graph of Workload Distribution

Source: U.S. Department of Justice, National Institute of Justice, *Patrol Deployment* (Washington, DC: U.S. Government Printing Office, 1985), p. 27.

TABLE 10–5   Sample Workload by Day of Week

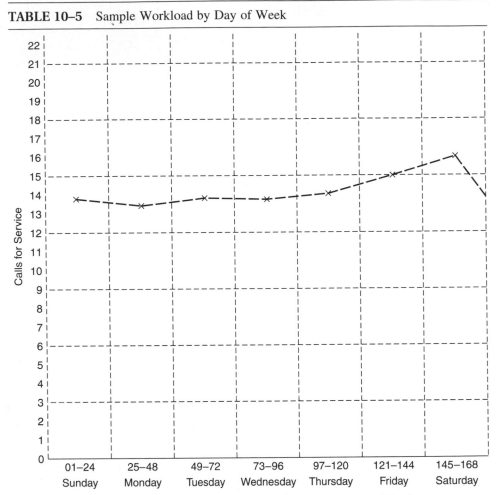

Source: U.S. Department of Justice, National Institute of Justice, *Patrol Deployment* (Washington, DC: U.S. Government Printing Office, 1985), p. 28.

Car Plans

After patrol personnel have been assigned according to needs of time and location, the supervisor or manager must deploy them to beats or patrol car districts. Separate car plans should be established for each shift to equalize workloads for all officers. The boundaries for the beats in a six-car plan on the day shift might be different from the boundaries in a six-car plan on the night shift because of changing needs at various times of the day. For example, a congested industrial area might present quite different problems on the day shift from those on the night shift when the businesses are closed (Iannone and Iannone, 2001). And, as we have seen earlier, the number of patrol vehicles in use will also vary by time of day and day of week.

The car plan in use will normally be dictated by the number of officers on duty and available for field patrol. If two-officer units are used, adjustments will be necessary. Using one-officer units, a nine-car plan will be required to cover nine beats, unless two of the beats use two-officer patrol units, in which case 11 officers would be required.

Patrol districts should ideally be grouped into beats so that each will contain as nearly as practicable an equal percentage of the total police work. Each beat in a 10-car plan would theoretically cover 10 percent of the work, each beat in a 5-car plan would ideally cover 20 percent of the work, and so on. By trying out different beats according to ideal percentage of workload and most desirable boundaries, the supervisor will eventually develop a variety of reasonably effective car plans from which he or she can select those that are most workable. Note that beats will not be equal in area, since area, as represented by street miles, is only one factor used in determining relative need for patrol (Iannone and Iannone, 2001).

Use of Computer Models

Computer-based analysis and allocation models were developed as early as the 1960s. These models assist administrators who often struggle with shift-related issues, such as fixed versus rotating schedules, one- versus two-officer cars, and compressed schedules. Some of the first programs developed were the Patrol Car Allocation Model (PCAM), by the RAND Corporation; Hypercube Queueing Model, by Public Systems Evaluation, Inc.; and Patrol Plan/Beat Plan, by the Institute of Public Program Analysis. These automated systems were capable of performing a number of staff distribution functions and could simplify the process of determining allocation needs and designing beats (Levine and McEwen, 1985).

The Statistical Package for Social Sciences (SPSS) can also be used to analyze workload and develop schedules. This comprehensive statistical package is personal–computer-based, inexpensive, and simple to run with some training. It may also be merged with mapping programs that are commonly used by police to obtain graphic representations of crime issues (e.g., location, population density, and reports of drug activity).

Clearly, a comprehensive workload analysis provides the foundation for determining allocation needs and deployment schemes. It provides the basic information for determining the number of patrol officers who are required to staff shifts each day of the week. Once an analysis is completed, managers can select the most appropriate deployment schemes to attain departmental objectives.

ALTERNATIVE PATROL RESPONSES

Why Respond to Every Call? Seeking Alternatives

Our discussion thus far assumes that every CFS requires the response of a uniformed patrol officer. However, increasing workloads, shrinking budgets, and increased public demands for service are key factors in police administrators' decisions to

Computer-aided dispatch (CAD) systems prioritize calls based on their seriousness, and send assigned beat officers to handle the call for service.
Courtesy NYPD Photo Unit

employ alternative methods for handling nonemergency CFS. Research (Scott, 1981) has shown that as much as 30 to 40 percent of CFS do not require dispatching a patrol unit to the scene and could be handled by alternative call-taking methods. These alternative response methods are commonly referred to as *differential police response* (DPR). They reduce patrol officers' workloads, allowing them to spend more time with directed patrol activities, initial investigations, case follow-up, and neighborhood problem-solving activities.

Differential response provides a tremendous opportunity for administrators to gain some control over limited resources. The potential savings in officers' hours can have a significant impact on allocation and deployment.

Beginning in the mid-1970s, police departments began to question whether a patrol officer's response to every CFS, especially nonemergency situations, was needed in order to produce effective outcomes. Several studies concerning the patrol function were conducted during the 1970s and 1980s and greatly affected managerial assumptions about traditional strategies for responding to citizen CFS. Following are descriptions of some of those key studies that led police administrators to consider alternative patrol responses:

Kansas City Preventive Patrol Experiment. This evaluation of the effectiveness of random preventive patrol challenged several traditional assumptions held by police. Normal, proactive (saturation), and reactive (emergencies only) patrols were conducted in 15 of 24 beats in the city's south patrol division. The normal strategy involved conventional single patrol car response to CFS. The proactive strategy involved increasing preventive patrol and police visibility by tripling the number of cars on patrol in another area. The reactive strategy was characterized by the virtual elimination of patrol cars. No significant differences in crime reduction were found in any of the experimental beat areas, regardless of the level of patrol. This experiment suggested that random police patrol was not a factor in deterring crime (Kelling, 1974).

Kansas City Response Time Study. This study evaluated whether rapid response to calls increased the likelihood of arresting offenders. It was discovered that the most important factor in arresting offenders was not the speed at which the police responded, but the delay in calling the police. Simply, the fastest response could not compensate for delays in reporting the incident (Bieck and Kessler, 1977).

RAND Study of Managing Investigations. This study cast a first critical eye on detective work. Findings suggested that the way detectives were organized had little effect on the results of investigations. Factors, such as case screening, that focus on those cases with the highest possibility of arrest, while weeding out those cases with few solveability factors, were more important. It also determined that the quality of patrol officers' initial investigation was a significant factor in making an arrest (Greenwood, 1975).

Team Policing Experiment. Team policing was a popular reform effort that sought to improve crime prevention and reduction efforts by assigning teams of officers to a particular neighborhood and giving them responsibility for all services in that area. An evaluation of its implementation in seven cities in the United States suggested that the experiment was largely a failure. Findings revealed that poor planning and implementation by chief administrators, confusion by officers about what they were supposed to do, and resistance by mid-managers who resented sharing their authority with sergeants and officers contributed to its failure (Sherman, 1973).

One- Versus Two-Officer Patrol Cars. In a study of the effectiveness of one- versus two-officer patrol cars, Hale (1981) suggested that officer productivity and operational efficiency were in fact increased by using one-officer patrol units. Officer safety concerns can be addressed by establishing a policy that requires the dispatching of two cars to high-risk CFS. Wrobleski and Hess (1993) added that one-officer patrol vehicles can patrol twice the area, and that solo officers are generally more cautious and more attentive to their patrol duties since they do not have a partner to engage in coversation.

Newark and Flint Foot Patrol Studies. Evidence on the effects of foot patrol is somewhat mixed. In Newark, New Jersey, findings suggested that citizen fear of crime was reduced while citizen satisfaction with the police increased; however, foot patrols had no significant impact on reported crime or victimization (Police Foundation, 1981). In Flint, Michigan, findings suggested that the neighborhood foot patrol program appeared to decrease crime, increase citizens' satisfaction with the police, and reduce public fear (Trojanowicz, 1986). The lack of sound experimental designs contributed to this inconsistent evidence regarding the effects of foot patrol (Green and Taylor, 1991). As a result, these findings should be interpreted with caution until more information is made available.

Newark and Houston Fear Reduction Studies. These jurisdictions tested several fear-reduction strategies, including citizen newsletters, victim recontact, neighborhood storefronts, increased citizen contact during patrol, community organizing, and coordinated comunity policing efforts. These studies were implemented to evaluate the impact of these efforts on the public's fear of crime. Findings indicated that these programs were least effective in reducing the public's concerns about property crime and most effective at reducing perceived civil disorder (Pate et al., 1986).

Newport News Problem Oriented Policing. This study examined whether police officers could employ more rigorous analysis of the underlying causes of crime problems and reduce the prevalence of multiple incidents. Officers were trained and provided a problem-solving model called S.A.R.A. (for *s*canning, *a*nalysis, *r*esponse, and *a*ssessment). The study showed that properly trained officers could employ problem solving as a daily practice. This study reported significant reductions in the burglary and prostitution (Eck and Spelman, 1987).

Later we discuss other methods for addressing nonemergency CFS.

Call Management: Prioritizing Calls for Service

Call management is a process for screening and prioritizing CFS. Today most police agencies have computer-aided dispatch (CAD) systems that are capable of prioritizing calls by their importance. Obviously, more dangerous and in-progress calls such as robberies and assaults would receive the highest priority and an immediate response from patrol units, while a general request for information may bring a delayed response. Police departments have clearly established dispatch protocols that determine the priority of call responses, such as the following:

Priority 1: Danger to life and/or property is imminent, or a crime of a serious nature is in progress. Examples include an armed robbery in progress, a shooting with the suspect on the scene, a major accident, and so on.

Priority 2: Threat to a person or property is possible or a breach of the peace is occurring. Examples include a loud argument or verbal disturbance, an unruly shoplifter in the custody of store security, loud music or party, and so on.

Priority 3: No threat to life or to property exists, and a delay in response would not cause undue inconvenience to the citizen. Examples include theft of property that occurred days ago, a request for a house watch, a dead animal in the road, and so on.

Oftentimes the volume of CFS will exceed the number of personnel who are available to respond. In this case, police agencies are forced to hold the calls and delay their response. Policies generally will guide the amount of time in which a call may be delayed. For example, Priority 1 calls may require an immediate response in all cases, Priority 2 calls can be held for 15 minutes, and Priority 3 can be held for 30 minutes. When a pending call cannot be assigned to an officer within the established time limit, it is usually the responsibility of the dispatcher to notify a field supervisor or watch commander. The supervisor may need to direct communications to relieve an officer from a nonessential activity, such as lunch or another less serious call, or to hold the call for the next available officer.

Other Alternative Responses

A number of alternatives are available to reduce officer workload and increase productivity. Nearly all of these alternatives to traditional mobile response contain some mechanism to produce more time for officers to perform other activities. They have been developed and tested by the National Institute of Justice, and they include telephone report units, delayed mobile response (stacking calls, setting appointments), walk-in reports, and use of nonsworn personnel in lieu of patrol officers (such as civilian evidence technicians, animal control officers, community service specialists). Each is discussed briefly next.

One of the major purposes of developing alternative response strategies is that those calls requiring rapid mobile response can receive priority, while other calls are handled by methods that both satisfy the citizen and accomplish the needs of the department.

Telephone Reporting

One of the most effective call alternative strategies for relieving officer workload is the Telephone Report Unit (TRU). Reports are handled over the telephone rather than by a patrol officer dispatched to the scene. TRUs provide several advantages for police agencies and the public. For example, a Priority 3 call (discussed earlier) can take 45 to 60 minutes for an officer to respond, while a telephone report can be handled in 10 to 15 minutes and at the convenience of the caller. A telephone reporting unit may handle as much as 25 to 50 percent of an agency's non-investigative reports. This accounts for a considerable amount of the workload and frees officers in the field to engage more in community problem solving.

In order to be effective, a call classification system and prioritization scheme are needed so that call takers can properly classify incoming calls. A training program is also required for call takers, dispatchers, and officers who must be familiar with the new procedures. Evaluations of this approach have consistently shown it to be efficient and without a loss in citizen satisfaction. In addition to the volume of work that can be handled by TRUs, experience has shown that they provide major savings in the amount of time taken to complete a report and also save money on vehicle maintenance costs. They also afford sworn officers more time for self-initiated activities and arrests (Levine and McEwen, 1985).

Delayed Response

Delayed response means that the presence of a police officer is required at the scene, but the incident is of sufficiently minor nature that a rapid dispatch is not necessary. Such instances include "cold" larcenies and burglaries, unoccupied suspicious vehicle calls, and vandalism calls. The trend today is to develop formal delayed response strategies that specify the types of calls that can be delayed, and for how long. Factors to be considered are the seriousness of the call, presence or absence of injuries, and amount of damage. Most departments' policies state a maximum delay time, such as 30 or 45 minutes, after which the closest available unit is assigned to the call (Levine and McEwen, 1985).

Although the delayed response does not directly reduce officer workload, it does help make the existing workload more manageable. It increases the likelihood that officers will receive calls in their area of assignment, resulting in fewer cross-beat dispatches, and prevents officers from being interrupted while on another assignment (such as COPPS activities).

The call taker must inform the citizen that an officer will not arrive immediately; studies have found that once the call taker informs the citizen of the expected police arrival time, citizen satisfaction is not adversely affected by the delay (Levine and McEwen, 1985).

Walk-in/Mail-in Reporting

Many police agencies also have instituted programs that encourage citizens to come to the nearest police facility at their convenience to file a report, or the police may send a report package to citizens to be completed and returned by mail. The recent trend by police agencies to decentralize patrol operations through various COPPS initiatives has resulted in an increase in neighborhood police mini-stations. These provide an excellent and convenient place for citizens to complete walk-in reports or to pick up or deliver reporting packages.

Use of Nonsworn Personnel

The use of volunteer and nonsworn personnel to handle nonemergency CFS has gained considerable popularity over the years. Many agencies utilize volunteers who have been trained in citizen police academies, reserve police academies, and senior volunteer programs to handle a bulk of the workload traditionally handled by uniformed officers.

Another concept used by many police agencies to reduce patrol officer workload is the Community Service Officer (CSO) program. This program uses nonsworn personnel in the field and to respond to CFS, thus eliminating the requirement for an officer's presence. A CSO may engage in traffic accident investigations, take vandalism reports, perform parking enforcement, conduct basic crime scene investigations and collect evidence, dust for fingerprints, and perform other related duties. In some agencies, CSOs also staff mini-stations to handle telephone and mail-in reporting requests, again eliminating the need for an officer at these locations.

The civilianization of police agencies is another area that should be explored. It makes little sense to assign a fully trained and qualified police officer to administrative or support duties when those responsibilities can be better handled by nonsworn personnel. Some of the areas being civilianized in police agencies include dispatching, research and planning, crime analysis, finance, parking enforcement, custody, technical/computer support, and animal control.

SHIFT SCHEDULING

General Recommendations

The question of whether or not to work around-the-clock shifts is not an option for the police. Police organizations are bound by their 24-hour responsibility to public problems to deploy officers to beats in shifts. What is most important is that departments develop shifts that assure the safety and longevity of officers and provide efficient and effective services to the public. Primary concerns are the physical and emotional health and productivity of officers. O'Neill and Cushing (1991:71–73) provided the following advice for administrators when creating shifts:

1. A system of steady shifts with selection based, at least in part, on fair and equitable criteria such as seniority grade. Shift selection could provide for 75 percent of the positions to be filled by seniority and 25 percent of the positions filled at management's discretion.

2. A steady midnight shift in which the workweek is limited to four consecutive days. Officer's court dates would be scheduled for the day preceding their first night of work, and this would be considered a workday.

3. Redeployment of personnel so that only the required minimum number of officers and supervisors are on duty from 2 A.M. to 6 P.M. This would more accurately reflect the demand for service by assigning more officers to shifts where they are needed most.

4. In general, no changing of shifts within a time period should be permitted without making allowances for proper rest. In those rare instances when this must be done, several days of advance notice must be given. There should be no changing of shifts for purely disciplinary reasons. Officers should be permitted to bid for another shift at least twice during a year, and vacancies should be announced.

Administrative decisions concerning shift scheduling can have significant impacts on officer performance and the quality of police service the community receives. The challenge for the supervisor is to employ a schedule that meets the needs of both the organization and the officers. An optimal shift schedule can minimize shortages by determining the correct starting times and days for the right number of officers so that, on an hourly basis, the number of officers on duty matches the patrol needs as closely as possible.

Traditionally, the patrol division has utilized a 3 eight-hour shift plan. For example, day shift officers would be assigned to work from 8 A.M. to 4 P.M., "swing" or evening shift officers work from 4 P.M. to 12 A.M., and night ("graveyard") shift officers are deployed from 12 A.M. to 8 A.M. In recent years, however, alternative 9-, 10-, and 12-hour shifts have become popular (these are discussed later). Regardless of the shift schedule that is employed, police administrators should ensure that it provides staffing levels and proper supervision, and that it improves patrol effectiveness.

Permanent Versus Rotating Shift Assignments: Advantages and Debilitating Effects

The issue of permanent versus rotating shifts has long been argued at length in police management literature. There are advantages and disadvantages to both methods. The primary advantages of having personnel work a permanent or fixed shift is its simplicity of scheduling and assignment of officers according to workload. Other advantages of fixed shifts include fewer physiological problems for personnel, fringe benefits for senior officers (such as better choice of days off), easier court scheduling, and the fact that studies have indicated that most officers prefer to work fixed shifts (Brunner, 1976). The disadvantages of fixed shifts include the time-honored tradition of placing rookie officers on the graveyard shift, which then has the greatest number of the least-experienced personnel; the stress on younger officers who may be assigned to higher workload shifts; and the officers' lack of experience of working various shifts. Officers may also argue that permanent shifts result in officers' losing touch with other shift activities or becoming stale.

Rotating shifts also offer some advantages, including the fact that rotating officers have an opportunity to experience the different kind of work that occurs on each shift and have different times of day off for their personal or family needs. But the disadvantages weigh heavily on the rotating-shift officers. The frequency of rotation (some agencies rotate as often as monthly or quarterly) creates disruptions in officers' homelife and their pursuit of higher education, as well as fatigue. The physical adjustment to rotating shifts may be the equivalent of "jet lag."

Because rotating shift work is debilitating and even dangerous, O'Neill and Cushing (1991) report that police departments are moving away from rotating shifts, and that most major departments are moving or have moved out of what some psychologists have termed the "dark ages" and into a fixed shift schedule or a more scientifically designed type of rotation. Departments are realizing that the rotating shift is to blame for poor performance, bad attitudes, absenteeism, and accidents.

Another reason for giving strong consideration to permanent shift assignments concerns the number of police agencies that are implementing COPPS. Under this philosophy, shift rotation can greatly frustrate the officers' attempts to solve neighborhood problems on their beats. Indeed, frequent shift rotation can be a death knell for COPPS's effectiveness. Goldstein (1990:160), the founder of the problem oriented policing concept, argued that

> The ultimate form of decentralization [occurs when] officers are assigned permanently, *for a minimum of several years,* to a specific area. Such an arrangement enables an officer to get to know the problems of a community, the strengths and weaknesses of existing systems of control, and the various resources that are useful in solving problems. Changes in the time during which a police officer works seriously detract from the potential to cement relationships between a police officer and [citizens]. If maintaining permanent assignments to both an area and a time of day is not possible, considerable effort must be invested in communications among officers serving the same area to ensure continuity and consistency in dealing with problems. (emphasis added)

The research on shift work strongly suggests that administrators should carefully consider the benefits and hazards of various shift schemes. Human beings are naturally day oriented or diurnal in their activity patterns. Shift work disrupts the body's complex biological clock, known as the *circadian rhythm,* and can result in stress-related illnesses, fatigue-induced accidents, family crises, and lower life expectancy. Furthermore, supervisors need to be aware of the higher probability of accidents and errors during shifts when officers may be fatigued. Moore-Ede and Richardson (1985) noted that the Exxon *Valdez* incident (11 million gallons of crude oil were dumped into Alaska's Prince William Sound in 1989), nuclear accidents at Three Mile Island (March 1979) and Russia's Chernobyl (April 1986, killing 45 people and affecting tens of thousands more because of the aftereffects), and the industrial chemical disaster in Bhopal (killing 6,000 people in India in 1984) all occurred during the early hours of the morning when the risk of employee fatigue was at its highest. A review of each of these accidents and scores more involving automobiles, airplanes, trains, and ferries has cited fatigue as a factor.

Assigning Officers to Shifts

Two principal forms of shift scheduling exist. The first is a *flat system* of scheduling that assigns an equal number of officers to each shift. The obvious problem with this type of scheduling is that demands vary across shifts. Most jurisdictions find the weekend late evening and early morning hours to be the busiest, thus presenting the most danger to officers from the types of calls during those time periods. The day shift may also be busy but involved in noninvestigative theft and burglary reports or traffic- and accident-related incidents that present little threat to officers. Also, a high percentage of typical day shift calls can be assigned to differential responses. One study showed that the typical distribution of calls by shift varied. In what the study termed a "typical city," approximately 22 percent of the CFS occurred between 12 A.M. and 8 A.M., while 33 percent of the CFS were received from 8 A.M. to 4 P.M. and 45 percent between 4 P.M. and 12 A.M. (O'Neill and Cushing, 1991).

Compressed Work Schedules

Compressed work schedules have gained considerable momentum, with the strong support of police employees and representative labor organizations. This support is prompted by a changing mood in the workplace that has resulted from numerous economic, legislative, and cultural changes (Williams and Eide, 1995). In both corporate America and government, employers are being forced to be more flexible in their work arrangements. The trend in law enforcement began in the 1970s, with many agencies, including the Huntington Beach, California, Police Department and the Sacramento County Sheriff's Department, moving toward 4/10 (officers work four days per week, 10 hours per day) plans.

Considerable debate has taken place among police practitioners about the benefits and problems associated with these 9-, 10-, and 12-hour compressed work schedules. While advocates claim improvements in the quality and quantity of work, reduced sick time, and lower attrition rates, managers remain skeptical and have voiced concerns to the contrary.

With each compressed schedule, certain benefits and concerns appear. Of utmost concern for the supervisor considering a compressed schedule is that the schedule meet the needs of the department and employee. Following are some of

During briefing sessions at the beginning of each shift, supervisors must properly assign and deploy personnel.
Courtesy Riverside, California, Police Department.

the types of compressed work schedules that have been implemented and tested by agencies across the United States:

5-day, 8-hour schedule (5–2 [8]). The 5–2 (8) work schedule remains the most common format used by police agencies. In some jurisdictions, an overlapping 7 P.M. to 3 A.M. shift is added to assist evening and night officers during what is traditionally the busiest time of their shifts—when bars and taverns empty, fights and domestic disturbances begin to occur, and buildings and residences are more often burglarized under cover of darkness.

4-day, 10-hour schedule (4–3 [10]). Under the 4–3 (10) shift plan, officers work four 10-hour days per week, with three days off. This shift configuration also has a built-in overlap during shifts (Table 10–6). When scheduled properly, the overlaps can be utilized to ensure that more employees are available during late afternoon and evening hours, which are typically peak workload times for agencies. Four/ten plans have been studied extensively by many police agencies. It has been found that officers generally favor the shorter

TABLE 10–6   A Basic 8- and 10-Hour Duty Shift Configurations

Type of Shift	Day	Evening (Swing)	Night (Graveyard)
Three	8 A.M.–4 P.M.	4 P.M.–12 P.M.	12 P.M.–8 A.M.
8-hour	or	or	or
shifts*	7 A.M.–3 P.M.	3 P.M.–11 P.M.	11 P.M.–7 A.M.
4–10 hr.-shift[†]	7 A.M.–5 P.M.	3 P.M.–1 A.M.	9 P.M.–7 A.M.

*Swing or relief officers may work all three shifts to cover as needed.
[†]This shift has built-in overlapping of personnel.
Source: M. J. Levine and J. T. McEwen, *Patrol Deployment* (Washington, DC: U.S. Department of Justice, 1985).

workweek because of the added time for leisure, education, and moonlighting. Nevertheless, many police executives have decided against implementing the 4/10 plan for a host of reasons, including the fatigue factor, the greater need to control officers' moonlighting, the need for more equipment to accommodate extra personnel during overlapping periods of duty, and the potential need for higher salary budgets to pay employees at overtime rates for exceeding eight hours per day (Iannone and Iannone, 2001). In addition, this schedule makes training for 10-hour blocks problematic. Table 10–6 depicts in simple terms the 8- and 10-hour shift configurations.

Table 10–7 presents a more detailed comparison of the 5–2 (8) and the 4–3 (10) duty shifts, using average types and amounts of days off that are taken by officers in a typical year. Several important aspects of the two shifts may be noted. First, 5–2 (8) personnel are on-duty 1,760 hours per year and can be scheduled to work for 220 shifts; 4–3 (10) personnel are on-duty for 1,680 hours per year and work 168 shifts. What is *not* shown in the table is that while both 5–2 (8) and 4–3 (10) personnel will earn about the same hourly wage (because they work about the same number of hours per year), 4–3 (10) personnel will earn much more compensation per shift worked as well as per overtime hour and shift.

3-day, 12-hour schedule (3–4 [12]). The 3/12 plan originated in the private sector nearly 40 years ago but has gained the attention of police only within the past decade. Unlike 9- and 10-hour plans, it fits neatly into a 24-hour day for scheduling. Normally, officers are assigned to work three days a week, with four days off for three weeks, and four days a week with three days off for the fourth week of a 28-day cycle. Again, proponents claim the benefits of increased productivity and employee morale as justification for 3/12 shifts (Schissler, 1996). Management voices concerns regarding increased fatigue and potential increased costs associated with the Fair Labor Standards Act,

TABLE 10–7   Comparisons of Scheduling Availability for the 8- and 10-Hour Duty Shifts

5–2 (8) Shift Scheduling Availability

BASE = 8 HRS./DAY × 365 DAYS PER YEAR = 2,920 HOURS

From the base, we subtract the following time off (averages are used; actual amount of time off taken per year will vary from agency to agency; officer to officer):

Days		Hours
Days off	2 days/week × 8 hrs./day × 52 wks./yr. =	832 hrs.
Vacation	16 days/week × 8 hrs./day =	128
Holidays	3 days/year =	24
Sick/Injury	7 days/year =	56
Training	5 days/year =	40
Compensatory	8 days/year =	64
Compassionate	1 day/year =	8
Other (military, discipline)	1 day/year =	8
		Total: 1,160 hrs.

Hours and shifts for which personnel may be expected to be on duty are as follows:
   2,920 hrs.(base) − 1,160 hrs. off duty = 1,760 hrs. (or 220 eight-hour shifts).

Note that an officer is available for duty only *60 percent* of the time.

4–3 (10) Shift Scheduling Availability

BASE = 10 HRS./DAY × 365 DAYS PER YEAR = 3,650 HOURS

From the base, we subtract the following time off (averages are used; actual amount of time off taken per year will of course vary from agency to agency, officer to officer):

Days		Hours
Days off	3 days/week × 10 hrs./day × 52 wks./yr. =	1,560 hrs.
Vacation	16 days/week × 10 hrs./day =	160
Holidays	3 days/year =	30
Sick/Injury	7 days/year =	70
Training	5 days/year =	50
Compensatory	8 days/year =	80
Compassionate	1 day/year =	10
Other (military, discipline)	1 day/year =	10
		Total: 1,970 hrs.

Hours and shifts for which personnel may be expected to be on-duty are as follows:
   3,650 hrs. (base) − 1,970 hrs. off duty = 1,680 hrs. (or 168 ten-hour shifts).
Note that an officer is available for duty only *46 percent* of the time.

discussed later, as primary issues. Nonetheless, the 12-hour plan is enjoying increased support, with many agencies now using and praising it (see, for example, Talley, 1995). It is touted by many agencies as resulting in higher officer morale and productivity, with reduced sick leave time taken.

5-day, 9-hour schedule (5–2 [9]). The 9-hour work schedule requires five working days followed by two days off, five workdays followed by three days off, and a final workday with another three days off. The 5/9 schedule is becoming popular with nonuniformed assignments, such as detective units and administration.

No single shift-scheduling configuration fits all needs, nor would we recommend one shift pattern over the others. Administrators should decide on the shift that accomplishes a balance between organizational objectives and employee needs. Maintaining staffing levels, productivity, fatigue, equipment, and overtime costs should be evaluated carefully before deciding on a compressed schedule.

Split and Overlapping Shifts

We should also mention that so-called "split shifts" in which officers work a few hours, are relieved for a period, and then return to complete their tour of duty should usually be avoided because of the adverse effects they have on morale. There are times, however, when such arrangements are desirable for officers wishing to further their education or to attend to other personal needs during the middle of their shift. Indeed, split shifts may be sought after by such personnel (Iannone and Iannone, 2001).

Also, on occasion, because of inordinately high workloads at certain peak periods, it may be desirable to institute overlapping shifts to meet this need. For example, if certain problems arise at about 8 P.M. each evening, a 6 P.M. to 2 A.M. shift might be implemented. Like split shifts, overlapping shifts should also be avoided because of possible adverse effects on morale and effectiveness, unless the problem in question is most prevalent at the end of one shift and the beginning of another. Such overlapping shifts should be eight consecutive hours in length (avoiding officers' working split shifts) (Iannone and Iannone, 2001).

Labor Considerations

For some police administrators, the Fair Labor Standards Act (FLSA) (at 29 U.S.C. 203 et seq.) has become a budgetary and operational nightmare (Randels, 1992). The act provides minimum pay and overtime provisions covering both public- and private-sector employees and contains special provisions for firefighters and police officers. Although there has been some discussion in Congress concerning the repeal or modification of the act, at the present time it is still a legislative force that administrators, mid-managers, and supervisors must reckon with. Indeed, one observer referred to the FLSA as the criminal justice administrator's "worst nightmare come true" (Lund, 1991:4).

The act was passed in 1938 to protect the rights and working conditions of employees in the private sector. During that time, long hours, poor wages, and substandard work conditions plagued most businesses. The FLSA placed a number of restrictions on employers to improve these conditions. Then, in 1985, the U.S. Supreme Court brought local police employees under the coverage of the FLSA. In this major (and costly) decision, *Garcia v. San Antonio Transit Authority,* the Court held, 5 to 4, that Congress legally imposed the requirements of the FLSA on state and local governments.

Criminal justice operations often require overtime and participation in off-duty activities such as court appearances and training sessions. The FLSA comes into play when overtime salaries must be paid. It provides that an employer must generally pay employees time and a half for all hours worked over 40 per week. Overtime must also be paid to personnel for all work in excess of 43 hours in a 7-day cycle or 171 hours in a 28-day period. Public safety employees may accrue a maximum of 480 hours of "comp" time, which, if not utilized as leave, must be paid off on separation from employment at the employee's final rate of pay or at the average pay over the last three years, whichever is greater (Swanson et al., 1993). Furthermore, employers usually cannot require employees to take compensatory time in lieu of cash. The primary issue with FLSA is the rigidity of application of what is compensable work. The act prohibits an agency from taking "volunteered time" from employees.

An officer who works the night shift must receive pay for attending training or testifying in court during the day. Further, officers who are ordered to remain at home in anticipation of emergency actions must be compensated. Notably, however, the FLSA's overtime provisions do not apply to persons employed in a bona fide executive, administrative, or professional capacity. In criminal justice, the act has generally been held to apply to detectives and sergeants but not to those of the rank of lieutenant and above.

Garcia prompted an onslaught of litigation by police and fire department employees of state and local governmental entities. The issues are broad but include paying overtime compensation to K-9 and equestrian officers who care for departmental animals while "off duty," overtime pay for officers who access their work computer and conduct business from home, pay for academy recruits who are given mandatory homework assignments, and standby and on-call pay for supervisors and officers who are assigned to units that require their unscheduled return to work. These are just a few of the many FLSA issues that are being litigated in courts across the nation.

The fiscal and operational repercussions of the FLSA could be staggering for some agencies, depending on past practices. For example, in one West Coast police department, the city was required to pay each of its six K-9 officers up to $35,000 in back pay for FLSA claims associated with the care, feeding, and training of the department's dogs. This example alone should be a warning to police administrators to review their department policies and practices and ensure that they conform with FLSA requirements.

A companion issue with respect to criminal justice pay and benefits is that of equal pay for equal work. Disparate treatment in pay and benefits can be litigated under Title VII or statutes such as the Equal Pay Act or the equal protection clause. An Ohio case involved matron/dispatchers who performed essentially the same job as jailers but were paid less. In *Jurich v. Mahoning County* (1983), this was found to be in violation of the Equal Pay Act and, since discriminatory intent was found, in violation of Title VII.

DEPLOYMENT STRATEGIES

Several methods for deploying officers to patrol duties have been explored over the years. The most common deployment schemes involve basic officer, split force, and special unit plans. Next, we briefly discuss each, as well as directed patrol. We conclude this section with a more in-depth look at the unique deployment requirements of a community policing and problem solving initiative.

Basic Officer Plan

Under this approach, officers are assigned to a geographic area that has been designed with neighborhoods in mind. This is the typical beat plan configuration described earlier. Most CAD systems adjust beat plans according to the number of officers available during any given shift. The basic officer plan assigns officers to fixed shifts.

Split Force

The split force plan splits patrol into two groups. One group consists of three-fourths of the patrol officers who handle CFS in a normal fashion. The second group of officers performs specialized functions in high-crime areas, often in plainclothes. The split force concept is used by many agencies to free officers to engage in COPPS activities. All officers respond to emergency calls under this plan. An evaluation conducted by the Wilmington, Delaware, Police Department found that police productivity increased by 20 percent, whereas crime decreased 18 percent during the first year of implementation (Krajick, 1978).

Special Units

Many agencies also have developed special teams to handle certain community concerns. These teams may be dedicated solely to COPPS, gang activities, adult repeat offenders, or traffic matters and may utilize a variety of patrol tactics, including bicycle patrol, footbeats, horse patrol, or other means of transportation. The key to the effectiveness of any specialized unit is that community problems drive the tactics. Departments must be sure that the various patrol tactics benefit the agency's responses to community problems. Few agencies can afford to implement these approaches purely to improve police-community relations.

Directed Patrol

Directed patrol efforts were implemented in an effort to increase patrol productivity. Directed patrol is used by supervisors to direct officers to use their available time in a more planned and rational manner than traditional random patrol. Directed patrol utilizes crime analysis and shift designs as a tool to accomplish its objectives. With this data, a patrol supervisor can deploy officers to attend to specific beat problems.

Community Policing and Problem Solving

As will be seen in Chapter 13, COPPS is less of a deployment strategy and more an overarching management philosophy that impacts how an entire organization addresses crime detection and prevention. One of the strongest needs of the COPPS strategy involves changes in how patrol officers are deployed, including an emphasis on geography, and not just on shift time. Officers must be given the requisite time for neighborhood interaction and relationships. Decisions must be made concerning matters such as duties and job descriptions of COPPS officers, functions to be performed, staffing levels, and neighborhood boundaries.

A new set of district and post boundaries might need to be created that match the major neighborhood areas of the city, ensuring that those areas generating the greatest number of CFS were in the middle of districts and posts, thus providing for strong accountability for policing those areas. Very often, some police officers have little uncommitted time during a tour of duty, while others have large blocks of uncommitted time. As a general rule, no more than 40 percent of an officer's time should be devoted to handling CFS.

The time between calls is the key element in determining if officers have time for problem solving. It is not uncommon to find that officers have more than three hours between calls for other activities. The available time is normally spread throughout the shift, however, varying from 10 minutes to 45 minutes between calls. If we assume a problem-solving project takes 45 minutes, then the officer may have few blocks of uninterrupted time for an assignment. Time between calls varies considerably depending on the number of calls for a particular shift, the types of calls, and how much time they require. One or two fewer calls can make a big difference in the availability of uninterrupted time.

Obviously, citizen calls are important and cannot be ignored. But the aim should be to handle citizen calls in an efficient and expedient manner. In addition to telephone reporting and walk-in/mail-in reporting, discussed earlier, there are three methods for overcoming the problem of finding time for problem solving while still handling calls effectively (Peak and Glensor, 2002:205–206):

1. Allow units to perform problem-solving assignments as self-initiated activities. Under this approach, a unit would contact the dispatcher and go out of service for a problem-solving assignment. The unit would be interrupted only for an emergency call in its area of responsibility.

2. Schedule one or two units to devote a predetermined part of their shift to problem solving. As an example, a supervisor could designate one or two units each day to devote the first half of their shift or even just one hour to problem solving. Their calls would be handled by other units so that they have an uninterrupted block of time.

3. Review the department policy on "assist" units. In some departments, several units show up at the scene of a call even though they are not needed. A department should undergo a detailed study of the types of calls for which assist units are actually appearing, with the aim of reducing the number of assists.

In summary, the overall aim should be to provide officers with uninterrupted amounts of time for problem-solving assignments. There are many ways to accomplish this aim, but they require a concerted planning effort by the department.

A RELATED CONSIDERATION: MANAGING OVERTIME

There is a sense both within and outside the police community that overtime by officers is overused, misused, and only halfheartedly controlled. It must be noted that a certain amount of overtime is inevitable, so supervisors and managers must be realistic about what can be achieved in controlling it. Some shifts must be extended because time-consuming problems occur at any time. Sensational crimes or natural disasters are impossible to predict; police work also entails court appearances, roll calls, meetings, holidays, and standby time (when supervisors and officers must be available in the event of an emergency or are waiting at home to be called into court).

How does a police agency control overtime? The answer is by recording, analyzing, managing, and supervising. The key element that overshadows all others is management. Useful records systems cannot be constructed unless managers anticipate what they need to know. Management is also essential for analysis, and analysis needs to be done before responsive data systems can be designed. Even new computer-based information systems cannot assist if they pour out data that is not used (Bayley and Worden, 1998).

An ongoing question for every police supervisor and manager is whether overtime is being abused. Supervision of overtime is often seen as the first line of defense against abuses. Managers often complain that one of their major responsibilities is controlling overtime; it is often critical to how they are judged as leaders. At the same time, first-line supervisors can be made the scapegoats for the failures of management, even though most of the factors that determine overtime, such as contract regulations, calls for service, crime emergencies, vacations, injuries, retirements, and special events, are beyond their control. Although first-line supervisors formally approve overtime, in some departments their ability to refuse is restricted. Furthermore, in many agencies, first-line supervisors frequently are not given the information needed to anticipate demands and to adjust work schedules.

Responsible overtime management requires leadership from the top. If the chief executive is indifferent about overtime, middle managers and supervisors will be at risk for criticism or even discipline if overtime problems occur. City councils and other outside persons should understand that overtime cannot be effectively controlled by supervisors and should not allow senior officers to pass the responsibility for managing overtime to junior officers.

It is also critical for the police agency to distinguish work done on paid overtime from work done on unpaid, or compensatory, overtime. Work paid on paid overtime generally increases policing activity, even though paid at time and a half. Compensatory time, conversely, represents less policing because every hour worked must be repaid at time and a half by an officer's being off duty; in short, compensatory time subtracts from the organization's existing capacity to do the job (Bayley and Worden, 1998).

THE INFLUENCE OF UNIONS

Police unions consider officer deployment and scheduling to be issues that should be negotiated with management, as a condition of work. The number of persons assigned to a patrol car or section of the community, how seniority and education will be used in assignments, and hours worked and shift selection by seniority are areas that were traditionally considered to be management prerogatives but are now negotiable. Critics argue that this kind of union activity is detrimental to the effective management of the department and the provision of services to the community (Bouza, 1985). Others, however, blame poor management and unfair treatment of employees as fostering such union activity (Kliesmet, 1985).

———— Case Studies ————————————————

Applying the materials presented in this chapter to the following case studies, the reader will get a "real-world" flavor of the issues confronting today's police supervisors and managers concerning personnel deployment and scheduling.

Letting the Count Determine the Amount

It is budget preparation time at Deer County Sheriff's Office. Sgt. Fitzpatrick is assigned as the administrative supervisor to the patrol captain. The captain needs to prepare a justification statement for a budget staff meeting in two weeks and defend to the chief the need for more positions. The captain asks Fitzpatrick to provide information on the total number of officers needed per shift. Sgt. Fitzpatrick gathers the following data from the computer-aided dispatch system:

	Midnights	**Days**	**Evenings**
Workload Data:			
Calls for Service	6,432	6,608	8,901
Assists	1,522	1,766	2,111
Traffic Accidents	615	713	991

Using these figures and the same procedure and general information presented in Table 10–1 and in the chapter itself, *as well as the same number of average time required to handle these calls per shift,* and assuming that data was collected over a 28-day period, how many total officers will Sgt. Fitzpatrick determine are needed (with a relief factor of *1.66*)?

"Who's on First?" (Or, Who Should Work When?)

Industry City is rapidly growing, and in the past five years, the police department has doubled its number of officers. As a result, it is not uncommon to find that the officers assigned to the evening and night shifts have less than three years of experience. There is also a shortage of qualified field training officers for the evening shifts, because the majority of veteran officers are on day shift or on a special assignment. All sworn officers work a straight 5-day, 8-hour week, with no shift rotation; all assignments are seniority based. Lately, a lot of unhappiness has been expressed by the union concerning the lack of opportunities for the younger officers to work other shifts and on special assignments. Some interest has also been expressed by the younger officers in the 4-day, 10-hour shift scheme. There have also been increased sick time usage and citizens' complaints against graveyard officers. The union has sent a letter to the chief requesting a discussion of these matters. The training supervisor, Sgt. O'Neal, has been directed to provide the chief with an evaluation of the benefits, costs, and concerns of various compressed shift configurations.

1. What suggestions might Sgt. O'Neal provide regarding shift rotation?

2. Would a compressed shift plan have any benefits over the current 5-day, 8-hour plan? Disadvantages?

3. What labor considerations might be posed by a shift rotation or compressed plan?

SUMMARY

As we noted at the outset of this chapter, the determination of the proper allocation of patrol personnel is of vital interest and concern to the police supervisor. This is due to the fact that the patrol function is the backbone of police work and requires the greatest number of personnel. Examining the need for patrol planning, methods of determining resource allocation needs and for performing a workload analysis, alternative patrol responses, types of compressed shift schedules, and deployment strategies, this chapter has demonstrated that ensuring 24-hour, 7-days-per-week shift coverage is not an easy task, with special challenges being posed by the spread of the problem-oriented policing initiative.

As the philosophical or qualitative approach to policing evolves, so will the deployment and scheduling of personnel. Today's police supervisors must therefore be more flexible and willing to modify their personnel deployment schemes to fit the needs of the department.

ITEMS FOR REVIEW

1. Describe the purposes of patrol planning and some of the factors that contribute to the overall lack of proper patrol planning in police agencies.

2. Discuss the three methods most often used by police departments to determine resource needs.

3. Explain the two plans for allocating patrol resources as shown in Table 10–2.

4. Describe some of the factors to be considered when attempting to properly deploy officers by time and location.

5. Discuss some alternative patrol responses that can be used by the police for handling citizen calls for service, thus reducing officers' workload.

6. Compare permanent versus rotating shift assignments, including advantages and debilitating effects of each.

7. Explain the benefits and drawbacks of the 5–2 (8) and the 4–3 (10) work shifts.

8. Describe how the Fair Labor Standards Act has affected shift scheduling.

9. Examine the primary methods for deploying officers, including the basic officer, split force, and special unit plans and directed patrol plans.

10. Explain why the police must be deployed differently with the community policing and problem solving strategy.

11. Explain why overtime management is so important, as well as the supervisors' and managers' roles in directing and controlling overtime.

REFERENCES

Aschoff, J. (1965). Circadian rhythms in man. *Science* 148:1427–1432.

Bayley, D. H., and Worden, R. E. (1998). *Police overtime: An examination of key issues.* Washington, DC: U.S. Department of Justice, National Institute of Justice Research in Brief.

Bieck, W., and Kessler, D. (1977). *Response time analysis.* Kansas City, MO: Board of Police Commissioners.

Bouza, A. V. (1985). Police unions: Paper tigers or roaring lions? In W. A. Geller, ed., *Police leadership in America: Crisis and opportunity.* New York: Praeger, pp. 241–280.

Brunner, G. D. (1976). Law enforcement officers' work schedules reactions. *The Police Chief* (January):30–31.

Eck, J., and Spelman, W. (1989). A problem-oriented approach to police service delivery. In Dennis Jay Kenney, ed., *Police and policing: Contemporary issues.* New York: Praeger, pp. 95–111.

Eck, J., and Spelman, W. (1987). *Problem-solving: Problem-oriented policing in Newport News.* Washington, DC: Police Executive Research Forum.

Garcia v. San Antonio Metropolitan Transit Authority, 469 U.S. 528 (1985).

Gay, W. G., Schell, T. H., and Schack, S. (1977). *Improving patrol productivity: Routing patrol, prescriptive package* (Vol. 1). Washington, DC: U.S. Department of Justice.

Goldstein, H. (1990). *Problem oriented policing.* New York: McGraw-Hill.

Green, J. R., and Taylor, R. B. (1991). Community-based policing and foot patrol: Issues of theory and evaluation. In Jack R. Greene and Stephen D. Mastrofski, eds., *Community policing: Rhetoric or reality?* New York: Praeger, pp. 195–223.

Greenwood, P. (1975). *The criminal investigation process.* Santa Monica, CA:RAND.

Hale, C. D. (1981). *Police operations and management.* New York: John Wiley.

Iannone, N. F., and Iannone, M. P. (2001). *Supervision of police personnel,* 6th ed. Upper Saddle River, NJ: Prentice Hall.

Jurich v. Mahoning County 31 Fair Emp. Prac. 1275 (BNA) (N.D. Ohio 1983).

Kelling, G. L. (1974). *The Kansas City preventive patrol experiment: A summary report.* Washington, DC: Police Foundation.

Kleismet, R. B. (1985). The chief and the union: May the force be with you. In W. A. Geller, ed., *Police leadership in America: Crisis and opportunity.* New York: Praeger, pp. 281–285.

Krajick, K. (1978). Does patrol prevent crime? *Police Magazine* 1 (September):4–16.

Levine, C. H. (1982). *Cutback management in the criminal justice system: A manual of readings.* Washington, DC: University Research Corporation.

Levine, M. J., and McEwen, J. T. (1985). *Patrol deployment.* Washington, DC: U.S. Department of Justice.

Lund, L. (1991). The "ten commandments" of risk management for jail administrators. *Detention Reporter* 4 (June):4.

McEwen, J. T., Conners, E., and Cohen, M. (1986). *Evaluation of the differential police response field test.* Washington, DC: National Institute of Justice.

Moore-Ede, M. C., and Richardson, G. S. (1985). Medical implications of shift work. *Annual Review of Medicine* 17:608.

O'Neill, J. L., and Cushing, M. A. (1991). *The impact of shift work on police officers.* Washington, DC: Police Executive Research Forum.

Pate, A. M., Wycoff, M. A., Skogan, W. G., and Sherman, L. W. (1986). *Reducing fear of crime in Houston and Newark: A summary report.* Washington, DC: Police Foundation and National Institute of Justice.

Peak, K. J., and Glensor, R. W. (2002). *Community policing and problem solving: Strategies and practices,* 3d ed. Upper Saddle River, NJ: Prentice Hall.

Police Foundation (1981). *The Newark foot patrol experiment.* Washington, DC: Author.

Randels, E. L. (1992). The Fair Labor Standards Act: An administrative nightmare. *The Police Chief* (5):28–32.

Roberg, R. R., and Kuykendall, J. (1995). *Police organization and management: Behavior, theory, and processes.* Pacific Grove, CA: Brooks/Cole.

Schissler, T. M. (1996). Shift work and police scheduling. *Law and Order* (May):61–64.

Scott, E. J. (1981). *Calls for service: Citizen demand and initial police response.* Washington, DC: U.S. Government Printing Office.

Sherman, L. (1973). *Team policing: Seven case studies.* Washington, DC: Police Foundation.

Swanson, C. R., Territo, L., and Taylor, R. W. (1993). *Police administration.* Upper Saddle River, NJ: Prentice Hall.

Talley, G. B. (1995). Twelve-hour shifts: Comments from the field. *The Police Chief* (December): 29.

Trojanowicz, R. C. (1986). Evaluating a neighborhood foot patrol program: The Flint, Michigan project. In Dennis P. Rosenbaum, ed., *Community crime prevention: Does it work?* Beverly Hills, CA: Sage, pp. 157–78.

U.S. Department of Justice, Federal Bureau of Investigation (2001). *Crime in the United States–2000: Uniform Crime Reports.* Washington, DC: U.S. Government Printing Office.

Williams, W. L., and Eide, R. W. (1995). LAPD conducts one year test. *The Police Chief* (December):18–27.

Wrobleski, H. M., and Hess, K. M. (1993). *Introduction to law enforcement and criminal justice.* St. Paul, MN: West.

11

On Patrol: Special Problems and Operations

LEARNING OBJECTIVES

After reading this chapter, the student will:

- know patrol officers' goals and objectives in addressing calls for service
- have a basic understanding of supervisory and management roles with potentially hazardous patrol problems
- be able to explain the supervisor's role and potential for liability in selected areas of problems on patrol
- understand some strategies for dealing with major patrol problems
- be knowledgeable about when supervisors and managers should be notified concerning unusual or critical incidents

*The best executive is the one who has sense enough to pick good men to
do what he wants done, and the self-restraint to keep from meddling
with them while they do it.*

—Theodore Roosevelt

*Big jobs usually go to the men who prove their ability to outgrow small
ones.*

—Ralph Waldo Emerson

*For one man that can stand prosperity, there are a hundred that will
stand adversity.*

—Thomas Carlyle

INTRODUCTION

Many situations and problems confront patrol supervisors and commanders as they direct their daily operations; they must also ensure that patrol officers' work activities are conducted according to agency expectations. During any tour of duty, police officers can encounter situations that are extraordinary and unique when compared with the majority of general calls for service and that require special attention.

This chapter begins with a general discussion of the scope of patrol operations, including the kinds of goals or objectives that patrol officers possess when responding to CFS. Then, six potentially deadly situations that confront police officers and leaders are addressed: domestic violence, crimes in progress, street drug enforcement, youth gangs, school violence, and vehicular pursuits. Each discussion includes a review of possible "leadership rejoinders"—replies or responses—for handling these problems. Then, because these and other kinds of critical incidents may be too overwhelming for street officers to handle, policy guidelines are considered for when a superior officer should be notified. The chapter concludes with two case studies.

It should also be noted that many of the incidents discussed in this chapter, such as crimes in progress, vehicular pursuits, and domestic disputes, are often addressed in city ordinances or agency policies and procedures, which spell out how officers are to deal with them. It is incumbent on supervisors and managers to ensure that officers adhere to those mandates as well.

Finally, because they have a far greater direct role in overseeing patrol officers, and because this chapter focuses on street crimes, the primary emphasis will be on first-line supervisory personnel, and less on middle managers.

THE SCOPE OF PATROL OPERATIONS

To understand the scope of patrol operations, we must consider the myriad possible CFS handled by police officers. These range from simple requests for information or assistance to emergency situations.

One of the primary responsibilities of supervisors is to manage and control the scene of dangerous calls and to supervise officers' handling of such incidents. Also, a number of calls can be classified as tactical or critical incidents (discussed in Chapter 12), which have the potential to become life threatening; supervisors must manage those calls as well. Any of these situations can take a turn for the worse and result in personal injury to citizens or officers. For this reason, the direct involvement of supervisors in such incidents is most important.

Police officers also have a number of resources at their disposal when responding to CFS, ranging from providing information or assistance to the use of deadly force. Both officers and supervisors must ensure that these responses meet the needs of the situation and that they do not go beyond the level that is necessary. If a situation calls for an arrest to be made, officers should take the suspect into custody.

It should be noted that when officers engage in various activities, they are attempting to achieve some goal or objective. Possible goals include (1) protecting an endangered citizen, (2) protecting the officer himself or herself or other officers, (3) preventing a crime, (4) defusing a potentially violent situation, (5) solving a crime, (6) serving court papers, (7) ensuring the orderly flow of traffic and pedestrians, (8) helping or serving citizens, or (9) collecting information. The goal that officers select is contingent on the situation; it is the ultimate responsibility of supervisors and managers to ensure that officers employ the proper response.

The following sections explore several types of CFS from operational and supervisory perspectives. These are the kinds of CFS that can require a leader's immediate attention and involvement.

DOMESTIC VIOLENCE SITUATIONS

Danger and Liability

Perhaps one of the most potentially problematic situations for police officers is a domestic violence call. Domestic or family violence refers to a number of situations, including spousal abuse, elder abuse, and child abuse. There is disagreement as to what constitutes domestic violence, but most agree that abuse must occur. Abuse can refer to overt acts of aggression against another (Feld and Straus, 1989) or the injuries incurred as a result of the assault (Berk et al., 1983).

Domestic violence, especially spousal abuse, was viewed in the past as being different from and less serious than other forms of assault, because the act was a private family matter. Indeed, domestic violence has been viewed so differently from other forms of assault and criminality that some observers postulate that it is accepted as normal family behavior in some circles (Gelles and Straus, 1988). "A man's home is his castle" was traditionally the prevailing notion, and the sanctity of the home was not to be violated by the police unless "significant" criminal acts occurred therein (Belknap, 1990; Fyfe and Flavin, 1991). No concrete data exists relative to the number of abuse cases that occur each year, but we know that spousal abuse and other forms of domestic violence remain a substantial problem for America's police.

Domestic violence CFS are difficult for police for two reasons. First, handling domestic violence calls is fairly dangerous. A significant number of police

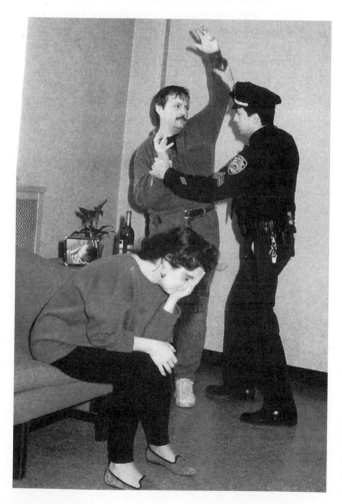

Role playing is one of the best methods for teaching officers how to handle difficult situations. Here a supervisor participates in domestic violence training. *Courtesy NYPD Photo Unit.*

officers are killed or injured each year while handling these calls (Figure 11–1), and officers are trained to exercise all due care when handling domestic situations.

Second, domestic violence represents a weighty area for police liability. Each year, a significant number of civil suits that originated from a domestic violence call are filed against the police: These suits commonly allege excessive force or false arrest or that police officers failed to take a suspect into custody who later returned to the scene of the disorder and assaulted or killed his or her spouse or other relatives. Officers are more likely to arrest citizens in confrontational situations, and such actions frequently lead to false arrest charges. Similarly, police officers are often accused of using excessive force in domestic violence situations. Since many domestic calls involve physical confrontations, police officers generally resort to some form of physical force to subdue arrestees or to break up fighting parties. Thus, by their very nature, domestic violence calls are conducive to the use of physical violence and to officers being accused of using excessive force. Officers and supervisors must ensure that officers' use of force is within acceptable limits.

Leadership Rejoinder

Research fails to provide police leadership with any concrete guidelines on how to handle domestic violence cases. Supervisors, however, should ensure that their officers follow the spirit of the law and provide victims with maximum protection. That is, if the jurisdiction has a mandatory arrest policy, it must be followed. If a mandatory arrest law or policy does not exist, officers should encourage and assist victims in obtaining warrants or restraining orders. Finally, officers should ensure that they accurately analyze domestic conflicts and make only appropriate arrests and refrain from using excessive force when making such arrests.

CRIMES IN PROGRESS

Lethal Potential

Responding to crimes in progress is one of the most dangerous types of CFS. Large numbers of police officers are killed answering crimes in progress calls each year. Between 1976 and 1998, of the 1,820 police officers who were murdered in the line of duty, 39 percent were killed during arrest situations, 16 percent were responding to disturbance calls, 14 percent were enforcing traffic laws, 14 percent were investigating suspicious persons or circumstances, and 11 percent were in ambush situations (Brown and Langan, 2001; see Figure 11–1).

The danger comes from the fact that in most cases, perpetrators know the police are coming and have time to seek a defensive advantage. Also, on arrival

Law enforcement officers feloniously killed
By circumstances at scene of incident, United States, 1978–2000

Circumstances at scene of incident	1978	1979	1980	1981	1982	1983	1984	1985	1986	1987	1988	1989	1990	1991	1992	1993	1994	1995	1996	1997	1998	1999	2000
Total	93	106	104	91	92	80	72	78	66	74	78	66	66	71	64	70	79	74	61	71	61	42	51
Disturbance calls	10	17	12	19	18	15	8	13	7	23	7	13	10	17	11	10	8	8	4	14	16	7	8
Bar fights, persons with firearms, etc.	5	13	6	14	11	10	7	6	5	10	4	5	5	8	2	5	4	2	1	3	7	6	4
Family quarrels	5	4	6	5	7	5	1	7	2	13	3	8	5	9	9	5	4	6	3	11	9	1	4
Arrest situations	39	47	49	38	36	31	33	29	26	27	33	24	30	14	27	28	33	21	26	22	16	12	12
Burglaries in progress/pursuing burglary suspects	3	7	8	6	3	4	2	4	1	6	3	0	1	3	5	1	4	4	3	5	0	0	2
Robberies in progress/pursuing robbery suspects	15	19	22	17	14	11	9	12	9	4	7	8	13	4	11	9	17	7	12	11	3	4	2
Drug-related matters	6	6	9	2	5	6	4	6	7	4	12	7	5	3	3	3	4	4	3	1	7	2	3
Attempting other arrests	15	15	10	13	14	10	18	7	9	13	11	9	11	4	8	15	8	6	8	5	6	6	5
Civil disorders (mass disobedience, riot, etc.)	0	0	0	0	1	0	0	0	0	0	0	0	0	0	0	0	0	0	0	0	0	0	0
Handling, transporting, custody of prisoners	7	3	1	1	3	3	3	4	5	6	2	6	2	6	2	1	1	4	0	4	4	2	2
Investigating suspicious persons/circumstances	8	9	16	10	11	10	12	9	11	5	23	10	9	10	7	15	15	17	13	10	6	7	6
Ambush situations	12	11	7	9	9	8	8	7	4	4	6	4	8	11	7	5	8	14	6	12	10	6	10
Entrapment/premeditation	11	8	2	5	7	6	4	5	2	3	2	2	2	5	5	3	1	6	2	5	4	4	2
Unprovoked attack	1	3	5	4	2	3	4	2	2	1	4	2	6	6	2	2	7	8	4	7	6	2	8
Mentally deranged assailants	3	4	2	2	2	1	0	0	3	1	1	2	1	0	0	1	4	1	1	1	0	0	0
Traffic pursuits/stops	14	15	17	12	12	11	8	16	10	8	6	7	6	13	10	10	10	9	11	8	9	3	13

Note: See Note, table 3.164. These data include Federal, State, and local law enforcement officers feloniously killed in the line of duty. Some data have been revised by the Source and may differ from previous editions of SOURCEBOOK.

Source: U.S. Department of Justice, Federal Bureau of Investigation, *Law Enforcement Officers Killed and Assaulted, 2000*, p. 30; FBI Uniform Crime Reports (Washington, DC: U.S. Department of Justice). http://www.albany.edu/sourcebook/1995/pdf/t3165.pdf (accessed 16 January 2003).

FIGURE 11–1 Police Officers Murdered by Felons (FBI).

the officers are extremely vulnerable as they exit their patrol vehicle, approach the location, attempt to obtain information, and search out any suspects.

Police officers frequently do not use their emergency equipment (lights and siren) in an effort to "run silent" and keep perpetrators from knowing of their response. This creates a dangerous situation, especially if officers are responding at a high rate of speed. Automobile accidents frequently occur, and police officers are held at fault. Therefore, police departments must ensure that when officers are not using their emergency equipment, they do not violate traffic laws and constantly have their vehicles under control. It is critical that supervisors ensure that officers follow state statutes and departmental policies in this regard.

Leadership Rejoinder

Once a crime has been reported, it is critical that call takers or dispatchers obtain as much information as possible. It is especially important that the exact location of the incident, descriptions of suspects and vehicles and their whereabouts, possible weapons involved, and witness and victim information are obtained. If a suspect is on the scene, the dispatcher should maintain contact with the caller and provide updated information to all responding officers.

Sufficient police units should be dispatched to the scene of a crime in progress. Supervisors should ensure that responding units converge on the scene from different directions so that as many getaway routes as possible can be observed by police officers. In fact, supervisors should coordinate and direct officers' responses to ensure that the maximum number of avenues of escape are covered. Even when a description of the perpetrators or their vehicle is not available, officers should look for suspicious vehicles and conduct field interviews. These field interviews often result in the capture of the suspects or the identification of witnesses.

When responding to a crime in progress, it is critical that the dispatcher and responding officers work as a team. Field supervisors must ensure that responding officers follow police procedures and are equipped with the best possible information. Every tactical action taken by officers is guided by information obtained by the dispatcher. It is the field supervisor's responsibility to ensure that both perform according to procedures.

STREET DRUG ENFORCEMENT

Relatively speaking, the use of illegal drugs in the United States is a rather recent phenomenon. Johnson et al. (1990) noted that in 1960, less than 5 percent of the nation's population and perhaps less than 25 percent of the criminal population had ever tried illegal drugs. However, the substantial increase in marijuana use after 1965, the heroin epidemic of 1965 through 1973, the cocaine epidemic of

1975 through 1984, and the more contemporary methamphetamine and crack cocaine epidemics have resulted in substantial numbers of citizens and criminals using illegal drugs. This increase has led to a complete rethinking of police tactical operations, and most everything police departments do today is directly or indirectly related to or affected by the drug problem.

Perhaps the best way to understand street drug enforcement is to consider the criminal activities associated with drugs, and then progress to enforcement tactics. The police can better assemble effective tactics if they first understand the problem. Also, it must be understood that there is no simple or even complex solution to drug-related criminality. Since there are a variety of types of drug dealers, drug users, and criminals involved in drug-related criminality, the police must devise and adopt tactics that target each type. In other words, there is no single panacea for addressing the problem.

Drug-Related Criminality

Many people in the law enforcement community have long operated under the assumption that drugs and crime are directly and undisputedly related. That is, drugs cause crime. People who use drugs ultimately become involved in criminal activities. This view has been supported by the fact that many criminals are drug abusers, and drug abusers are disproportionately represented in the jail and prison populations.

Drug abuse is a major factor in crime and violence; more than 277,000 offenders are in prison for drug law violations—21 percent of state prisoners and more than 60 percent of federal prisoners. More than 80 percent of state prisoners and 70 percent of federal prisoners have engaged in some form of illicit drug use. One-third of state prison inmates and 22 percent of federal prisoners report they were under the influence of drugs when they committed the crime for which they are in prison (U.S. Department of Justice, 1999).

Several classes of criminals must receive special attention from the police. The first class is street drug dealers. Research shows that many drug dealers are not dangerous and drift in and out of selling; they tend to use drug selling as supplemental income or to obtain drugs for themselves (Johnson et al., 1985). Those drug dealers who openly sell drugs in the streets, however, tend to commit high rates of predatory crimes and are much more dangerous to society. Even though all drug dealers should be police targets, street-level dealers should receive special attention.

A second type of drug offender includes juvenile drug users. When drug abuse begins at an early age, the abuse tends to extend into adulthood and abusers often graduate to more addictive drugs. A large percentage of these individuals who commit significant numbers of predatory crimes also are drug abusers. Drug abuse does not necessarily lead to criminality, but the two problems seem to co-exist. Regardless, early intervention would quite possibly reduce criminality and drug abuse.

Finally, a third type of offender that deserves special police attention is the heroin addict, who tends to commit large numbers of crimes in an effort to produce the income needed to maintain the drug habit. Although the vast majority of these crimes are property crimes, some addicts become involved in crimes against persons such as robbery. Because of their high rates of criminality, these offenders should be considered dangerous when developing police operational tactics.

Leadership Rejoinder

The selection and implementation of enforcement tactics largely depend on the nature and the setting of the drug problem. For example, in rural communities the problem tends to be dispersed across jurisdictional boundaries, and law enforcement agencies have responded with multijurisdictional enforcement teams (Chaiken, Chaiken, and Karchmer, 1990; Schlegel and McGarrell, 1991). Larger jurisdictions have more concentrated problems and tend to deploy a variety of tactics to counteract the problem. Regardless, all jurisdictions tend to use the same basic tactics.

Hayslip (1989) noted that law enforcement has adopted a number of new tactics in the war against drugs. Traditionally, the police tended to concentrate on arresting persons in possession of drugs when targeting the user and used undercover surveillance, buy-busts, and criminal possession when concentrating on street dealers. Police leaders now have expanded these approaches. In terms of the user, the police are using reverse stings, street sweeps or concentrated enforcement, and asset seizure. Tactics aimed at the street dealer include concentrated street sweeps and enforcement, eradication of crack houses and other drug-selling locations through concentrated enforcement and demolition, asset seizure, and community and problem-oriented policing. Street drug enforcement usually focuses on concentrated areas where drug problems are the greatest. When concentrated problem areas are identified, the police can deploy a variety of tactics, including buy-busts, street sweeps, undercover surveillance, sting operations, and problem solving.

Buy-busts represent one of the most frequently used police drug tactics. Police undercover officers essentially locate dealers, purchase drugs, and then later arrest the dealer. A team of officers in an area with a large number of drug dealers can make numerous cases. The problem is that once the police arrest one dealer, others are alerted and leave the area, or other dealers are alerted and no other arrests can be made.

Street sweeps occur when the police identify a problem area and attempt to solve the problem by making large numbers of arrests. The police make every possible arrest, no matter how minor the charge, in an effort to rid the area of drug dealers and disorder. Street sweeps not only deter and obstruct street-level drug dealing, they also discourage buyers from entering an area.

Critics of street sweeps note that such operations result in short-term results. For example, Zimmer (1990) examined a program in the borough of Queens in New York City and found that drug dealers reentered the area just days after the end of the project. Sherman (1990), however, argues that even though street sweeps do not totally clean up the drug and crime problem, they do have an immediate effect and it may take an extended period of time for the drug dealers and buyers to return and reestablish their business at the normal rates. Sherman also notes that intermittent sweeps can have substantial effects on the drug trade in a particular area.

YOUTH GANGS

Extent, Nature, Activities

A youth gang is an association of individuals who have a gang name and recognizable symbols, a geographic territory, a regular meeting pattern, and an organized and continuous course of criminality (Block and Block, 1993:2). The critical point in identifying a gang is that members are willing to use violence to defend their territory, and it is this violence that separates gangs from other groups of juveniles.

Juveniles join gangs for reasons aside from poverty or the pursuit of wealth. A study of the two largest youth gangs, the Crips and the Bloods, determined that most young men who join gangs "grow up in dangerous family environments," and that members may affiliate with gangs "to escape the violence of home, or drift away because they are abandoned or neglected by their parents" (Spergel, 1990:173).

Gang members are becoming younger. The most typical age range of gang members has been approximately 14 to 24; youngsters generally begin hanging out with gangs at 12 or 13 years of age, join the gang at 13 or 14, and are first arrested at 14 (Huff, 1998).

Gangs are now a substantial problem in most American cities. A recent federal survey found 26,000 active gangs in the United States, nearly half of which are in large cities. Nearly half of all gang members (47 percent) are Hispanic youth, 31 percent are African American, 13 percent are Caucasian, and 7 percent are Asian (Egley, 2000). Gang members are also violent: Gang homicides normally exceed 1,000 in number per year (Curry, Maxson, and Howell, 2001:1).

Gang members usually join the gang either by committing a crime or undergoing an initiation procedure. Members use automatic weapons and sawed-off shotguns in violent drive-by shootings, while becoming more sophisticated in their criminal activities and accumulating more wealth.

Gangs are composed of three types of members: hardcore (those who commit violent acts and defend the reputation of the gang), associates (members who frequently affiliate with known gang members for status and recognition but move in and out on the basis of interest in gang functions), and peripherals (non-members who identify with gang members for protection—usually with the dominant gang in their neighborhood). Most females fall into this latter category. Although researchers have been unable to determine with any precision the proportion of gang members in the United States who are female (estimates ranging from three or four percent [Curry et al., 2001] to 10 percent [Miller, 1992]), surveys have suggested an increase in independent female gangs (Curry et al., 2001). These gangs typically do not have a rigid structure like their male counterparts, but do engage in criminal activities.

Several levels of gun-toting "gang-bangers" want to earn their stripes. The "wannabe" begins by having target practice and handling guns. The next level is the gang-involved youth who wants a tough-guy reputation; he will eventually kill somebody, but he is not seen as a hard-core violent person. When a teenager reaches that level—the crazed killer—he does not care about himself or his victims; his violence is random and cold blooded.

Police agencies in jurisdictions experiencing gang problems must develop expertise in gang movements, activities, and all forms of nonverbal communication.

Graffiti provides gang officers with important intelligence information.

Police have also developed intelligence files on known or suspected gang members that should be maintained.

Gangs create problems for police as a result of their violence and criminality, particularly in drug trafficking; the percentage of gangs that are considered drug gangs is 40 percent (Egley, 2000). Basically, gangs participate in three types of violence: random violence, intergang violence, and intragang violence. Random violence occurs when gang members attack nongang civilians as part of a criminal act or to impress their superiors with their savagery (Klein and Maxson, 1989). Intergang violence refers to the violence between different gangs as they (1) retaliate for past aggression or acts, (2) protect or compete for territory, or (3) recruit new members, especially in another gang's territory.

About two-thirds of all large cities (more than 200,000 population) in the United States have a specialized gang unit, while about half of all smaller cities (less than 200,000) have a gang unit (Weisel and Painter, 1997).

Leadership Rejoinder

It must be reiterated that gangs remain one of the most potentially significant problems facing the police. As such, no effort or resource should be spared in combating their presence. If police efforts are to be effective, the police—with the policy input and oversight by supervisors and managers—must use multiple strategies, including community building, social intervention, juvenile development programs, and law enforcement suppression.

The first step in containing a gang problem is the assembling of gang-related intelligence. Most major police departments now have Gang Intelligence Units (GIUs) that perform this function. The critical task for the GIU is to identify the core members of the gang and target them for enforcement. Intelligence is collected by questioning suspected gang members who are arrested, talking with rival gang members, and talking with residents in gang neighborhoods.

Another relatively new, promising strategy is "designing out" gang violence and other activities. When a systematic pattern of opportunity was found in one community, drive-by shootings and violent gang encounters that occurred in clusters on the periphery of neighborhoods linked to major thoroughfares, the police closed all major roads leading to and from the identified hot spots; they placed cement freeway dividers at the end of streets that led directly to these roads. An evaluation determined that blocking opportunities reduced homicides and street assaults significantly and that crime was not displaced to other areas (Lasley, 1998).

If these strategies are to be effective, however, supervisors and managers must participate in identifying problem areas or where such programs should be implemented, and they must ensure that officers adequately fulfill expectations and assignments when working in such programs.

Societal Responses

Determining the best course of action for dealing with street gangs is not easy. Most experts believe that programs in communities with gangs should include some combination of the following:

- *Fundamental changes in the way schools operate.* Schools should broaden their scope of services and act as community centers involved in teaching, providing services, and serving as locations for activities before and after the school day.
- *Job skills development for youths and young adults accompanied by improvements in the labor market.* Many youths have dropped out of school and do not have the skills to find employment. Attention needs to be focused on ways to expand the labor market, including the development of indigenous businesses in these communities, and on providing job skills for those in and out of school.
- *Assistance to families.* A range of family services including parent training, child care, health care, and crisis intervention must be made available in communities with gangs.
- *Changes in criminal justice system responses—particularly in policing.* Many people believe that police agencies need to increase their commitment to understanding the communities they serve and to solving problems. This shift is currently being addressed through the proactive, community oriented policing and problem solving approach. COPPS brings the community and police together in a partnership to work toward reducing neighborhood disorder and fear of crime (see, for example, Goldstein, 1990; Peak and Glensor, 2002; Trojanowicz and Bucqueroux, 1990). Case studies about successes with the COPPS approach to gangs are becoming more numerous.
- *Intervention with and control of known gang members.* Illegal gang activity must be controlled by diverting peripheral members from gang involvement and criminal activity. Achieving control may mean making a clear statement, such as by arresting and incapacitating hard-core gang members, that communities will not tolerate intimidating, violent, and/or criminal gang activity. (Conly et al., 1993)

Obviously, something more than police work alone is needed to break the cycle of gang delinquency. It can become easy for a community to tolerate gang violence as long as gang members victimize each other and do not bother the rest of society (Horowitz, 1987). Without community support, the current cycle of youth gang activities will continue.

Over time, however, many police agencies have shifted from an emphasis on suppression to one on education. A well-known police response to gangs is the Gang Resistance Education and Training (GREAT) program, which originated in 1991 in Phoenix, Arizona. GREAT emphasizes the acquisition of information and skills needed by students to resist peer pressure and gang influences; the curriculum contains nine-hour lessons offered to middle-school students, mostly seventh graders.

SCHOOL VIOLENCE

"What's Happened to Our Children?"

Recent shootings and other forms of violence on school campuses have Americans wondering what has happened to their children. In one six-year period, 1992 to 1998, there were 225 school-associated violent deaths (Marlin and Vogt, 1999). (This figure excludes the April 1999 massacre of 13 people at Columbine High School in Littleton, Colorado.)

Today, the possibility that a disagreement among students will be settled with some type of weapon has increased significantly. About 5 percent of today's students are chronic rule breakers and are generally out of control most of the time. Students in schools where violence occurs will not focus on studies, perform at high academic levels, or even stay in school ("An overview of violence in the schools," 2001).

Common traits among the perpetrators of school violence include an orientation toward violent shows, videos, and music; a feeling of inferiority or of being picked on, with a grudge against some student or teacher; easy access to weapons; suicidal tendencies and above-average intelligence; and the presence of ample warning signs, either in writing or talking about killing others (Egan, 1998).

Leadership Rejoinder

Police leaders can partner with school administrators toward being prepared for acts of school violence and creating safer schools. First, they can ensure that basic crime prevention techniques are being employed: having all school visitors check in at the office; monitoring campus perimeters and hallways; making certain that area police agencies have maps or site plans of schools as well as master keys to all school classrooms and offices; having a warning signal when a school encounters a threat or emergency; and ensuring that the police and school personnel remain in constant contact during a crisis (Bridges, 1999).

It is also recommended that representatives from the police, the schools, and the community come together to sign memoranda of understanding (MOU) that clearly define what each organization or agency will do from the beginning if a school-violence crisis occurs (Band and Harpold, 1999).

An interesting approach to school violence was recently attempted in Charlotte, North Carolina, where the National Institute of Justice sponsored a research project on school safety in a high school. The program had three major components: regular meetings among faculty, administrators, and the police; problem-solving classes for the students; and regular reviews by the police and teachers to identify problem students. The curriculum was based on the S.A.R.A. problem-solving process (discussed in Chapter 13) to be student driven with teachers acting as mentors and facilitators. Students identified fighting and disorder in the lunchroom as a major issue. The root of the problem was that the entire school population—as many as 1,500 students—were released for lunch at the same time. Students proposed several solutions (an open campus policy was rejected by the administration); students met with lunchroom workers, who agreed to open additional lines and improve the food-serving system. Police calls for service at the school, fear levels of students, and actual incidents of violence dropped, as did incidents of vandalism, theft, and obscene threats and gestures (Kenney, 1998).

Furthermore, police can (and often must) take their gang-suppression measures into the elementary and secondary schools. Studies have found that the percentage of 12- to 17-year-old students reporting the presence of gangs at school nearly doubled during the mid-1990s; indeed, about 8 percent of students surveyed reported that gangs are involved in three types of crimes at their schools: violence, drug sales, or gun possession (Howell and Lynch, 2000).

Other strategies have been suggested toward helping to prevent school violence:

- Publicizing the philosophy that a gang presence will not be tolerated, and institutionalizing a code of conduct
- Alerting students and parents about school rules and punishments for infractions
- Creating alternative schools for those students who cannot function in a regular classroom
- Training teachers, parents, and school staff to identify children who are most at risk for violent behavior
- Developing community initiatives focused on breaking family cycles of violence, and providing programs on parenting, conflict resolution, anger management, and recovery from substance abuse
- Establishing peer counseling in schools to give troubled youths the opportunity to talk to someone their own age
- Teaching children that it is not "tattling" to go to a school teacher or staff member if they know someone who is discussing "killing" (Marlin and Vogt, 1999)

VEHICULAR PURSUITS

A High-Stakes Operation

Few patrol operational issues are of greater concern to police leadership than police pursuits. Civil litigation arising out of collisions involving police pursuits reveal it to be a high-stakes undertaking with serious and sometimes tragic results (Hill, 2002). Several hundred people are killed each year during police pursuits (National Highway Traffic Safety Administration, 1995); many of the resulting deaths and injuries involve innocent third parties or stem from minor traffic violations. The U.S. Supreme Court, as seen later, has strengthened most progressive chase policies; but the Court has also conferred a responsibility that must be borne by the police.

Pursuits place the police in a delicate balancing act: On one hand, they need to show that flight from the law is no way to freedom. If a police agency completely bans high-speed pursuits, its credibility with both law-abiding citizens and law violators might suffer; public knowledge that the agency has a no-pursuit policy may encourage people to flee, decreasing the probability of apprehension (Eisenberg, 1999). Still, according to Belotto (1999:86), because of safety and

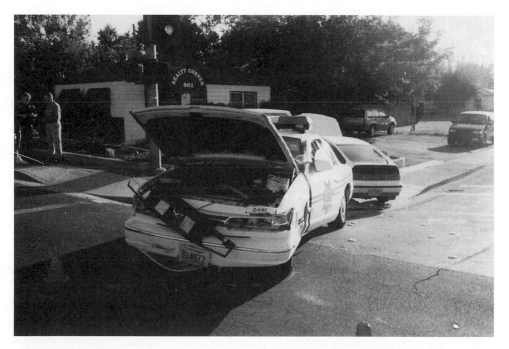

The danger of high-speed police pursuits is all too evident in the number that result in accidents, with injuries or death.
Courtesy Sparks, Nevada, Police Department.

liability concerns, "a growing number of agencies have the position that if the bad guy puts the pedal to the metal, it's a 'freebie.' They will not pursue him."

On the other hand, there is indeed the high-speed threat to everyone within range of the pursuit, including suspects, their passengers, or other drivers or bystanders. One police trainer asks a simple question of officers to determine whether or not to continue a pursuit: "Is this person a threat to the public safety other than the fact the police are chasing him?" If the officer cannot objectively answer "yes," the pursuit should be terminated (Williams, 1997).

The Supreme Court's View

In May 1990, two Sacramento County, California, deputies responded to a fight call. At the scene, they observed a motorcyle with two riders approaching their vehicle at high speed; turning on their red lights, the deputies ordered the driver to stop. The motorcycle operator began to elude the officers, who initiated a pursuit reaching speeds of more than 100 miles per hour over about 1.3 miles. The pursuit ended when the motorcycle crashed; when that occurred, the deputies' vehicle could not stop in time and struck the bike's passenger, killing him; his family brought suit, claiming the pursuit violated the crash victim's due process rights under the Fourteenth Amendment.

In May 1998, the U.S. Supreme Court, in *County of Sacramento v. Lewis* (118 S.Ct. 1708), ruled in this case, holding that the proper standard to be employed in these cases is whether the officer's conduct during the pursuit was "conscience-shocking" (conduct or character that is offensive to a reasonable person's sense of moral goodness); it further determined that high-speed chases with no intent to harm suspects do not give rise to liability under the Fourteenth Amendment (at p. 1720). The Court closed the door on the liability for officers involved in pursuits that do not shock the conscience. (But the Court left unanswered many important questions, such as whether it will allow an innocent third party to file a claim against the police for damages, or whether a municipality can be held liable for its failure to train officers in pursuit issues.)

The following incidents also demonstrate the dangerous nature of police pursuits:

- In Omaha, Nebraska, a 70-mile-per-hour pursuit through a residential neighborhood of a motorcyclist for an expired license plate ended when the motorcyclist ran a stop sign, crashing into another vehicle and killing the female passenger on the motorcycle.
- A sheriff's deputy in Florida intentionally rammed a vehicle during a pursuit for an outstanding misdemeanor warrant, causing a collision and killing a backseat passenger.
- A police officer pursuing a shoplifter in Mobile, Alabama, crashed into a mall security vehicle, seriously injuring the guard.

These and other tragic stories are all too common, and certainly the onus is on police chief executives to develop pursuit policies that consider input from line personnel, supervisors and managers, and attorneys versed in civil liability and remain vigilant in seeing that they are enforced. Pursuit policies provide general guidelines for the officer and supervisor. The courts will evaluate these policy issues when considering whether or not an agency or its officers or supervisors should be held culpable for damages or injuries resulting from pursuits.

At the International Association of Chiefs of Police Annual Conference in 1996, its membership adopted a resolution and model pursuit policy to serve as a guideline for police executives. The resolution and policy, based on recommendations from the National Commission on Law Enforcement Driving Safety, was provided to the IACP's Highway Safety Committee. The resolution and policy as shown in Figure 11–2 are purposely generic in nature so that agencies can individualize them to their specific needs.

Supervisory Roles and Liability

The responsibility falls to the field supervisor to see that proper methods are employed by patrol officers during pursuits—whether the pursuit simply involves a primary pursuing officer and a backup, or more elaborate methods, such as the following.

Two rather elaborate methods of pursuit termination may be used that involve police vehicles. The first is "boxing": Three police vehicles are positioned during the chase at the front, rear, and side of the suspect vehicle; the three police vehicles slow in unison, causing the offender to slow and eventually stop. This technique can result in damage to any or all of the vehicles involved. The second termination tactic, "precision immobilization technique," involves a police vehicle making contact with a suspect vehicle. The officer gently pushes one of the rear quarter panels of the suspect vehicle in order to displace its forward motion, causing it to spin. This technique also involves considerable risk to the officer and suspect (Eisenberg, 1999). Both of these methods and other tactics employed during pursuits are obviously potentially perilous and require extensive officer training to obtain proficiency.

Oversight of pursuits enables a third party—the supervisor—who is not emotionally involved to guard against what has been termed a *pursuit fixation,* wherein pursuing officers throw caution to the wind (Sweeney, 1997). Supervisors need to set the rules on what will be tolerated and what level of performance is expected during a pursuit. They must clearly establish that once the pursuit team is in place, other officers not directly involved should calm down and drive parallel to the pursuit, obeying all traffic laws (Belotto, 1999).

Supervisors depend on the communications of other officers for the information needed to make the decisions demanded by the courts. The supervisor should ask by radio for the following information: the speed and direction of the

Following are selected portions of the Sample Vehicular Pursuit Policy that was approved at the 103rd Annual Conference of the International Association of Chiefs of Police in Phoenix, Arizona, on September 30, 1996. Note the responsibilities of the supervisor as they pertain to communications, coordination, participation, and possible termination as they relate to the pursuit:

I. *Purpose*

The purpose of this policy is to establish guidelines for making decisions with regard to pursuits.

II. *Policy*

Vehicular pursuit of fleeing suspects can present a danger to the lives of the public, officers, and suspects involved in the pursuit. It is the responsibility of the agency to assist officers in the safe performance of their duties. To fulfill these obligations, it shall be the policy of this law enforcement agency to regulate the manner in which vehicular pursuits are undertaken and performed.

III. *Procedures*

A. Initiation of Pursuit

1. The decision to initiate pursuit must be based on the pursuing officer's conclusion that the immediate danger to the officer and the public created by the pursuit is less than the immediate or potential danger to the public should the suspect remain at large.

2. Any law enforcement officer in an authorized emergency vehicle may initiate a vehicular pursuit when the suspect exhibits the intention to avoid apprehension by refusing to stop when properly directed to do so. Pursuit may also be justified if the officer reasonably believes that the suspect, if allowed to flee, would present a danger to human life or cause serious injury.

3. In deciding whether to initiate pursuit, the officer shall take into consideration:

a. Road, weather, and environmental conditions.

b. Population density and vehicular and pedestrian traffic.

c. The relative performance capabilities of the pursuit vehicle and the vehicle being pursued.

d. The seriousness of the offense.

e. The presence of other persons in the police vehicle.

Upon engaging in a pursuit, the officer shall notify communications of the location, direction, and speed of the pursuit, the description of the pursued vehicle, and the initial purpose of the stop. When engaged in pursuit, officers shall not drive with reckless disregard for the safety of other road users.

B. Supervisory Responsibilities

1. When made aware of a vehicular pursuit, the appropriate supervisor shall monitor incoming information, coordinate and direct activities as needed to ensure that proper procedures are used, and have the discretion to terminate the pursuit.

2. Where possible a supervisory officer shall respond to the location where a vehicle has been stopped following a pursuit.

FIGURE 11–2   IACP Model Pursuit Policy

Source: Reprinted from *The Police Chief,* Vol. 64, No. 1, pp. 20–21, 1997. Copyright held by the International Association of Chiefs of Police, 515 North Washington Street, Alexandria, VA 22314, USA. Further reproduction without express written permission from IACP is strictly prohibited.

fleeing suspect vehicle; the offense, suspected offense, or status (i.e., warrants) of the suspect; the number of police units involved in the pursuit; and the suspect's actions (is he close to putting others in danger with his driving?) (Williams, 1997). Supervisors are to serve as the "safety officer" of the pursuit, a role they may not wish to take because they do not want to be unpopular with their officers, but one that is far better than attending an officer's funeral or visiting one in the hospital.

It is obvious the liabilities associated with police pursuits should be a primary concern of every police chief executive officer. The courts have awarded numerous six- and seven-figure settlements to plaintiffs seeking redress for injuries, damages, or deaths resulting from police pursuits. The development of pursuit policies and officer and supervisor training can help to protect agencies against liability suits.

It is the responsibility of command personnel and supervisors to ensure that officers thoroughly understand and comply with pursuit policies. In addition to the policy issues and supervisory information identified earlier, other factors considered by the courts to evaluate pursuit liability involve the following:

The Reason for the Pursuit. Does it justify the actions taken by the officer?

Driving Conditions. Any factor that could hinder an officer's ability to safely conduct a pursuit should be considered sufficient reason to terminate.

The Use of Police Warning Devices. Typically, lights and siren are required by state statutes.

Excessive Speed. This often depends on conditions of the environment. For example, a 30-mile-per-hour pursuit in a school zone may be considered excessive and dangerous.

Demonstrations of Due Regard in Officers' Actions. Officers who choose the course of safety will create the least danger to all parties affected and maintain the highest degree of protection from liability.

The Use of Deadly Force. There are few instances in which officers can justify driving tactics that result in the death of a fleeing driver; such situations include roadblocks, boxing in, and ramming.

Departmental Policies and State Law. These must be obeyed; to do otherwise greatly increases the potential liability of both the officer and department.

Appropriate Supervision and Training. In the absence of such measures, the department will be subject to a finding of negligence, and liability will attach. (Falcone, Charles, and Wells, 1994:60)

Police pursuits represent an ongoing, hazardous problem. Therefore, efforts must continue to develop electromagnetic-field devices that officers can place on the roadway and use to interrupt the electronic ignition systems in suspect vehicles and terminate pursuits. In the meantime, tire deflation devices, which can end chases by slowly deflating one or more tires of a suspect's vehicle, have been welcomed by the police.

WHEN ALL HELL BREAKS LOOSE: NOTIFYING MANAGERS AND SUPERVISORS

Police managers and supervisors cannot work 24 hours a day, 7 days per week. Nonetheless, critical incidents may well be occasions when ranking personnel should be notified, as the task at hand is too overwhelming for subordinates only. This is known as the "exception principle" of management: Each rank should handle only the situations that its subordinate officers lack the authority and capacity to handle or one that may have further implications. Then, a superior officer must be notified for future guidance or simply to inform him or her of what is going on (Fulton, 1998).

Although subject to change depending on local custom and guidelines (which should be put in writing), police supervisors and/or managers should be appropriately notified when incidents involve

- Serious injuries to officers or employees
- Use of force (when serious death or injury occurs as a result of officer actions)
- Multijurisdictional officers (officers from other jurisdictions within the geographic boundaries assigned to a particular police manager or commander; such notification can prevent jurisdictional or "turf" problems from flaring up later)
- Off-duty officer conduct that is unusual or unlawful in nature
- Serious crimes (the term *serious* will vary in meaning from one jurisdiction to the next)
- Prominent public figures (from politicians to rock stars, the interest generated by such incidents often becomes highly publicized) (Fulton, 1998)

⎯⎯ Case Studies ⎯⎯⎯⎯⎯⎯⎯⎯⎯⎯⎯⎯⎯⎯⎯⎯⎯⎯⎯⎯⎯

The following two case studies deal with some of the issues that supervisors and managers must confront concerning patrol.

Another Day, Another (Seemingly) Drab Domestic Dispute

Officers Ben Collins and Earl James respond to a domestic violence call at the Knox household. The officers are very familiar with the Knoxes. It seems that every Friday night the husband and wife get drunk and eventually begin to assault each other. The state has enacted a mandatory arrest law for domestic violence that requires that the primary aggressor be arrested. Who exactly is the primary aggressor can never be determined in the case of the Knoxes, because they are uncooperative with the police. In fact, in the 38 previous responses to their home, only three arrests have been made—for assaults on the police officers, not domestic violence. Tonight was no different. Officers Collins and James arrived at the Knoxes' home to face an onslaught of vulgarities from both of them. Both were quite drunk and displayed the usual matching bruises. Sgt. Caplan also responds and observes his officers' vain attempts to resolve the situation. After witnessing the normal discord, drunkenness, and vulgarities, and believing his officers have other more pressing problems to deal with, Sgt. Caplan orders them to leave the home and return back to their patrol duties. Three hours later, a neighbor calls police dispatch to report the sound of gunshots from the Knox residence; they respond and find that Mrs. Knox has killed her husband with a shotgun.

1. Could this situation have been prevented? How?
2. Is the supervisor liable in any manner?
3. Which, if any, laws were violated by the manner in which the police addressed the problem?

Can "The Long Arm of the Law" Reach Too Far?

Saturday night downtown is usually hectic, with the teenage cruisers, drunks, and "fender bender" accidents. Motorcycle officers have little time to relax on those nights. During the beginning of a shift, Officer Thompson observes a blue 1996 Camaro go through a stop sign at Second and Main Avenues. When he attempts to stop the vehicle, a high-speed pursuit ensues. Thompson radios the license plate of the vehicle as it accelerates to more than 70 miles per hour, away from the downtown area and into a residential neighborhood. Thompson continues to pursue the vehicle at speeds exceeding 50 miles per hour when the dispatcher advises him that there are no wants or warrants on the vehicle or its owner. At that point, Sgt. Bevins, in accordance with departmental policy, orders Thompson to terminate the pursuit, which Thompson does. About an hour later, while on an unrelated traffic stop, Thompson observes a blue 1996 Camaro pass by. He runs to his motorcycle and gets close to the Camaro as it enters an industrial park. Thompson, now determined not to lose the vehicle, and knowing there are no other exits from that portion of the park, decides to wait at the park's entrance for the vehicle to exit, with the motorcycle's lights turned off. Suddenly, the Camaro speeds toward Thompson, who immediately turns his headlights on and activates his siren and red lights. The driver of the Camaro, startled by the lights and siren, swerves to miss Thompson's motorcycle and crashes into a ditch, seriously injuring all four juvenile passengers. The ensuing investigation reveals that the Camaro was *not* the same vehicle that Thompson had pursued earlier in the evening; the driver had taken his father's car and gone to the industrial park, which was a popular place to race.

1. What, if any, errors in judgment did Thompson commit?
2. Evaluate the supervisor's decision in this matter.
3. Might claims of negligence and liability be filed against Thompson? The supervisor? The city (for any lack of training and control over its officers)? Will such claims be successful?

SUMMARY

This chapter has addressed several situations that pose substantial danger in terms of life and property. If police agencies are to effectively address these situations, supervisors and managers must apply the proper control and guidance to ensure officers follow departmental procedures and the law.

As we noted at the chapter's beginning, the supervisor is at the heart of the police response to patrol operations. Since supervisors back up officers on potentially dangerous and complex calls, they are ultimately responsible for successful outcomes and for ensuring that commanders are notified of situations and that adequate resources are provided. Supervisors must also take charge at the scene until other support units arrive.

ITEMS FOR REVIEW

1. Describe the problems and potential for liability that can occur when the police deal with domestic violence situations.
2. Explain the supervisor's role when police respond to crimes in progress.
3. Compare the enforcement tactics that are used by police for dealing with the drug problem.
4. Define a gang, and explain why people become members of gangs; describe the two major trends that have been identified in police responses to gangs.
5. Explain the supervisor's role with vehicular pursuits, as well as factors considered by the courts to evaluate pursuit liability.

REFERENCES

An overview of violence in the schools (2001). http://eric-web.tc.columbia.edu/monographs/uds107/preventing_introduction.html (accessed 14 June).

Band, S. R., and Harpold, J. A. (1999). School violence: Lessons learned. *FBI Law Enforcement Bulletin* (September):10.

Belknap, J. (1990). Police training in domestic violence: Perceptions of training and knowledge of the law. *American Justice Society* 14:248–267.

Belotto, A. (1999). Supervisors govern pursuits. *Law and Order* (January):86.

Berk, R. A., Berk, S. F., Loseke, D. R., and Raume, D. (1983). Mutual combat and other family violence myths. In D. Finkelhor, R. Gelles, G. Hotaling, and M. Straus, eds., *The dark side of families: Current family violence research*. Beverly Hills: Sage, pp. 197–212.

Block, C. R., and Block, R. (1993). *Street gang crime in Chicago*. Washington, DC: National Institute of Justice, Research in Brief.

Bridges, D. (1999). Safeguarding our schools. *FBI Law Enforcement Bulletin* (September):21–23.

Brown, J. M., and Langan, P. A. (2001, March). *Policing and homicide, 1976–1998: Justifiable homicide by police, police officers murdered by felons*. Washington, DC: U.S. Department of Justice, Bureau of Justice Statistics.

Chaiken, J. M., Chaiken, M. R., and Karchmer, C. (1990). *Multijurisdictional drug law enforcement strategies: Reducing supply and demand*. Washington, DC: U.S. Department of Justice.

Conly, C. H., Kelly, P., Mahanna, P., and Warner, L. (1993). *Street gangs: Current knowledge and strategies*. Washington, DC: U.S. Department of Justice, National Institute of Justice.

Curry, G. D., Maxson, C. L., and Howell, J. C. (2001, March). *Youth gang homicides in the 1990s*. Washington, DC: U.S. Department of Justice, Office of Juvenile Justice and Delinquency Prevention.

Egan, T. (1998). Killing sprees at nation's schools share number of common traits. *The Springfield State-Journal Register* (June):9.

Egley, A., Jr. (2000, November). *Highlights of the 1999 national youth gang survey*. Washington, DC: U.S. Department of Justice, Office of Juvenile Justice and Delinquency Prevention.

Eisenberg, C. B. (1999). Pursuit management. *Law and Order* (March):73–77.

Falcone, D. N., Charles, M. T., and Wells, E. (1994). A study of pursuits in Illinois. *The Police Chief*, 61(March):59–64.

Feld, S. L., and Straus, M. A. (1989). Escalation and desistance of wife assault in marriage. *Criminology* 25:141–161.

Fulton, R. (1998). Supervisory notifications. *Law Enforcement Technology* (November):66.

Fyfe, J., and Flavin, J. (1991). Differential police processing of domestic assault complaints. Paper presented at the annual meeting of the Academy of Criminal Justice Sciences, Nashville.

Gelles, R. J., and Straus, M. A. (1988). *Intimate violence*. New York: Simon & Schuster.

Goldstein, H. (1990). *Problem-oriented policing*. New York: McGraw-Hill.

Hayslip, D. (1989). *Local-level drug enforcement: New strategies*. (NIJ Reports/No. 213, April/May). Washington, DC: National Institute of Justice.

Hill, John (2002). High-speed police pursuits: Dangers, dynamics, and risk reduction. *FBI Law Enforcement Bulletin* (July):14–18.

Horowitz, R. (1987). Community tolerance of gang violence. *Social Problems* 34 (December):437–450.

Howell, J. C., and Lynch, J. P. (2000, August). *Youth gangs in schools*. Washington, DC: U.S. Department of Justice, Office of Juvenile Justice and Delinquency Prevention Programs.

Huff, C. R. (1998). *Comparing the criminal behavior of youth gangs and at-risk youths*. Washington, DC: National Institute of Justice Research in Brief.

Johnson, B. D., Goldstein, P., Preble, E., Schmeidler, J., Lipton, D. S., Spunt, B., and Miller, T. (1985). *Taking care of business: The economics of crime by heroin abusers*. Lexington, MA: Lexington Books.

Johnson, B. D., Williams, T., Dei, K. A., and Sanabria, H. (1990). Drug abuse in the inner city: Impact on hard-drug users and the community. In M. Tonry and J. Q. Wilson, eds., *Drugs and crime*. Chicago: University of Chicago Press, pp. 10–44.

Kenney, D. (1998, August). *Crime in the schools: A problem-solving approach*. Washington, DC: National Institute of Justice Research Preview.

Kleiman, M. (1988). Crackdowns: The effects of intensive enforcement on retail heroin dealing. In M. Chaiken, ed., *Street-level drug enforcement: Examining the issues*. Washington, DC: National Institute of Justice.

Klein, M. W., and Maxson, C. L. (1990). Street gang violence. In N. Weiner and M. Wolfgang, eds., *Violent crime, Violent criminals*. Newbury Park, CA: Sage, pp. 114–134.

Lasley, J. (1998). *"Designing out" gang homicides and street assaults*. Washington, DC: U.S. Department of Justice, National Institute of Justice Research in Brief (November):1–4.

Marlin, G., and Vogt, B. (1999). Violence in the schools. *The Police Chief* (April):169–172.

Miller, W. B. (1992). *Crimes by youth gangs and groups in the United States*. Washington, DC: U.S. Department of Justice, Office of Juvenile Justice and Delinquency Prevention.

National Highway Traffic Safety Administration (1995). *National Highway Traffic Safety Administration statistics*. Washington, DC: Author.

Peak, K. J., and Glensor, R. W. (2002). *Community policing and problem solving: Strategies and practices,* 3d ed. Upper Saddle River, NJ: Prentice Hall.

Schlegel, K., and McGarrell, E. F. (1991). An examination of arrest practices in regions served by multijurisdictional drug task forces. *Crime & Delinquency,* 37(3):408–426.

Sherman, L. (1990, March/April). *Police crackdowns*. NIJ Reports. Washington, DC: National Institute of Justice.

Spergel, I. A. (1990). Youth gangs: Continuity and change. In M. Tonry and N. Morris, eds., *Crime and justice: A review of research,* Vol. 12. Chicago: University of Chicago Press, pp. 171–275.

Sweeney, E. M. (1997). Vehicular pursuit: A serious—and ongoing—problem. *The Police Chief* (January):16–21.

Trojanowicz, R., and Bucqueroux, B. (1990). *Community policing: A contemporary perspective*. Cincinnati: Anderson.

U.S. Department of Justice, Bureau of Justice Statistics Press Release (1999). More than three-quarters of prisoners had abused drugs in the past. (January):1.

Weisel, D. L., and Painter, E. (1997). *The police response to gangs: Case studies of five cities*. Washington, DC: Police Executive Research Forum.

Williams, G. T. (1997). When do we keep pursuing? Justifying high-speed pursuits. *The Police Chief* (March):24–27.

Zimmer, L. (1990). Proactive policing against street-level drug trafficking. *American Journal of Police* 9:43–74.

12

Disasters, Critical Incidents, and Homeland Defense

LEARNING OBJECTIVES

After reading this chapter, the student will:

- be able to define and identify critical incidents, disasters, and terrorist acts
- understand the key elements of an Incident Command System in planning for and dealing with crises
- have a basic understanding of some tactical responses for dealing with crises, and the kinds of technologies needed for combating them
- be able to explain why tactical police units were formed and their general composition and efficacy
- be knowledgeable about mutual aid agreements and memoranda of understanding, and their importance for addressing crises

You gain strength, courage, and confidence by every experience in which you really stop to look fear in the face. You are able to say to yourself, "I lived through this horror. I can take the next thing that comes along." . . . You must do the thing you think you cannot do.

—Eleanor Roosevelt

I am more afraid of an army of 100 sheep led by a lion that an army of 100 lions led by a sheep.

—Talleyrand

INTRODUCTION

A devastating earthquake. Massive flooding. Mudslides. Wildfires. These natural disasters occurred during the 1990s in the state of California alone, causing pain and suffering for hundreds of thousands of Americans, and even death for some others. Such disasters present the utmost challenges to the police in terms of saving lives and protecting property. (California, of course, also experienced a disaster of human origin in the early 1990s—widespread rioting following the trials connected with the Rodney King incident.) These kinds of catastrophic events happen nearly everywhere; no locale in this country is immune from such acts of nature. Other incidents may occur by some form of accident (such as a train or plane crash) or environmental hazard (such as chemical spills).

Critical incidents also arise. A *critical incident* may be defined as "any high-risk encounter with police-civilian contacts when officers reasonably believe they are legally justified in using deadly force, regardless of whether they use such force" (Stevens, 1999:48). Examples of such incidents involve emotionally disturbed offenders, domestic terrorism, hostage takers, barricaded subjects, riots, high-risk warrant service, and sniper incidents. All such events pose serious threats to the police and citizens alike.

The newest threat that challenges local, statewide, and national police is domestic terrorism and homeland defense. Command and control by police supervisors during the first few critical minutes of such incidents will often determine the incidents' ultimate outcomes and the safety of those involved (Kaiser, 1990). The incident commander or officer in charge (terms used in this chapter to include both supervisors [sergeants] and managers [lieutenants] who are often given the responsibility for command and control at such scenes) must be familiar with the agency's (and, in many cases, multiagency and regional) basic operating procedures for handling critical incidents as well as the procurement of necessary personnel and equipment to prevent the further escalation of a crisis.

This chapter explores several types of critical situations from operational and command and control perspectives. We begin with a review of the Incident Command System that has been developed to assist public agencies to respond to major occurrences. Then, we examine selected disasters (major fires, airplane crashes, and misuse of hazardous materials), critical incidents (including barricaded persons and hostage situations, civil disorders and riots, bombing incidents, and the use of police tactical units), and terrorism and homeland defense measures. Two case studies are provided at chapter's end to illustrate the complexities of being in command when such incidents arise.

An underlying theme is that incident commanders must see that the preparatory foundation is laid for such catastrophic occurrences, as well as know and understand the resources that are available to them from federal, state, and local agencies; they must also be cognizant of the protocols for working within established interagency cooperative procedures, as set forth in mutual aid agreements, all of which are discussed in this chapter.

ESTABLISHING COMMAND AND CONTROL: THE INCIDENT COMMAND SYSTEM

Need for an Incident Command System

A key element to command and control is the development of comprehensive policies and procedures for handling a variety of major occurrences. As a result of its history with disasters and critical incidents, California has developed a renowned Incident Command System (ICS) to coordinate response personnel from more than one agency or teams from more than one jurisdiction. ICS has more recently been adopted to help local police agencies respond to terrorist incidents.

A key strength of ICS is its unified command component, which is composed of four sections: operations, planning, logistics, and finance. In the past, each responding agency would set up its own command post with no regard for where other agencies were; under ICS, all agencies go to the same location and establish a unified command post (Buntin, 2001). The Federal Bureau of Investigation also has adopted a four-phase framework for deploying personnel and equipment with tactical situations; this process is discussed later in this chapter.

The most critical period of time for controlling a crisis is those initial moments when first responders arrive at the scene. They must quickly contain the

The bombing of the Alfred P. Murrah Federal Building in Oklahoma City required a tremendous amount of command and control.
Courtesy Captain Jim Nadeau, Washoe County, Nevada, Sheriff's Office.

situation, analyze the extent of the crisis, request additional resources and special teams if needed, and communicate available information and intelligence to senior personnel at headquarters. Their initial actions provide a vital link to the total police response and will often determine its outcome.

Initial Duties and Responsibilities

The following checklist provides the necessary information for quickly assessing the personnel, equipment, and other resources needed during the initial stages of any critical incident:

1. What is the exact nature and size of the incident (e.g., flood, barricaded suspect holding two hostages, civil disorder involving 500 persons, suspected bioterrorism)?
2. What is the exact location and its surroundings?
3. Are dangers to persons and property present, such as armed suspects, fire, or hazardous materials?

4. Are there any unusual circumstances, such as snipers, explosives, or broken utilities present?

5. Is there a need to evacuate, and are antilooting measures required?

6. Is traffic control needed?

7. Is an inner perimeter needed to control the immediate scene?

8. Are additional personnel for inner and outer perimeter, evacuation, rescue, special weapons and tactics (SWAT, discussed later), negotiators, or other specialists needed?

9. Will a command post (CP) and staging area for additional personnel and emergency support be needed?

10. What emergency equipment and personnel are needed, and what safe routes are available for their response to the staging area?

11. What other equipment, supplies, and facilities will be needed?

12. Are there any dead or injured persons who require medical assistance or transport to the hospital?

13. What other needs are there (food and drink for long-term incidents, tactical units, rescue operations, bomb squad, K-9, tow trucks, and so on)? (Iannone and Ianonne, 2001)

It is often difficult to predict how long it will take to bring a major occurrence under control. The catastrophic terrorist attack on New York City's World Trade Center not only resulted in heavy loss of life but also necessitated almost one year to clean up the debris; rebuilding the site will require more years to come. Some hostage situations may be concluded within minutes, while others may last much longer (e.g., the 1993 incident in Waco, Texas, involving the Branch Davidians and several federal law enforcement agencies lasted for 51 days). Natural disasters present another problem. While tornadoes and earthquakes may occur in only minutes, the cleanup and restoration of damaged bridges, freeways, and buildings can take months or even years. De Jong (1994) recommends that supervisors and managers adhere to the principles of containment, communication, coordination, and control when responding to critical incidents:

Containment. Containment ensures that a crisis does not escalate beyond police control or resources. Containment also protects innocent people from entering areas of danger and allows police to isolate a suspect for apprehension in a tactical situation.

Communication. Communicating the status of a crisis to headquarters and other responding personnel is a first priority for the on-scene commander and may be accomplished by answering the questions listed earlier. For more prolonged operations, an emergency operations center (EOC) and/or CP should be established as a single point for command and control and centralized communications during critical incidents.

Coordination. Once effective communications have been established, the coordination of ongoing logistical needs becomes a priority for the on-scene commander. This would involve requests for additional personnel, equipment, and specialized units such as SWAT, hostage negotiators, hazardous materials team, and so on.

Control. At this stage, personnel and equipment are deployed to the incident. The three previous elements should be implemented before any response is attempted.

Tactical Concerns

Tactical problems present many unique concerns and dangers for the incident commander's consideration. FBI training for managing confrontational situations adopts De Jong's principles into a four-phase framework for organization and deploying personnel and resources to tactical incidents:

Preconfrontation/Preparation Phase. When preparing for a situation that may be confrontational and may require a tactical response, preparation and planning are key to successful outcomes. Training should address individual officers' tactical skills, team skills (such as hostage negotiators, SWAT, and command post staff), and systems skills (agency's capabilities to manage a command post). Multiagency exercises provide one method for training and testing an agency's preparation and capabilities.

Contingency Planning. Contingency planning focuses on identifying any potential problems, logistical requirements, strategies and tactics, communications needs, and command and control requirements for any potential tactical situation. Contingency planning provides a basis for developing standard operating procedures.

Immediate Response Phase. Control of the scene and isolating the threat are paramount in any response to a tactical situation. An initial assessment of the situation may be provided by answering the questions provided earlier. Establishing an inner and outer perimeter will help isolate the suspect and keep all nonessential personnel a safe distance from danger. As a situation progresses in severity or time, attention must be given to a variety of concerns, including ongoing intelligence about suspects and hostages; establishing a command post to handle logistics, tactics, and negotiations separately; and documenting all actions taken.

Deliberate/Specific Planning Phase. During this phase, strategies for responding to the incident are developed. These may include maintaining negotiations, emergency or deliberate assault, or surrender. Tactical response plans are carefully briefed by all tactical personnel and coordinated with all other responses before initiation.

Resolution Phase. Resolution entails maintaining control, negotiations, and intelligence during an incident. The goal of this phase is to end the incident without injury to anyone involved. Surrender is preferred, but assault may be necessary, depending on the circumstances. Assault tactics should consider all available intelligence information. A direct assault is often the last resort and consideration. An after-action report should be completed following every tactical incident, identifying which tactics were successful and which were not, so that appropriate changes can be made for future operations.

These matters will guide incident commanders during the first few minutes of their arrival at scenes requiring tactical operations; the type of situation will dictate further measures that need to be taken.

A number of federal, state, and local organizations exist to help prepare for, respond to, and recover from major disasters. Of particular note at the federal level is the National Domestic Preparedness Office, which is run through the FBI and coordinates all efforts of the Department of Defense, the Federal Emergency Management Agency (FEMA), the Department of Health and Human Services, the Department of Energy, and the Environmental Protection Agency to assist state and local first responders with planning, training, and equipment necessary to deal with a conventional weapon or a weapon of mass destruction incident (U.S. Department of Justice, 2001).

Mutual Aid Agreements

Interagency mutual aid agreements are essential for responding to disasters. This point was proven during a May 2000 drill to simulate a terrorist attack, sponsored by the federal government in California. Often, the agencies involved, including the FBI, state attorney general's office, and department of public health, would look to one another to come up with a way to respond to the crisis; decisions were often made in cumbersome conference calls involving up to a hundred people who lacked agendas or clear guidance. It is that kind of confusion that an emergency management system is designed to avoid (Buntin, 2001).

Mutual aid agreements provide a coalition of reinforcements from neighboring agencies for jurisdictions that have been struck by a natural disaster. In many jurisdictions, written mutual aid agreements are developed within the planning process for emergency responses. These joint powers agreements allow for the sharing of resources among participating agencies and the establishment of clear policies concerning command and control when a disaster occurs. Mutual aid agreements are commonly used to share personnel and equipment in a major tactical situation. Few agencies have the capability of handling a major tactical incident alone and must rely on the assistance of larger neighboring metropolitan agencies, county sheriff's departments, or state and federal agencies for assistance.

DISASTERS: NATURAL AND ACCIDENTAL CALAMITIES

When Nature Rages . . .

Every year, millions of people throughout the United States are victims of natural disasters. The aftermath of an earthquake, tornado, flood, or fire presents many challenges for the police.

As noted in the chapter introduction, natural disasters do not discriminate by jurisdiction; the largest and smallest of communities may be victim to the catastrophic effects of a natural disaster. Within minutes of such events, large numbers of people may be endangered and police and emergency services personnel face a variety of complex problems; these events also require significant coordination and efforts to control and reduce the aftereffects of these unusual situations.

Figure 12–1 shows the life cycle of disasters and describes the process through which managers prepare for emergencies and disasters, respond to them when they occur, help people and institutions recover from them, mitigate their effects, reduce the risk of loss, and prevent disasters from occurring.

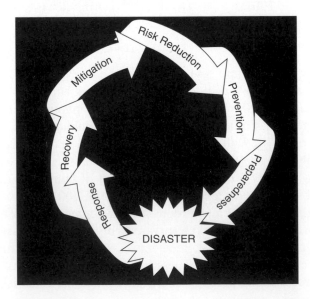

FIGURE 12–1   Life Cycle of Disasters
Source: Federal Emergency Management Agency (FEMA)
http://www.fema.gov/about/what.
October 20, 1997.

The effective management of disaster situations requires that incident commanders know what to do and how to respond quickly. Lifesaving measures, rescues, and evacuations will occupy much of the decision making during the initial stages of a disaster. Coordinating the responses of other emergency and fire personnel and support agencies will also be a concern.

Major Fires, Airplane Crashes, Hazardous Materials

Major Fires

The magnitude and scope of a major fire present immediate dangers to the public as well as police and fire personnel responding to such incidents. During any major fire, the incident commander should meet with his or her counterpart in the fire department to determine what police control measures may be required. The police commander should direct any resources necessary to support the fire department in its immediate rescue and evacuation efforts. Additionally, personnel should be assigned to the perimeter to control traffic and crowds of onlookers and protect fire apparatus and hoses. A vehicle driving over a fire hose can rupture it and risk the lives of firefighters who may be inside a structure using the hose for protection and suppression of the fire.

Nature challenges the police in many ways. Floods can quickly destroy bridges and roads, making it very difficult for police to respond to citizens' needs.
Courtesy Washoe County, Nevada, Sheriff's Office Photo Unit.

When a fire is extinguished, the scene should be protected for investigation. The police are also responsible for the protection of the property from looters. In some cases, police may have to establish a perimeter around an entire neighborhood affected by a fire and check the identification of persons asking to enter the property to retrieve personal belongings.

The Oakland Hills, California, fire in the early 1990s provides a good example of the complexities and dangers involved in major fires. On that day, hot and dry gusts of winds swept the Monterey pine- and eucalyptus-covered upscale neighborhoods in the Oakland-Berkeley hills. Twenty-five firefighters were on-scene overhauling hot spots from a fire the previous day when embers blew into dry areas and quickly ignited a fire that was soon out of control. Immediate evacuation efforts were initiated by police and fire officials and mutual aid was requested. Twenty-five persons died, 150 were injured, more than 3,000 residences were destroyed in a 5.25-mile area, totaling more than $1.5 billion in damages. An after-action report pointed to the need for enhanced mutual aid, increased availability of water, stricter fire codes and ordinances, improved communications, and vegetation management (Parker, 1992).

Airplane Crashes

The aftermath of an airplane falling from the sky with passengers and scattering plane parts is catastrophic. Police and fire personnel are usually the first to arrive at the scene of an airplane crash; they must assume the gruesome task of fire suppression, lifesaving, containment, and protection of the scene until the responsible investigators arrive. Police leaders must also be concerned with crowd and traffic control and the looting of the personal effects of passengers.

The containment of a crash scene is often complicated by the large area or type of geography involved; sometimes planes plunge into swamps or large areas of water.

Military aircraft are particularly problematic and present many potential dangers for the on-scene commanders and officers. Depending on the type of military aircraft involved, the existence of conventional and nuclear weapons, explosives charges for ejection canopies, and the presence of classified or top secret materials make the handling of a military aircraft accident additionally difficult. As a result, many agencies located near military bases conduct joint crash response exercises and have developed mutual aid agreements for handling such occurrences.

An incident commander's primary tasks in these cases are similar to those for any aircraft accident and include coordinating immediate lifesaving and rescue operations and containing and protecting the scene until responsible authorities arrive. In most cases, and in accordance with National Transportation Safety Board (NTSB) regulations, Federal Aviation Administration (FAA) investigators will respond and assume responsibility for the investigation and coordinate their efforts with the assistance of local authorities.

The wheels from downed TWA Flight 800—which killed 230 people in 1996 off Long Island, New York—are carefully brought to shore.
Courtesy NYPD Photo Unit.

Hazardous Materials

The U.S. Department of Transportation estimates that a half million interstate shipments of hazardous materials are transported daily across the United States (Donahue, 1993). This creates a tremendous potential for accidents to occur in any small town or large metropolitan area. The following news articles illustrate the potential dangers involved in hazardous materials accidents:

> Three pipefitters at the Newport News, Virginia, shipyard were found dead after lethal gas and raw sewage flooded a pump room in the aircraft carrier U.S.S. *Harry S. Truman*. About 1,800 sailors had to be evacuated. ("Three shipworkers die," 1997)

> Two warehouse workers in Port Fourchon, Louisiana, were hospitalized for exposure to toxic fumes after hundreds of barrels of drilling fluids and other chemicals caught fire. ("Port Fourchon," 1997)

> A fire and explosion at a farm chemical distribution plant in West Helena, Arkansas, killed three firefighters and injured 16 others. Nearby residents had to be evacuated due to the threat of danger caused by burning toxic chemicals. ("Three die," 1997)

A toxic gas explosion at the Accra Pac Aerosol packaging plant in Elkhart, Indiana, killed one worker and sent 34 others to the hospital. ("Indiana blast," 1997)

These incidents reinforce the need for police education and training concerning hazardous materials. Police are often one of the first responders to hazardous materials accidents and can quickly become victims themselves if the proper precautions are not taken. Recently, however, the need for such training has been recognized, and hazardous materials training (HAZMAT) is now included in mandated Peace Officers Standards and Training curriculums.

Police are considered first responders, and their responsibility is simply to recognize and report any suspected HAZMAT condition to the proper authorities. Many local fire departments now have a special HAZMAT team trained to deal with these conditions. More extensive situations may require the response of state or federal agencies for assistance.

When on the scene of a suspected HAZMAT situation, the incident commander should quickly evaluate the threat, notify the proper authorities, and establish a perimeter large enough to protect the public and officers from the effects of the hazard or spill. The commander should determine how large a perimeter is needed, as winds, water, and other environmental conditions may aggravate a problem. Some hazardous materials are also susceptible to fire or explosion.

A HAZMAT incident of any size will require the response of several agencies, including police, fire, specialized HAZMAT response teams, and ambulance services for those injured. It is recommended that agencies develop response plans that account for the many different types of emergencies that may occur. These plans should include the following issues:

1. Preemergency planning and coordination with outside parties
2. Personnel roles, lines of authority, training, and communication
3. Emergency prevention
4. Determining safe distances
5. Site security and control
6. Evacuation routes and procedures
7. Decontamination procedures
8. Emergency medical treatment and first aid
9. Critiques of response and follow up
10. Proper use of personnel and equipment (Donahue, 1993:5)

A hazardous materials accident in Casa Grande, Arizona, serves as an example of how a lack of preplanning, misunderstandings about command and control, and communications problems can lead to major problems. Police and fire units responded to reports of smoke coming from a railcar that was parked near the city's downtown area. Railroad officials failed to inform responding personnel that the car contained chemical white phosphorous. Decisions to evacuate were delayed for 40 minutes, and no formal system was established for evacuation of households in imminent danger. A command post was never established, and information about the dangers involved was not transmitted to additional responding units. Subsequently, five police officers succumbed to toxic smoke as a result of the absence of self-contained breathing apparatuses. Despite the availability of six HAZMAT teams in the state, none were called for assistance. Crowd problems developed because police failed to announce the dangers through the media. Obviously, this occurrence serves as a case study in how *not* to treat a critical incident involving hazardous materials.

CRITICAL INCIDENTS: HOSTAGE, RIOT, AND BOMB SITUATIONS

Barricaded Persons and Hostages

Armed suspects who take hostages or barricade themselves represent one of the most dangerous situations confronting the police. By virtue of their motives, hostage takers are extremely dangerous to police officers and citizens. The four categories of hostage takers are (1) traditional (criminal trapped at the scene of a crime or while escaping from a crime scene), (2) terrorists, (3) prisoners who take a hostage(s) while escaping, and (4) the mentally disturbed (Peak, 2000).

The traditional or criminal type often takes hostages to gain leverage to bargain for freedom. The second type, terrorists, are probably the most dangerous of the four types. When terrorists take hostages, the operation is usually well planned and executed; furthermore, terrorists are often prepared to die for their cause and will quickly kill hostages, may be sophisticated fighters, and have probably studied antiterrorist strategies used by police.

The third type of hostage situation involves prisoners who take hostages, usually correctional personnel, to get publicity for perceived inhumane conditions and other grievances. The final type of hostage taker, the mentally disturbed person, is the most prevalent and perhaps least dangerous, if properly trained police personnel are dealing with them. They can be paranoid schizophrenic; have a bipolar disorder; be antisocial personality types; or suffer from hallucinations, feelings of persecution, or depression (Peak, 2000).

Remsberg (1986) has identified four reasons why people take hostages:

1. *Persons seeking attention:* This is often the motivation for gang members, criminals, or persons with mental disorders taking hostages; for example, four gunmen who took 30 hostages in a 1991 Sacramento electronics store were attempting to obtain recognition and respect for their gang.

2. *Power:* The hostage taker has a psychological need to control or dominate. For example, an employee may take hostages in the workplace to prevent his dismissal.

3. *Revenge:* The hostage taker is attempting to right some wrong. Many hostage situations involving families are the result of revenge.

4. *Despair:* The perpetrator is hopeless because of his or her job or financial or family situation. Hostage takers acting from despair commonly commit suicide or force the issue so that the police will kill them. Many hostage takers are experiencing multiple stressors. They frequently lack family support systems and therefore have no emotional outlets. They often feel isolated, alienated, and desperate. (Fuselier, Van Zandt, and Lanceley, 1991)

These incidents are high profile in terms of media coverage; every detail of the event is usually reported in the news. Therefore, the police must follow proper procedures in barricade and hostage situations. Police officials must proceed deliberately but cautiously, and an assault should be conducted only as a last resort or if absolute safety can be ensured.

Although no hard and fast rules apply to such cases, the incident commander at the scene must decide whether or not to accede to the hostage taker's demands. Generally, no deals will be made. But the incident commander must judge each case on its own merits and recognize that the successful negotiation of a hostage's release will take considerable time and patience.

Incident commanders should also evaluate the situation and ensure that they respond accordingly. For example, if the hostage taker's motive is attention, negotiators should respond in a firm, caring manner. Getting tough only exacerbates the situation. The power-motivated hostage taker requires a different approach. The negotiator must display power and force but also must be willing to give and take. When revenge is involved, homicide is even more likely. Negotiators should express compassion but should be prepared to move at the slightest opportunity. Finally, the despair-motivated hostage taker is the most difficult. The negotiator must realistically provide encouragement and support as opposed to false hope, which can backfire and result in violence. The negotiator must also communicate with the incident commander, in order that tactical decisions can be made.

As part of a tactical plan for neutralizing and arresting the hostage taker, the incident commander should ensure that the following tasks are being performed (adapted from Iannone and Iannone, 2001:272):

1. *Secure the premises:* Officers should be posted at the front and rear of the premises and in other locations to prevent an escape.

2. *Command post:* Locate in a safe, strategic area upwind from the scene to avoid contamination if gas is used.

3. *Injured persons:* Give aid, interview, and remove.

4. *Communications:* Notify headquarters of the situation.

5. *Personnel support:* Acquire necessary personnel to cordon off the area and for operations at the scene.

6. *Special equipment:* Request gas grenades, masks, body armor, sharp-shooters and rifles, portable communications equipment, loudspeakers for communicating with the suspect, portable lights and generators, helicopter patrol, ambulance and fire vehicles as needed.

7. *Staging area:* Locate staging area where officers and equipment are to report upwind from scene of incident.

8. *Identify officers as they report:* Assign them to positions where they can secure escape routes without exposing themselves to crossfire.

9. *Evacuation:* Persons in the area who may be endangered by gunfire or other police operations should be removed to a safe location.

10. *Field intelligence:* Collate intelligence from police and civilians regarding the suspect, victim, and location. Determine the type of crimes committed, the purpose in barricading or seizing a hostage, the suspect's physical and mental condition and attitudes concerning police and society, and a physical description. Disseminate the latter information to personnel, so they will not mistake the hostage for the suspect.

Negotiations, for the most part, are extremely effective in bringing hostage situations to a successful end; however, the police must be tactically prepared if negotiations fail and the lives of hostages are endangered. When negotiations fail, the incident commander will turn to the tactical commander to initiate a tactical plan for assaulting the barricade (negotiators and SWAT personnel often have separate command posts and plans). Entry into a barricade absolutely is the last resort.

The FBI and other entities conduct excellent training programs for professional hostage negotiators; this is a delicate and difficult subject that requires much more training and in-depth analysis than we are able to do here.

Civil Disorders and Riot Control

Civil disorder is a natural part of our society and has been present ever since there were governments. Our country was born out of civil disorder; the Boston Tea Party, which helped to initiate the War of Independence, was an act of civil disobedience as a result of an unfair tax on imported tea. In 1863, a riot in New York City left approximately 2,000 people dead. More recently, the riots as a result of the civil rights movement and the Vietnam War affected every American citizen. Many of our major cities have experienced devastating riots, and many of our best-known universities had major riots and demonstrations that pitted students against university administrators and the police.

Civil disorders are far more common today than most people realize. They can erupt as a result of a variety of causes, such as the aftermath of a court decision, a variety of police actions (effecting an arrest or keeping peace at an abortion clinic), or even a major sporting event, making planning and reacting more difficult. In 1992, in the wake of the Rodney King verdicts in Los Angeles, the country witnessed one of the worst riots since the 1960s. Although such disorders are not commonplace, there is a strong potential for several riots each year in the United States. Furthermore, they are not limited to our large cities; many riots and disorders occur in medium-sized cities and towns.

Adams (1994) noted that crowds develop into unruly mobs through a series of three stages. During the first stage, the crowd consists of a conglomeration of individuals who are together because of the excitement or a feeling of some impending event. They tend to be individualistic, but they have the potential to rapidly band together, especially if some event causes them to focus their attention. The second stage occurs when leaders or agitators are able to gain individuals' attention and cause them to focus on some objective or perceived threat. Primary leaders attempt to provide a focus, while secondary leaders move through the crowd encouraging action. These leaders generally develop informally based on opportunity. The third stage occurs when the mob reaches critical mass and focuses on some objective. At this point, the crowd likely will get out of control, resulting in destruction of property and injury to citizens.

When a crowd situation occurs, the police have four primary objectives: containment, dispersal, reentry prevention, and arrest of violators (Adams, 1994). Anytime there is a disorder, the police should first attempt to contain it or prevent it from growing larger. Containment is achieved by establishing blockades and barriers to prevent others from entering into the area. This should be accomplished only when the police have adequate personnel on the scene. To attempt containment without adequate resources can only worsen the situation. Tactically, the police should passively observe the rioters until adequate resources are available.

Once adequate resources are there, the police should quickly contain the situation and begin to disperse members of the crowd. This is accomplished by forcing the passive participants on the edges to leave the area. Some will resist and move back into the core of the crowd, while others will leave peaceably. Reducing the size of the crowd will effectively lessen the remaining participants' courage. As the crowd becomes smaller, it will be easier for the police to deal with the core or more troublesome members.

Finally, the police should attempt to arrest those persons who are responsible for inciting the riot or disorder and the individuals who cause personal injury or property damage. The decision to make an on-scene arrest must be weighed against the potential that the arrest will further incite the rioters and cause more harm. Also, a physical arrest should not be attempted unless the police have the resources to ensure that the arrest can be effected. The police should also conspicuously take video and still photographs of the crowd; photographs serve to discourage rioters from criminal behavior and to frighten the more timid into leaving the area. They also serve as evidence and can be used in court to document individuals' behavior. Finally, they can be used at a later period to identify those who violated laws for arrest purposes.

Bomb Incidents

Bombs have traditionally been one of the weapons of choice for urban terrorist groups because of the damage they inflict to life and property. In addition to the World Trade Center and Oklahoma City bombings, the past few years have witnessed two other notable bombing cases in the United States:

> *The Unabomber.* In April 1996, federal agents arrested Theodore Kaczynski and charged him with the crimes committed by the so-called "Unabomber." The Unabomber targeted university and airline employees among others and had evaded authorities for more than 18 years, during which time 3 people were killed and 23 others injured in mail-package bombing incidents.

> *Olympic Bombing.* During the Summer Olympic Games in July 1996, a pipe bomb exploded at Centennial Olympic Park in Atlanta, Georgia, killing two people and injuring more than 100. The FBI reported that the device was a homemade pipe bomb.

These horrific incidents provide graphic examples of the potential devastation and loss of life that a bombing can cause.

While the number of actual bombing incidents has been declining in the United States in recent years, the 5-year period of 1993 to 1997 saw 8,056 such incidents, resulting in 329 people killed, 2,773 injured, and more than $600 million in damages (U.S. Department of Treasury, Bureau of Alcohol, Tobacco and Firearms, 2003).

The initial response and responsibility for lives and property at these incidents often rest with a commander and officers assigned to the beat where the incident occurred. The ability of the commander to control and protect the scene and direct necessary resources to the area is often critical to the investigation's outcome.

Explosive devices may be easily concealed. A search should be organized that is systematic and thorough so that it can be completed in the least amount of time possible. Some agencies have trained dogs to search for explosives. The dogs' speed is particularly useful for such a situation. One method for searching is to match a police officer with an employee of the establishment. An employee is more likely to be familiar with the premises and be able to identify suspicious packages or out-of-place items. For example, a lunchbox or package on a desk may not look out of place to a police officer but may be obviously suspicious to an employee. Police should caution any employees assisting in the search not to touch any suspected device and to summon an officer if one is found.

If a device is not found, the person who is responsible for the premises should be advised. Police personnel should avoid telling anyone the building is safe or suggesting that employees may return to work. This is the duty of the responsible employee on the scene, and for the police to do so could incur a tremendous liability if a bomb were to explode and injure anyone.

If a suspected bomb is found, the officer in charge should ensure that trained bomb specialists are summoned to the scene. There should be no attempt by on-scene officers to remove or disarm the device while waiting for expert assistance. Officers should be directed to establish a perimeter a safe distance around the device in the event of an explosion so that no one would suffer injuries if the bomb exploded.

The dangers inherent in any bomb incident or other crisis require that a decision be made concerning the evacuation of persons from a business or their residence. Under many circumstances, the police do not have the legal authority to force people to leave their personal property or business. Exceptions occur when police encounter persons who are mentally incompetent, crippled, aged, young, or sick. In these instances, the police may assume responsibility for their safe removal from danger.

Every police agency should request an opinion from a legal advisor concerning its authority and responsibility for evacuating citizens and should develop clear departmental policies and procedures for personnel to follow during such incidents. On one hand, an incident commander's failure to take action that might ensure a person's safety could result in criticism and liability; on the other, the decision to force the evacuation of persons from their residence or business assumes the responsibility for the protection of their property from theft or damage.

Use of Tactical Units

The Los Angeles Police Department developed the first special weapons and tactics (SWAT) units in 1967, following increased incidences of "urban violence, including snipings, political assassinations, and urban guerrilla warfare" (Los Angeles Police Department, 1974:101). Following its lead, a large number of police agencies have had SWAT teams since the 1970s, although many use a softer, more expansive title for their team, such as Special Operations and Response Team, or "SORT."

Since their inception, such teams have been trained to address critical incidents. Team members are normally highly trained, wear distinctive clothing, are well equipped with automatic weapons and gear, may be accompanied by a mobile command post with elaborate communications systems, and are often highly specialized (including, for example, a leader, scout, sharpshooter, observer, rear guard, and so on) (Center for Research on Criminal Justice, 1975).

In a critical incident today, it is recommended that most teams have 21 officers: a commander, a four-officer entry team, another four-officer secondary entry or emergency response team, a four-officer sniper complement, and eight officers to provide a containment function/perimeter team (Green, 2001). Obviously, many small agencies would be unable to maintain a well-trained unit of this size.

A national survey of 51 law enforcement agencies with SWAT units was recently completed; together, the units reported 92 critical incidents over a three-year period. In terms of outcomes, they reported surrender or arrest of the suspect in 71 (65 percent) of the incidents without gunfire or lethal force being employed. Those findings were compared with 106 agencies in the same survey that did not have a SWAT unit; they had 212 critical incidents over the same three-year period. In those incidents, suspects surrendered or were arrested without gunfire or lethal force in 93 (44 percent) of the incidents. Therefore, the study concluded that agencies with police tactical units resolve critical incidents far more safely than those agencies without such units and suggested that the reason for this finding is the greater adequacy in resources and tactics when dealing with such incidents (Stevens, 1999).

TERRORISM AND HOMELAND DEFENSE

A Nation Changed and Challenged

Unquestionably, historians of the future will maintain that terroristic acts of the early twenty-first century forever changed the nature of policing and security efforts in the United States. Words are almost inadequate to describe how the events of September 11, 2001, forever modified and heightened the fears and concerns of all Americans with regard to domestic security and the methods and technologies necessary for securing the general public.

The ongoing conflict between Israel and the Palestinians, the antigovernment narcoterrorists in several South American countries, the spread of radical Islamic fundamentalism, and our own homegrown terrorist groups strongly suggest that North Americans will face the threat of terrorism for some time to come (Tully and Willoughby, 2002) and that the local police departments are our first line of defense. Within the 50 states, 3,000 counties and 18,000 cities must be protected. The job of getting law enforcement, emergency services, public health agencies, and private enterprises coordinated and working together at local, state, and federal levels is a daunting task (Meisler, 2002).

We now focus on how the federal government and local law enforcement agencies are responding to this comparatively new challenge.

Definitions and Types

Title 22, Section 265f(d) of the U.S. Code states the following: "Terrorism means premeditated, politically motivated violence perpetrated against noncombatant targets by subnational groups or clandestine agents, usually intended to influence an audience" (Jylland-Halverson, Stoner, and Till, 2000). The FBI defines terrorism as "The unlawful use of force against persons or property to intimidate or coerce a government, the civilian population, or any segment thereof, in furtherance of political or social objectives" (quoted in Rehm and Rehm, 2000):38.

The threat of terrorism has changed and become more deadly. Over the past several years, a new trend has developed in terrorism within the United States: a transition from more numerous low-level incidents to less frequent but more destructive attacks, with a goal to produce mass casualties and attract intense media coverage. Although the number of terrorist attacks in the United States declined during the 1990s, the number of persons killed and injured increased (Lewis, 1999).

Police officers confronting terrorists in the United States now find themselves vulnerable in six types of situations (Garrett, 2002):

1. *Traffic stops:* Law enforcement lacks prior knowledge of the individual being stopped; the officer may be isolated and the potential terrorist may be in a heightened state of suspicion or anger as a result of the stop.

2. *Residence visits:* Officers are on the extremists' home turf, putting them at a disadvantage; the visit may be routine, but the extremist may not view it as such, and the home may be armed and fortified.

The terrorist attacks on New York's World Trade Center greatly intensified the issue of homeland defense for the nation's police.

3. *Rallies/marches:* The risk to police usually comes not from the group holding the event, but from protestors, often anarchists who hate the police and believe that the best way to confront the demonstrators is through physical violence.

4. *Confrontations/standoffs:* All such incidents can arise from the three previous situations.

5. *Revenge and retaliation:* A terrorist may be motivated by personal benefit or revenge, such as one who attempts to blow up an Internal Revenue Service office because he was audited.

6. *Incident responses:* These can take many forms, ranging from activities of terrorists to acts of nature.

Terrorist attacks in the United States are perpetrated by both foreign and domestic terrorists. Examples of the former are the attacks in September 2001 with hijacked jetliners on the World Trade Center building in New York and the Pentagon in Virginia, with more than 3,000 people killed or missing. Another example is the bombing of the World Trade Center in New York City in February 1993, killing six and injuring 1,000 people. An example of the latter is the April 1995 bombing of the Murrah Building in Oklahoma City by Timothy McVeigh, killing 168 people and injuring more than 500 (Lewis, 1999). (McVeigh was executed in June 2001.)

Chasing terrorists is expensive: The U.S. Congress appropriated more than $60 billion from September 2001 to January 2002 to combat terrorism at home and abroad, including $1.5 billion for the new Homeland Security Office (Fram, 2002). Law enforcement resources available for the task have also greatly increased. From 1993 to 2001, the FBI, which created a new Counterterrorism Division in April 2000, saw its counterterrorism budget increase from $77 million to $376 million or 388 percent; the most significant increase followed the Oklahoma City bombing (Ragavan, 2001). The cost of trying to secure the nation's people and places is projected to skyrocket even more in the aftermath of 9/11 with $150 billion more by 2010 (Fram, 2002). In February 2002, President Bush announced his "Plan to Strengthen Our Homeland Security," which proposed allocating $3.5 billion for the nation's first responders—police, firefighters, and medical teams—as well as $11 billion for border security, $700 million to improve intelligence gathering and sharing abilities, and $230 million to create a citizens' initiative to help communities be better prepared for an attack; this plan was posted on the World Wide Web (http://www.whitehouse.gov.news/releases/2002/02/2002/20204-2.html).

Terrorism can take many forms and does not always involve bombs and guns. For example, the Earth Liberation Front (ELF) and a sister organization, the Animal Liberation Front, have been responsible for the majority of terrorist acts committed in the United States for several years. These "ecoterrorists" have burned greenhouses, tree farms, logging sites, ski resorts, and new housing developments. The groups' members have eluded capture, have no centralized organization or leadership, and are so secretive as to be described as "ghosts" who are more difficult to infiltrate than organized crime (Westneat, 2001).

U.S. embassies abroad have also been singled out for terrorist attacks; in 1998, bombings of embassies in Kenya and Tanzania left 224 dead and resulted in the placement of Saudi millionaire Osama bin Laden at the top of the FBI's most wanted list, as well as the conviction in June 2001 of four of bin Laden's foot soldiers (Doane, 2001).

The FBI divides the current international terrorist threat into three categories:

1. *Foreign sponsors of international terrorism.* Seven countries—Iran, Iraq, Syria, Sudan, Libya, Cuba, and North Korea—are designated as such sponsors and view terrorism as a tool of foreign policy. They fund, organize, network, and provide other support to formal terrorist groups and extremists.

2. *Formalized terrorist groups.* Autonomous organizations (such as bin Laden's al Qaeda, Afghanistan's Taliban, Iranian-backed Hezbollah, Egyptian Al-Gama'a Al-Islamiyya, and Palestinian HAMAS) have their own infrastructures, personnel, finances, and training facilities. Examples of this type are the al Qaeda terrorists who attacked the World Trade Center and the Pentagon in 2001.

3. *Loosely affiliated international radical extremists.* As noted, examples are the persons who bombed the World Trade Center in 1993. They do not represent a particular nation but may pose the most urgent threat to the United States because they remain relatively unknown to law enforcement agencies. (Lewis, 1999)

These international groups now pose another source of concern to law enforcement agencies: They are cooperating among themselves. For example, a terrorist manual is circulating among some of them, and al Qaeda is known to maintain close ties with Hezbollah (Doane, 2001). Another concern is their choice of weapons; although terrorists continue to rely on conventional weapons such as bombs and small arms, indications are that terrorists and other criminals may consider using unconventional chemical (including nerve gas, sarin, or other chemical cocktails whose ingredients are readily available) or biological weapons in an attack in the United States at some point in the future (Lewis, 1999).

With regard to domestic terrorism, many people living in the United States are determined to use violence to advance their agendas. Domestic terrorism seems to have hit a high-water mark from 1982 to 1992, when a majority of the 165 terrorist incidents were conducted by domestic terrorist groups. One current troubling branch of right-wing extremism is the militia or patriot movement. They generally are law-abiding citizens who have become intolerant of what they perceive as violations of their constitutional rights (Lewis, 1999).

A Looming Threat: Bioterrorism

The use of anthrax in the United States in late 2001 left no doubt about people's vulnerability to biological weapons—and the intention of some people to develop and use them. Smallpox, botulism, and plague also constitute major threats, and many experts believe that it is only a matter of time before biological weapons get into the wrong hands and are used like explosives in the past (Strandberg, 2001).

All of this brings to mind the *Andromeda Strain* movie scenario: a toxic agent being genetically engineered in large quantities and sprayed into the population; that agent then reproducing itself and killing many people. The person who controls this toxin could then sell it to terrorists. One has to wonder why international terrorists have not already done so. This form of terrorism can wipe out an entire civilization. All that is required is a toxin that can be cultured and put into a spray form that can be weaponized and disseminated into the population. Fortunately, they *are* extremely difficult for all but specially trained individuals to make in large quantities and in the correct dosage; they are tricky to transport, because live organisms are delicate; and they must be dispersed in a proper molecule size to infect the lungs of the target. Like chemical weapons, they are also dependent on the wind and the weather and are difficult to control (Rogers, 2001).

Some police responses to attacks by biological agents are discussed next.

Local Law Enforcement Responses

Police have several possible means by which to address domestic terrorism, particularly following the 2001 attacks in New York City. First, and perhaps the most fruitful, is military support of domestic law enforcement. The Posse Comitatus Act of 1878 prohibits using the military to execute the laws, generally; the military may be called on, however, to provide personnel and equipment for certain special support activities, such as domestic terrorist events involving weapons of mass destruction (Bolgiano, 2001).

Other means that have been considered (Pincus and Eggen, 2001) include lifting a 1976 executive order banning U.S. involvement in foreign assassinations; loosening restrictions on FBI surveillance; more power for law enforcement agencies to conduct wiretaps, detain foreigners, and track money-laundering cases; recruiting and paying overseas agents linked to terrorist groups, for the purpose of infiltration; having a counter-terrorism czar within the White House; and expanding the intelligence community's ability to intercept and translate messages in Arabic, Farsi, and other languages. Other measures now in use involve the aviation industry, such as the fortification of cockpits to prevent access by hijackers, placing federal air marshals on commercial flights, eliminating curbside check in, and more intensive screening of luggage (Morris, 2001).

On a larger level, four major aspects are involved in dealing with terrorist organizations:

1. Gathering raw intelligence on the organization's structure, its members, and its plans (or potential for the use of violence)

2. Determining what measures can be taken to counter, or thwart, terrorist activities

3. Assessing how the damage caused by terrorists can be minimized through rapid response and containment of the damage

4. Apprehending and convicting individual terrorists and dismantling their organizations (Tully and Willoughby, 2002)

Emergency Response Checklist and Lessons Learned

Following ICS rationale, recently the U.S. Department of Justice and the Federal Emergency Management Agency issued a lengthy *Emergency Response to Terrorism Job Aid* checklist detailing the actions that are to be taken by law enforcement and rescue agencies in the event of terrorist attack. This manual's section on law enforcement's activities when responding to terrorism is shown in Exhibit 12–1.

Several fundamental lessons have been learned and "articles of faith" developed concerning critical incident management following terrorist acts. A federal report stated the following: "Emergencies can only be managed by people at the site. They can't be managed back in Washington. Expect the unexpected and be prepared to adjust accordingly" (Carlson, 1999:19).

With respect to biological agents, the role of the police will vary depending on whether or not they are the first responder. In either event, they must become knowledgeable about bioweapons, and how to ascertain if the agent is transmittable, as well as the appropriate agencies to get involved. Then, if an agent is deployed overtly and therefore discovered quickly, the police will respond immediately; if covert (and, say, the hospitals do not begin to see cases until many days after the agent is released), the police will be responsible for conducting a later investigation. If hundreds of people are showing up at hospitals, then the police will also have to maintain order (Strandberg, 2001).

Exhibit 12–1

LAW ENFORCEMENT'S EMERGENCY RESPONSE TO TERRORISM*

If First on Scene:
- Isolate/secure the scene, establish control zone
- Establish command
- Stage incoming units

If Command Has Been Established:
- Report to Command Post
- Evaluate scene safety/security (ongoing criminal activity, secondary devices, additional threats)
- Gather witness statements and document
- Institute notifications (FBI, explosive ordinance squad, private security, and so forth)
- Request additional resources
- Secure outer perimeter
- Control traffic
- Use appropriate self-protective measures
- Initiate public safety measures (evacuations as necessary)
- Assist with control/isolation of patients
- Preserve evidence
- Participate in a unified command system with fire, medical, hospital, and public works agencies

*Adapted from U.S. Department of Justice, Federal Emergency Management Agency, *Emergency Response to Terrorism: Self-Study*. Washington, DC: Author, June 1999.

Technology Needs

Of particular concern among the law enforcement community is the gap between technologies available to the police and those used by persons and groups planning terrorist acts. The National Institute of Justice conducted a survey of law enforcement technology needs for combating terrorism, interviewing 198 individuals representing 138 agencies from 50 states. The interviewees were queried about their needs in areas such as intelligence gathering; surveillance; command, control, and communication (C3); site hardening; detecting, disabling, and containing explosive devices; and defending against weapons of mass destruction (i.e., nuclear, biological, chemical [NBC] devices) and cyberterrorism (U.S. Department of Justice, 1999).

By far, the most pressing technology needs concerned ready access to current intelligence, a national terrorism intelligence database accessible to all state and local law enforcement agencies, improved means to detect and analyze explosive devices, and better NBC protective gear (such as masks, suits, and

EXHIBIT 12–2_____

MOST FREQUENTLY CITED TECHNOLOGY NEEDS

Need	Function	Total Times Mentioned	Top Five*
National intergovernmental information system with current intelligence on terrorism	Intelligence	58	47
Improved means of detecting explosives	Detecting, disabling, and containing explosive devices	58	21
Improved and more readily available secure communications	Command, control, and communications	53	19
Improved means of detecting and categorizing nuclear, biological, and chemical threats	Defending against weapons of mass destruction	51	24
Improved interagency communi- cations	Command, control, and communications	48	26
Improved robots for disarming and disabling explosive devices	Detecting, disabling, and containing explosive devices	47	9
Improved affordable protective gear	Defending against weapons of mass destruction	45	16
Improved nonlethal weapons	Apprehending terrorists; crowd and riot control	40	8
Improved "see-through-the-wall" capability	Surveillance	34	18
Improved long-range video monitoring	Surveillance	34	13
Improved detection and tracing mechanisms and countermeasures for cyberattacks	Defending against cyber- terrorism	33	4
Improved electronic listening devices	Surveillance	32	15
Improved training to combat terrorism	Training	31	18
Improved containment vessels and vehicles for explosive devices	Detecting, disabling, and containing explosive devices; defending against weapons of mass destruction	31	6
Improved night vision devices	Surveillance	30	15

*Indicates the total number of times mentioned as being among an agency's top five needs.

Source: U.S. Department of Justice, National Institute of Justice, *Inventory of State and Local Law Enforcement Technology Needs to Combat Terrorism,* Washington, DC: Author, January 1999, p. 4.

gloves); C3 was another area of greatest need. Exhibit 12–2 shows the complete listing of the 15 most frequently cited needs.

___ Case Studies ___

The following two case studies afford the reader a small taste of the kinds of tactical operations that are confronted by the police all too frequently.

When the Going Gets Tough . . .

An estranged husband, Donald Blair, goes to his ex-wife's school, where she is a fifth-grade teacher. A residential area borders the school on the north side; on the south side is a large shopping center with a restaurant and several other small stores; a four-lane thoroughfare borders the school on the west side; and a daycare center and a retirement home are on the east. Blair enters the cafeteria, where the majority of the school's children, teachers, and the principal are having lunch. He pulls out an AR-15 automatic weapon, screams to his ex-wife that she's made his life miserable, and threatens to kill her. He also states that no one is to leave the room, or he will kill them. The school nurse, passing by in the hallway, overhears the commotion and immediately contacts the police. Sgt. Hawthorne is in charge of this district and responds to the scene. The first officers to arrive see several teachers and kids running away from the school building. One of the teachers points out Blair's pickup truck, parked in front of the school; inside the truck are several survival guides, empty ammunition boxes, and pipe bomb materials.

1. As supervisor on the scene, use the checklist provided earlier and identify what Sgt. Hawthorne would need to do during the initial stages to gain control of this situation.

2. What additional personnel, equipment, and other resources might be needed?

Dealing with Spills That Kill

Metro City is a medium-sized community located in the Midwest. Three smaller incorporated cities border its jurisdiction. Union Rails, Inc., has informed the police chief of Metro City that it plans to increase the number of trains going daily through the downtown area, and that several of those trains will be carrying hazardous industrial materials. Each rail car containing such materials will be appropriately marked, and bills of lading identifying the cargo and its hazard will be available. The railroad is requesting a meeting with local officials to discuss the area's HAZMAT response capabilities in the event of an accident. Metro City has no such plan. As a police supervisor for planning and development, Sgt. Young has been directed to provide the police chief with recommendations concerning the impact on the cities of transporting HAZMAT materials through the urban area; Young must also determine what the jurisdictions need to do to prepare for the increase in rail traffic.

1. Which governmental agencies in the tri-city area would need to be involved in developing this plan?
2. What types of personnel training would be required, and where could the police agencies acquire this training for their officers?
3. Are there any other issues or concerns that Sgt. Young would need to identify for the chief?

SUMMARY

This chapter has examined the supervisor's and manager's roles in both human- and nature-generated critical incident management, including disasters of all types and terrorist attacks.

These kinds of occurrences require preplanned responses. It simply will not do for incident commanders to await their occurrence before developing plans for coping with them; the cost in human lives and property is too potentially great to be left to on-the-job training. It behooves all police personnel, especially incident commanders as well as the first responders at such scenes, to know and understand their own agency's and existing multiagency, regional protocol and procedures as well as mutual aid agreements for addressing these situations. Anything less would be a disservice to the public they serve.

ITEMS FOR REVIEW

1. Define an Incident Command System.
2. Describe some of the personnel, equipment, and other resources that are needed during the initial stages of any critical incident.
3. Explain what is involved with the principles of containment, communication, coordination, and control when police supervisors and managers respond to critical incidents.
4. Explain the four-phase framework for organizing and deploying personnel and resources for tactical problems.
5. Define terrorism, and what law enforcement agencies are doing to combat it.
6. Describe the six kinds of situations involving terrorism/extremists in which the police are vulnerable.

7. List the four types of hostage takers, and some of the approaches taken by the police in dealing with them.

8. Describe the primary objectives of the police in dealing with civil disorder.

9. Explain the duties of an officer in charge during a bomb search.

10. Discuss the kinds of natural disasters that can occur, and how supervisors and managers can help to ensure that their agencies are prepared to deal with them.

11. Explain how a tactical unit's officers, role, and equipment are different from those of standard police personnel.

12. Explain what the term hazardous materials includes, and how the police respond to incidents involving such materials.

REFERENCES

Adams, T. F. (1994). *Police field operations.* Upper Saddle River, NJ: Prentice Hall.

Begert, M. (1998). The threat of domestic terrorism. *The Police Chief* (November):36–38.

Bolgiano, D. G. (2001). Military support of domestic law enforcement operations: Working within Posse Comitatus. *FBI Law Enforcement Bulletin* (December):16–24.

Buntin, J. (2001). Disaster master. *Governing* (December):34–38.

Carlson, J. (1999). Critical incident management in the ultimate crisis. *FBI Law Enforcement Bulletin* (March):19.

Center for Research on Criminal Justice (1975). *The iron fist and the velvet glove: An analysis of the U.S. police.* Berkeley, CA: Author.

De Jong, D. (1994). Civil disorder: Preparing for the worst. *FBI Law Enforcement Bulletin* (3):1–7.

Doane, K. R. (2001). It's hardly Terror, Inc. *U.S. News and World Report* (June 11):31.

Donahue, M. L. (1993). Hazardous materials training: A necessity for today's law enforcement. *FBI Law Enforcement Bulletin* 11:1–6.

Fram, A. (2002, 7 January). Terror's $60 billion price tag. Associated Press.

Fuselier, G. D., Van Zandt, C. R., and Lanceley, F. J. (1991). Hostage/barricade incidents: High-risk factors and actions criteria. *FBI Law Enforcement Bulletin* (1):6–12.

Garrett, K. (2002). Terrorism on the homefront. *Law Enforcement Technology* (July):22–26.

Green, D. (2001). Implementing a multi-jurisdictional SWAT team. *Law and Order* (March):68–73.

Iannone, N. F., and Iannone, M. P. (2001). *Supervision of police personnel,* 6th ed. Upper Saddle River, NJ: Prentice Hall.

Indiana blast kills 1, forces evacuation (1997). *USA Today* (25 June):3A.

Jylland-Halverson, C., Stoner, R., and Till, S. (2000). Terrorism: The hostage negotiator's ultimate challenge. *Law Enforcement Trainer* (January/February):14–43.

Kaiser, N. (1990). The tactical incident: A total police response. *FBI Law Enforcement Bulletin* 8:14–18.

Lewis, J. F., Jr. (1999). Fighting terrorism in the 21st century. *FBI Law Enforcement Bulletin* (March):3.

Los Angeles Police Department (1974). *Special weapons and tactics.* Los Angeles: Author.

Meisler, J. (2002). The new frontier of homeland security. *Government Technology's Tech Trends 2002: Combined Effort* (August):26–30.

Morris, J. (2001). Task forces formed to recommend means to improve aviation security. *The Dallas Morning News* (September 16):1A.

Parker, D. R. (1992). *Report of the Oakland Berkeley hills fire.* Oakland, CA.: Oakland Office of Fire Services.

Peak, K. J. (2000). *Policing America: Methods, issues, challenges,* 3d ed. Upper Saddle River, NJ: Prentice Hall.

Pincus, W., and Eggen, D. (2001). Ashcroft seeks new surveillance powers. *The Washington Post* (16 September):1A.

Port Fourchon, Louisiana (1997). *USA Today* (4 June):8A.

Ragavan, C. (2001). FBI, Inc.: How the world's premier police corporation totally hit the skids. *U.S. News and World Report* (June 18):14.

Rehm, M. K., and Rehm, W. R. (2000). Terrorism preparedness calls for proactive approach. *The Police Chief* (December):38–43.

Remsberg, C. (1986). *The tactical edge: Surviving high risk patrol.* Northbrook, IL: Calibre Press.

Rogers, D. (2001). A nation tested: What is the terrorist threat we face and how can we train for it? *Law Enforcement Technology* (November):16–21.

Stevens, D. J. (1999). Police tactical units and community response. *Law and Order* (March):48–52.

Strandberg, K. (2001). Bioterrorism: A real or imagined threat? *Law Enforcement Technology* (June):88–97.

Three die, 16 injured in Arkansas blast, fire (1997). *Washington Post* (9 May):A15.

Three shipworkers die in leak of methane gas (1997). *New York Times* (14 July):A7.

Tully, E. J., and Willoughby, E. L. (2002). Terrorism: The role of local and state police agencies. http://www.neiassociates.org/state-local.htm (accessed 31 July 2002).

U.S. Department of Justice, Federal Bureau of Investigation, National Domestic Preparedness Office (2001). http://www.fas.org/irp/agency/doj/fbi/ndpo/ (accessed 5 January).

U.S. Department of Justice, National Institute of Justice Research in Brief (1999, January). *Inventory of state and local law enforcement technology needs to combat terrorism.* Washington, DC: Author.

U.S. Department of Treasury, Bureau of Alcohol, Tobacco and Firearms (2003). Total number of explosives incidents by type. http://www/atf.treas.gov.aexis2/type_files/f_aexis_report.html (accessed 5 January).

Westneat, D. (2001). Terrorists go green. *U.S. News and World Report* (June 4):28.

13

Community Policing
and Problem Solving

LEARNING OBJECTIVES

After reading this chapter, the student will:

- know how community oriented policing and problem solving differs from traditional policing, and the four-step process used by police to address crime and neighborhood disorder
- understand the key roles of first-line supervisors and middle managers in implementing and maintaining community policing and problem solving, and list the characteristics of a good problem-solving supervisor
- be able to explain how the street officer must be viewed by supervisors and managers under the community policing philosophy and be granted considerably more freedom and trust for problem-solving activities
- be able to delineate how police officers may obtain the time necessary for engaging in problem-solving activities
- comprehend some of the means by which police leaders might doom community policing to failure

The difficulty lies, not in the new ideas, but in escaping from old ones.

—John Maynard Keynes

We are continually faced with a series of opportunities, brilliantly disguised as insoluble problems.

—John Gardner

INTRODUCTION

In several of the previous chapters, we discussed many aspects of policing that applied to this chapter's main topic: community oriented policing and problem solving (COPPS). In effect we set up this chapter. Therefore, we locate this discussion of COPPS toward the book's end not because COPPS is less important, but because this chapter's content naturally flows from that of the others. As will be seen, COPPS is spreading rapidly around the world and has become the prevailing strategy of policing today.

As stated by one source, community oriented policing has "become a mantra for police chiefs and mayors in cities big and small across the country" (Witkin and McGraw, 1993:28) and is rapidly becoming entrenched as the new era of policing. This chapter provides a closer look at COPPS and examines the important roles of supervisors and managers within this strategy.

First, we discuss how COPPS rapidly became the prevailing philosophy and practice in local police agencies in the nation. The percentage of local police departments with community policing officers (64 percent) nearly doubled from 1997 to 1999 (Hickman and Reaves, 2001). Then, an illustration is used to demonstrate how this strategy differs from the traditional, reactive policing model. The four-step problem-solving process is then presented next.

Following is a discussion of several implementation and leadership issues as they relate to the COPPS philosophy, focusing on the key roles of first-line supervisors, middle managers, and executives. It will be seen that the importance of these individuals—particularly the sergeants, lieutenants, and captains—in the successful launching and maintenance of COPPS cannot be overstated. Next is a discussion of the importance of giving freedom and prominence to the street officer, and following that are several means by which adequate time may be obtained for officers to engage in problem solving. Other important implementation considerations are presented, followed by a somewhat tongue-in-check view of how police leaders can allow COPPS to fail.

The chapter concludes with two case studies.

THE EXTENT AND NATURE OF COMMUNITY POLICING AND PROBLEM SOLVING PRACTICES: AN OVERVIEW

A "Sweep" of the Nation

A recent survey by the U.S. Department of Justice, Bureau of Justice Statistics, found that COPPS is indeed sweeping the nation. State and local police agencies now have about 113,000 community policing officers, compared to about 21,000 in 1997; nearly two-thirds (64 percent) of local police departments serving 86 percent of all U.S. residents have full-time officers engaged in community policing activities (compared to 34 percent in 1997). And 87 percent of local police officers now work in an agency that provides community policing training for some or all of its new recruits (Figure 13–1; Hickman and Reaves, 2001).

Furthermore, about two-thirds of all local police departments have some type of community policing plan (Table 13–1); such plans generally indicate that community policing approaches and goals are incorporated into the overall agency strategic plan (Hickman and Reaves, 2001). Specifically, these plans normally include strategies such as geographic patrol assignments, support for problem-solving projects, community policing training for citizens, and problem-solving partnerships (Figure 13–2; Hickman and Reaves, 2001).

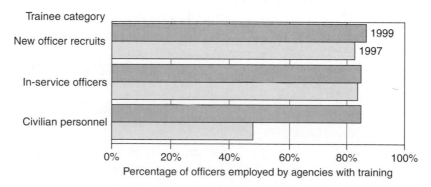

FIGURE 13–1 Percent of Local Police Officers Employed by a Department Providing Community Police Training to Some or All Employees (NIJ)

TABLE 13–1   Local police departments with a community policing plan, by size of population served, 1997 and 1999

Population served	Percent of agencies with a community policing plan					
	1997			1999		
	Total	Formally written	Informal, unwritten	Total	Formally written	Informal, unwritten
All sizes	69%	16%	52%	65%	17%	48%
1,000,000 or more	94%	75%	19%	94%	56%	37%
500,000–999,999	92	71	21	96	67	29
250,000–499,999	95	65	30	95	69	26
150,000–249,999	97	65	32	96	69	27
50,000–149,999	95	55	41	94	55	39
25,000–49,999	91	37	54	90	38	52
10,000–24,999	85	28	56	81	28	53
2,500–9,999	72	16	56	73	16	58
Under 2,500	56	6	50	50	9	40

Note: Detail may not add to total because of rounding.

Finally, it is also clear that the use of technology for COPPS is rapidly expanding. Nearly twice as many local police departments now use computers for crime-mapping purposes as in 1997 (32 percent versus 17 percent, respectively). Technology can also assist in community outreach. About 18 percent of all local police agencies, covering 62 percent of all residents served by a local police

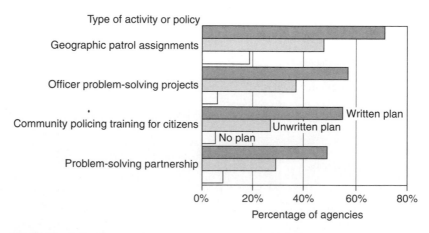

FIGURE 13–2   Community Oriented Activities and Policies of Local Police Departments, by Type of Community Policing Plan (NIJ)

TABLE 13–2   Local police departments with an Internet home page, by size of population served, 1997 and 1999

Population served	Percent of agencies with a home page on the Internet	
	1997	**1999**
All sizes	11%	18%
1,000,000 or more	69%	88%
500,000–999,999	88	100
250,000–499,999	70	85
150,000–249,999	63	79
50,000–149,999	46	66
25,000–49,999	34	47
10,000–24,999	19	36
2,500–9,999	13	17
Under 2,500	2	4

department, maintain an agency home page on the Internet (Table 13–2; Hickman and Reaves, 2001).

A Change in Philosophy and Methods: An Illustration

COPPS represents a dramatic shift from the traditional methods of policing. A brief overview of that shift would be advantageous, prior to discussing the role of leadership under this strategy.

During policing's professional era (roughly from the 1930s to the 1980s), the emphases were on law, technology, and crime fighting, and some of the accoutrements that remain yet today: officers' response time, number of arrests and calls for service, random patrol, and retrospective investigations; departments also employed performance measurements such as number of citations, arrests, and clearance rates. As Goldstein (1987:2) observed, "More attention [was] being focused on how quickly officers responded to a call than on what they did when they got to their destination." Officers were reactive, did what they were told to do, followed policies and procedures to the letter, and accomplished little in the way of long-term problem solving.

A primary weakness with the traditional model was a failure of leadership to provide the patrol officer with the necessary tools, training, and incentives to go beyond mere pinball-like police work—work in which rank-and-file officers were "automatons" (Goldstein, 1990:27). Nor were street officers given the *time* to do much problem-solving work. Indeed, many veteran officers can recall a time when they were judged by how many miles they drove during a tour of duty—the more, the better—and how officers were viewed with disdain when a supervisor found them outside their patrol cars, mingling with citizens.

The professional era of policing emphasized crime fighting. Shown are officers of NYPD's
Emergency Services, formed in 1926 to drive criminals from the streets.
Courtesy NYPD Photo Unit.

As a result of frustration with the dominant model of policing, Herman
Goldstein (1987) formulated the concept of *problem-oriented policing* while
exploring new methods for improving policing; he argued for a radical change in
the direction of efforts to improving policing. Now, when street officers are given
the necessary resources for what Goldstein (1990:68–69) termed *street-level
analysis,* they can have a significant impact on crime and disorder.

What exactly is COPPS? Following is a definition that captures the essence
of this concept:

> Community oriented policing and problem solving (COPPS) is a proactive philosophy that
> promotes solving problems that are criminal, affect our quality of life, or increase our fear
> of crime, as well as other community issues. COPPS involves identifying, analyzing, and
> addressing community problems at their source. (Peak and Glensor, 2002:99)

One of the strongest advocates of this approach to policing is the California
Department of Justice, which has published several monographs on the subject
and has taken the position that

> Community Oriented Policing and Problem Solving is a concept whose time has come.
> This movement holds tremendous promise for creating effective police-community
> partnerships to reclaim our communities and keep our streets safe. COPPS is not "soft"
> on crime; in fact, it is tougher on crime because it is smarter and more creative.
> Community input focuses police activities; and, with better information, officers are able

to respond more effectively with arrests or other appropriate actions. COPPS can unite our communities and promote pride in our police forces. (California Department of Justice, 1993:iii)

Two principal and interrelated components emerge from these two definitions: community engagement (partnerships) and problem solving. Although separate and distinct, they are not mutually exclusive. Engaging the community without problem solving provides no meaningful service to the public. Problem solving without partnerships risks overlooking the most pressing community concerns. Thus, the partnership between police departments and the communities they serve is essential for implementing a successful program in community policing.

COPPS, with its focus on collaborative problem solving, seeks to improve the quality of policing. This is no simple task, however, and several steps must be taken to accomplish it: (1) Police must be equipped to define more clearly and to understand more fully the problems they are expected to handle, (2) the police must develop a commitment to analyzing problems, and (3) police must be encouraged to conduct an uninhibited search for the most effective response to each problem (Goldstein, 1987:5–6). The S.A.R.A. process (discussed later) provides the police with the tools necessary to accomplish these steps.

To assist in understanding this definition, following is an example of how a neighborhood problem is treated under the traditional, reactive style of policing versus the community problem-solving approach:

> Police noted a series of disturbances in a relatively quiet and previously stable residential neighborhood. Although the neighborhood's zoning had for years provided for late-night cabaret-style businesses, none had existed until the "Nite Life," a live-music dance club, opened. Within a few weeks, the police dispatcher received an increased number of complaints about loud music and voices, fighting, and screeching tires late into the night. Within a month's time, at least 50 calls for service had been dispatched to the club to restore order. Evening shift officers responded to calls and restored order prior to midnight, but graveyard shift officers would have to again restore order when called back to the scene by complaining neighbors after midnight.

Under the COPPS approach, this same matter might be handled in the following manner:

> The evening-shift area patrol sergeant identified the disturbances as a problem. The initial information-gathering phase revealed the following: large increases in CFS in the area on both the evening and graveyard shifts; several realtors had contacted council members to complain about declining market interest in the area and to say that they were considering suing both the owner of the new business and the city for the degradation of the neighborhood; a local newspaper was about to run a story on the increase in vehicle burglaries and damage done to parked vehicles in and around the cabaret's parking lot. The team also determined that the consolidated narcotics unit was investigating both employees and some of the late-night clientele of the business as a result of several tips that narcotics were being used and sold in the parking lot and inside the business.

The officers and their sergeant gathered information from crime reports, a news reporter about to publish the story, neighboring business owners, and the department's crime analysis unit. Information was also gathered concerning possible zoning and health department violations. Officers then met with the business owner to work out an agreement for reestablishing the quality of life in the neighborhood to its previous levels and to decrease the department's CFS. First, the business licensing division and the owner were brought together to both reestablish the ground rules and provide for a proper licensing of all the players. This resulted in the instant removal of an unsavory partner and in turn his "following" of drug users and other characters at the business. The landlord agreed to hasten landscaping and lighting of the parking lots and provide a "sound wall" around the business to buffer the area residents. Agreements were reached to limit the hours of operation of the live music of the business. The cabaret's owner and all of his employees were trained by the area patrol teams in pertinent aspects of the city code (such as disturbing the peace, minors in liquor establishments, and trespassing laws). The police experienced a reduction in CFS in the area. Area residents, although not entirely happy with the continuing existence of the business, acknowledged satisfaction of their complaints; no further newspaper stories appeared regarding the noise and disorder in the neighborhood.

In this example, the police not only responded to the concerns of the neighborhood residents, they also developed a better understanding of both the area's businesses and residents and established a working relationship with all involved. By co-opting the services of the other municipal entities, police also learned of new and valuable resources with which to share some of the burden of future demands for governmental service.

The S.A.R.A. Process

This illustration of COPPS at work employed four steps toward solving the problems created by the Nite Life club. These four steps comprise the problem-solving process called S.A.R.A.:

Scanning: the initial information-gathering stage by the supervisor

Analysis: the more in-depth information-gathering stage, involving crime reports, the crime analysis unit, a news reporter, and zoning and health departments

Response: Involved a number of meetings, improved the lighting and landscaping, agreements

Assessment: A follow-up look at CFS in the area

Figure 13–3 shows the S.A.R.A. process. This process provides officers with a logical step-by-step framework to identify, analyze, respond to, and evaluate crime, the fear of crime, and neighborhood disorder. This approach, with its emphasis on in-depth analysis and collaboration, replaces officers' short-term, reactive responses with a process vested in longer-term outcomes.

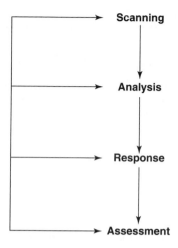

FIGURE 13–3   S.A.R.A. Problem Solving Process
Source: John E. Eck and William Spelman, *Problem Solving: Problem-Oriented Policing in Newport News* (Washington, DC: U.S. Department of Justice, National Institute of Justice, 1987), p. 43.

Next, we briefly discuss each component of the S.A.R.A. process in more detail (for a more complete discussion of this process, see Peak and Glensor, 2002, Chapter 4).

Scanning: Problem Identification

Scanning means problem identification. It initiates the problem-solving process by conducting a preliminary inquiry to determine if a problem really exists and whether further analysis is needed. A problem is different from an isolated incident, which is something police are called to or happen on that is unrelated to any other incidents in the community. A problem can be defined as a cluster of two or more similar or related incidents that are of substantive concern to the community and to the police.

If the incidents to which the police respond do not fall within the definition of a problem, then the problem-solving process is not applicable and the officers should handle the incident according to normal procedure (crime report, advisement, referral, and so on). The problems derived from repeated incidents may vary and include

- A series of burglaries at an apartment complex
- Drug activity at a city park
- Thefts of a particular type of car from several lots
- Graffiti at a particular location or jurisdiction
- Parking and traffic problems
- A series of gang-related drive-by shootings
- Robberies of convenience stores
- Juvenile loitering–related crime at a mall

- Aggressive panhandling at a downtown center
- Repeat alarms to commercial businesses

Numerous resources are available to the police for identifying problems, including calls for service data (especially repeat calls), crime analysis information, police reports, and officers' own experiences. Other sources of information include other governmental agencies, public and private agencies, businesses, media reports, and information obtained from the public. Scanning helps the officer determine whether a problem really exists before moving on to more in-depth analysis.

When considering how problems may be similar, officers should consider the following:

Behaviors. Behaviors can relate to specific crimes such as bank robberies, auto thefts, and burglaries, or numerous crimes resulting from specific behaviors such as juvenile loitering, gang activity, and cruising.

Location. Research indicates that a relatively few "hot spots" (5 percent) account for nearly 49 percent of all calls for service (Sherman, 1993). This may include concentrations of crime at a public housing project due to gang violence, a street corner where there are open-market drug sales, or downtown juvenile cruising that is contributing to fights, vandalism, and thefts.

Persons. Research shows that 20 percent of repeat or "career" offenders account for 80 percent of all crimes (Spelman, 1990). Victimization research reveals that a mere 4 percent of victims account for 44 percent of total crime (or, put another way, a small number of people are the same individuals who are victimized in about half of all crimes) (Farrell and Pease, 1993).

Time. Chapter 10 discussed how crime and calls for service vary by time of day and day of week. We also know that seasonal changes may impact crime, especially in communities where winter sports or summer vacations bring large numbers of people to the area.

As indicated, crime is often concentrated. By identifying those incidents that are similar in nature by one or more of these characteristics, officers may then explore the extent of the problem using more comprehensive analysis.

Analysis: Determining the Extent of the Problem

Analysis is the heart of the problem-solving process. It is the *most difficult* and *most important* step in the S.A.R.A. process. A common criticism of incident-driven policing is that officers often skip analysis in their haste to find solutions. Without analysis, long-term solutions are limited and the problem is likely to persist.

In this step, officers gather as much information as possible from a variety of sources. A complete and thorough analysis consists of officers identifying the seriousness of the problem, all persons affected, and the underlying causes. Officers should also assess the effectiveness of current responses.

Many tools are available to assist with analysis. Crime analysis may be useful in collecting, collating, analyzing, and disseminating data relating to crime, incidents not requiring a report, criminal offenders, victims, and locations. Mapping and geographic information systems (GIS) can identify patterns of crime and hot spots. Police offense reports can also be analyzed for suspect characteristics, MOs, victim characteristics, and information about high-crime areas and addresses. Computer-aided dispatch is also a reliable source of information, because it collects data on all incidents and specific locations from which an unusual number of events require a police response.

One explanation of crime may be found in routine activity theory (Cohen and Felson, 1979), which postulates that a crime will occur when three elements are present: (1) a suitable victim, (2) a motivated offender, and (3) a location. If one of these three elements is addressed or removed, the crime will not occur. The problem analysis triangle (Figure 13–4) helps officers to visualize the complexities of crime and the relationship among its three elements.

Response: Formulating Tailor-Made Strategies

Once a problem has been clearly defined, officers may seek the most effective responses. Responses should be developed in consideration of each side of the problem analysis triangle. Focusing solely on the offender leaves room for new offenders because the location or victims have not been changed.

We have stressed the importance of long-term solutions; however, officers cannot ignore the fact that more serious situations may require immediate action.

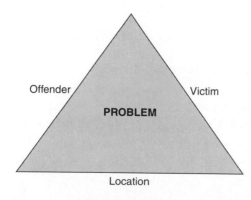

FIGURE 13–4 Problem Analysis Triangle
Source: Bureau of Justice Assistance, U.S. Department of Justice, *Comprehensive Gang Initiative: Operations Manual for Implementing Local Gang Prevention and Control Programs,* draft (October 1993), pp. 3–10.

For example, in the case of an open-air drug market involving rival gang violence, police may initially increase the number of patrols in the area to arrest offenders, gain control of public space, and secure the safety of residents and officers. Once this is accomplished, longer-term responses that include the collaborative efforts of officers, residents, and other agencies may be considered.

Responses to substantive problems rarely involve a single agency or tactic or quick fix. For example, arrest is often viewed as the only response to a problem even though it is rarely sufficient to provide more permanent resolutions. More appropriate responses often involve the police and public and other appropriate entities, including businesses, private and social service organizations, and other governmental agencies.

Officers have many options to respond to problems; however, they should not expect to eliminate every problem they take on. With some social problems, such as gangs and homelessness, elimination is impractical and improbable.

Another important prevention tool for COPPS is crime prevention through environmental design (CPTED). CPTED teaches officers how building space, architectural design, lighting, and other features of the environment contribute to criminal opportunities. Both situational crime prevention and CPTED provide officers with tools necessary to employ comprehensive prevention strategies.

Assessment: Evaluating Overall Effectiveness

The final stage is assessment. Officers evaluate the effectiveness of their responses and use the results to revise their responses, collect more data, or even redefine the problem. For some problems, assessment is simple: observing a location to see if a problem resurfaces. For example, in one East Coast city, when asked how he determined that his COPPS efforts in a local park were successful, an officer simply mentioned that more families were using the park.

In most cases, however, assessments should be comprehensive and include measures such as before/after comparisons of crime and calls for service data, environmental crime prevention surveys, and neighborhood fear reduction surveys. The nature of the problem often dictates the method of assessment.

IMPLEMENTATION AND LEADERSHIP ISSUES

To make COPPS a part of an organization's philosophy and practice requires an entire organizational transformation that cannot be accomplished overnight. Gaining the support of the agency's supervisors and managers represents a major step in implementing COPPS. Next, we discuss some of the needs and problems of accomplishing this task.

The Key to Success: First-Line Supervisors

The successful implementation of COPPS requires the support of the first-line supervisor. This can be a daunting task, however, and the sergeant is arguably the most important ranking individual within the police organization in terms of whether or not COPPS will succeed or fail. The link between street officers and the organization is the sergeant; however, there is some cause for supervisors' reluctance to change. As Goldstein (1990:29) noted:

> Changing the operating philosophy of rank-and-file officers is easier than altering a first-line supervisor's perspective of his or her job, because the work of a sergeant is greatly simplified by the traditional form of policing. The more routinized the work, the easier it is for the sergeant to check. The more emphasis placed on rank and the symbols of position, the easier it is for the sergeant to rely on authority—rather than intellect and personal skills—to carry out their duties. [S]ergeants are usually appalled by descriptions of the freedom and independence suggested in problem oriented policing for rank-and-file officers. The concept can be very threatening to them. This . . . can create an enormous block to implementation.

Supervisors often cannot overcome the idea that giving officers the opportunity to be creative and take risks does not diminish their own role or authority.

Supervising in a COPPS environment means a change from being a "controller," primarily concerned with rules, to being a "facilitator" and "coach" for officers involved in problem solving. Supervisors must learn to encourage innovation and risk taking among their officers and be well skilled in problem solving, especially in the analysis of problems and evaluation of efforts. Conducting a workload analysis (discussed in Chapter 10) and finding the time for officers to problem solve and engage with the community (discussed later) are important aspects of supervision.

The St. Petersburg, Florida, police department identified the characteristics of the "ideal" sergeant under the COPPS philosophy (Quire, 1998:8):

Availability	Leadership
Flexibility	Champion
Innovative	Trustworthy
Widely experienced	Good speaker
Facilitator	Respected
Open minded	Risk taker
Sense of humor	Coach
Supportive	Dependable
Buffer	

The Police Executive Research Forum (1990:4) also provided a list of characteristics for a good COPPS supervisor:

1. Allows officers the freedom to experiment with new approaches
2. Insists on good, accurate analyses of problems
3. Grants flexibility in work schedules when requests are appropriate
4. Allows officers to make most contacts directly and paves the way when they are having trouble getting cooperation
5. Protects officers from pressures within the department to revert to traditional methods
6. Runs interference for officers to secure resources and protects them from criticism
7. Knows what problems officers are working on and whether the problems are real
8. Knows officers' beats and important citizens in them, and expects subordinates to know them even better
9. Coaches officers through the S.A.R.A. process, giving advice and helping to manage their time
10. Monitors officers' progress and, as necessary, prods them along or slows them down
11. Supports officers, even if their strategies fail, as long as something useful is learned in the process—and the process was well thought through
12. Manages problem-solving efforts over a long period of time; does not allow efforts to end just because they get sidetracked by competing demands for time and attention
13. Gives credit to officers and lets others know about their good work
14. Allows officers to talk with visitors or at conferences about their work
15. Identifies new resources and shares them with officers
16. Stresses cooperation, coordination, and communication within and outside the unit
17. Coordinates efforts across shifts and beats and with outside units and agencies
18. Realizes that this style of policing cannot simply be ordered; officers and detectives must come to believe in it

COPPS supervisors should also understand that not all patrol officers or detectives will like this kind of work or be good at it. Supervisors must also realize that they need to avoid isolating the problem-solving function from the rest of

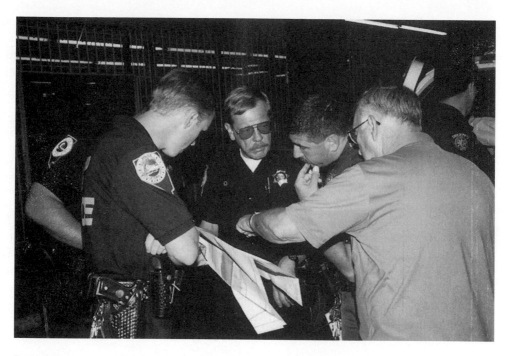

Interagency cooperation is essential for solving community problems.
Courtesy Washoe County, Nevada, Sheriff's Office Photo Unit.

the department. This could create the illusion that the problem solving unit is composed of "privileged prima donnas" who receive benefits that other officers do not. Also, supervisors should not allow the COPPS initiative to become a mere public-relations campaign; the emphasis is always on results (Police Executive Research Forum, 1990).

Executives and Managers

COPPS requires changing the philosophy of leadership and management throughout the entire organization. First, the agency's executive leadership, with input from managers and supervisors, should develop a new *vision/values/ mission statement*. All *policies and procedures* should be reviewed to ensure they conform to the department's COPPS objectives. The organization should also invest in *information systems* that will assist officers in identifying patterns of crime and support the problem-solving process. Progressive leaders will need to prepare for this millennium by engaging in *long-term strategic planning* and continuous *evaluation processes*.

Regarding managers, Robinette (1993) asserted that the traditional police middle manager (as well as the first-line supervisor) is largely unprepared by training and experience for the requirements of the COPPS strategy. Indeed, few street officers see their managers as sources of guidance and direction, but rather as authority figures to be satisfied by numbers of arrests and citations, the manner in which reports are completed, and so on. Normandeau and Leighton (1990:49) explained what must be done:

> Like most large, public service agencies, the requirements for innovation in policing include: changing the formal corporate values as well as the subculture of "front-line" policing; having an inspired chief executive who is committed to the new approach; having a motivated and experienced level of middle management which can implement the new approach in operational terms; recognizing innovations that come from the street level of policing; and obtaining support for the new approach and the risks that it runs from the police governing authorities and from the local community.

In many instances, the ultimate challenge to a police organization is to change its hierarchical, paramilitary structure. Managers and executives working within a flattened, COPPS-oriented organization often require new skills to ensure the successful adaptation and functioning of the police organization (Province of British Columbia, 1993:56). Exhibit 13–1 is an example of an attempt by one agency—the Seattle, Washington, Police Department—to support leadership in its transition to COPPS.

EXHIBIT 13–1

AMBITIOUS IN SEATTLE: LEADERSHIP CONFERENCING AND TOOL KITS

The Seattle, Washington, Police Department (SPD), in collaboration with the Police Executive Research Forum, has offered a three-day conference entitled "Leadership Sessions to Support Problem Oriented Policing." The purpose of the conference is to "provide a forum for inspiration, motivation, guidance, and practical tools to leaders who are committed to supporting problem solving in their agencies." Invitees include police supervisors, managers, and researchers. Topics include ethical challenges for leaders, politics inside and outside the organization, examining the organization from top to bottom to see how every system and structure supported problem oriented policing, and leadership.

Included is a three-day course entitled "Leadership Skills" for field training officers, supervisors, and managers; it includes coaching, feedback, facilitation, leadership, and cultural competency. Also, a "Training of Trainers" for police and community academies was developed to assist community and police instructors to incorporate the mission and values of the organization into every phase of academy training. The course also includes adult learning theory, gender inclusiveness, and facilitation skills.

Source: Norm Stamper, "A Training Menu to Support Problem Oriented Policing" (Seattle, WA: Seattle Police Department, 1997).

Valuing the Line Officer

The shift to COPPS centers on those singular individuals who comprise the "backbone" of policing—the patrol officers. The most powerful resources an organization possesses are thinking, creative, and innovative police officers who, when supported by information, the community, training (in problem identification, analysis, and response), and internal support systems that reward and motivate them, are capable of providing long-term solutions to problems.

A major departure of COPPS from the conventional style of policing lies with the view that the line officer is given much more discretion and decision-making ability and is trusted with a much broader array of responsibilities. The necessary shift to a COPPS perspective centers on supervisors, who should encourage officers to take the initiative in identifying and responding to beat problems. This recognizes the potential of college-educated officers "who have been smothered in the atmosphere of traditional policing" (Goldstein, 1987:17). It also gives officers a new sense of identity and self-respect; they are more challenged and have opportunities to follow through on individual cases and analyze and solve problems, which will give them greater job satisfaction. Using patrol officers in this manner also allows the agency to provide sufficient challenges not only for the better educated officers, but also for those officers who remain unpromoted throughout their careers. We ought to be recruiting as police officers people who can "serve as mediators, as dispensers of information, and as community organizers" (Goldstein, 1987:21).

COPPS appeals to the reasons why most officers chose policing as a profession. When asked why they originally wanted to join police forces, police officers consistently say they joined in order to help people (Sparrow, 1988). By emphasizing work that addresses people's concerns, and giving officers the discretion to develop solutions, COPPS helps make police work more rewarding.

Another Management and Supervisory Dilemma: Gaining Time for Officers to Solve Problems

One of the debates often heard with respect to COPPS is whether officers have enough time to engage in problem-solving activities. On the one hand, officers complain that they are going from call to call and have little time for anything else. On the other hand, police executives and managers might contend that there is plenty of time for problem solving because calls account for only 50 to 60 percent of an officer's time. The supervisor would seem to be caught in the middle of this debate and is certainly in a key position to determine whether or not adequate time is indeed available to the patrol officers and, if not, that it be made so.

Obviously, citizens' calls for service are important and cannot be ignored. But the aim should be to handle these calls in an efficient and expedient manner. There are four methods for overcoming the problem of finding time for problem solving while still handling calls effectively:

1. *Allow units to perform problem-solving assignments as self-initiated activities.* Under this approach, a unit would contact the dispatcher and go out of service for a problem-solving assignment. The unit would be interrupted only for an emergency call in its area of responsibility. Otherwise, the dispatcher would hold nonemergency calls until the unit becomes available, or send a unit from an adjacent area after holding the call for a predetermined amount of time.

2. *Schedule one or two units to devote a predetermined part of their shift to problem solving.* As an example, a supervisor could designate one or two units each day to devote the first half of their shift or even just one hour to problem solving. Their calls would be handled by other units so that they have an uninterrupted block of time for problems. Of course, this approach means that the other units will be busier. The tradeoff is that problem solving gets done and the supervisor can rotate the units designated for these activities.

3. *Take more reports over the telephone.* The information in nonemergency incidents is recorded on a department report form and entered in the department's information system as an incident or crime. The average telephone report taker can process four times as many report calls per hour compared to a field unit.

4. *Review the department policy on "assist" units.* In some departments, several units show up at the scene of a call even though they are not needed. This problem is particularly acute with alarm calls. A department should undergo a detailed study on the types of calls for which assist units are actually appearing, with the aim of reducing the number of assists. In addition, officers should be discouraged from assisting other units unless it is necessary.

As a more general approach, a department should review its patrol plan to determine whether units are fielded in proportion to workload. Time between calls is a function not just of the number of incoming calls, but also of the number of units in the field. More units result in more time between calls.

As noted in Chapter 10, delaying response time to calls for service can also provide more time for officers. Response time research has determined that rapid responses are not needed for most calls. Slower police responses to nonemergency calls has been found satisfactory to citizens if dispatchers tell citizens an

1. Assemble a group of patrol officers and emergency communications center personnel representing each shift.
2. Have each of them write down three to five locations where the police respond repeatedly to deal with the same general problem and people.
3. Determine the average number of responses to those locations per month and approximately how long the problem has existed.
4. Determine the average number of officers who respond each time to those incidents.
5. Determine the average length of time involved in handling the incidents.
6. Using the information from points 3, 4, and 5, determine the total number of staff hours devoted to each of these problem locations. Do this for the week, month, and year.
7. Identify all the key players who either participate in or are affected by the problem—all direct and indirect participants and groups such as the complaining parties, victims, witnesses, property owners and managers, bystanders, and so forth.
8. Through a roundtable discussion, decide what it is about the particular location that allows, or encourages, the problem to exist and continue.
9. Develop a list of things that have been done in the past to deal with the problem, and a candid assessment of why each has not worked.
10. In a free-flowing brainstorming session, develop as many traditional and nontraditional solutions to the problem as possible. Include alternative sources such as other government and private agencies that could be involved in the solution. Encourage creative thinking and risk taking.
11. After you have completed the brainstorming session, consider which of those solutions are (a) illegal, (b) immoral, (c) impractical, (d) unrealistic, or (e) unaffordable.
12. Eliminate all those that fall in categories (a) and (b).
13. For those that fall in categories (c), (d), and (e), figure out if those reasons derive from thinking in conventional terms like "We've never done it this way," "It won't work," "It can't be done." If you are satisfied that those solutions truly are impractical, unrealistic, or unaffordable, then eliminate them, too. If there is a glimmer of hope that some may have merit with just a little different thinking or approach, then leave them.
14. For each remaining possible solution, list what would have to be done and who would have to be involved to make it happen. Which of those solutions and actions could be implemented relatively soon and with a minimum of difficulty?
15. If the solution were successful, consider the productive things officers could do with the time that would be recaptured from not having to deal with the problem anymore.

FIGURE 13–5   15-Step Exercise to Recapture Officers' Time
Source: Jerald R. Vaughn, *Community-Oriented Policing: You Can Make it Happen* (Clearwater, FL: National Law Enforcement Leadership Institute, n.d.), pp. 6–7. Used with permission.

officer might not arrive at their home right away, and nonsworn employees can handle noncrime incidents (Eck and Spelman, 1989). Figure 13–5 provides a 15-step exercise that may help supervisors capture more time for officers to engage in problem solving (Vaughn, n.d.).

Other Important Considerations

In addition to leadership, organizational culture, field operations, and external relations are also important for the successful implementation of COPPS (Glensor and Peak, 1996). We briefly examine those three elements next.

Organizational Culture

Human resources is the "heart and soul" of organizational culture. For employees, it answers the question, "What's in it for me?" Any major change in an organization requires that a review of all human resources is conducted. Community engagement and problem solving require new skills, knowledge, and abilities for everyone in the organization. Therefore, areas such as *recruiting, selection, training, performance evaluations, promotions, honors and awards,* and *discipline* should be reviewed to ensure they promote and support the organization's transition to COPPS. Agencies must also work closely with the various *labor organizations,* which will be concerned with any proposed changes in shifts, beats, criteria for selection, promotion, and discipline. It is wise to include labor representatives in the planning and implementation process from the beginning.

Field Operations

The primary concern with field operations is to structure the delivery of patrol services so as to assist officers in dealing with the root causes of persistent community problems. The first issue raised is whether a *specialist vs. generalist* approach will be used. It is not uncommon, especially in larger police agencies, to begin COPPS implementation with an experimental district composed of a team of specially trained officers. The experience of many agencies, however, suggests that departmentwide implementation should occur as quickly as possible. This will eliminate the common criticism that COPPS officers do not do "real police work" and receive special privileges. If allowed to fester, this attitude can quickly impair any implementation efforts. The need for available time presents a supervisory challenge that begins with *managing calls for service,* which requires comprehensive workload analysis, call prioritization, alternative call handling, and differential response methods discussed in Chapter 10. A *decentralized approach* to field operations involves assigning officers for a minimum of one year to a beat and shift to learn more about a neighborhood's problems.

External Relations

Collaborative responses to neighborhood crime and disorder are essential to the success of COPPS. This requires new relationships and the sharing of information and resources among the police and community, local governmental agencies, service providers, and businesses. It requires that agencies educate and inform their external partners about police resources and neighborhood problems using surveys, newsletters, community meetings, and public service announcements. The *media* also provide an excellent resource for police to educate the community. Press releases about collaborative problem-solving efforts should be sent to the media and news conferences held to discuss major crime reduction efforts.

An officer works with citizens to improve the overall safety of a shopping mall. *Courtesy Community Policing Consortium.*

HOW TO FAIL

We conclude this chapter with a satirical and wry yet insightful list of tips on how the "tradition-bound chief" may undermine the successful implementation of COPPS (Eck, 1992). *Following these suggestions will guarantee failure!*

1. *Oversell It:* COPPS should be sold as a panacea for every ill that plagues the city, the nation, and civilization. Some of the evils you may want to claim that COPPS will eliminate are crime, fear of crime, racism, police misuse of force, homelessness, drug abuse, gangs, and other social problems. By building up the hopes and expectations of the public, the press, and politicians, you can set the stage for later attacks on COPPS when it does not deliver.

2. *Don't Be Specific:* This suggestion is a corollary of the first principle. Never define what you mean by the following terms: *community, service, effectiveness, empowerment, neighborhood, communication,* or *problem solving.* Use these and other terms indiscriminately, interchangeably, and

whenever possible. At first, people will think the department is going to do something meaningful and won't ask for details. Once people catch on, you can blame the amorphous nature of COPPS and go back to what you were doing before.

3. *Create a Special Unit or Group:* Less than 10 percent of the department should be engaged in this effort, lest COPPS really catches on. Since the "grand design" is possibly the return to conventional policing anyway (once everyone has attacked COPPS), there is no sense in involving more than a few officers. Also, special units are popular with the press and politicians.

4. *Create a Soft Image:* The best image for COPPS will be a uniformed female hugging a small child. This caring and maternal image will warm the hearts of community members suspicious of police, play to traditional stereotypes of sexism in policing, and turn off most cops.

5. *Leave the Impression That COPPS Is Only for Minority Neighborhoods:* This is a corollary of items 3 and 4. Since a small group of officers will be involved, only a few neighborhoods can receive their services. Place the token COPPS officers in areas like public housing. With any luck, racial antagonism will undercut the approach. It will appear that minority, poor neighborhoods are not getting the "tough-on-crime" approach they need.

6. *Divorce COPPS Officers from "Regular" Police Work:* This is an expansion of the soft image concept. If the COPPS officers do not handle calls or make arrests, but instead throw block parties, speak to community groups, walk around talking to kids, and visit schools, they will not be perceived as "real" police officers by their colleagues. This will further undermine their credibility and ability to accomplish anything of significance.

7. *Obfuscate Means and Ends:* Whenever describing COPPS, never make the methods for accomplishing the objective subordinate to the objective. Instead, make the means more important than the ends, or at least put them on equal footing. For example, to reduce drug dealing in a neighborhood, make certain that the tactics necessary (arrests, community meetings, etc.) are as important as or more important than the objective. These tactics can occupy everyone's time but still leave the drug problem unresolved.

8. *Present Community Members with Problems and Plans:* In meetings with community members, officers should listen carefully and politely and then elaborate on how the department will enforce the law. If the community members like the plan, go ahead. If they do not, continue to be polite and ask them to go on a ride-a-long or witness a drug raid. This avoids having to change the department's operations while

demonstrating how difficult police work is, and why nothing can be accomplished. In the end, they will not get their problems solved but will see how nice the police are.

9. *Never Try to Understand Why Problems Occur:* Do not let officers gain knowledge about the underlying causes of the problems; COPPS should not include any analysis of the problem and as little information as possible should be sought from the community. Keep officers away from computer terminals; mandate that officers get permission to talk to members of any other agency; do not allow officers to go off their assigned areas to collect information; prevent access to research conducted on similar problems; suppress listening skills.

10. *Never Publicize a Success:* Some rogue officers will not get the message and will go out anyway and gather enough information to solve problems. Try to ignore these examples of effective policing and make sure that no one else hears about them. When you cannot ignore them, describe them in the least meaningful way (item 2). Talk about the wonders of empowerment and community meetings. Describe the hours of foot patrol, the new mountain of bikes, or shoulder patches. In every problem solved, there is usually some tactic or piece of equipment that can be highlighted at the expense of the accomplishment itself.

——— Case Studies ————————————————

Following are two case studies that will provide the reader with opportunities to apply S.A.R.A. and to see how COPPS differs from the traditional reactive policing approach.

Problems Plague the Park

Paxton Park holds tremendous significance for the predominately older African American and Hispanic residents of the city's Hillsborough District. Referred to as "instant park," it was literally constructed within a day by residents during the late 1960s. Since then, it has deteriorated and become a haven for drug dealers and gang members. Today, few residents dare use the park. Residents frequently report to the police all manner of suspicious activities in the park, including sightings of persons under the influence harassing children and houses bordering the park that are being used as crash pads for drug users. In most instances, the police response is to send a police unit by the park to disperse the drug dealers. Few arrests are ever made. On occasion, the county-wide consolidated narcotics unit and the department's special weapons and tactics unit initiate a program to make massive arrests. This approach usually involves a large number of arrests, but it also generates complaints of excessive force and racism by offenders and residents alike. The department has also initiated a narcotics tip line for residents, but few calls have been made since it was installed six months ago. Sgt. Brewer was recently assigned to the Hillsborough District. She has recently attended a COPPS training seminar and believes that the drug and other problems at the park could be handled in a different manner than in the past. She calls a team meeting to discuss how they might approach the problem.

1. Use the problem analysis triangle to thoroughly identify the problem.
2. What responses might be considered by the team (be sure to include all organizations that could help)?
3. How could Sgt. Brewer evaluate their successes?

The Horrendous Highway Hangout

The Burger Barn is the most popular fast-food restaurant in town and it is open 24 hours a day. It is located in the middle sector of town where two highways intersect; this is a busy four-lane commercial area that is adjacent to a low-income residential area consisting of mobile homes, apartment complexes, and small single-family homes. Sgt. Maas has noticed a tremendous increase in calls for service at the location and on checking computer-aided dispatch records, discovers that CFS to the Burger Barn had indeed increased to nearly 90 per month. Further analysis reveals that the majority of CFS occur during the late night/early morning hours, peaking between 1:00 A.M. and 3:00 A.M. The CFS mostly involve large crowds of juveniles, fights, noise disturbances, shots fired, and traffic congestion and accidents. A few police officers have even been injured while attempting to break up fights. The restaurant's manager has attempted to limit access to the building during the peak hours, allowing only five juveniles inside at any one time. This approach has resulted in long lines forming outside and has increased the number of disturbances and fights. Employees are frequently harassed by angry customers waiting for service in the building. Many of the juveniles are cruising and driving carelessly, paying little attention to the traffic signals and contributing significantly to congestion, which is creating a backup on the adjoining highway, generating a letter of complaint from the state highway patrol to the police chief.

1. Use the problem analysis triangle to thoroughly identify the problem.
2. What responses may be considered (be sure to include all organizations that could help)?
3. How could Sgt. Maas evaluate their successes?

SUMMARY

It has become clear to this nation's nearly 113,000 community policing officers that they cannot singlehandedly contain the crime and neighborhood disorder problems that afflict society, create fear, and drain our federal, state, and local resources. These officers have discovered that COPPS—with its emphasis on community engagement and problem solving—carries the best potential for success in resolving substantive and recurring community problems.

It was also made clear in this chapter that police supervisors and managers are key to making this strategy work. It was shown that if these leaders are not viewed as a major part of the implementation and maintenance of the COPPS strategy, and do not provide officers with the kind of prominent role and freedom they require to be able to analyze and respond to community problems, then this approach to crime and disorder will inevitably fail.

ITEMS FOR REVIEW

1. Describe COPPS in general, focusing on how it differs in philosophy and practice from the traditional, reactive policing model.

2. Explain the four-step S.A.R.A. problem-solving process.

3. Describe the important role of the first-line supervisors and managers in the implementation and ongoing maintenance of COPPS; include a list of at least 10 characteristics of a good problem-solving supervisor.

4. Explain how the street officer must be viewed by supervisors and managers in terms of being granted freedom and trust for problem-solving activities.

5. Delineate how police officers may obtain the time necessary for engaging in problem-solving activities.

6. Explain some of the means by which a police executive might ensure that COPPS will fail.

REFERENCES

California Department of Justice, Attorney General's Office (1993). *Community oriented policing and problem solving: Definitions and principles.* Sacramento, CA: Author.

Cohen, L. E., and Felson, M. (1979). Social change and crime rate trends: A routine activity approach. *American Sociological Review* 44 (August):588–608.

Eck, J. E. (1992). Helpful hints for the tradition bound chief. *Fresh Perspectives.* Washington, DC: Police Executive Research Forum (6):1–7.

Eck, J., and Spelman, W. (1989). A problem-oriented approach to police service delivery. In Dennis Jay Kenney, ed., *Police and policing: Contemporary issues.* New York: Praeger, pp. 87–119.

Farrell, G., and Pease, K. (1993). *Once bitten, twice bitten: Repeat victimisation and its implications for crime prevention.* Crime Prevention Unit Paper 46, London: Home Office.

Glensor, R. W., and Peak, K. J. (1996). Implementing change: Community-oriented policing and problem solving. *FBI Law Enforcement Bulletin* 7:14–20.

Goldstein, H. (1990). *Problem-oriented policing*. New York: McGraw-Hill.

Goldstein, H. (1987, 12 June). Problem-oriented policing. Paper presented at the Conference on Policing: State of the Art III, National Institute of Justice, Phoenix, AZ.

Hickman, M. J., and Reaves, B. A. (2001). *Community policing in local police departments, 1997 and 1999*. Washington, DC: U.S. Department of Justice, Bureau of Justice Statistics Special Report (February):1–3.

Normandeau, A., and Leighton, B. (1990). *A vision of the future of policing in Canada: Police-challenge 2000, background document*. Ottawa: Solicitor General Canada, Police and Security Branch (October):49.

Peak, K. J., and Glensor, R. W. (2002). *Community policing and problem solving: Strategies and practices*, 3d ed. Upper Saddle River, NJ: Prentice Hall.

Police Executive Research Forum (1990). Supervising problem-solving. Washington, DC: Author, training outline.

Province of British Columbia, Ministry of Attorney General, Police Services Branch (1993). *Community policing advisory committee report*. Victoria, British Columbia, Canada: Author, p. 56.

Quire, D. S. (1998). Officers select "ideal" supervisors. Washington, DC: Community Policing Consortium, *Community Policing Exchange* (March/April):8.

Robinette, H. M. (1993). Supervising tomorrow. *Virginia Police Chief* (Spring):10.

Sherman, L. W. (1993). Repeat calls for service: Policing the "hot spots." In Dennis Jay Kenney, ed., *Police and policing: Contemporary issues*. New York: Praeger, pp. 42–76.

Sparrow, M. K. (1988). Implementing community policing. National Institute of Justice. *Perspectives on Policing*, No. 9 (November):6.

Spelman, W. (1990). *Repeat offender programs for law enforcement*. Washington, DC: Police Executive Research Forum, pp. 5–6.

Vaughn, J. R. (n.d.). *Community-oriented policing: You can make it happen*. Clearwater, FL: National Law Enforcement Leadership Institute.

Witkin, G., and McGraw, D. (1993). Beyond "Just the facts, ma'am." *U.S. News and World Report* (2 August):28.

PART FOUR

Epilogue

14

Future Trends and Challenges

❖

LEARNING OBJECTIVES

After reading this chapter, the student will:

- understand why it is important for police supervisors and managers to predict the future, and some methods for doing so

- know how futurists predict our society will change with respect to demographics and crime

- know how policing will likely change, particularly in the areas of community policing

- bc able to delineate new developments in technology, and how technology will have a major impact on policing—including some of the major problems that technology will bring

- be knowledgeable about how supervisors and managers of the future will be challenged by major shifts in the nature of rank-and-file officers, organizational structure, and general quality of life in their agencies

At every crossing on the road, each progressive spirit is opposed by a thousand appointed to guard the gates of the past.

—Maurice Maeterlinck

Some men see things as they are, and ask why? I dream things that never were, and ask why not?

—Robert F. Kennedy

INTRODUCTION

"What does the future hold?" "What is going to happen to our nation?" These are questions that probably all of us have asked ourselves, especially following the catastrophic events of September 11, 2001. One thing is for certain: Our society is constantly changing, and, as Postman (1989:19) said, we cannot afford to [be in the new millennium] with our eyes firmly fixed on the rearview mirror. Anticipating what the future holds with any degree of certainty is a complex undertaking; absent our ability to employ a crystal ball, or rely on palm reading or a Ouija board, we can look to other, more tangible and credible means of determining what the future holds.

Another point to be remembered, now and for always: The real role of a police officer is that of a peacekeeper, first and foremost; when all else fails, the police officer should be viewed as the one person to whom we can go when in trouble. This mandate and role definition *absolutely* color everything the police do and require the application of problem-solving skills, a focus on the prevention of crime, and a commitment to ensuring that every citizen is treated with dignity and respect. The common theme throughout this chapter is how supervisors and managers are affected by and will affect the future of their agencies and policing in general.

This chapter opens by examining the need for studying and anticipating the future in policing, to make the unknown more predictable. Then, some methods for forecasting our future are considered. We next examine what the experts predict in terms of anticipated changes in demographics and crime in the twenty-first century. Then, a review is presented of several factors within policing that may bring about major change, including community oriented policing and problem solving, high technology, the rank-and-file officers, participative management, flattening the organization, and quality of life within police agencies. The chapter concludes with two case studies.

THE NEED FOR A FUTURISTIC VIEW

Historically, in the eyes of many people, the role of the police has been to maintain the status quo. But reliance on the status quo will not prepare the police for the future. Previous chapters of this book, dealing with all kinds of personnel issues and critical incidents, have made clear the need for laying the groundwork for the inevitable catastrophes; we have learned from riots, financial cutbacks, natural and caused disasters, strikes, and other exigencies that the police simply must anticipate the worst. Police supervisors and managers, in particular, must be prepared for the unknown and expect the unforeseen.

The police have traditionally remained largely uninterested in futures research. A survey by Conser and Diller (1994) determined that nearly one half (44 percent) of 126 respondents believed that their police departments were resistant to change. According to Swanson et al. (2001:649), there are three possible reasons for this disinterest: (1) a time horizon, for many police agencies, no longer than the next budget cycle; (2) a "hot stove" approach to managing, meaning that "we'll handle today's crisis now and worry about tomorrow when it gets here"; and (3) a lack of any perceived need to consider what conditions may be like in 10 to 20 years.

These reasons for a lack of futures thinking seem to generally be true of policing, notwithstanding the spread of COPPS (discussed in Chapter 13) and the fact that many police leaders seem immersed in the multitude of problems that face their agencies on a daily basis. As one author (Tafoya, 1983:14) put it, "Most disciplines are almost totally absorbed with the problems of today and steeped in the tradition of yesterday."

More recently, however, there has been a growing interest among police executives in futures research; this interest has been fueled largely by the growing imperative to make sense out of a turbulent and sometimes chaotic environment, as well as the work of police futurists such as William Tafoya, who developed the nation's first graduate- and doctoral-level police futures courses and founded the Society of Police Futurists International. Some police departments have even created a futures research unit that stands alone or is within their planning division; these units assess trends, countertrends, shifting values, and other indicators and attempt to provide an understanding of what they mean, where a department is going, and what should be done.

Futurists think in terms of time frames of five years and beyond. Many police leaders, however, tend to focus on the immediate future—from the present to two years ahead, dealing with problems that need resolution, trying to "stay on top of things," and "putting out fires." Future outcomes *can* be influenced by decisions made today. This axiom is critical for police leaders to understand; the choices that are made today will affect their agencies throughout this century.

PREDICTING THE FUTURE

Scanning, Scenario Writing, Drivers

The past quarter century has seen a surging interest in forecasting the future of policing. Tafoya (1983) called forecasting the "purest form of futuristics," likening it to the headlights of a car being driven in a snowstorm. The lights provide enough illumination to continue, but not enough so the driver can proceed without caution. What lies ahead is unknown. We next examine some of the methods that are employed by persons engaged in futures research in their efforts to make the unknown more predictable.

Contemporary futures research has two major aspects: environmental scanning and scenario writing. *Environmental scanning* is an effort to put a social problem under a microscope, with an eye toward the future. We may consult experts, such as demographers, social scientists, technologists, and economists. A Delphi process (a brainstorming technique where forecasters envision and plan for different scenarios) may also assist, gathering experts, looking at all possible factors, and getting an idea of what will happen in the future. Thus, environmental scanning permits us to identify, track, and assess changes in the environment (Peak, 2000).

Through scanning, we can examine the factors that seem likely to "drive" the environment. *Drivers* are factors or variables (such as economic conditions, demographic shifts, governmental policies, social attitudes, and technological advances) that will have a bearing on future conditions. Three categories of drivers identify possible trends and impacts on the American criminal justice system: (1) social and economic conditions (e.g., size and age of the population, immigration patterns, nature of employment, and lifestyle characteristics), (2) shifts in the amount and types of crimes (including the potential for new types of criminality and for technological advances that might be used for illegal behavior), and (3) possible developments in the criminal justice system itself (e.g., changes in the way the police, courts, and corrections subsystems operate; important innovations) (Peak, 2000).

Scenario writing is simply the application of drivers to three primary situations: public tolerance for crime, amount of crime, and the capacity of the criminal justice system to deal with crime. An important consideration is whether each scenario will occur in a high or low degree. For example, drivers may be analyzed in a scenario of *low* public tolerance for crime, a *high* amount of crime, and a *high* capacity of the criminal justice system to deal with crime. Conversely, a scenario may include a view of the future that has a *high* tolerance for crime, a *low* amount of crime, and a *low* capacity for the system to cope with crime.

The nature of crime, as will be seen later, is rapidly changing. We are witnessing a decline in several types of crime. As we see the increase in the "graying

The spoils of war—gangs, guns, and drug-related violence—will continue to challenge the police in the twenty-first century.
Courtesy NYPD Photo Unit.

of America," however, the young criminals will increasingly prey on the elderly and flourish. The growing number of crime-prone youths in our metropolitan areas virtually ensures that high crime rates will continue in the inner city (Peak, 2003).

A CHANGING SOCIETY, A CHANGING FUTURE

Demographics

Future police recruiting and leadership efforts will be greatly affected by the nation's shift in demographic makeup. A change toward older workers, fewer entry-level workers, and more women, minorities, and immigrants in the population will force criminal justice and private industry to become more flexible to compete for qualified applicants. Agencies must devise new strategies to attract 21- to 35-year-olds and offer better wage and benefits packages in order to compete with private businesses. Packages will need to include daycare, flexible hours, and paid maternity leave (McCord and Wicker, 1990).

We are rapidly becoming a more diverse and older society. By 2010, one in every four Americans will be 55 or older. The elderly are more likely to suffer the harmful consequences of a victimization, such as sustaining injury or requiring medical care (Peak, 2000).

The minority population is also increasing rapidly; in less than 100 years, we can expect the white majority in the United States to end, as the growing number of blacks, Hispanics, and Asians together become the new majority. And when these various minority groups are forced to compete for increasingly scarce, low-paying service jobs, intergroup relations can be damaged and even become combative, as has already occurred in several large American cities. The gap between the "haves" and "have-nots" is widening. An underclass of people, those who are chronically poor and live outside society's rules, is growing (Peak, 2000).

The demographic makeup of the nation poses additional challenges for the police. For example, single-occupant households represented 17 percent of the total in 1970 and 25 percent in 1997 and are projected to increase to 27 percent in 2010; average household size has been steadily decreasing from 3.14 in 1970 to 2.64 in 1997. Likewise, the percentage of married couples has gone from 70 percent in 1970 to 53 percent in 1997, with a continued decline predicted (Police Futurists International, 2000). These figures represent threats to societal stability, because the smaller the household, the less the commitment of people to one another, and the less likely deviance will be managed at the household level, thus necessitating governmental intervention. Marriage is our most stable family structure; between 1980 and 1997, however, there was a 20 percent increase in the never-married category, which was highest among blacks and Hispanics (Police Futurists International, 2000).

Another destabilizing force is the number of people who in a given year change where they live. The average person moves once every six years. But approximately 17 percent of the population moves each year. Thus, long-term neighborhood stability is the exception rather than the rule. Home ownership—another stability factor—is a concern, with 72 percent of blacks and Hispanics and 38 percent of whites unable to afford a modestly priced home (Police Futurists International, 2000).

Crime

The nation's crime rate fell for an unprecedented nine consecutive years from 1992 to 2001, to its lowest point in a generation. Certainly a robust economy (prior to the recession that began following the September 11, 2001, incident) and the overall aging of the country (including the failure of the predicted "superpredator" juvenile offender to materialize in the mid-1990s) contributed in large fashion to those declines. More and more, however, experts are also pointing to the methods used by police as a substantial cause for the decline in the nation's crime levels—community oriented policing and problem solving being prominent among them.

The nature of crime is also changing rapidly in the United States, due in great measure to the introduction of high technology, including software piracy, industrial espionage, bank card counterfeiting, and embezzlement by computer. These crimes will compel the development of new investigative techniques, specialized training for police investigators, and the employment of individuals with specialized, highly technological backgrounds. The distribution and use of narcotics, which is spreading in numbers and throughout various social classes, will also continue.

It is a foregone conclusion that new criminal types will dot the national landscape in the future: They will be better educated, upscale, older, and increasingly female. Computer crimes will increase dramatically, including cyberterrorism, identity theft, credit card fraud, consumer fraud, stock market–related fraud, and industrial espionage; these crimes may well become the next national crime-fighting obsession. To meet these challenges, the police must become better educated, adaptable, and equipped. Training will have to be virtually continuous to address complex threats to society (Pettinari, 2001).

The growing rift between this country's haves and have-nots is fostered in part by the differences between people in terms of access to and knowledge of computer technology. As a result, street crimes and other crimes by the underclass may also increase dramatically, as the underclass sees hope decline even further. The poor will become poorer, which could contribute to still-alarming levels of youth violence (Peak and Glensor, 2002).

ANTICIPATED CHANGES IN POLICING

Three important developments likely to affect police supervision and management in the future are agency diversification, COPPS, and high technology. These trends, and others discussed here, will significantly affect how supervisors function in the years ahead.

Diversifying the Organization

As our society becomes more diversified, so too must the ranks of the police, including its supervisory and management levels. The proportion of sworn female employees in local police agencies has risen to about 11 percent (Horne, 1999), with about 14 percent of all sworn federal officers being women (Reaves and Hart, 2000). But challenges remain. The number of women holding top command positions (captain and higher) is only 7.5 percent, and they compose only

Female and minority officers are more commonplace today. Their representation will hopefully increase as agencies strive to recruit officers who are more representative of a community's diversity.
Courtesy Washoe County, Nevada, Sheriff's Office Photo Unit.

1.6 percent of supervisory positions (sergeant and lieutenant) (Reaves and Hart, 2000). Several key issues need to be addressed:

Recruitment: Unfocused, random recruiting is unlikely to attract women and minorities; agencies should go to several locations (local colleges, women's groups, female community leaders, gyms, martial arts schools) and use all types of media to attract qualified applicants.

Academy training: Recruits must be trained in integrated academy classes to insure full integration between officers of both sexes. Female instructors are especially important during academy training, both as positive role models and to help female rookies develop skills and confidence.

Assignments: If women are removed from patrol and placed in special assignments early on in their careers, they will miss vital field patrol experience. The majority of supervisory positions exist in the patrol division, and departments generally feel that field supervisors must have had adequate field experience in order to be effective and respected by subordinates.

Promotions: As indicated above, for a number of reasons women are not getting promoted in proportion to their numbers. The so-called "glass ceiling" continues to restrict women's progress through the ranks. The more subjective the promotional process, the less likely women are to pass it.

Mentoring: Women officers have a higher turnover rate (about 6 percent) than men (about 4 percent). Transitioning into the organization can be critical to whether or not the employee remains with the organization. Formal mentoring programs can help to raise retention rates of women by having a veteran employee provide new hires with information concerning what to expect at the academy and beyond (Reaves and Hart, 2000).

Increasing the number of women in supervisory and management levels could also influence police policy and serve as role models for younger female officers.

African American police officers face problems similar to those of women who attempt to enter and prosper in police work. Until more African American officers are promoted and can affect police policy and serve as role models, they are likely to be treated unequally and have difficulty being promoted—a classic "Catch-22" situation.

Community Oriented Policing and Problem Solving

At various points throughout this book, primarily in Chapter 13, we have discussed how supervisors and managers and their subordinates must adapt to the new way of thinking and acting under the spreading COPPS philosophy of policing. We now address this concept from a futures perspective.

As noted in Chapter 13, until recently the traditional police first-line supervisor has been largely unprepared by training or experience for the COPPS strategy. The command and control model of policing during the past 50 years measured the supervisor's and manager's success in terms of the statistical accomplishments of his or her unit. Arrests, citations, calls for service, response time, and case closings were all counted in this quantitative approach. Good line officers followed orders and stayed out of trouble, filled out forms and reports correctly, and did not abuse citizens. Orders came down from the top. Sergeants checked the accuracy and compliance of paperwork going up and down the chain of command, doing more and more of the lieutenant's administrative work and spending less and less time on the street. As a result, the sergeant saw his or her officers only once during the shift, at roll call (Robinette, 1993).

The COPPS strategy requires a different leadership methodology. Cultural, gender, and ethnic diversity will characterize the police work group of the future as well as the community, making it difficult for leadership to manage according to traditional standards. In those departments that implement the COPPS strategy, supervisors and managers will have more freedom to intervene, innovate, and reallocate resources and task personnel. They will need to set clear, achievable goals and define outcomes; recognize and accommodate differences; and provide recognition, visibility, celebration, and rewards for team accomplishment. The new supervisor will be in the neighborhood talking to people, taking reports, and meeting with policing team members regularly (Robinette, 1993).

Will COPPS endure in the twenty-first century? As we noted earlier, more than any other single factor, the critical determinant is expected to be the kind of people who enter policing in the next decade. The most significant question that should be asked by police supervisors and administrators is, "What will be the predominant characteristics of tomorrow's police candidates?"

If past practices of selecting police candidates based on perceived physical prowess and propensity to be "good soldiers" continue, policing is likely to regress to the norm: the legalistic style of policing. If, however, the majority of people selected to enter policing in the future are disposed to share decision making and are flexible, resilient, and well educated, the foundations of COPPS will endure, and this nation will serve as a positive model for emerging nations looking for guidance from the most democratic nation in the world (Tafoya, 1997).

Some futurists also see COPPS undergoing a metamorphosis, including the following changes:

- Ethics will be woven into everything the police do: hiring processes, FTO programs, decision-making processes. Emphasis will increase on accountability and integrity within police agencies as policing is elevated to a higher standing, reaching more toward being a true profession, and, concomitantly, the majority of officers will be required to possess a college degree.
- Formal awards ceremonies will concentrate as much or more on acts that improve citizens' quality of life than on felony arrests or other high-risk activities.
- Communications will be greatly improved through internal Intranets that contain local and agency operational data, phone books, maps, calendars, calls for service, crime data sheets, speeches, newsletters, news releases, and so on (Pettinari, 2001).
- Major cities will no longer require policing experience in order to be the chief police executive, who can be recruited from private industry. The head of the future police agency will essentially be recognized as a CEO with good business sense, as a trend toward privatization of certain

services becomes more prevalent. Knowledge will continue to increase at lightning speed, forcing the CEO to be involved in trend analysis and forecasting in order to keep ahead of the curve.

- The rigid paramilitary style currently used will become obsolete, replaced by work teams consisting of line officers, community members, and business and corporation representatives.
- The current squad structure will give way to more productive, creative teams of officers who, having been empowered with more autonomy, will become efficient problem solvers, thus strengthening ties between the police and the citizenry.
- Neighborhoods will more actively participate in the identification, location, and capture of criminals.

High Technology: New Developments—and Problems

Certainly, the advent of new technologies has changed—and will continue to affect—the manner in which the police do business and solve crimes. Conversely, the police are compelled to develop new technological skills in order to meet the challenges posed by the *criminals* who are quite sophisticated in their use of high technology.

The rapid expansion in computer technology, while certainly a strong advantage for society overall, may carry problems as well. The first problem with this technology is that to many Americans, it is so complex to operate as to be "fiendish instruments of mental torture" (Lardner, LaGesse, and Rae-Dupree, 2001:31–32). Most people use about a third of the capacity of any one technology employed. The problem is apparently due to the fact that "these products are engineered by engineers, for the sake of engineering, as opposed to the sake of the person at the end" (Lardner et al., 2001:32). This need for technology that is more user friendly is certainly a problem for the police, because many departments lack the in-house expertise to install or run software and equipment. Many police executives believe they should hire only people to be sworn police officers—not to be computer programmers or database experts. But the nature of policing is obviously changing; officers with such skills are not only desirable and valuable, but are also increasingly and rapidly becoming a *necessity*.

In a related vein, in many police agencies the technology staff are civilians, who are generally kept away from the operational side of the organization. They understand what computers do, but not necessarily how that capability supports the operational needs of the police officer on the street. Thus, the sworn officer or detective is often playing catch-up to counter passwords, digital compression, steganography, remote storage, audit disabling, anonymous remailers, digital cash, computer penetration and looping, cellular phone cloning and phone cards, and a host of other evasive criminal schemes (Peak and Glensor, 2002).

Before embracing any new technology, agencies should spend a significant amount of time planning how it will be applied and what impact it will have on the agency. A committee that is representative of all stakeholders—especially supervisors and managers—should be formed to conduct a needs assessment and to identify the agency's specific requirements and expectations. This committee should continue its work even before implementation and after the technology is operational; it can assist with the user training to be conducted, evaluations that should be performed of its functions, and policies that need to be developed concerning the technology's use. For example, with respect to laptop computers in cars (Schoenle, 2001), which calls should still be sent via voice by dispatch? What are the logging-on and logging-off requirements? Are laptops to be taken out of the vehicles?

Following are some of the major technological developments that are now occurring in policing.

New Developments

Police Laptop and Handheld Computer Technology.   A growing number of police agencies, including small ones, are using laptop and handheld computers with wireless connections to crime and motor vehicle databases. Officers can access court documents and in-house police department records, as well as enter license numbers into their laptop computers. And, through a national network of motor vehicle and criminal history databases, they can locate drivers with outstanding warrants, expired or suspended licenses, and other information. Furthermore, rather than using open radio communications, today's police officers often use their computers to communicate with one another via e-mail (Ghaemian, 1996). Systems also exist that place a touch-screen display and a handheld remote unit in the officer's easy reach; lights, siren, radar, video camera, and global positioning equipment later are in a programmed sequence on the touch screen.

Geographic Information System.   Some cities are also developing a Geographic Information System (GIS), enabling officers to plot criminal activity on an electronic map. Layers of information can then be added to the map to create a picture of crime trends. One unique way officers can use community policing strategies is to develop a database of problems and solutions. When an officer answers a call for service or encounters a problem, he or she can enter it into the database, along with all information about the problem, the action taken, and a list of resources that were applied to the problem. The next time officers confront a similar problem, they can search the database and get a report on everything that was done with that problem in the past (Kavanaugh, 1996).

Electronics in Traffic Investigations and Enforcement.   A multicar accident can turn a street or highway into a parking lot for many hours, sometimes days. Police need to collect evidence relating to the accident, including measurements and sketches of the scene and vehicle and body positions, skid marks, street or highway elevations, intersections, and curves. These tasks typically involve a measuring wheel, steel tape, pad, and pencil. The cost of traffic delays, especially for commercial truck operators, for every hour traffic is stalled is substantial.

Some police agencies have begun using a version of a surveyor's "total station," electronically measuring and recording distances, angles, elevations, and the names and features of objects.

Several companies now manufacture and provide traffic cameras to the police.

Imaged Fingerprints and Mugshots. Instead of transporting prisoners to a central booking facility in downtown Boston—a task that took 40,000 hours of officers' time per year—officers at the 11 district police stations can electronically scan a prisoner's fingerprints, take digital photographs, and then route the images to a central server for easy storage and access. This network gives investigators timely access to information and mugshot lineups and is saving the police department $1 million in labor and transportation costs while freeing officers from prisoner transportation duties (Newcombe, 1996).

Computerized Mapping for Crime Control. Computerized mapping is an effective tool to help police departments track criminal activity in neighborhoods, known in community policing as hot spots. Sophisticated crime-specific mapping software exists, for example, for burglaries and can track not only geographic areas, but types

Computerized latent fingerprint systems are being used by many agencies today. Here, detectives use a computerized latent fingerprint system to capture a serial attacker.
Courtesy NYPD Photo Unit.

of property taken, time of day, means and method of entry, offender and victim oriented behaviors, vehicle description, and so on (Baker, 2001). Combined with a technique known as geocoding (which verifies addresses and links other geographic information with them), computer-mapping software can combine data sets to provide a multidimensional view of crime and its potential contributing factors.

Three-Dimensional Crime Scene Drafting.   Today, three-dimensional computer-aided drafting (3-D CAD) software can be purchased for a few hundred dollars. By working in 3-D, CAD users can create scenes that can be viewed from any angle. Suddenly, technical evidence can be visualized by nontechnical people. Juries can "view" crime scenes and see the location of evidence; they can view just what the witness says he or she saw.

Gunshot Locator System.   A primary goal for the police is to determine the location of gunshots. Technology is now being tested that is similar to that used to determine the strength and epicenter of earthquakes. Known as a Gunshot Locator System, it uses microphone-like sensors placed on rooftops and telephone poles to record and transmit the sound of gunshots by radio waves or telephone lines.

Firearms Training.   A device known as FATS, for Firearms Training System, is said to be "as close to real life as you can get" (Joyce, 1995). Recruits and in-service officers alike use the system, which ranges in cost from $32,000 to a military model selling for $5 million. The students are given a high-tech lesson in firearms and can be shown a wide variety of computer-generated scenarios on a movie screen. An instructor at a console can control the scene. Using laser-firing replicas of their actual weapons, they learn not only sharpshooting but also judgment—when to shoot and when not to shoot.

Artificial intelligence (AI) refers to computers programmed to exhibit charac-teristics of human intelligence. AI expert systems (programs that capture the knowledge of experts for use with new situations), virtual reality (AI that combines computers and sensory apparatus to create simulated, controlled environments and experiences), robotics (using computers to accomplish a useful action), and speech recognition (the interface between people and computers) are some additional tools that can be put in place in policing, provided that the public will accept their use.

OTHER INTERNAL FACTORS THAT WILL AFFECT POLICING

Four additional factors within policing—the rank-and-file officers, participative management, flattening the organization, and the quality of life within police agencies—will loom large on the horizon and require considerable attention by police leaders. These factors are discussed next.

The Rank and File

It would be a tremendous oversight to omit mention of the role of rank-and-file officers among the changes in future police service. For several reasons, future generations of police officers will be vastly different from those of the past. These reasons include the need for future generations to be at ease and fluent with information technologies, as well as their entering a police service that is much more involved with collective bargaining.

In the past, particularly under the professional model of policing, during the academy phase of their training, recruits adopted a new identity and a system of discipline. They learned to take orders and not to question authority. Indeed, much of the emphasis was on submission to authority. Recruits learned that loyalty to fellow officers, a professional demeanor and bearing, and respect for authority are highly valued qualities. That theme and the police executive's set of expectations for recruits must change, however. Officers of the future must be hired for their ability to critically think, plan, and evaluate. At the same time, chiefs, sheriffs, commanders, and even sergeants will wield less power and control and filter less information; instead, they will move into enhanced roles as coaches, supporters, and resource developers (Pettinari, 2001).

Police officers of the future will also function in different ways and on different terms than officers of the past. Given the kinds of existing technologies just discussed, and what they bode for the future, every officer will function with few time and space constraints because all officers will be equipped with new technologies. Before going on the streets, every rookie will be thoroughly computer literate and able to use crime analysis software (Pettinari, 2001).

With such tools, it is easy to envision an officer's home or car becoming his or her workplace. Identification of suspects in the field will take a quantum leap with electronic telecommunication of fingerprints, scanning of retinal patterns, and facial ratio and heat patterns that say positively, "This is the bad guy." Officers will also access maps and data; be able to bring up any call, crime type, or problem by geographic area; and sort out this information and compare similar incidents. They will be able to touch their computer keys and ask for the top 10 crimes in their beat area, while receiving instant crime analysis for use in deployment and other operational decisions (Pettinari, 2001).

Participative Management

In the past, the emphasis of police supervision and management was on submission to authority. A different set of values and expectations has been established for the future. The autocratic leader of the past will not work in the future. As Witham (1991:30) noted, "The watchwords of the new leadership paradigm are coach, inspire, gain commitment, empower, affirm, flexibility, responsibility, self-management, shared power, autonomous teams, and entrepreneurial units."

Because police officers of the future will not normally possess military experience and its inherent obedience to authority, but will have higher levels of education, they will tend to be more independent and less responsive to traditional authoritative approaches to their work. They will have been exposed to more participative, supportive, and humanistic approaches. These officers will want more opportunities to provide input in their work and to address the challenges posed by neighborhood problem solving. In short, they will not want to function like automatons during their tour of duty, blindly following general orders, policies and procedures, and rules and regulations. These officers will be, according to Metts (1985:31), "bright, resourceful, and versatile, cross-trained in law enforcement, firefighting, and paramedical services. Administrators will care less about marksmanship and physical size and more about mental capacity and diplomas."

Flattening the Organization

An area of concern among futurists is policing's organizational structure. Increasing numbers of police executives are beginning to question whether or not the traditional pyramid-shaped police bureaucracy will be effective in the future. Hillary Robinette (1989), retired special agent of the Management Science Unit of the Federal Bureau of Investigation, believes that the typical departmental organizational chart of the future will no longer resemble a pyramid. Instead, he maintains that the top will be pushed down and the sides will expand at the very base of what used to look like a pyramid. Advancement will be across the organization and not up.

Indeed, the spread of COPPS has allowed many police executives to flatten their organizations. Communication within the pyramid structure is often confronted with many barriers and frustrated by the levels of bureaucracy; perhaps the organizational structure, the argument goes, could be changed to a more horizontal design to facilitate the flow of information and ideas.

Quality of Life Within Police Agencies

The quality of life within police agencies will present new management challenges for the future. The increase in older workers will be reflected in the police workforce and will call for different motivational incentives and management practices. Older officers will be less willing to change tasks or assignments.

Supervisors and managers will advise and assist their team members in their professional development. Some of the officers will need assistance in learning a second language; all will need training in technology. Management training for newly promoted or promotable supervisors will be critical to the success of improved quality of life in the department.

Tomorrow's supervisor or manager will be a team builder who will be guided by five principles (Robinette, 1993:15–16):

1. *Free and equal access to police service:* The supervisor must test each decision against its equity effect and ask, "Is the action I am about to take, or the decision I am about to make, equitable and fair to those affected?"

2. *Fidelity to the public trust:* The supervisor or manager asks, "Is it the right thing to do?"

3. *Balancing the needs of safety and security with the needs of enforcement:* The supervisor or manager must determine whether his or her choice is lawful or involves unnecessary risks to life and property.

4. *Cooperation and coordination of activity with the community and other public agencies:* The supervisor or manager must query whether or not the choice of action or decision is based on the best possible beneficial outcome for all the parties involved, and whether or not the action is defensible in the public forum.

5. *The final test, which may be the most difficult, is that of objectivity:* This test examines one's personal motives for choice and action and forces the supervisor or manager to ask why a particular action or decision is being chosen over others, and whether his or her intentions are honorable.

Despite the fact that increasing specialization is likely to characterize policing in the next century, patrol officers will remain the backbone of policing, as a result of sheer numbers and frequency of contact with the public. The importance of retaining competent patrol officers becomes increasingly apparent as COPPS spreads, as officers become less isolated from the public, and as cooperative efforts between the public and other citizens expand. Police officers who continue to serve and be perceived as soldiers of occupation in minority neighborhoods are unlikely to be effective in either crime control or order maintenance.

IN SUM: QUESTIONS FOR THE FUTURE

Policing has certainly changed in the past 20 years, under the COPPS strategy. Indeed, it would seem that much of the future of policing revolves around the continuing use of this approach, as opposed to the traditional, reactive, "professional" model of policing (see Peak and Glensor, 2002). Although COPPS appears to be sweeping the nation, it has not yet been embraced by all of the

17,000 police agencies across the nation. So we end this chapter and the book with several questions that, for those agencies, will require answers in the future:

- Will those departments come to believe that they alone cannot control crime and enlist the aid of the community in this endeavor?
- Will those chief executives acquire the innovative drive necessary to change the culture of their departments, implement COPPS, flatten the organizational structure of their department, and see that officers' work is properly evaluated?
- Will those police executives have the necessary job security to accommodate COPPS?
- Will those departments work with their communities, other city agencies, businesses, elected officials, and the media to sustain COPPS?
- Will those police executives, managers, and supervisors come to develop the necessary policies and support mechanisms to support COPPS, including recruitment, selection, training, performance appraisals, and reward and promotional systems?
- Will those police executives, managers, and supervisors begin viewing the patrol officer as a problem-solving specialist? Will they give street officers enough free time and latitude to engage in proactive policing?
- Will those police departments come to view COPPS as a department- and citywide strategy? Will they invest in technology to support problem-oriented policing?
- Will those agencies attempt to bring diversity into their ranks, reflecting the changing demographics and cultural customs of our society?

_____ Case Studies _____

Following are two case studies that will compel the reader to think in futuristic terms.

Loganville Looks Beyond the Horizon

The city of Loganville has a number of new department heads, with varying levels of experience. Furthermore, recent crime, budget, and other crises have underscored the need for the city's departments to work more collaboratively and address problems of the future. Accordingly, the city manager is convening a strategic (long-term) planning workshop in one week to bring all department heads together to orient them concerning the city council's long-term priorities and to discuss and address these problems. Of course, the chief of police will attend and represent the police department. Sgt. Jennifer Smith, with nine years on the force and three years in the planning and research division, has been assigned by the chief to locate and prepare the requisite information that will be necessary for this workshop.

1. What kind of information does the chief need? Where will the sergeant obtain this information?
2. Using the data that is collected, what are the factors (drivers) that will affect the future of *your* city in its changing environment?
3. What kinds of future challenges would those factors pose for the police in your community?

A Futures Forum

Devonshire is a medium-sized, industrial community with a progressive mayor and council. Together, they have implemented a new program called Leadership Devonshire, which is a one-year program to bring professionals together from the business and governmental sectors to discuss common issues, challenges, methods, and concerns. Sgt. Dale Williams is a patrol supervisor with 10 years' total experience, including four years as a supervisor. He has just graduated from the local university and also just completed a supervision course (using this textbook). He has applied to be a participant at Leadership Devonshire and received notification from the project's director that he has been selected to attend and represent the police department. He was advised that the first meeting will be in two weeks, and he is to make a 10-minute presentation on his profession, his position, and its future challenges.

1. Using some of the materials discussed throughout this book, how would *you* explain the role of a police supervisor to this diverse group?
2. If you were in Sgt. Williams's position, what would be some of the important *current* themes and issues that you would take to the forum concerning a supervisor's job and its complexities and challenges?
3. How would you describe how the supervisor's role is changing, and the *future* issues and challenges of this position?

SUMMARY

This chapter has examined the future, including the need for police generally to plan for it as well as some methods for forecasting its future. It also reviewed some anticipated changes in policing and the impact of demographics, crime, and high-technology on the field.

The years ahead are not likely to be tranquil, either inside or outside the halls of the police agency. Such matters as age discrimination, employee misconduct, sexism, new employee attitudes, and poor work habits will not be resolved in the near future.

For 45,000 years, humankind was largely huddled in the darkness of caves, afraid to venture into the light of day. Today's police leaders must not wait for someone else to set the pace. Bold leadership is essential today, to prepare for the future of police reform (Tafoya, 1990). More than ever before, police leaders must shoulder the responsibility for seeing that the best and brightest individuals are recruited and trained and then become the best they possibly can be in their performance. Tomorrow's police supervisors and managers must know more than their predecessors and be both flexible and principled as well as careful listeners, with confidence in their decisions. But such challenges have always been presented to the men and women of policing who have chosen to wear the gold badge of leadership.

ITEMS FOR REVIEW

1. Explain why it is important for the police to study the future and to engage in futures research.

2. Describe some of the methods used by futurists to predict the future.

3. Delineate some of the anticipated changes in policing, particularly with respect to technology and crime; focus on the changes that are most likely to affect police supervision and management in the future.

4. List some of the problems for the police that can accompany the development of high technology.

5. Describe the kinds of changes that are anticipated with the rank-and-file officers of the future, and the challenges to supervisors and managers that will be posed.

6. Explain how community policing will change both policing in general and supervision and management in particular.

REFERENCES

Baker, T. E. (2001). Burglary mapping: A 2001 cyberspace odyssey. *Law and Order* (June):30–35.

Conser, J. A., and Diller, J. J. (1994, 14–16 September). From theory to practice: The implementation of futuristics in selected policing agencies. Paper presented at the annual meeting of the Midwestern Criminal Justice Association, Chicago.

Ghaemian, K. (1996). Small-town cops wield big-city data. *Government Technology* 9 (September):38.

Horne, P. (1999, November). Policewomen: 2000 A.D. redux. *Law and Order,* p. 53.

Joyce, P. (1995). Firearms training: As close to real as it gets. *Government Technology* 8 (July):14–15.

Kavanaugh, J. (1996). Community oriented policing and technology. *Government Technology* 9 (March):14.

Lardner, J., LaGesse, D., and Rae-Dupree, J. (2001). Overwhelmed by tech. *U.S. News and World Report* (January 15):31–36.

McCord, R., and Wicker, E. (1990). Tomorrow's America: Law enforcement's coming challenge. *FBI Law Enforcement Bulletin* 59 (January):31–33.

Metts, J. R. (1985). Super cops: The police force of tomorrow. *The Futurist* (October):31–36.

Newcombe, T. (1996). Imaged prints go online, cops return to streets. *Government Technology* 9 (April):1, 31.

Peak, K. J. (2003). *Policing America: Methods, issues, challenges,* 4th ed. Upper Saddle River, NJ: Prentice Hall.

Peak, K. J. (2000). *Policing America: Methods, issues, challenges,* 3d ed. Upper Saddle River, NJ: Prentice Hall.

Peak, K. J., and Glensor, R. W. (2002). *Community policing and problem solving: Strategies and practices,* 3d ed. Upper Saddle River, NJ: Prentice Hall.

Pettinari, D. (2001). Are we there yet? The future of policing/sheriffing in Pueblo or in Anywhere, America. http://www.policefuturists.org/files/yet.html (accessed 13 February 2001).

Police Futurists International (2000). Visioning 21st century crime and justice. http://www.policefuturists.org/fall99/21crime.htm (accessed 20 October 2000):1–2.

Postman, N. (1989). Quoted in David Osborne and Ted Gaebler, *Reinventing government: How the entrepreneurial spirit is transforming the public sector.* Reading, MA: Addison-Wesley.

Reaves, B. A., and Hart, T. C. (2000). *Federal law enforcement officers, 1998.* Washington, DC: U.S. Department of Justice, Bureau of Justice Statistics Bulletin, p. 6.

Robinette, H. (1993). Supervising tomorrow. *Virginia Police Chief* (Spring):10–16.

Robinette, H. (1989). Operational streamlining. *FBI Law Enforcement Bulletin* (September):7–11.

Schoenle, G. W., Jr. (2001). Mobile computing police perspectives: The Buffalo experience. *The Police Chief* (September):36–42.

Story, D. (1992). What happens after all the dinosaurs are gone? (The passing of the torch). *Law and Order* (October):47–48.

Swanson, C. R., Territo, L., and Taylor, R. W. (2001). *Police administration.* 5th ed. Upper Saddle River, NJ: Prentice Hall.

Tafoya, W. L. (1997). The future of community policing. *Crime and Justice International* 13 (July):4–6.

Tafoya, W. L. (1990). The changing nature of the police: Approaching the 21st century. *Vital Speeches of the Day* 56 (February):244–246.

Tafoya, W. L. (1983, 22–26 March). Futuristics: New tools for criminal justice executives, part I. Paper presented at the 1983 annual meeting of the Academy of Criminal Justice Sciences, San Antonio, TX.

Witham, D. C. (1991). Environmental scanning pays off. *The Police Chief* (March):26–31.

Appendix

Advice That has Stood the Test of Time: Some Practical Counsel

---

❖

This book has covered many facets of supervision and management in its 14 chapters. Perhaps at its simplest level, the book is saying that a successful supervisor or manager influences others by example and gains the willing obedience, confidence, respect, and loyalty of subordinates. This characteristic of leadership was recognized in the sixth century B.C. by Lao-Tzu, when he wrote:

> The superior leader gets things done
> With very little motion.
> He imparts instruction not through many words
> But through a few deeds.
> He keeps informed about everything
> But interferes hardly at all.
> He is a catalyst.
> And although things wouldn't get done as well
> If he weren't there,
> When they succeed he takes no credit.
> And because he takes no credit
> Credit never leaves him. (quoted in Bennett and Hess, 2001:56)

ANALECTS OF CONFUCIUS AND MACHIAVELLI

The writings of two other major figures have stood the test of time. The analects (or brief passages) of Confucius (551–479 B.C.) and the writings of Machiavelli (A.D. 1469–1527) are still popular today. Many college and university students in a variety of academic disciplines have analyzed the writings of both, especially Machiavelli's *The Prince,* written in 1513. Both of these philosophers tended to agree on many points regarding the means of governance, as the following will demonstrate. After reading some quotations from each philosopher, we consider their application to police supervision and management.

Confucius often emphasized the moralism of leaders, saying,

He who rules by moral force is like the pole-star, which remains in its place while all the lesser stars do homage to it. Govern the people by regulations, keep order among them by chastisements, and they will flee from you, and lose all self-respect. Govern them by moral force, keep order among them . . . , and they will . . . come to you of their own accord. If the ruler is upright, all will go well even though he does not give orders. But if he himself is not upright, even though he gives orders, they will not be obeyed. (Waley, 1938:88, 173)

Confucius also believed that those people whom the leader promotes are of no small importance: "Promote those who are worthy, train those who are incompetent; that is the best form of encouragement" (Waley, 1938:92). He also believed that leaders should learn from and emulate good administrators:

In the presence of a good man, think all the time how you may learn to equal him. In the presence of a bad man, turn your gaze within! . . . Even when I am walking in a party of no more than three I can always be certain of learning from those I am with. There will be good qualities that I can select for imitation and bad ones that will teach me what requires correction in myself. (Waley, 1938:105, 127)

Unlike Confucius, Machiavelli is often maligned for being cruel; the "ends justify the means" philosophy imputed to him even today has cast a pall over his writings. Although often as biting as the "point of a stiletto" (Machiavelli, 1992:xvii) and seemingly ruthless at times ["Men ought either to be caressed or destroyed, since they will seek revenge for minor hurts but will not be able to revenge major ones," and "If you have to make a choice, to be feared is much safer than to be loved" (Machiavelli, 1992:7, 46], he, like Confucius, often spoke of the leader's need to possess character and compassion. For all of his blunt, management-oriented notions of administration, Machiavelli was prudent and pragmatic.

Like Confucius, Machiavelli believed that administrators would do well to follow examples set by other great leaders (we would encourage the reader to take some literary license with Machiavelli's writings and substitute "supervisor" and/or "manager" for "prince"):

Men almost always prefer to walk in paths marked out by others and pattern their actions through imitation. A prudent man should always follow the footsteps of the great and

> imitate those who have been supreme. . . A prince should read history and reflect on the actions of great men. (Machiavelli, 1992:15, 41)

On the need for developing and maintaining good relations with subordinates, he wrote:

> If . . . a prince . . . puts his trust in the people, knows how to command, is a man of courage and doesn't lose his head in adversity, and can rouse his people to action by his own example and orders, he will never find himself betrayed, and his foundations will prove to have been well laid. The best fortress of all consists in not being hated by your people. Every prince should prefer to be considered merciful rather than cruel. . . The prince must have people well disposed toward him; otherwise in times of adversity there's no hope. (Machiavelli, 1992:29, 60)

In a related, more contemporary vein, we might briefly note other writers' views of today's supervisors and managers. For example, Peter Drucker provided a compelling opinion of the importance of a supervisor: "Supervisors are, so to speak, the ligaments, the tendons and sinews of an organization. They provide the articulation. Without them, no joint can move" (quoted in Bennett and Hess, 2001:41). Similarly, the critical importance of supervisors and managers was noted by Bock (1993:39), who drew an analogy from the military:

> The old saying, "generals win battles but sergeants win wars," is true of millions of organizations—and of police departments. What a department is, to the officer on the street and the citizens of your community, is a direct result of what sergeants are and do.

As police organizations struggle with the complexities of a rapidly changing world and ever-demanding workforce, their leaders might do well to heed the analects of Confucius and the work of Machiavelli, as well as other, more contemporary observers.

CUES FOR TODAY'S SUPERVISORS AND MANAGERS

Several implications for contemporary supervisors and managers come from these philosophers. First, supervisors must lead by example, including by appearance, and occupy several roles. Lao-Tzu tells us that the successful leader is one who keeps informed, does not rant and rave, and prefers to "condemn in private, praise in public." Confucius tells us that one who leads must, above all, be moral and upright, advance subordinates, and try to learn something from each human contact.

Machiavelli also teaches us that supervisors and managers should emulate successful leaders; recruit and train competent subordinates; be able, upon newly assuming a leadership role, to maintain an adequate amount of professional distance between themselves and their subordinates, some of whom were formerly good friends with the new supervisor or manager and may now attempt to see how much they can get away with; and be able to say "no" to underlings while being compassionate toward them.

REFERENCES

Bennett, W. W., and Hess, K. (2001). *Management and supervision in law enforcement,* 3d ed. Belmont, CA: Wadsworth.

Bock, W. (1993). Generals win battles but sergeants win wars. *Law and Order* (May):39–40.

Machiavelli, N. (1992). *The prince.* R. M. Adams, trans. New York: Norton. (Original work published in 1513.)

Waley, A., trans. (1938). *The analects of Confucius.* London: Allen and Unwin.

Index